Ireland under the Union

T. W. Moody

Ireland under the Union

Varieties of tension

ESSAYS IN HONOUR OF T. W. MOODY

EDITED BY

F. S. L. LYONS & R. A. J. HAWKINS

CLARENDON PRESS · OXFORD

1980

Oxford University Press, Walton Street, Oxford OX2 6DP

OXFORD   LONDON   GLASGOW
NEW YORK   TORONTO   MELBOURNE   WELLINGTON
KUALA LUMPUR   SINGAPORE   JAKARTA   HONG KONG   TOKYO
DELHI   BOMBAY   CALCUTTA   MADRAS   KARACHI
NAIROBI   DAR ES SALAAM   CAPE TOWN

Published in the United States by Oxford University Press, New York
© F. S. L. Lyons and R. A. J. Hawkins 1980

British Library Cataloguing in Publication Data

Ireland under the Union.
  1. Ireland — History — 19th century — Addresses,
  essays, lectures
  I. Moody, Theodore William   II. Lyons, Francis
  Stewart Leland   III. Hawkins, R A J
  941.5081   DA950   79–40386
  ISBN 0–19–822469–9

Set in Monotype Bembo by Eta Services (Typesetters) Ltd., Beccles, Suffolk

Reproduced from copy supplied
printed and bound in Great Britain
by Billing and Sons Limited and Kemp Hall Bindery
Guildford, London, Oxford, Worcester

Preface

The *Festschrift* in honour of a revered professor was never perhaps an art form that commanded a wide audience, but until recently it was a tradition that was faithfully observed in academic circles. Now adverse economic circumstances have made such tributes increasingly rare, so that it is with deep appreciation that we, the editors of this volume, acknowledge the generosity of the Delegates of the Oxford University Press in allowing it to appear under the Clarendon imprint.

One of the most notorious difficulties about producing a volume of essays of this kind is to achieve a unity of theme which will be neither forced nor spurious. Complete integration is impossible without unreasonably constricting one's authors; on the other hand, to allow them unfettered freedom is a recipe for complete disintegration. We have sought a middle ground by choosing the Irish nineteenth century as a broad unifying theme while encouraging our writers to select whatever aspects of 'Ireland under the union' particularly engage their attention.

The nineteenth-century emphasis seemed appropriate to us because this is the field in which most of Dr Moody's own recent work has been done. But it was appropriate also for another reason. The essayists are united not only by the fact that they are composing variations on a theme, but also because they are all either products of, or have been in close contact with, the graduate seminar which has been the main training ground in Trinity College, Dublin, for young scholars in modern Irish history. It would have been easy for us to recruit innumerable eminent historians to contribute to a volume in honour of Dr Moody, but we believe that it is closest to his wishes, and consonant with his lifelong commitment to encouraging new talent, that this book should be almost entirely written by men and women most of whom are at the beginning of their careers.

As to the others who have taken part—Dr J. G. Simms was an old and valued friend and colleague; Mrs K. M. Davies, who drew the

[v]

map on p. 293, has worked with Dr Moody on the cartography for the *New history of Ireland* now in course of publication by the Clarendon Press; Mr Richard Hawkins is not only secretary to the *New history*, but has been closely associated with Dr Moody in various kinds of editorial work; and the provost of Trinity College, as will be clear from the introductory personal memoir of 'T.W.M.', is not only the senior pupil of Professor Moody's to appear in these pages, but also the one most deeply in his debt.

All of us offer our homage to a great historian for the splendid uniqueness of his contribution to our subject.

F. S. L. LYONS

RICHARD HAWKINS

Contents

Contributors

Richard Vincent Comerford, B.A., M.A. (N.U.I.), Ph.D. (Dubl.); lecturer in modern history, St Patrick's College, Maynooth

Robert Fitzroy Foster, B.A., M.A., Ph.D. (Dubl.); lecturer in modern history, Birkbeck College, University of London

David Nigel Haire, B.A., M.Litt. (Dubl.); teacher of history, Preston Lodge High School, Prestonpans

Jacqueline Rhoda Hill, B.A., Ph.D. (Leeds); junior lecturer in history, St Patrick's College, Maynooth

Robert Wybrants Kirkpatrick, B.A., H.Dip.Ed., Ph.D. (Dubl.); teacher of history, Alexandra College, Dublin

Francis Stewart Leland Lyons, F.B.A.; provost of Trinity College, Dublin

Elizabeth Malcolm, B.A. (N.S.W.), M.A. (Sydney); lecturer in English, University of Tromsø, Norway

John Gerald Simms, M.A. (Dubl., Oxon.), Ph.D. (Dubl.), M.R.I.A.; late fellow emeritus, Trinity College, Dublin

William Edward Vaughan, B.A., Ph.D. (Dubl.); lecturer in modern history, Trinity College, Dublin

Christopher John Woods, B.A., M.A. (Cantab.), Ph.D. (Nottingham); assistant editor, Royal Irish Academy; part-time lecturer in modern history, St Patrick's College, Maynooth

Abbreviations

B.M.	Library of the British Museum (now British Library)
B.M., Add. MS	—, Additional MS
C.S.O.	Chief Secretary's Office (papers, at S.P.O.)
C.S.O., R.P.	—, registered papers
Census Ire., 1841 [etc.]	[This title denotes the reports and other material relating to the censuses of Ireland in the years shown, published in parliamentary papers]
ch.	chapter
D.M.P.	Dublin Metropolitan Police
E.H.R.	*English Historical Review* (London, 1886–)
ed.	edited by, edition, editor(s)
F.J.	*Freeman's Journal* (Dublin, 1763–1924)
Glos. R.O.	Gloucestershire Record Office
H.C.	house of commons
H.L.	house of lords
H.L.R.O.	House of Lords Record Office
Hansard 3, i [etc.]	*Hansard's parliamentary debates*, third series, 1830–91 (vols i–ccclvi, London, 1831–91)
I.H.S.	*Irish Historical Studies: the joint journal of the Irish Historical Society and the Ulster Society for Irish Historical Studies* (Dublin, 1938–)
N.L.I.	National Library of Ireland
P.R.O.	Public Record Office of England
P.R.O.I.	Public Record Office of Ireland
P.R.O.N.I.	Public Record Office of Northern Ireland
R.C.P.	Lord Randolph Churchill papers, Churchill College, Cambridge
R.I.A., H.P.	Royal Irish Academy, Halliday pamphlets
R.I.C.	Royal Irish Constabulary

R.M.	resident magistrate
S.P.O.	State Paper Office of Ireland, Dublin Castle
Thom's directory 1841 [etc.]	*Thom's Irish Almanac and Official Directory for the year 1841* [etc.] (Dublin, 1841–) [subsequent changes of title]

References to British parliamentary papers are in the forms prescribed in T. W. Moody, *Irish Historical Studies: rules for contributors* (2nd rev. ed., Dublin, 1975), pp 5–6.

'T.W.M.'

F. S. L. LYONS

OF late years the phrase 'the Irish historiographical revolution' has been used so often that it is in danger of becoming a cliché to which everyone subscribes, but which nobody pauses to analyse. Perhaps the revolution is too recent to be analysed, for it is still going on, and must go on until it has penetrated the schools as it has already penetrated the universities and colleges of Ireland. To that continuing process many individuals have contributed, but by the universal acclaim of his peers the name of T. W. Moody leads all the rest. This volume of essays by some of his students is offered as a tribute to his achievement, and I, as one of the first to be both a pupil and a friend, have been honoured by being asked to preface the book with a personal memoir.

Theodore William Moody (henceforth to be designated by the familiar initials T.W.M.) was born in Belfast on 26 November 1907. His father, who came from County Londonderry, was of Ulster presbyterian stock, and his mother, of Scottish–huguenot descent on her father's side, was born in Jarrow-on-Tyne, but lived most of her long life in Belfast. Both families were connected with ship-building. T.W.M.'s paternal grandfather was an unskilled worker who could give his only child no more than an elementary education. That child, T.W.M.'s father, became an iron-turner in the engineering works of the great Belfast shipbuilders, Harland and Wolff; but, though a highly competent craftsman, he never rose above the ranks, perhaps because he was an active trade unionist in a milieu where such tendencies were still suspect. His earnings had to be supplemented by those of his wife, who taught dressmaking at the Belfast College of Technology.

T.W.M.'s childhood was thus a frugal one, but in two respects characteristic of the city and the time. His grandparents and his parents were deeply religious people for whom the bible was 'the book of books', and this early influence was to have a lasting effect upon their two children—Theodore and a sister, Doris, who was six years his senior. Next to religion in the household ranked a Victorian belief in self-improvement through education, a belief which impelled them to send the boy to the best day school available, the Royal Belfast Academical Institution. His period there (1920–26) was decisive for his development, though chance might easily have dictated otherwise. At the age of fifteen he passed an examination for admission to Harland and Wolff as a draughtsman, and in the summer of 1923 actually began work there as an apprentice. But before he had signed his indentures his excellent results in the junior intermediate examination persuaded his parents that he should continue at school. Their self-sacrifice was quickly rewarded. At that time T.W.M.'s strongest subjects were science, Latin and English. But when he began to work for a scholarship to the Queen's University, he fell under the spell of an outstanding history teacher, Archie Douglas, who turned his thoughts, and ultimately his career, in a whole new direction.

When T.W.M. entered Queen's in the autumn of 1926, the professor of history was James Eadie Todd. Todd, though not a prolific writer, exercised a powerful influence upon the young men whom he taught. T.W.M. has recorded that 'to Todd's inspiration and friendship I owe more than I can ever express', and in an autobiographical fragment, written at my request, he identifies three of his professor's qualities which affected him profoundly—that he was 'brimful of historical learning', that in his lectures 'he gave significant form to whatever subject he treated', and that he 'professed history as a high and holy calling'.[1]

A brilliant undergraduate career led, under Todd's inspiration, to T.W.M.'s first steps in more advanced work, which at that epoch

---

[1] T. W. Moody, 'Notes on my career as a historian', p. 2.

meant almost inevitably a period at the Institute of Historical Research in London. There, between 1930 and 1932, he launched into his pioneer work on the Londonderry plantation in Ulster of the early seventeenth century, which earned him his doctorate of philosophy in 1934. Out of this detailed and elaborate investigation came a series of articles and a book, *The Londonderry plantation, 1609–41: the city of London and the plantation in Ulster* (Belfast, 1939). This established new standards of thoroughness and objectivity in a field of Ulster history which, like so many other fields in the tangled history of that province, had long been the preserve of myth and rhetoric. Although T.W.M.'s name is probably best known to the modern generation in the context of nineteenth-century studies, a glance at the bibliography at the end of this volume will show that his interest in seventeenth-century Ireland has never waned. Throughout his career, range as well as depth have been characteristic of his approach to history.

Those years at the Institute of Historical Research were important to T.W.M.'s development in two quite different ways. First, it was in London that he met the girl, a law student named Margaret Robertson, who was to become his wife. They met through the sheer accident of both having rooms in the same lodgings. Margaret Moody has lately recalled for me that she first heard her future husband's name when asking her landlady what the rustling noise was in the room next door. 'Oh', was the reply, 'that's the mouse in Mr Moody's wastepaper basket.' 'Mr Moody's mouse' having broken the ice, they became engaged in June 1932, though they did not marry until after he had been appointed to a permanent post in Belfast. Margaret Moody, in addition to possessing a first-class mind of her own, was well versed in the values and the vagaries of the academic profession, since her father was a distinguished professor of electrical engineering in the university of Bristol.

This happy marriage has been the bedrock upon which all T.W.M.'s achievements have been founded. It has given him the joys of a close and intimate family life, with five children and all the stir and bustle and vivacity which that involves. The eldest, David

Robertson, was born in 1937, and there followed Ann Sheila in 1940, Catherine Margaret in 1943, Janet Lucy in 1945 and Susan Rosemary in 1952. It would be impertinent to comment on a partnership which remains a joy to all their friends, but any one who has known Margaret Moody will understand how much her common sense, forthrightness and steadiness in adversity, as well as in triumph, have contributed to the inner peace which, in his later years especially, has lain at the heart of T.W.M.'s personality.

At the institute, meanwhile, T.W.M. was coming into contact with senior scholars and with contemporaries who were to influence him all his life. His supervisor was Eliza Jeffries Davis, a pioneer in London history and an invaluable guide to the records of the London companies, though, like everyone else at the institute at that time, blissfully ignorant of Irish history. A more potent force was R. H. Tawney, whose seminar T.W.M. attended and who was the first to subject the young scholar's writing to the detailed critical comment that every thesis demands but not all receive. Among other established historians whom T.W.M. met during this fruitful period were A. P. Newton, J. E. Neale and that frequent and genial bird of passage from America, Wallace Notestein. His fellow-students included S. T. Bindoff, Taylor Milne, Mark Thomson, and a young Irish historian, R. Dudley Edwards, whom T.W.M. had first met in the National Library in Dublin in 1931 and with whose fortunes his own were to be intertwined for many years to come. One may perhaps best sum up T.W.M.'s experience at the institute by saying that it placed him on terms of intimacy with many of the best minds outside Oxford and Cambridge who were then advancing the frontiers of British historical scholarship. This, to a historian whose destiny was to lie in Ireland, with all the perils of provincial isolation which that implied, was of incalculable value not only to his own growing maturity as a scholar, but to the historiographical revolution he was soon to initiate.

That revolution began quietly and tentatively enough. T.W.M. returned to Belfast in 1932 as assistant to Professor Todd. With his support, and with that of Professor R. M. Henry, a Latinist, who had also written authoritatively on Sinn Féin, he became in 1935 a lecturer with special responsibility for Irish history. This was a new departure for Queen's, though Irish history had of course figured prominently in the curricula of the colleges of the National University of Ireland, and was also being taught at Trinity College, Dublin, by the distinguished scholar, Edmund Curtis. But although historians like Curtis in Trinity, or George O'Brien and Mary Hayden in University College, Dublin, had certainly prepared the way for the radical changes that were to come, their weakness had been that they were individuals, striving to achieve proper standards of objectivity in a society which was more interested in illusion than in reality. What was needed was to establish some sort of institutional framework for the study of Irish history and also, if possible, a means of publication for the new work which younger scholars were beginning to accumulate.

It was due primarily to T.W.M. that both these aims began to be achieved in the dark and unpromising years just before the second world war. In February 1936, with the help not only of Todd, but also of an enthusiastic amateur, Samuel Simms, a Belfast doctor and insatiable collector of books, he founded the Ulster Society for Irish Historical Studies. In November of that year his friend and fellow-student at the Institute of Historical Research, Robin Dudley Edwards, established the Irish Historical Society in Dublin, in pursuit of a strategy for developing the study of Irish history which they had often discussed in London.[1] Within two years the Ulster and the Irish societies had agreed to collaborate in two important projects, each of which is still in full career. One was the Irish Committee of Historical Sciences, created in March 1938. Brought into being originally so that Ireland might be represented on the Comité International des Sciences Historiques, the Irish committee soon became both a meeting-place for scholars from different parts of the island and a forum in which ideas and plans for furthering the

[1] See the editorial, 'Twenty years after', signed T.W.M., in *I.H.S.*, xi, no. 41 (Mar. 1958), pp 1–4. The names of the original officers and committees of both societies are printed in *I.H.S.*, i, no. 1 (Mar. 1938), p. 119.

study of Irish history were often discussed and clarified before being realised by other, more formal, means.

The second initiative taken at this time was of even greater significance. This was the foundation of *Irish Historical Studies*, which not only gave Ireland the first professional journal of history it had ever possessed, but from the outset established standards of scholarship that secured international recognition. The first number bore the date March 1938, and the aim has ever since been to produce two numbers a year. Broadly, this aim has been faithfully fulfilled, though human frailty and the usual hazards inseparable from periodical publishing have sometimes caused unconscionable delays. The normal pattern has been to group four numbers in a volume, and the first of these volumes appeared in 1939 under the imprints of Messrs Hodges, Figgis and Co., of Dublin, and B. H. Blackwell Ltd, of Oxford. *I.H.S.* has been from the beginning the joint journal of the Irish Historical Society and the Ulster Society for Irish Historical Studies. Its regular appearance has been made possible by a judicious blend of financial assistance from the Irish universities, modest advertising, subscriptions from libraries, and the faithful support of the members of the two societies and a number of scholars from abroad. For many years the journal was edited by T.W.M. and R. Dudley Edwards, not without the occasional explosions which are virtually certain when two men of marked ability and strong character work together in close proximity. But, though some changes in personnel have occurred in recent years, *I.H.S.* has always been produced by a duumvirate of which T.W.M. has been, so to speak, the constant member. His retirement after the publication of the eightieth issue, therefore, marks the end of a continuous editorial tenure lasting for forty years; though he will remain associated with the journal as chairman of the committee of management. This very continuity has enabled T.W.M. to set his stamp upon the journal and to make it the foremost agent of the revolution in Irish historiography. The appearance and the structure of *I.H.S.* have changed little in the four decades of its existence, though during that time succeeding generations of scholars, inside and outside Ireland, have made their first appearances in print, and sometimes built their whole careers, within its green covers. The strength of the journal has partly been the strength of its chief editor, partly its fidelity to the diverse aims it has pursued from the start. As editor, T.W.M. combined to a rare degree three qualities seldom seen together so abundantly—a catholicity of taste which enabled him to separate the permanent from the ephemeral over a wide spectrum of subjects and periods; a sensitivity towards language which ensured that even the dullest submission left his hands so elegantly attired as sometimes to be almost unrecognisable to its dazzled author; and finally, an eye for detail which made him one of the most formidable proof-readers in these islands, imposing upon all contributors the strictest adherence to the strictest of rules governing punctuation, capitalisation (or rather non-capitalisation) and syntax.

As for the purposes the journal was intended to achieve, these were set out in the preface to the first number and they have guided editorial practice ever since. It has always been necessary, given the conspicuous absence of serious rivals until very recently, for *I.H.S.* to perform two functions. On the one hand, it has encouraged original research and also reinterpretations of accepted views on particular topics. And on the other hand, in the effort to pass on the results of modern scholarship to teachers in colleges and schools, and to other interested persons, it has regularly found space for articles on the scope and teaching of Irish history or on research methods and problems, for select documents with editorial comment, and of course for a great deal of bibliographical material as well as a comprehensive section of reviews and short notices.

T.W.M.'s central position in Irish historical scholarship was much strengthened by what has proved to be the decisive event of his life. This was his election to a fellowship in history at Trinity College, Dublin, on 5 June 1939. By a curious chance this was followed a few months later by appointment to a full professorship, arising from the sudden retirement of W. Alison Phillips from the Erasmus Smith chair of modern history (a foundation dating from 1762), with which was combined at that time the Erasmus Smith chair of oratory. The latter involved few duties, the chief of these being the somewhat penitential task of judging the sermons delivered by aspirants for prizes in the divinity school, but the chair of history was another matter.

At that time the college was small and poor. There were only about 1500 undergraduates, and the number taking the four-year honour (moderatorship) degree course in modern history and political science seldom went above ten or fifteen in any one year. To deal with these classes, and with the additional pass degree teaching, there were no more than three other full-time dons with some part-time assistance. The three full-time teachers did indeed make up for their fewness by their quality. At their head was Edmund Curtis, author of a well-established *History of Ireland* and of a some-what less popular, but possibly more valuable, *History of medieval Ireland*. Curtis, almost single-handedly, had been attempting for years to raise the standard of research in Trinity, and had attracted a band of devoted pupils. Though also well known in Dublin literary circles, he had drifted helplessly in the cross-currents of Trinity academic life, and to the shame of the college had never been elected to a fellowship. Even as Erasmus Smith professor, or as Lecky professor after Alison Phillips's retirement in 1939, Curtis was excluded from the centre of power and the fountain of such meagre wealth as Trinity possessed.[1] Of the remaining two historians in post, one, Miss A. J. Otway-Ruthven, Curtis's most outstanding pupil, had recently returned from Cambridge to take up a lecture-ship, and the other was Miss Constantia Elizabeth Maxwell. Miss Maxwell was something of a pioneer in social history (G. M. Trevelyan's kind of social history), and although her work might nowadays be found wanting in rigour of research and analysis, she had achieved undeniable fame as the author of *Dublin under the Georges* and several other studies of eighteenth-century Irish life.

[1] When T.W.M. was elected to fellowship in 1939 his salary was £500 a year, and when he succeeded Curtis as Erasmus Smith professor later that year, his additional salary was only £100 a year.

When T.W.M. arrived in Trinity, Curtis was, if not a dying man, at any rate a spent force. Soon he fell ill of pernicious anaemia, to which he succumbed in March 1943. While Miss Maxwell succeeded him as Lecky professor, the responsibility for running the school of history devolved upon T.W.M., who was to remain chairman of the school committee until 1977, though the school divided into two autonomous departments of modern and medieval history in 1965. During his long period of office the moderatorship course was much expanded and many times revised, the number of honour students rose so steeply that an upper limit of forty in any one year had to be imposed, and although the staff did not increase *pari passu*, it was steadily enlarged and included at one time or another many of the foremost Irish historians of the past thirty years. It was within this framework that Trinity began to acquire the reputation it still holds as a major centre of research, both in medieval and in modern Irish history. At first this was loosely organised, but in recent years T.W.M. has developed a graduate seminar which has become famous and in which all the contributors to this volume have participated in one way or another.

Perhaps this is the point at which something should be said about T.W.M. as a teacher. Entering Trinity College in 1941, I was one of the first to experience his reforms, and in particular to take his final year special option on the American revolution. In the earlier years of the honour course, shortage of staff had meant that most teaching was done by lectures, reinforced by essay classes which, though infrequent by modern standards, were searching enough to ensure a standard of literacy also unfashionable by modern standards. The final year special option, though it necessitated some lecturing, was based firmly on contemporary documents, and to most of us, by then rather bored with survey courses, it was an exhilarating experience. T.W.M. as a lecturer could be two different people, and sometimes both at the same time. By sheer force of will he had conquered a speech impediment in his youth, but this had left an occasional hesitancy in his delivery, which was liable to be accentuated when he was tired or preoccupied. On the other hand, his lectures, just because they did not flow as his written words flowed, conveyed a sense of earnestness and commitment, as of a man wrestling with problems of expression and overcoming them in the presence of the class. We respected him for this, but we admired him much more for his treatment of the documents through which, we felt, we had at last reached to the roots of history. In patient explanation, in subtle analysis, in the re-creation of dead men through the words living after them, he gave us an example which I for one have never forgotten.

For most of us that was the end of the road and, having taken our examinations, we went the way of our contemporaries, which, in the Trinity of those days, was generally straight out of the country. But a few, of whom I was privileged to be one, stayed on to work for our higher degrees under his supervision. To me, who knew hardly any Irish history, this was a revelation, a whole new world for which my undergraduate course, though respectable so far as results went, had scarcely begun to prepare me. Thus began an apprenticeship which has continued to this day—a training in how to define one's subject, how to locate one's sources, how to evaluate different kinds of evidence, how to progress from description to analysis, how to handle footnotes and bibliographies, and at the end how to set out one's conclusions clearly, reasonably and, if all went well, even with some degree of style. Everyone who has sat at the feet of a great master will know what the experience is like (though its full impact may not be felt until long afterwards), but few can ever explain it satisfactorily to those who have not had the chance to fall under the spell. Suffice it to say that in acknowledging T.W.M. as a great master, I am not alone. Year by year, decade by decade, young men and women have passed through his hands, grown to maturity under his critical eye, and gone on to do him credit after their fashion, though never enough to pay the debt they owe.

To produce graduates of calibre and offer them no outlet for their talents save an arid thesis which struts and frets its hour on an examiner's desk and then is heard no more, was not T.W.M.'s idea of how a school of Irish history should be conducted. He had already, of course, in *I.H.S.*, provided one important forum for new writers. But just after the end of the second world war, together with R. Dudley Edwards (since 1945 professor of modern Irish history in University College, Dublin) and David B. Quinn (then professor of history at Queen's University, Belfast, and later professor of history at Liverpool University), he persuaded Messrs Faber and Faber to launch a series entitled 'Studies in Irish history', to consist of monographs by young or newly emerging scholars. The first of these, R. B. McDowell's *Irish public opinion, 1750–1800*, appeared in 1948 and others followed in rapid succession. In 1960 a second series was inaugurated, this time published by Routledge and Kegan Paul, by my *The fall of Parnell, 1890–91*. Although economic factors have slowed the rate of production in recent years, the series still continues, its tenth volume, R. B. McDowell's *The Church of Ireland, 1869–1969*, having been published in 1975. It is symptomatic of the widening of the scope of Irish historical research that the editorial board now consists of scholars drawn not only from Dublin and Belfast, but also from the U.S.A. and Australia. The driving force behind the project, however, is still T.W.M.

To establish professional scholarship at the highest level was undoubtedly T.W.M.'s principal objective. But he had others when he came to Dublin nearly forty years ago and these he has defined as follows:

When I was elected to fellowship in Trinity in 1939 the broad pattern of my work as an academic historian had been established: it was to teach history in various fields, including the history of Ireland to undergraduates; to encourage and direct research on Irish history, especially by young history graduates; to set new standards of objectivity and technical excellence in the conduct of that research and in the presentation of its results; to promote and assist the publication of articles and books based on such work and thus to bring a new historiography to bear on the teaching of Irish history and on public thinking about the Irish past; to encourage cooperation among historians and communication between the historians and the concerned public; and to contribute directly to the new historiography.[1]

[1] T.W.M., 'Notes on my career as a historian', pp 4–5.

To realise the ideal of linking the new historians with 'the concerned public' has absorbed a great deal of T.W.M.'s almost inexhaustible energy for the past thirty years. No one who knows the modern history of Ireland, or how that history has been distorted by myth and subverted by prejudice, will be in any doubt about the vital importance of establishing direct communication between the scholars and the busy world. The first attempt to bring this about was made where the need was even then greatest, in Ulster. Between 6 October and 22 December 1954, twelve talks on Ulster since 1800 were broadcast on the Northern Ireland programme of the B.B.C. on successive Wednesday evenings. The series was conceived by T.W.M. and was so successful that the talks were immediately issued in paperback form, edited by T.W.M. and J. C. Beckett, who had been one of his first graduate students at the Queen's University, where, after a spell of schoolteaching, he became first a lecturer and then a most respected professor of Irish history. All the lecturers save two were Ulstermen by origin, and although the series was subtitled 'a political and economic survey', it covered many matters, including religion and its bearing on politics, now a harsh commonplace of discussion but then almost taboo. The demand created by the series could not be satisfied simply by publishing the twelve talks. A second series was commissioned and this, consisting of twenty-two broadcasts under the same general title 'Ulster since 1800', went out during 1957 on the Northern Ireland home service of the B.B.C.; it was published, with the same editors, before the end of that year. Many of the original contributors reappeared and, though others were added, the series still spoke with an Ulster voice. Or rather several Ulster voices, for different traditions, different religions, different cultures, were all explored by historians from different backgrounds but with a common concern for truth and honesty. This series, more penetrating than the first in its treatment of potentially controversial subjects, still offers valuable insights into the problems of the north.

The Ulster experiment was the prelude to a more ambitious attempt to use radio in the republic of Ireland as a means of publicising as widely as possible the results of modern scholarship. In 1953 a new director of broadcasting, Mr Maurice Gorham, was appointed to Radio Éireann, and to assist him an advisory committee was set up. This committee investigated, but found impracticable, a suggestion that a 'university of the air' be established to transmit various courses to a possibly bemused public for three hours at a time each week for twenty-six weeks in each year. T.W.M., who was a member of the committee, suggested instead a series of regular half-hour talks in which the best of contemporary Irish research in a number of fields—mainly historical and literary—would be presented to the non-specialist listener as stimulatingly as possible. It was T.W.M., also, who suggested that these talks be called the Thomas Davis lectures, thus commemorating the Young Irelander of the mid-nineteenth century who had preached the reconciliation of the different Irish cultures and had urged his generation to 'educate that you may be free'.[1]

It was decided that the lectures should normally be broadcast on Sunday evenings in the autumn and winter months; also that they should be concerned wholly with Irish themes and given mainly by Irish lecturers. Although individual lectures have been given from time to time, it has been general practice to group them in series dealing with specific topics. Each series has had a general editor, and for the first dozen years they and their contributors were fortunate to work under the direction of Francis MacManus who, until his death in 1965, was guide, philosopher and friend to every nervous lecturer facing the ordeal of holding the attention of his invisible audience for thirty inexorable minutes. The first series was entitled 'Early Irish society', and its general editor, the late Myles Dillon, gave the initial lecture himself on 27 September 1953.

The success, not only of that series but of the whole conception, exceeded all expectations. The lectures rapidly became an institution in themselves, growing rapidly both in scope and in extent. In 1966, for example, when grappling with the delicate problems created by

[1] F. X. Martin, 'The Thomas Davis lectures, 1953–67', in *I.H.S.*, xv, no. 59 (Mar. 1967), pp 276–302.

the fiftieth anniversary of the Easter rising, the series 'Leaders and men of the Easter rising: Dublin 1916', contained nineteen contributions, including one from virtually every major historian competent to write on the subject. So popular were the lectures that from the outset there was a lively demand for their publication. Not every series has gone into print, but a great many have; a few have been published in hardback by London publishers, but the majority have appeared cheaply and attractively in paperbacks produced mainly by the Mercier Press of Cork. While they have not in themselves carried the historiographical revolution from the study to the street, there can be no doubt that they had a considerable and cumulative effect in creating in non-academic minds a more mature and reflective response to the literature and history of Ireland.

While the Thomas Davis lectures continued to thrive, their vehicle, radio, came under increasing competition from television. But T.W.M. was equal to this emergency also, bringing his energy and determination to bear upon a project which many regarded at the time as impossible. Between January and June 1966 Radio Telefís Éireann transmitted twenty-one programmes, each of about half an hour's duration, under the title 'The course of Irish history'. The series was mounted and edited by T.W.M. and Professor F. X. Martin, O.S.A., the gifted and versatile professor of medieval history in University College, Dublin, who that same year was responsible for the Thomas Davis lectures on the Easter rising. The aim of this television series, as the editors observed, was 'to present a survey of Irish history that would be both popular and authoritative, concise but comprehensive, highly selective while at the same time balanced and fair-minded, critical but constructive and sympathetic'. The result may not have been the acme of television—the lecture formula seems to have been rather too rigid to be easily translated into visual images—but 'the book of the film' was an immediate success. *The course of Irish history* (Mercier Press, Cork, 1967), edited by T.W.M. and F. X. Martin, rapidly became the general history in paperback form for which students in colleges and schools had long been hungering. That it has held its place as essential reading for the young is due primarily to its brevity and clarity, which elucidate often complex episodes in Irish history with a freshness all too rare in the prescribed reading that had been the indigestible diet of Irish schoolchildren for many generations.

While T.W.M.'s flair for *haute vulgarisation* has undoubtedly made a considerable impact upon educated Irish opinion, north and south, it would be wrong to give the impression that he was deflected from his own researches by the demands of the non-specialist public. Although it has to be said that he was indeed being deflected, this, as we shall see presently, was for weightier reasons. But the deflection was so far from being absolute that in the years after his move to Dublin he began to develop the nineteenth-century studies which have ever since remained his principal preoccupation, while not excluding characteristic forays into the seventeenth and eighteenth centuries. The impulse towards the nineteenth century was partly supplied by the family of Michael Davitt, founder of the Irish land league and for many years in the forefront of nationalist and labour movements in the last decades of the nineteenth century and the early years of the twentieth. T.W.M. was entrusted with Davitt's voluminous papers in the hope that these would form the basis of a biography. It is the tragedy of his many-sided career that despite his titanic energy he has still to complete, as he has said, 'a book on that great man, Michael Davitt, that shall be worthy of the subject'.[1] It is only proper to add, however, that not only has a whole series of articles and essays on Davitt appeared during the last twenty years, but I myself have been privileged to see a draft in typescript of a large work on Davitt and the land war which, for anyone less of a perfectionist than T.W.M., would seem to be in an advanced state of preparation. The long delay in producing the *magnum opus*, though vexing to the author and to two generations of scholars, has given time for a considerable revision of T.W.M.'s view of his hero. The Davitt we shall get, in whatever form we may get him, will be a very different Davitt from the one we might have got a quarter of

---

[1] T.W.M., 'Notes on my career as a historian', p. 7.

a century ago. The eyes regarding him will not be less sympathetic, but the judgement passed will be by a mind which in the interval has absorbed, and contributed to, much critical revision of nineteenth-century history.

Davitt, it must be said, has had to compete with many rivals for T.W.M.'s attention. These have included both the Fenians and Parnell, but a more persistent competitor even than these has been Thomas Davis. Davis, a protestant of mixed Irish and English parentage, was a graduate of Dublin University (Trinity College, Dublin) at a time when that institution was rigidly 'ascendancy' in its attitudes. During the short time that remained to him after graduation (he died in 1845 at the age of 31) Davis sought to unite his fellow countrymen of different creeds and origins by giving them a common pride in the Irish civilisation they had inherited and thus leading them to discover a common identity for the future. In a centenary lecture given in the presence of Mr de Valera in 1945, T.W.M. emphasised the reconciling role of Davis with a fervour that reflected his own commitment to that tradition.[1] Just over twenty years later, in another lecture, also delivered before Mr de Valera, he was still faithful to the reconciling ideal which indeed has been his own guiding star all his life.[2]

This phase, running roughly from 1945 to 1965, was for T.W.M., as for most Irish historians, a period when the rewriting of Irish political history in a more objective fashion seemed the most important task to be tackled. But he never lost sight of the fact that there were other kinds of history, and into one of these—the history of the Irish university question in the nineteenth century—he flung himself with an almost frenetic ardour. This was partly, as we shall see, because of his public involvement with the Irish university

[1] T.W.M., *Thomas Davis, 1814–45: a centenary address delivered in Trinity College, Dublin, on 12 June 1945 at a public meeting of the college historical society* (Dublin, 1945).

[2] T.W.M., 'Thomas Davis and the Irish nation', in *Hermathena*, ciii (1966), pp 5–31. The lecture was delivered in the public examination hall of Trinity College, Dublin, on 20 April 1966, in association with the golden jubilee of the 1916 rising.

question in the twentieth century, but partly also because the centenary of his own Queen's University, Belfast, was approaching and he was asked, together with his friend and frequent colleague, J. C. Beckett, to write its history. The resulting two volumes, amounting to almost a thousand pages and published by Faber and Faber in 1959, when the centenary (1945) was a rather distant memory, constituted a monumental task almost beyond the endurance of the authors. Nevertheless, the book they produced was not only a model for all historians of universities, but also a major contribution to the history of modern Ireland.

The strain imposed by the writing of the history of Queen's was not just peculiar to that book, but was inherent in the situation confronting T.W.M. from the time he took up his duties in Trinity College. Two points about the college during his early years there are fundamental to an understanding of the predicament in which he soon found himself. One was that when he joined it, and for a long time afterwards, it had virtually no administrative machinery. Nearly everything, down to the most minute detail, had to be dealt with by the fellows, whose whole training had in many cases ideally unfitted them for this kind of work. The tradition was not wholly bad, of course. It was in origin a humane tradition, based upon the assumption that in a civilised community civilised standards would be best maintained by the amateurs of an amiable academia rather than by the professionals of a sinister bureaucracy. Up to a point, and while the college remained small and poor, this assumption was justified. More especially, it was justified by the institution of tutorship, whereby every undergraduate was assigned on entry to a tutor (at that time necessarily also a fellow) who stood to him *in loco parentis*. A tutor might also teach his pupils, but often he did not, and much time had to be spent by new incumbents in learning how to 'play the system', so that they could advise their pupils in a dozen different disciplines how best to manipulate the college regulations to their advantage. T.W.M. was a tutor for twelve years, and I was among his first pupils in the technical sense, as well as being a history student under his instruction. I can testify to the care and sympathy he lavished on his charges, and it was evident even to brash young people like us that, as he has since observed, he found tutoring 'valuable and congenial'. But he also found it time-consuming, and in 1952 he exchanged this burden for that of senior tutor for admissions.

T.W.M. held that post for six years, and for a further six years was responsible, as senior lecturer, for the academic functioning of the college. In Trinity usage, senior tutor and senior lecturer were not stages on the ladder of promotion, but the titles of 'officers' appointed annually by the board of the college on the nomination of the provost to oversee various aspects of administration. During these twelve years (1952–64), T.W.M. played a notable part in drawing the college out of its old amateurism and into a new era of professionalism. This was achieved in a typically Trinity way by ensuring that the heads of the two main administrative divisions— financial and secretarial—should themselves be graduates of the college who had gained experience of management in the world outside. Even so, the tradition remained intact—as it still does—of entrusting major offices to academics, though nowadays, and so that they may not be too long divorced from their subjects, it is customary for the 'annual officers' to hold their posts for much shorter periods than in T.W.M.'s time.

As an officeholder T.W.M. revealed great strengths and a few defects which were perhaps the obverse of those strengths. His has always been a classifying mind, though this instinct for order has been combined to an unusual degree with a capacity for innovation. In this combination he curiously resembled Gladstone, even to the extent of producing on occasion a characteristically Gladstonian blend of far-sighted reform and administrative congestion. Thus, he completely reorganised and extended the offices first of senior tutor and then of senior lecturer, bringing both to a high pitch of efficiency in the performance of a whole range of new functions. But at the same time, because of his passion for exactness of detail and a certain reluctance to delegate, he soon became submerged in trivia which not only involved him unwillingly in the broils dear to a particular kind of academic heart, but sometimes also blunted the effectiveness of the reforms he himself had carried out.

A single illustration must suffice. As senior lecturer T.W.M. is most famous in the college for his invention, 'the senior lecturer's exercise'. Starting from the assumption that the duty owed by every full-time academic to the college in term-time was sixteen hours of teaching per week, he introduced a system of 'credits', whereby this commitment would be reduced in proportion to the time spent on official administration of one kind or another. The enlightened object of this exercise was a fairer apportionment of burdens in a college where the staff was never numerous enough to meet all the demands made upon it; but the calculations needed to do justice to each individual case were so intricate as to tax a modern computer, let alone a single officer with one or two assistants. Nevertheless, the system worked satisfactorily for some years, and although the growth of the college eventually made its continuance impossible, it stands as a monument to a daring attempt at solving that most intractable of all problems, how to ensure a proper balance between humane administration and academic excellence.

For T.W.M. this problem was complicated by the second fundamental fact about Trinity when he first came to the college. This was its isolation from the life of the city and the country that flowed round its walls but seemed to penetrate very little inside those walls. In part this was a consequence of history. In the nineteenth century, the period of its greatest international reputation, the college had been identified by the majority of Irishmen as the home of an arrogant and complacent ascendancy spirit. With the coming of political independence, Trinity shrank back into itself. It was not, indeed, menaced by government hostility, but the already existing prohibition by the Irish Roman Catholic hierarchy upon students going there was strictly enforced and did not finally disappear until 1970. Moreover, the college had for many years to exist on its own resources, derived mainly from fees and from its much diminished endowments, and the results of this were only too evident in academic as well as in architectural dilapidation.

This situation began to change in the late 1940s, when government assistance was made available by Mr de Valera. From a modest beginning, the stream of public money has swelled to such an extent that Trinity is now largely state-supported. It was in these hopeful circumstances that a new generation of Trinity dons began to work for a closer integration between the college and the society with which it had to identify itself or perish. Among those who accepted this challenge T.W.M. took a foremost part. Mention has already been made of his contribution to the establishment of the Thomas Davis lectures. His connection with broadcasting, however, went much further than that. Between 1953 and 1960 he was a member of Comhairle Radio Éireann (the Irish Broadcasting Council) and from 1960 to 1972 (the period when television was being introduced into Ireland) he was a member of the successor body, the Irish Broadcasting Authority. This last appointment ended sadly, indeed tragically. In November 1972 the entire authority was dismissed by the government of the day for allegedly contravening a directive by the minister for posts and telegraphs not to broadcast 'any matter that could be calculated to promote the aims or activities of any organisation which engages in, promotes, encourages or advocates the attaining of any particular objective by violent means'. It was the broadcasting of a radio interview interpreted by the government as incompatible with the directive that led to this drastic action. In a public statement T.W.M., while agreeing that the radio interview was misjudged, made an eloquent plea for the freedom of responsible broadcasting, more necessary than ever, as he pointed out, at a period of great political tension. In the Irish context, he said, what was desperately needed was the kind of open-minded investigation which Irish radio and television had done their best to promote:

Much of our problem springs from a refusal to face unpalatable facts, an addiction to make-believe, a tendency to prefer myths to truth. But a new realism, a new questioning of case-hardened assumptions has emerged, and this has been greatly, perhaps decisively, encouraged and stimulated by the development of broadcasting. If the measure of freedom that R.T.E. [Radio

Telefís Eireann] has had is now to be drastically reduced, one of the first casualties will be truth, and the process of awakening the public mind to the realities of the Irish predicament may be disastrously halted. We need more, not less, real communication in Ireland.[1]

Side by side with these preoccupations went his membership of the Irish Manuscripts Commission, which he has attended regularly since 1943, of the advisory committee on cultural relations (a body set up by the department of external relations, as it then was) from 1949 to 1963, and above all, of the government-appointed commission on higher education between 1960 and 1967.

This last was at once the most important and the most frustrating episode of T.W.M.'s public life. As his own researches had shown, the tangled history of the university question in the nineteenth century had bequeathed to Ireland a variety of institutions of higher learning which, while overlapping in certain respects, had left some areas of study and some parts of the country inadequately provided for. During its lengthy deliberations the commission investigated the whole complex situation with unexampled thoroughness and produced a massive report. Its precise recommendations need not trouble us, for hard on the publication of a summary of them the then minister for education produced his own solution for the most difficult aspect of the problem, the existence in Dublin of two universities, separate, independent and both intensely proud of their very different traditions. The minister's *coup de théâtre* was to decree a merger of the two into one large university of Dublin; but he died before he could achieve this, and in face of the hostility which his proposal evoked in both universities it is doubtful that he could have succeeded had he lived to be as old as Methuselah. In the event, while the concept of an outright merger was relegated to the wings, successive governments have addressed themselves to the broader issues of higher education in Ireland with little visible effect as yet, save to confound confusion still further.

To T.W.M. this outcome was a peculiarly bitter blow, since he

[1] *Irish Times*, 27 Nov. 1972.

had invested an enormous expenditure of time and energy in the affairs of the commission. Not only did he devote a long series of Fridays and Saturdays to its full meetings, but, together with the chairman (the then chief justice, Cearbhaill Ó Dálaigh) and Professor Eoin O'Malley of University College, Dublin, he spent many hundreds of hours in drafting the final report, the details of which were discussed at innumerable meetings in the Four Courts, often extending far past midnight. Yet T.W.M. has never regretted these labours, or regarded them as wasted. 'The outcome', he has written,

with all its disappointments, has been far from fruitless. We worked with eyes on the future and with no thought of earning present favour. Some at least of our recommendations have been implemented, and others doubtless will be. But, quite apart from this, our report, with its supporting corpus of evidence and other documentation, embodies a comprehensive view and assessment of higher education in the republic of Ireland, the first of its kind ever made in this country; and as such it will, I believe, have lasting value.[1]

This is true, and T.W.M.'s own commission papers, now in the library of Trinity College, Dublin, will undoubtedly be a major source for future historians of Irish higher education. But the price paid for this arduous labour, piled as it was on top of all T.W.M.'s other commitments, was high. To offset the endless flow of paper and the crushing burden of committee-work, there was only one brief intermission—an idyllic sabbatical year at the Institute of Advanced Studies at Princeton in 1965, made possible by the Leverhulme research fellowship T.W.M. held at that time. This, it is worth recording for the benefit of a generation which orders these things differently, was the sole study leave he obtained in the whole of his professional career. Naturally, his own research suffered from the pressure of these other demands upon his time. It suffered, not in the sense of absolute disruption, for articles and reviews continued to appear in *I.H.S.* and elsewhere, but chiefly, as already indicated, by the continuing postponement of the long-awaited, and still longer striven for, life of Davitt.

---

[1] T.W.M., 'Notes on my career as a historian', pp 6–7.

Yet such has been T.W.M.'s reservoir of stamina that even while still immersed in many of his existing commitments he embarked on one more which may yet prove to be his most enduring monument. On 4 December 1962 he read a presidential address to the Irish Historical Society entitled 'Towards a new history of Ireland'. In this he advanced the view that after a generation of specialised research the next and most urgent task of historians would be 'to give a new impetus to Irish history by promoting a history of Ireland that would span its entire course, would be broadly concerned in social, economic and cultural, as well as in political and constitutional, terms, would fully exploit the new scholarship and the new materials now available, and, finally, would be as authoritative as possible'.[1] His conception, though it was to undergo several changes later, was from the beginning nothing less than gigantic. In its original form it envisaged twelve to fourteen volumes embracing every imaginable kind of history, requiring the close collaboration of a multitude of scholars and, of course, demanding a special organisation and a degree of financial support from the state such as had never before been given to any historical enterprise in Ireland. This scheme was enthusiastically received by the meeting which heard T.W.M.'s address, but there was also a certain amount of the criticism that is inseparable from the launching of any new endeavour in Ireland. He recalled this seven years later with wry amusement:

There was, it was claimed, no need for such a project. It smacked of monopoly and would discourage private enterprise. It would be disastrous to accept money from the state, and, in any case, it was unnecessary to create a special organisation for something that could be done on a purely voluntary basis. The time was not ripe for such a project: far too much specialised research had yet to be done. Besides, political history could safely be left to individual enterprise, and if there was to be a cooperative effort it should concentrate on economic and social history, in which progress has been specially slow. It would be exceedingly difficult to get Irish historians to

---

[1] T.W.M., 'Towards a new history of Ireland', in *I.H.S.*, xvi, no. 63 (Mar. 1969), p. 243.

work to any agreed plan and impossible to extract contributions from them by any fixed dates.[1]

Many of these criticisms, it has to be said, were founded on a realistic assessment of the history of Irish historical writing. It was perfectly true that undue concentration on political history had left large areas of social and economic history, and virtually the whole of *Kulturgeschichte*, unworked by specialists. It was no less true that Irish historians were difficult to lead and impossible to drive. While many were, and are, active and admirably punctual, others, and these not the least senior, have been apt to subside into what Harold Laski, addressing them, once memorably described as 'that state of resentful coma which historians call research'. In the event, and as the project got under way, some proved amenable to discipline, but others found the constraints intolerable and in due course fell out of the ranks.

Nevertheless, the project was driven ahead with strong determination. The scheme presented by T.W.M. was formally adopted by the Irish Historical Society in October 1963, though in June 1964 the society transferred its sponsorship to the Irish Committee of Historical Sciences, of which, as we have already seen, T.W.M. had been an active member since its inception in 1938. In November 1964 this body set up the skeleton of a working organisation and appointed four editors—T. Desmond Williams, professor of modern history in University College, Dublin; F. X. Martin; J. C. Beckett; and T.W.M. himself. There was also to be an editorial committee consisting of the four editors and nine other members, and a larger advisory board of historians who were either to become contributors or had, at the very least, indicated their support for the project. In the course of these developments the nature of the project had changed considerably. In place of the twelve or fourteen volumes originally proposed, the history was to be written in two stages. Stage 1 was to be produced at high speed (in no more than five years, it was hoped) and was to consist of a general history of Ireland in

[1] Ibid., pp 243–4.

two or more volumes of text, together with a volume of reference material. The volumes constituting stage 1 were to be published simultaneously, whereas stage 2, which was to embody the original multi-volume project, would be spread over a much longer span of time and would be published volume by volume as circumstances dictated.

At the heart of the New History, as it was already beginning to be called, was the permanent secretariat which was essential if continuity and momentum were both to be maintained. But a secretariat presupposed a regular home, and that, in turn, presupposed a regular income. To lay the basis for the latter the important, and in some eyes hazardous, decision was taken to approach the government of the republic of Ireland for an annual grant-in-aid. The then minister for education, Dr Patrick Hillery (now president of Ireland) was sympathetic, and in May 1965 the editors received a firm promise of support. As often happens in such affairs, economic stringency delayed the implementation of the promise, and therefore of the project also, until May 1967, when a small initial grant was at last made. The following year this was substantially increased by a new minister, the late Donogh O'Malley—ironically, the same minister who had played havoc with the report of the commission on higher education—and subsequent ministers and governments have been faithful to the original pledge. Even so, the New History could hardly have been set in motion without the additional help of a munificent private benefaction from Dr John A. Mulcahy of New York. It was however a disappointment that, despite the personal involvement of several Ulster historians in the scheme, the then government of Northern Ireland was unable to make a contribution.

The problem of residence was solved by transferring the New History in July 1968 from the auspices of the Irish Committee of Historical Sciences to those of the Royal Irish Academy. The latter body, which has been since the end of the eighteenth century the source of much fundamental research into the language, literature and history of Ireland, found suitable accommodation in its own house in Dawson Street, Dublin, where the headquarters of the New

History has ever since remained. And it was there, in the Academy, in the summer of 1976, almost exactly eight years after the transfer and nearly fourteen years after T.W.M.'s original initiative, that Irish historians gathered to celebrate the publication of the first volume of the great work—or rather, and in true Hibernian style, not the first but the third, dealing with the history of early modern Ireland, 1534–1691. As that volume makes plain, further changes in the grand design had taken place over the years. Although stage 2 has not been formally abandoned, it may be said to have receded over the rim of the horizon. In place of the fairly modest general history of the first version of stage 1, there are to be ten volumes, of which the last three will consist of chronology, maps, other reference matter, bibliographical material, and illustrations. And instead of four editors, there are now three. Professors Williams and Beckett have dropped out and Professor F. J. Byrne, a leading authority on early Irish history, has come in. The other two editors, F. X. Martin and T.W.M., are still at the helm, but, as his editorial colleagues gracefully pointed out at the launching of volume III, the heaviest burden has always been carried, and is still being carried, by T.W.M.

The *New history* is being published by the Oxford University Press, and in appearance somewhat resembles the *Oxford history of England*, with which, no doubt, it will eventually be compared. In composition and layout, however, a comparison with the *New Cambridge modern history* might be more apt, since each volume is the work of several contributors and different chapters are devoted to politics, economics and society, and a variety of cultural topics. Since the stage is obviously much more constricted, it would not be unreasonable to expect a higher degree of cohesion from the Irish *New history* than from the *New Cambridge modern history*, and that has certainly been the aim of the editors. 'This history', they state in their preface, 'though the work of many scholars, has been conceived as a unity, based on a detailed plan for the nine volumes as a whole. . . . Though each volume has been designed to cover an identifiable period of Irish history, the work is not a series of isolated volumes but a harvesting of the best contemporary scholarship for each period up to the end of 1974'.[1]

Obviously, it is too soon yet to assess the *New history*. The next volumes scheduled to appear are two reference volumes containing chronology, maps, and other reference material, and they will probably be before the public not long after this book of essays is published. But only when the whole project has been completed will it be possible to measure its full magnitude. Two things, however, may already be said in the light of the much-praised volume III. One is that it promises, in rigorous comprehensiveness, to live up to the standards proclaimed by T.W.M. some fifteen years ago. And the other is that this rigour, combined as it is with a notable elegance of production, bears the hallmark which has been stamped upon every piece of historical work that T.W.M. has undertaken. Cooperative work it undoubtedly is, but as 'Moody's history' posterity will know it.

It would be difficult to imagine that anything more could be crammed into a scholar's life than the creation of the *New history* simultaneously with the other labours glanced at in this memoir. Yet the fact remains that while continuing with the editorship of *I.H.S.*, while still running his department, and while developing the graduate seminar in Irish history, T.W.M. has found time to complete one further piece of writing. This grew out of a paper delivered at St Patrick's College, Dublin, in July 1973 at a course on the teaching of history in Great Britain and Ireland. It became a paperback of some hundred pages, entitled *The Ulster question, 1603–1973*. In part this was a historical survey in the author's most careful and conscientious manner, a retracing of ground which in places had been first marked out by himself forty years earlier. As such, it deserves more attention that it seems to have received, but, paradoxically, it has received less attention because it was also in part a product of the contemporary political situation by which in

---

[1] *A new history of Ireland, iii: early modern Ireland, 1534–1691* (Oxford, 1976), p. v.

fact it was dominated. T.W.M. found time to write the book because he was still at heart an Ulsterman, deeply affected by the tragedy that had beset his province since the outbreak of the 'troubles' in the autumn of 1968. As he completed the book in December 1973 the Sunningdale agreement to form a power-sharing executive in Northern Ireland had just been concluded, and T.W.M. had allowed himself to indulge the hope shared by many that a significant turning-point had at last been reached. 'The violence and the killings continue', he wrote,

and the British army remains in Northern Ireland. But after five anguished years there is an unprecedented change in the northern situation: a government is to take office on 1 January 1974 in which the elected representatives of the minority will share power with those of the majority, a government committed to restoring peace and promoting social justice and human welfare with the assurance of cooperation and support from the government of the Irish republic and of Britain.[1]

Alas for these high hopes. When, a few months later, I received an advance copy from T.W.M. the power-sharing experiment was already doomed and was soon to vanish into the capacious limbo reserved for futile attempts to solve the Ulster question.

T.W.M.'s book seems to have suffered almost the same eclipse as the Sunningdale agreement itself, but it has an importance in his work transcending the crisis that evoked it. It is important because it is the most modern instance of certain qualities that have always distinguished his scholarship. Some of these qualities he has impressed upon the historians he has trained to succeed him, but some, I suspect, may divide him more deeply from his successors than either he or they have yet fully realised. The qualities he has sought to transmit are those of accuracy, clarity, absolute fairness, and objectivity of interpretation, so far as these are possible within the obvious human limitations under which all historians labour. The qualities which his pupils admire, but find harder to reproduce, are those that derive from a view of history at once moral, rational and,

---

[1] T.W.M., *The Ulster question, 1603–1973* (Dublin and Cork, 1974), p. vii.

in a deep, non-technical sense, religious. Like every writer, T.W.M. is strongly marked by his upbringing and early environment. Both in his serious and frugal home, and in his serious and frugal student days, he learned to think of men and women as responsible human beings, making choices and taking decisions more or less according to a code of conduct to which society at large subscribed.

Of course, as any historian must be, he is aware of the dark side of the moon, and he has never excluded from his calculations H. A. L. Fisher's 'play of the contingent and unforeseen'. But it would not be unfair to say that he has generally proceeded on the assumption that, when men and women have made their historical choices and decisions, such imponderables as conscience and compassion have to some degree entered in. Two examples will indicate this tendency in his thinking. The first is his steadfast devotion to Michael Davitt, who was one of the few leading figures in the political history of nineteenth-century Ireland to base his career upon social concern. Social concern, in fact, has always been an activating motive in T.W.M.'s own conduct of life. When he came to Trinity, one of those whom he grew to revere was R. M. Gwynn, a saintly fellow of the college who for many years had spent himself in unobtrusively doing what he could to improve the lot of the Dublin poor. And he admired no less another don, Owen Sheehy-Skeffington, who, though often in a seeming minority of one, spoke out fearlessly against callousness and injustice in Irish society wherever he saw it. It was characteristic of T.W.M. that his contribution to the cause of conscience should have been eminently practical. In 1942 he became treasurer of the T.C.D. Social Service Company, an organisation formed to run a home (at the time of writing, three homes) for old people, and since 1953 he has been chairman of the company. Himself holding such a view of man's responsibility for man, he has always been particularly drawn to those aspects of history where responsibility can be identified and observed in action.

My second example is of precisely such a case. Anyone who works in the history of nineteenth-century Ireland has to come to terms sooner or later with Gladstone. For the generation to which

T.W.M. belongs (at least for those of them who were liberally inclined; the conservatives had a different view) Gladstone's Irish policy was a prime example of enlightened moral purpose triumphing over the baser and more corrupt passions of ordinary mankind. This was the Gladstone of J. L. Hammond's *Gladstone and the Irish nation*, first published in 1938, the very year in which *I.H.S.* was launched. But the Gladstone of more modern writers—for example of A. B. Cooke's and John Vincent's *The governing passion* (Brighton, 1974)—is another kind of Gladstone altogether, a calculating politician for whom the *summum bonum* is to stay in office and hold the liberal party together. T.W.M. certainly prefers the older to the newer version, though he would probably not dissent from the verdict that both versions distort through over-simplification and that, as historians comfortably say when they want to indulge in ritual purification, the truth 'lies somewhere in between'.

Yet that is not really the point. The point rather is that a historian who grew to maturity between the wars necessarily has a different view of life, and therefore of history, from one who has grown to maturity after 1945. Another way of putting this is to suggest that when T.W.M. was completing his training the liberal—more strictly, perhaps, one should say the whig—interpretation of history, to which Lord Acton had given such an impulse, was still, if only just, holding the field. There have been times, indeed, when reading T.W.M.'s work, or listening to him in full flight, that I have seemed to hear the voice of Acton exhorting us all 'never to debase the moral currency or to lower the standard of rectitude'. This is not to say that T.W.M. followed Acton to the extreme of believing that the historian should assume the authority of a judge (though in his inquest into *The Times*'s behaviour in the matter of the Pigott forgeries he comes close to doing just that[1]), but it does imply that his disposition is to maintain the moral currency and the standard of rectitude when assessing such historical figures as Davis, or

---

[1] T.W.M., '*The Times* versus Parnell and Co., 1887–90', in *Historical Studies*, vi (London, 1968), pp 147–82.

Davitt, or Gladstone. In T.W.M. there remains a good deal of the
liberal historian of the old school who still cherishes a lingering
belief, if not in the perfectibility of man, at least in his improvability,
and who has not entirely discarded the idea of progress from his
mental equipment. His students, on the other hand, inhabit a world
where such liberalism begins to seem increasingly an intellectual
luxury which they can scarcely afford. Too much has happened to
our society, too many axes have been laid to the roots of the tree of
knowledge, for us easily to ascribe any longer purity of aim and
disinterestedness of motive to men and women who, we sense, were
as muddled and vulnerable in their day as we are in ours.

I must not be taken as suggesting that the example of a life
devoted to rigorous and unselfish scholarship has not had an impact
upon the students whom T.W.M. has passed through his hands.
The impact has never been less than immense and no graduate
student who has been exposed to his influence has escaped being
marked permanently and beneficially. Only part of that influence
has been exerted through the 'official' channels of the seminar room
or the direct supervision of research. A no less important part has
derived from the unforgettable experience of coming into direct
personal contact with a man of exceptional powers who has always
lived life to the full. T.W.M. has been blessed in many ways, but
most of all, as I have already indicated, in his happy married and
family life. This, aided in recent years by his and his wife's membership of the Society of Friends, has given an inner and most admired
tranquillity to an outer life that has certainly been no stranger to
storms. Like most men of resolute character and strong conviction,
T.W.M. has known his share of controversy, inside and outside his
college. No one can govern a department for nearly forty years on
the centralised lines favoured by professors of his generation without
colliding from time to time with other colleagues of similar
temperament but possibly less stamina. And no one, assuredly, can
undertake to prod Irish historians into prompt delivery of their copy
without encountering a great deal of opposition and acrimony.

Yet, though there have been many battles (and some disappoint-

ments, of which the most wounding was his failure to be appointed
to the Lecky chair of history after Miss Maxwell's retirement), it
would be altogether false to the essence of the man to end by
conveying an impression simply of restless and combative energy.
To those who really came to know him his outstanding characteristics have always been quite otherwise. They have found in him a
man of great courtesy and gentleness; a man of taste and discern-
ment in the arts, especially in his adored music; a man who gloried
in the Irish countryside and with whom to walk therein was a
never-failing joy; a man who delighted in children and was, and is,
to be seen at his best by his own fireside, submitting with the best
grace imaginable to the blandishments of daughters who were
clearly devoted to him, but no less clearly expert in winning his
support for whatever their hearts were set on.

Now, his children are almost all married and scattered, and their
children in turn are beginning to invade the familiar house in
Healthfield Road. But neither children nor grandchildren mono-
polise T.W.M.'s attention. Always there is the larger family of
students, old ones and new ones, whose problems and interests he
has never ceased to share. To them he has given much and from them
he has expected much. In the giving and receiving, bonds have been
established which no differences of interpretation can slacken. When
the contributors to this volume were invited to participate, their
replies without exception expressed enthusiasm, affection and pride.
Enthusiasm to share in a tribute, however modest, to a revered
teacher; affection for one who has been to them much more than a
teacher; pride in belonging to the famous school of history he has so
largely created.

T.W.M. retired from the Erasmus Smith chair of history on
30 September 1977, a year earlier than he would ordinarily have
done if reasons of health had not made it desirable to shed the ad-
minstrative duties he has carried for so long. But for him retirement
is a relative term, meaning simply freedom to concentrate his still
formidable powers upon the long-suffering Davitt and, of course,
upon completing the massive edifice of the *New history*. Yet it is

entirely characteristic of this extraordinary man that even as I sat down to write this memoir there should have arrived on my desk one more document bearing the familiar initials, T.W.M. It was a proposition for the establishment of an institute of historical research, designed to build upon the foundations laid by the *New history* and to prepare the way for the further development of Irish historiography for many generations to come. It is too soon to say whether or not this will come into being, and if it does, it may well fall to others to carry it through. But whatever the outcome, there is surely a symbolic aptness in the fact that the earliest initiatives in this latest and most important project should have been taken by the man who has done more to transform his subject and its place in Irish intellectual life than any other since history first began to be written on this island.

The protestant response to repeal: the case of the Dublin working class

JACQUELINE HILL

HISTORIANS have now generally accepted that the great majority of Irish protestants failed to support the repeal movement initiated by Daniel O'Connell in 1840. Various explanations have been advanced to account for this, including the effect of economic prosperity on northern protestants, the development among protestants of a British rather than an Irish sense of nationality, and the fear of catholic political control in an independent Irish parliament. Such explanations can be helpful, but they are often applied in a sweeping way to protestants in general with little account taken of variations in attitude arising from local circumstances or differences in social class. In this respect, the protestant working class of Dublin represents a particularly interesting case, because for several reasons it might have been expected to support the repeal movement. According to economic arguments prevalent in the 1840s, and apparently widely accepted among catholic tradesmen, Dublin had suffered a severe setback in her trade and industry through the effects of the union:[1] decline was particularly noticeable in some of the industries, like silk, which were traditionally identified with protestants. Moreover, the headquarters of the repeal movement was in the capital, able to bombard the working class with arguments about the merits of repeal. Furthermore, protestants were already outnumbered by catholics in Dublin by about three to one (in contrast to the situation in Belfast, where their numbers were much more even); Dublin protestants might have been expected to

---

[1] L. M. Cullen, 'Irish economic history: fact and myth' in L. M. Cullen (ed.), *The formation of the Irish economy* (Cork, 1969), pp 113–24.

see the writing on the wall and agree to cooperate with the majority so as to make their own terms before repeal was achieved.[1] Yet instead of joining the repeal movement, a substantial number— between two and three thousand—preferred the political leadership of an evangelical clergyman whose apocalyptic interpretation of current events earned him and his followers the ridicule of repealers and the contempt of middle- and upper-class protestants. The clergyman was the Reverend Tresham Dames Gregg, and the politico-religious association he led was the Dublin Protestant Operative Association and Reformation Society (hereafter D.P.O.A.).[2] The D.P.O.A. stood out consistently against any cooperation with catholics for political ends.

In his historical record *Eighty-five years of Irish history* the veteran repealer, W. J. O'Neill Daunt, placed the blame for the failure of working-class protestants in Dublin to cooperate with the repealers in 1848 on

preachers, orators, and writers, whose idea of Christianity appeared to be confined to the duty of hating the papists and shouting 'To hell with the pope!' . . . [who] bellowed about Antichrist, romanced about apocalyptic numerals, . . . [and] threatened that if repeal were obtained the papists would ride roughshod over the protestants . . .[3]

There is little doubt that Daunt was referring principally to Gregg, whose influence over working-class protestants was notorious, and who did indeed counsel them not to support the repeal movement.

---

[1] Dublin's protestant inhabitants (excluding quakers and Jews) numbered 65,736, or about 27 per cent of Dublin's population. These figures are based on statistics collected in the late 1830s and reprinted in *Dublin Almanac and General Register of Ireland for the year . . . 1841* (Dublin, n.d.), p. 575.

[2] Gregg was chaplain to the chapel of St Mary in the parish church of St Nicholas Within: he had been chosen by the parishioners against the wishes of the archbishop of Dublin. See *Letter of Rev. Tresham D. Gregg, A.M., to the churchwardens and parishioners of St Nicholas Within, Dublin* (Dublin, n.d.), R.I.A., H.P., vol. 1799 (1841). The D.P.O.A. was founded in 1841; it added the words 'and Reformation Society' to its title in 1842 (*Warder*, 15 Oct. 1842).

[3] William Joseph O'Neill Daunt, *Eighty-five years of Irish history 1800–1885* (2nd ed., 2 vols, London, 1886), ii, 147.

Other writers since Daunt have noted that from the mid-nineteenth century onwards demagogic protestant clergymen (more familiar in the context of Belfast than of Dublin) used their influence over the protestant working class to inflame sectarian passions, often with violent results.[1] However, the question that is seldom asked— Daunt did not raise it at all—is why the protestant working class should prove so receptive to the influence of such clergymen; why they should have accepted their arguments and interpretation of events rather than those of less fanatical clergymen, or, indeed, of non-sectarian nationalists.

It is the purpose of this paper to consider these questions in relation to the protestant working class of Dublin in the 1840s. First, the background to the emergence of the D.P.O.A. will be analysed, in particular the prevailing religious climate and social and economic conditions at the time of its foundation, in an attempt to show why Gregg's leadership proved attractive to working-class protestants. The second part of the paper will consider the various arguments the repealers used to persuade these protestants to join them, and the D.P.O.A.'s response. In conclusion, an attempt will be made to assess the broader significance of the D.P.O.A. for the national movement.

The starting-point for any discussion of the reasons for the foundation of the D.P.O.A. is the prevailing religious climate in Ireland in the 1830s and 1840s. In Europe generally it was a period of heightened interest in apocalyptic prophecies. The Napoleonic wars, bringing political, social and economic upheaval, had created conditions of bewilderment and anxiety conducive to apocalyptic speculation, which was particularly marked among protestants.[2] Its prevalence among protestants may probably be attributed to their emphasis on the need for each individual to have a personal relationship with God, achieved through familiarity with scripture, the scriptures

---

[1] See, for instance, Constantine Fitzgibbon, *Red hand: the Ulster colony* (London, 1971), pp 200–4, 226–31.

[2] Bryan Wilson, *Religious sects* (London, 1970), p. 94.

being a rich source of apocalyptic speculation. In Ireland, the prophecies of Pastorini evoked interest among catholics in the 1820s, while protestants (often laymen), published tracts speculating on the approach of Armageddon and the millennium.[1] Irish protestants shared a tendency, common in England and America, to revive an older protestant tradition (prevalent in early seventeenth-century England) in which the papacy was identified with the beast (Antichrist) mentioned in the Book of Revelation.[2] Such speculation has traditionally attracted great interest among the poor, and Irish journals began to appear in the mid-1830s dedicated to expounding an apocalyptic interpretation of events in terms poor protestants could understand.[3] These journals included the *Protestant Penny Magazine* (1834–6) and the *Watchman* (1836–7). Two similar journals (the *Protestant Watchman* and the *Protestant Penny Journal*) made their appearance in 1848, a year in which millennial speculation received another boost from the European revolutions. In all these journals Roman Catholicism was habitually identified with Antichrist.

Meanwhile, in the early nineteenth century, Ireland was increasingly regarded as a suitable field for the activities of evangelical protestants. The evangelical approach stressed the need for personal conversion, and took it for granted that dramatic changes in religious and moral conduct could be achieved through exposure to the teaching of scripture. Such was the optimism engendered by the apparent success of this approach that numerous evangelical societies were established, both in England and in Ireland, to carry out the work of preaching and teaching, among catholics as well as protestants. However, by the late 1830s it had become clear that

[1] Millennial attitudes in both catholic and protestant communities in Ireland have recently been explored by Patrick O'Farrell. See his article 'Millenialism, messianism and utopianism in Irish history' in P. J. Drudy (ed.), *Anglo–Irish Studies*, ii (1976), pp 45–68.

[2] Wilson, *Religious sects*, pp 93–5.

[3] Such journals were among the earliest cheap Irish periodicals. See Barbara Hayley, 'Irish periodicals from the union to the *Nation*' in P. J. Drudy (ed.), *Anglo–Irish Studies*, ii (1976), pp 83–108.

preaching the Word had made relatively little impact in Ireland. Disappointment and frustration at the poor results had the effect, in some quarters, of reinforcing apocalyptic beliefs, for those who had hoped for dramatic conversions were tempted to explain their limited success in terms of opposition which was not merely human but supernatural. It is not accidental that the key figure in organising and leading the D.P.O.A., the Reverend Tresham Gregg, was a Church of Ireland clergyman who had a history of trying to convert catholics by evangelical methods.

Gregg was a champion of public theological debate, in which each protagonist set out to prove from scriptural sources the truth of his own church's principles. In 1838 he had participated in public debate with the catholic advocate, Fr Tom Maguire. The debate had aroused tremendous public interest, but although Gregg claimed a victory for protestantism, Maguire had claimed a similar one for the catholic church, and no dramatic conversion of catholics had ensued.[1] In Gregg's religious creed, which was to provide the basis for the outlook of the D.P.O.A., apocalyptic beliefs and evangelism reinforced each other. The tenacity with which catholics clung to their own church seemed to suggest that supernatural forces were sustaining them; it was all the more necessary, therefore, to employ 'evangelical weapons' in order to convert them.[2] However, Gregg's religious duties also brought him into close contact with working-class protestants of Dublin, who were strong supporters of the orange institution; it seems likely that this contact with orangeism also contributed to his obsession with popery. But while there were plenty of clergymen who were more closely associated with orangeism than Gregg, few could emulate his achievements in the

---

[1] See *An authentic report of the great protestant meeting, held in . . . Dublin, on 29th June 1838, to express the feelings of the protestants of Ireland on the result of the discussion between Messrs Gregg and Maguire . . .* (Dublin, 1838), R.I.A., H.P., vol. 1726 (1838).

[2] *Protestant ascendancy vindicated, and national regeneration, through the instrumentality of national religion, urged in a series of letters to the corporation of Dublin, by the Rev. T. D. Gregg, A.M.* (Dublin, 1840), R.I.A., H.P., vol. 1764 (1840), especially letters 8 (24 Sept. 1839), 12 (16 Oct. 1839), and 13 (24 Oct. 1839).

field of scriptural exegesis, designed to establish the truth of protestantism and the falsehood of Roman Catholicism.[1] Gregg saw his task as one of awakening protestants to the dangers facing them: specifically, the progress of popery since the passing of the catholic emancipation act. Although he did not see himself as a messianic figure, he did take on a prophetic role, persistently urging protestants to end their policy of conciliation towards catholics.[2] He also warned protestants against accepting the arguments being put forward in the late 1830s by adherents of the Oxford movement in England, which appeared to diminish the differences between protestantism and Roman Catholicism.[3]

Turning to the political background, it is necessary to consider the development within the conservative party, in both Ireland and Britain, of a movement which emphasised the threat to church and state arising from the alliance between the reforming whig governments and O'Connell's Irish party. Modest reform of the established church in Ireland (including the abolition of ten bishoprics),[4] together with a proposal to reform the house of lords, led to the formation of a rash of organisations designed to defend protestant interests.[5] In Ireland the Protestant Conservative Society, the Protestant Association of Ireland and the Metropolitan Conservative Society were founded between 1832 and 1836. These organisations

---

[1] See Gregg's pamphlet *Free thoughts on protestant matters* (n.p., n.d.), R.I.A., H.P., vol. 1946 (1845), especially chs 9, 12, and 15: Gregg's published works are listed at the back of this pamphlet. He was in great demand as a lecturer in both Ireland and England.

[2] Others made claims on his behalf: the dean of Ardagh believed that the Lord had raised Gregg up to be a great protestant champion. See *An authentic report of the great protestant meeting, held in . . . Dublin, on 29th June 1838*, p. 9.

[3] Such warnings occur in *Free thoughts on protestant matters*, pp 65–74.

[4] Gregg's parish stood to suffer directly from this reforming trend; the parish church of St Nicholas Within was in a ruinous condition, but the church commissioners would not allow it to be rebuilt. See *Warder*, 3 Apr. 1841, and *Letter of Rev. Tresham D. Gregg to the churchwardens and parishioners of St Nicholas Within*, pp 3–4.

[5] Gilbert A. Cahill, 'Some nineteenth-century roots of the Ulster problem, 1829–48' in *Irish University Review*, i, no. 2 (spring 1971), pp 215–37.

sought to mobilise public opinion against the government, and in this task the old cry of 'no popery' with its emotional and patriotic overtones was a useful ally. The public were warned that popery was once again endangering their liberties in church and state. Stock images of Roman Catholicism were resurrected for party political use. Allegedly, it was opposed to the use of the bible; it persecuted its opponents; it represented a conspiracy on a world-wide scale which aimed to establish universal papal power.[1] Such images harked back to popular fears of popery in the seventeenth century. Sophisticated and educated protestants, such as those who read the London *Times*, did not care to resurrect the apocalyptic atmosphere which had accompanied popular anti-catholicism at that time, and *The Times* criticised Gregg for arguing that the papacy was Antichrist.[2] But it was the conservatives' own appeal to seventeenth-century prejudices which helped to ensure that at the popular level the whole seventeenth-century tradition, not just part of it, would be revived.

In England the years after 1835 saw the formation of many local protestant operative associations in alliance with the conservative political movement. However, in Ireland there was little attempt to set up such associations until the 1840s, though one was established in Cork in 1837.[3] The Irish conservative societies did draw the attention of propertied protestants to the interests of the lower classes,[4] but with only limited results. During the 1840s few members of the gentry were prepared to support the D.P.O.A.'s activities. Indeed, working-class protestants felt even more neglected after 1836, for in

[1] See, for instance, the speeches made in *Report of the proceedings at the first public meeting of the Irish Metropolitan Conservative Society . . . held . . . on the 16th of November, 1836* (Dublin, n.d.), R.I.A., H.P., vol. 1677 (1836).

[2] *Warder*, 22 May 1841.

[3] Ian D'Alton, 'A contrast in crises: southern Irish protestantism, 1820–43 and 1885–1910' (paper read to the thirteenth Irish conference of historians, Coleraine, 25–8 May 1977), pp 1–13 (p. 5). This association apparently lapsed, for another was founded in 1841 (*Warder*, 25 Sept. 1841).

[4] *Report of the proceedings at the first public meeting of the Irish Metropolitan Conservative Society*, p. 5.

that year the Grand Orange Lodge was dissolved, and the orange lodges which traditionally helped to sustain protestant morale were driven underground.[1]

In the economic field, the single most important factor affecting working-class protestants in Dublin at the time the D.P.O.A. was formed was the severe economic depression which hit Ireland along with the rest of the United Kingdom in the period 1839–42. Among the worst affected in Dublin were the hand-loom weavers and other textile workers who lived and worked in the notoriously over-crowded area of the Liberties.[2] In this area working-class catholics and protestants lived in close proximity to each other, and violent sectarian clashes had recurred throughout the eighteenth century.[3] The textile trades included some, such as silk weaving and tabinet and poplin manufacture, in which protestants were traditionally strong. Silk had once been one of Dublin's most important industries, but it had been declining since the late eighteenth century, and especially since about 1830, through competition from English silks produced on better machinery.[4] It seems likely that protestants in those trades were having to emigrate to find work; certainly some of the silk manufacturers had gone out of business.[5] By 1838 there were only 400 silk weavers left in Dublin, and when the depression came some workers were sacked, while the rest were under-employed.[6]

The depression affected both protestants and catholics and drew appeals for help from spokesmen for both communities. The official poor law was in a state of reorganisation, for the new poor law had

[1] Hereward Senior, 'The early Orange Order 1795–1870' in T. Desmond Williams (ed.), *Secret societies in Ireland* (Dublin, 1973), pp 36–45 (p. 43).

[2] *Warder*, 16 Jan. 1841; T. W. Freeman, *Pre-famine Ireland* (Manchester, 1957), p. 88.

[3] Maurice Craig, *Dublin 1660–1860* (Dublin, 1969), pp 88–9.

[4] John J. Webb, *Industrial Dublin since 1698, & the silk industry in Dublin* (Dublin, 1913), p. 37.

[5] One of them sent a subscription to the repeal association (*Pilot*, 12 June 1840).

[6] Freeman, *Pre-famine Ireland*, p. 88.

been introduced in Dublin in 1839, substituting the workhouse test for outdoor relief; protestants and catholics were to be treated alike, and in the elections for poor-law guardians in Dublin, catholics had won a majority of the new posts.[1] Appeals produced little beyond some charitable donations which did not tackle the underlying problem—the scarcity of employment. Meanwhile, the repeal association had been founded in April 1840, and there is evidence that during its first six months some working-class Dublin protestants in the textile trades sent in contributions. These included some silk weavers and some operatives at a cotton factory.[2] This would seem to indicate some support for repeal in the protestant working class, but two considerations should be borne in mind. First, it was not until July 1840 that O'Connell announced that the association, originally called 'the National Association of Ireland for full and prompt justice, or repeal', was henceforth to stand unequivocally for repeal.[3] Secondly, during the summer of 1840 O'Connell was working for the cooperation of members of the Ulster Association who were known to have doubts about the full repeal programme.[4] Hence O'Connell was prepared to play down the demand for repeal. The attraction of the association to any member of the Dublin working class was that its leading figures (apart from O'Connell) were then almost entirely preoccupied with the distressing conditions of the Dublin working class.[5] After September 1840, there is very little evidence of support for the repeal association from the protestant working class of Dublin, whether dissenters or members of the established church. By the end of the year they were in any

[1] *The case of the city of Dublin: the speeches delivered by counsel at the bar of the house of lords, in defence of the city of Dublin, on the motion for going into committee on the Irish municipal reform bill* (Dublin, 1840), pp 135–6.
[2] *Pilot*, 10, 19 June, and 30 Sept. 1840. The cotton workers included at least one presbyterian.
[3] Repeal association meeting, *Pilot*, 15 July 1840.
[4] Ibid. The Ulster Association was supported by northern liberal protestants, one of the most prominent being William Sharman Crawford.
[5] Jacqueline R. Hill, 'The role of Dublin in the Irish national movement, 1840–48' (Ph.D. thesis, University of Leeds, 1973), pp 91–4.

case to have a more useful forum for tackling their problems: a board of trade, which was to encourage the manufacture and sale of Irish-made goods. The 'Irish manufacture' movement, as it became known, represented an attempt by the working classes to improve their situation by purely economic means: politics were to be excluded from the board.[1]

Initially, working-class members of both religious communities joined the Irish manufacture movement, and for some months it represented real cooperation (not without difficulties) between protestants and catholics, liberals and conservatives. But the lack of sympathy from their social superiors was brought home by the scorn poured on the movement by the conservative journal, the *Dublin Evening Mail*, and by the lack of response to appeals for support directed towards clergymen of the Church of Ireland.[2] However, a protestant silk-weaver named Farrell became secretary to the operative board of trade. The parliamentary elections of 1841 brought to the surface underlying sectarian tensions and revealed the tremendous difficulty involved in keeping politics out of such a movement. The Dublin election was held in July 1841, and resulted in O'Connell losing the contest to the conservatives. Among O'Connell's supporters there was considerable resentment against protestants who had voted for the conservatives; especially against those from humble backgrounds who had a vote by virtue of being freemen.[3] In this context Farrell resigned his position as secretary in July, following criticism of his having voted for the conservative candidates. He was also accused of having tried to reserve work for protestant operatives.[4] In the following month, O'Connell decided to turn the Irish manufacture movement to the advantage of repeal and announced that he wished to ally it with the repeal movement.[5]

[1] *Pilot*, 11 Nov. and 11 Dec. 1840. The president of the board was Fr Matthew Flanagan, P.P., St Nicholas Without.

[2] *Freeman's Journal (F.J.)* 1 and 15 July 1841.

[3] See the report of a meeting of Dublin citizens, *F.J.*, 7 July 1841, and the editorial in *F.J.*, 22 July 1841.

[4] *F.J.*, 16 July 1841.

[5] *F.J.*, 5 Aug. 1841.

The protestant corporation of silk-weavers had already made it clear that its members rejected any involvement with politics on the part of the board,[1] and from September 1841, when the board became the repeal board of trade, there is no evidence that protestants continued to participate in it. The depression, then, meant that working-class protestants were thrown back on their own resources. For a time they had managed to cooperate (for purely economic ends) with catholics who were in a similar position, in an organisation which was actually led by a catholic priest. But the increase in political tensions as the elections approached, together with the lack of trust between the two communities, showed how difficult it was to achieve real cooperation between them. Despised by the propertied classes, attacked by resentful catholics, the protestant working class were bound to experience a sense of isolation in the face of these events.

The last aspect that must be considered in the background to the emergence of the D.P.O.A. is a social and political one, arising from the passing in 1840 of the municipal reform act, which swept away the old corporation of Dublin—so exclusive that even liberal protestants were kept out. The corporation had been elected by a body of protestant freemen—some four thousand in all—which included members of the Dublin guilds and others who had become freemen through birth or marriage; some were from very humble backgrounds.[2] The Irish parliamentary reform bill had proposed to remove the freemen's parliamentary vote, but this had been prevented in the house of lords. Under the terms of the municipal reform act, however, the freemen were to lose their civic franchise. The franchise was to be extended instead to all ten-pound householders, among whom catholics outnumbered protestants by two to one.[3]

---

[1] *Warder*, 24 July 1841.

[2] *Municipal corporations (Ireland). Appendix to the first report of the commissioners: report on the city of Dublin, pt I*, p. 8, H.C. 1835, xxvii, 90.

[3] This was an estimate made in 1839 by Mr G. A. Hamilton; *An epitome of the case of Irish corporations, intended for the perusal of protestants generally . . .* (Dublin, 1839), pp 19–28. See also *Warder*, 24 July 1841.

Moreover, the property belonging to the protestant guilds was to be vested in the new corporation; in effect, the guilds were to be dissolved. Although some freemen may have retained a civic vote by qualifying under the new regulations, they could no longer prevent the corporation being dominated by catholics. This represented a blow at their social status and political importance; it may even have affected their economic prospects, for the unreformed corporation was notoriously corrupt and freemen were said to receive bribes of jobs or money in return for their votes.[1] Moreover, the unreformed corporation had enjoyed substantial powers in the fields of policing, taxation and administration of justice. These powers had not been exercised impartially, and the abolition of the old corporation confirmed a liberalising trend which had begun at central government level under the Drummond administration in the late 1830s.[2] During the 1840s the D.P.O.A. was frequently to complain that local police and magistrates came down heavily on those who used orange slogans.[3]

In one other way, the municipal reform act helped produce a climate favourable to the establishment of the D.P.O.A. The wrangles over municipal reform for Ireland were accompanied by an upsurge of appeals to sectarian prejudice by the opponents of the bill. Isaac Butt, the protestant barrister and later leader of the home-rule movement, was at this time still identified with the exclusive protestant party. In his speeches against the bill he employed the sectarian language which had become a feature of the extreme wing of the conservative party, arguing that if the bill passed it would create a 'popish ascendancy' in all the corporate towns in Ireland, and that this would be the prelude to the destruction of the Church of Ireland.[4] Such sentiments were echoed by Tresham Gregg, who

[1] Repeal association meeting, *F.J.*, 6 Jan. 1842.

[2] Gearóid Ó'Tuathaigh, *Ireland before the famine, 1798–1848* (Dublin, 1972), pp 183–4.

[3] *Warder*, 8 June 1844. Also Memorial of the members of the D.P.O.A. & R.S. and other protestant inhabitants of Dublin . . . on the 31st October, 1844 (S.P.O. (Ireland) O.P./1844/19).

[4] *An epitome of the case of Irish corporations*, p. 50.

took part in a public meeting held in February 1839 to protest against the proposed reforms; he contended that Ireland's miseries were caused solely by popery, since God's curse was on every catholic country.[1]

The D.P.O.A. itself was founded as the climax of a series of protestant meetings held in March and April 1841. Gregg was the chief activist and did most of the talking at the meetings. At the first meeting, described in the *Warder* as very crowded,[2] his main pre-occupation was the need to reverse the decline of the 'protestant cause', which had come about, he asserted, as a result of catholic emancipation and the municipal reform act. He suggested that the means to reverse the decline of the cause was a protestant operative association, organised on the lines of those in England. Other operative associations could also be set up in towns outside Dublin; like their English counterparts, they would fulfil a political as well as a religious role. At the second meeting—also crowded—Gregg issued a challenge to Fr Maguire, who was planning to visit Dublin again.[3] Gregg also deplored the condition of poor protestants: the answer to their difficulties was to cooperate, to combine, and pro-claim the truth. Finally, the D.P.O.A. was established at a meeting held at the end of April, attended by scarcely any members of the propertied class, but by a few sympathetic clergymen and other protestants. According to Gregg, the association's aim was to spread protestantism and to agitate against state support for anything detrimental to it, especially popery. This aim would be achieved by the use of the right to petition.[4] When the association's rules were drawn up it appeared that nine M.P.s had been willing to act as presidents or patrons of the association.[5] However, their acceptance did not lead them to take an active part in its activities.

The D.P.O.A. adopted Gregg's own blend of evangelical and

---

[1] Ibid., pp 33–4.
[2] *Warder*, 27 Mar. 1841. The *Warder* (weekly) was one of the few Dublin newspapers to support the interests of working-class protestants and to report fully the activities of the D.P.O.A.
[3] *Warder*, 3 Apr. 1841.   [4] *Warder*, 1 May 1841.   [5] *Warder*, 24 July 1841.

apocalyptic beliefs. Ireland's miseries were the result of God's wrath because protestants had not prevented the advance of popery (the great famine was later to be interpreted as a further visitation of divine anger).[1] Members of the association saw themselves as the small remnant of protestants who had remained true to their principles. Although their numbers might be small, they believed that God was on their side and Antichrist was doomed: their own duty was to arouse their fellow protestants to the dangers they were in, and convince them of the need to reverse the recent concessions to popery. God's wrath would then be alleviated, and a protestant 'theological polity' would be established, with God's blessing.[2] While the association occasionally discussed economic matters (on one occasion the M.P. for Dublin, W. H. Gregory, was criticised for his vote on a factory bill)[3] it was the state's apparent indulgence towards popery which was its overwhelming preoccupation.

What made Gregg's leadership attractive to working-class protestants in Dublin? It must be remembered that they had experienced very rapid social, economic and political change, detrimental to their interests, in a relatively short period of time. In the 1830s, Dublin was still a 'protestant city', in which even a working-class protestant could feel a sense of superiority simply on account of his protestantism: the emancipation act had made only a limited impact on city life because the corporation had remained exclusively protestant. But within the space of three years (1839–41) working-class protestants had not only experienced a loss of status and influence as a result of the municipal reform act, but had faced severe economic depression, which in certain trades had come as the culmination of a long period of decline. Their social superiors had shown little concern for their plight. At the same time, catholics,

---

[1] *Annual report of the Dublin Protestant Association and Reformation Society, . . . for the year ending 31st December, 1845* (Dublin, 1846), R.I.A., H.P., vol. 1914 (1846), p. 10.

[2] *Two addresses to the protestants of Ireland, adopted at public meetings at the Rotundo, by the D.P.O.A. & R.S.* (Dublin, 1843), R.I.A., H.P., vol. 1868 (1843); address no. I (17 Aug. 1843), pp 5–7.

[3] *Warder*, 29 June 1844.

whom these protestants had been taught to regard as inferior, were apparently advancing rapidly (and with the sanction of the state) as the corporation and local administration of the poor law passed into their hands, and as catholic champions publicly defended their faith. It has been recognised that rapid change of this kind produces the conditions in which new religious sects are formed, since poor and uneducated people are often unable 'to perceive exactly what social processes are at work', and are tempted to look for super-natural explanations.[1] It is suggested here that the working-class protestants of Dublin failed to understand the real causes of their plight, and in their bewilderment and anxiety were only too ready to believe that there was a connection between the two processes they could see going on simultaneously: their own sufferings and the advance of Roman Catholicism. Hence the attraction of Gregg's explanation of events, which also linked these two processes in the context of a supernatural struggle between the forces of good and evil.

Gregg's interpretation offered these protestants three major sources of support. First, all their troubles were attributed to the progress of popery/Antichrist.[2] This elevated their sufferings to a higher plane and removed some of the burden of responsibility from the human to the divine sphere. It was for them a credible explanation, for it merely added one more dimension to their orange interpretation of Irish history and to the anti-catholic sentiments they heard from the lips of conservative orators. Secondly, it helped restore self-confi-dence and hope for the future. Although in everyday life they might be downtrodden and despised, in fact they represented the true church, 'the faithful followers of Jesus Christ'; and God was on their side: 'we then, being faithful, are the Israel of God, our foes Canaan-ites, Philistines, idolatrous Gentiles.'[3] The forces of Antichrist were

[1] Wilson, *Religious sects*, p. 232.

[2] *Protestant ascendancy vindicated*, preface, p. vii.

[3] Memorial of the D.P.O.A. to the lords justices of Ireland, 31 Aug. 1843, S.P.O (Ireland), C.S.O., R.P. 1843 E12786. Also *Two addresses to the protestants of Ireland*, no. II (24 Aug. 1843), p. 10.

doomed, and this doom might come at any time. Conviction of the literal truth of this prediction explains the D.P.O.A.'s confidence that despite the evidence before their very eyes of the progress of the catholic church, in the form of the building of new catholic chapels in Dublin, protestants would in the end get these 'mass houses', as they had in the past taken over St Patrick's and Christ Church cathedrals and other Dublin churches.[1] Thirdly, Gregg's interpretation also suggested a means by which they could hasten on the overthrow of popery. In contrast to many millennial religious movements, revolutionary means were not required, for they could simply petition the state to end its concession to popery and work instead for the conversion of the catholics. Britain was, after all, officially a protestant country; her statesmen were regarded as potential recruits to the cause of evangelism. This outlook helps explain the D.P.O.A.'s sense of outrage when Peel proposed to raise the grant to the catholic seminary at Maynooth; far from working to stamp out popery, this was giving it positive encouragement.[2]

Before turning to the relations between the D.P.O.A. and the repeal movement, it will be useful to consider briefly the size and social background of its membership. First, the question of numbers. No list of members of the association was published, but it seems unlikely that the actual membership exceeded 500 at any time, and it was probably less. In September 1842—rather more than a year after it had been founded—it certainly had fewer than 500 members,[3] and a reference by its Cork counterpart to 1000 electors in the Dublin branch in 1844 was probably an exaggeration.[4] However, it did attract interest and support from a broader section of the working class; the highest estimate for attendance at any single

---

[1] *Address of the Dublin Protestant Operatives' Association, to the Hon. and Rev. George Spencer, on his apostacy to the church of Antichrist* . . . (Dublin, 1842), R.I.A., H.P., vol. 1827 (1842), pp 14–15.

[2] *Warder*, 27 July 1844.

[3] *Warder*, 17 Sept. 1842.

[4] *Warder*, 13 July 1844.

meeting was 2500.[1] Moreover, the association's petitions frequently received several hundred signatures; 2000 people signed one protesting to parliament against the increase of the Maynooth grant.[2]

The social background of members is much harder to establish, although the description 'operatives and tradesmen' (whom the association was originally set up to serve)[3] provides a broadly reliable guide. It is clear that Gregg had influence over a considerable number of parliamentary voters, for his opposition in 1847 to the conservative member for Dublin, W. H. Gregory, encouraged his followers to refuse Gregory their second votes. Gregory lost some 228 votes, and the second seat went to the repealer, John Reynolds.[4] However, these voters were not necessarily ten-pound householders, for there were still 3000–4000 voters who possessed the franchise because they were freemen.[5] Indeed, scrutiny of the signatures on D.P.O.A. petitions suggests that very few of its supporters were householders of any description. Among the several hundred people who signed one petition, complaining about the dismissal of a policeman who had used language offensive to catholics, only about one in twenty were householders.[6] Their occupations included those of carpenter, builder, cabinet-maker, coal factor, vintner, house-painter, watchmaker and scrivener. A handful were graduates of Trinity College, Dublin. Many gave the address of commercial premises, and these were probably artisans, shop assistants and general labourers. Others, giving a private address, were probably servants. The addresses were spread all over the city, together with a few from outside Dublin and one or two from England. The only occasion on which the D.P.O.A. attracted support from outside the

---

[1] *Warder*, 6 May 1848. In 1842 Gregg claimed that the D.P.O.A.'s meetings were usually attended by 2000 or more people (*Warder*, 15 Oct. 1842).

[2] *Nation*, 12 Apr. 1845.

[3] *Warder*, 3 Apr. 1841.

[4] *Warder*, 7 Aug. 1847. It is not clear whether Gregg's followers actually voted for Reynolds as was claimed in the *Nation*, 7 Aug. 1847.

[5] *F. J.* (22 July 1841) estimated that there were some 2180 Dublin voters who did not possess the necessary property qualification.

[6] Memorial of the members of the D.P.O.A. & R.S. .... 31st October 1844.

lower classes was when the grant to Maynooth was increased; this produced a reaction among the middle and upper classes, and in the ensuing atmosphere of protestant unity the D.P.O.A. decided to drop the class distinction in its title.[1] However, the expected influx of members from outside the working class never came, and in 1848 the association restored the word 'operative' to its title.

The religious background of members and supporters was primarily the evangelical wing of the established church, although it is possible that methodists were also attracted by the association; methodist ministers occasionally addressed its meetings.[2] Gregg's own congregations at Swift's Alley free church and the parish church of St Nicholas Within evidently valued his religious services, and it is probable that they also supported the D.P.O.A.[3] The evangelical movement was not well supported in Dublin by either clergy or laity, but the relatively few evangelical clergymen were said to attract devoted support from their congregations.[4] The final point which must be made about the members and supporters of the association is their close identification with the orange institution. This was referred to on several occasions. In July 1844 the association replied to an address from the repealers to the orangemen, and made the point that although the D.P.O.A. could not speak for the orangemen, it did comprise 'almost without exception' the orangemen of Dublin.[5] In October of the same year the Schomberg orange lodge of Dublin congratulated the D.P.O.A. on its stand on federalism, and mentioned that its members were

---

[1] *Annual report of the Dublin Protestant Association and Reformation Society, for the year ending 31st December, 1845*, p. 10.

[2] See, for instance, *Soirée of the Dublin Protestant Association and Reformation Society: at Whitefriar's Hall, January 14, 1846* (n.p., n.d.) R.I.A., H.P., vol. 1814 (1841), p. 1.

[3] *A voice from the protestants of Ireland to the Rev. Tresham Dames Gregg, the faithful and intrepid defender of protestant truth and liberty* . . . (Dublin, 1846), R.I.A., H.P., vol. 1982 (1846), pp 31–2.

[4] See the letter signed 'Theophilus' in *Protestant Watchman* (*P.W.*), 4 Aug. 1848.

[5] *Warder*, 13 July 1844.

individually members of the association.[1] Certainly the D.P.O.A. made a point of celebrating orange anniversaries, in a quiet way while such celebrations were officially banned (until 1845), but more ostentatiously thereafter. When the decision was taken to dissolve the association in May 1848, its members were urged to join 'the orange society'.[2]

We now turn to the response of the D.P.O.A. to the repeal movement in the 1840s. It should be stated at the outset that both repealers and the D.P.O.A. agreed on one thing: the crucial position of the Irish protestants as the potential arbiters of repeal. On occasion O'Connell admitted that repeal would be won only when the protestants joined the movement; the orangemen represented a 'serious obstacle' to repeal.[3] The Young Irelanders were even more emphatic: a peaceful measure of repeal was a hopeless goal until the protestants joined.[4] The D.P.O.A. also perceived the importance of the protestant response to repeal. This clearly emerges from two addresses drawn up in August 1843, when O'Connell's 'monster meetings' were demonstrating the mass popular support from catholics for repeal. Recognising that the progress of the repeal movement had brought Ireland to the brink of an 'important crisis', the first address argued that if the Irish protestants were to join, 'not all the power of England could prevent its success. Were England, on the other hand, to consent to the measure of "repeal", it is in our power to forbid it . . .'[5] According to the D.P.O.A., no physical force in Ireland was stronger than that of the protestants; no petty sectarian differences would prevent their unity of action, and the Lord was on their side. The same consciousness of their role as arbiters of the national question prevailed in 1848, when they were faced with the prospect of a national rising.[6]

---

[1] *Warder*, 26 Oct. 1844.   [2] *Warder*, 6 May 1848.

[3] See the repeal association committee's second report on the state and prospects of the repeal cause, *F.J.*, 9 Nov. 1842.

[4] *Nation*, 28 Sept. 1844.

[5] *Two addresses to the protestants of Ireland*, no. I (17 Aug. 1843), p. 3.

[6] 'Manifesto of the protestant operatives of Dublin in public meeting lawfully assembled' in *Warder*, 6 May 1848.

The protestant response to repeal: the case of the Dublin working class

Dublin's working-class protestants were wooed by the repealers; partly because they lived in the capital itself, partly because Dublin working-class catholics were such enthusiastic repealers, and partly because, despite their lowly station, any protestant support was welcome. Various means, ranging from reasoned argument to intimidation, were adopted to induce them to join the repealers. Intimidation was occasionally employed at the popular level, for instance, by causing disturbances at protestant meetings;[1] but to judge by D.P.O.A. reports this was not a serious problem in Dublin. A more insidious method of intimidation was the system of 'exclusive dealing', which involved a form of boycott of tradesmen, shopkeepers and other commercial dealers who were dependent on the patronage of the public. To judge by the complaints made at the D.P.O.A., exclusive dealing caused protestant tradesmen considerable hardship.[2] However, such forms of intimidation were not new; they were a reflection of community divisions which had existed long before the repeal movement, and it does not appear that they had the backing of the repeal leadership.

The leaders of the repeal movement confined themselves to the use of argument in order to induce Gregg's supporters to join them. One of their favourite arguments was that the union was the cause of the decline of Irish trade and industry, and so repeal would bring great benefits to the trade and industry of Ireland generally and Dublin in particular. O'Connell used this argument again and again in the period 1840–41, when the effects of the economic depression on the working class were so severe.[3] The Young Irelanders added their voice in 1843 when the *Nation* carried a report that the tradesmen of Dublin were to meet to affirm their support for repeal. The

[1] Interruptions at a protestant meeting are noted in *Warder*, 27 Mar. 1841. The Cork operative association complained of more serious disturbances: *Warder*, 6, 13 July 1844.

[2] Letter II from Rev. T. D. Gregg to the Right Hon. Fredrick Shaw, M.P., *Warder*, 31 July 1841. Also address no. II from the D.P.O.A. & R.S. to Sir Robert Peel, *Warder*, 15 June 1844.

[3] O'Connell's speech at the board of trade, *F.J.*, 5 Aug. 1841. Also *F.J.*, 5 July 1841.

article went on: 'The Dublin tradesman who is not a repealer is half mad. Of the benefit repeal would be to Dublin no doubt was ever expressed, even by the opponents of that measure . . .'[1] In conclusion, the hope was expressed that workmen of all creeds would join the demonstration. But although this argument seemed so persuasive to catholic tradesmen—at least, during the early 1840s[2]— two considerations prevented the supporters of the D.P.O.A. from accepting it. In the first place, as we have seen, they were convinced that it was not the union, but popery, which was the cause of Ireland's difficulties: repeal of the union, then, would not attack the underlying causes of Ireland's problems. Secondly, the greater economic prosperity of England and Ulster seemed to uphold their interpretation that, where protestantism was in the ascendancy, prosperity would follow.[3] It was not until 1848, amid the heightened tensions over the national question, that a more authentic refutation of the repealers' economic arguments began to circulate among working-class protestants. In June of that year, a letter from 'Veritas' appeared in the *Protestant Watchman*, pointing out that there had been great misery and depression in certain trades before the act of union, under an Irish parliament.[4]

The Young Irelanders, with their vision of a non-sectarian nationalism, made greater efforts to win over conservatives and orangemen than did O'Connell, who, more realistically, directed most of his propaganda towards the liberal protestants.[5] The Young

---

[1] *Nation*, 1 July 1843.

[2] In the mid-1840s the Dublin trades were less inclined to seek political solutions to their problems. F. A. D'Arcy, 'Dublin artisan activity, opinion and organisation, 1820–50' (M.A. thesis, U.C.D., 1968), p. 71.

[3] See *Warder*, 14 Sept. 1844.

[4] *P.W.*, 30 June 1848.

[5] Paradoxically, O'Connell and Gregg developed a grudging respect for each other, based on mutual recognition of an uncompromising and straight-forward opponent. See *A voice from the protestants of Ireland*, pp 58–64. It was in this context that Gregg was prepared to admit that while he was identified with the orangemen, he also loved the green. In other words, he knew where he was with a catholic repealer: what he could not tolerate was 'loathsome neutralism in religion and politics', ibid., p. 42.

Irelanders attempted to exploit the evident gulf between the protestant working class and their social superiors. The D.P.O.A. frequently complained of lack of support from the propertied classes, and that their views were ignored. In November 1844 matters came to a head when representatives of the D.P.O.A. were excluded from a conservative meeting held to discuss the forthcoming registration of voters. A sub-committee of the D.P.O.A. condemned this action in strong terms; the conservatives had displayed 'cowardice', 'illiberality', and 'exclusiveness'.[1] The *Nation* strove to drive the two sides further apart, and held out an alluring bait to the working class. 'Were Ireland a nation, the protestant democracy would not be excluded from protestant counsels, nor be the standing joke of the Castle.'[2] If the *Nation* meant that an Irish government would be more democratic than the existing one, then this was a somewhat disingenuous statement, for the Young Irelanders themselves were opposed to the principle of universal suffrage.[3] However, their appeal was not likely to carry much weight with the D.P.O.A., since its members were not in favour of universal suffrage either. Like Gregg, they were conservatives who were not seeking confrontation with the upper classes but trying to win them over to their views.[4] In fact, the social aims of the D.P.O.A. and Young Ireland had much in common: both wanted an essentially conservative social order, with the nobility and gentry at the head of the people, respected and venerated; a contented peasantry, and happy tradesmen. It was over politico-religious issues that they differed.

The Young Irelanders, however, devoted relatively little time to appealing to these protestants' self-interest. Their main concern was to communicate their conviction that nationalism, with its goal of

[1] *Warder*, 9 Nov. 1844.
[2] *Nation*, 9 Nov. 1844.
[3] Young Ireland's position on universal suffrage is discussed at length in [W. H. Dyott] *Reasons for seceding from the 'seceders', by an ex-member of the Irish Confederation* (Dublin, 1847).
[4] For Gregg's views, see *Warder*, 24 July 1841.

self-government for every nation, was both an inevitable feature of modern society, and also intrinsically desirable in a moral sense.[1] This carried great weight with a generation which was particularly susceptible to appeals based on moral grounds. The D.P.O.A., through Gregg, admitted to admiration for the 'genius' and the 'eloquence' which appeared each week in the *Nation*.[2] In the autumn of 1844, when it looked as if a substantial number of protestants might announce their support for a federal union, and when certain northern presbyterians had sent contributions to the repeal association, a member of the D.P.O.A. attempted to show that there could be an alternative object of national loyalty. A Mr Rogers said at one of the association's weekly meetings that 'nationality' was a very high-sounding word. The grandeur of becoming a nation, he admitted, was over-powering. 'But', he continued,

are we less a people, because amalgamated and identified with the greatest, the most powerful, and the most intellectual on the earth? Is our nationality destroyed, because absorbed in and one with that round which, in unfading lustre, beams the glory of Blenheim and Waterloo?... What narrow-minded, crawling patriotism is that which, resting its jaundiced eye on the scanty tract that may surround it, is lost to that lofty sentiment... that delights to see, not merely an island, but an empire, nay, a world of compatriots.[3]

The D.P.O.A. thus countered Young Ireland's appeal to the glorious and moral nature of nationalism, not by denying these qualities but by suggesting that they were attached to the wrong object.

Such glowing references to Britain may give the impression that members of the D.P.O.A. were straightforward British nationalists, with little concern for their own country of birth. This interpretation would be extremely misleading. In order to counter Young Ireland's glorification of nationalism, they were bound to exaggerate the glories of the British connection. In fact, the D.P.O.A. did have great affection for Ireland, and a deep sense of attachment to their

[1] See, for instance, 'The movement of nationality' in *Nation*, 10 Aug. 1844.
[2] *A voice from the protestants of Ireland*, p. 60.
[3] *Warder*, 14 Sept. 1844.

native land. These qualities emerge clearly in Gregg's writings. 'Our own beloved land', he wrote, 'Old Ireland, Green Erin, the land of song, of sunshine, and hilarity'.[1] Nor was this attachment confined to the physical landscape and people of Ireland; addressing the protestant youth of Ireland, the D.P.O.A. urged them to rally 'for old Ireland—for the land of Patrick and of the saints'.[2] But while both the repeal association and the D.P.O.A. could agree on the landscape and the qualities of the Irish people, the traditions they looked back to were interpreted in radically different ways. For in the eyes of the D.P.O.A. St Patrick was a forerunner not of the catholic church but of the protestant one. It had become accepted in some circles in the evangelical wing of the Church of Ireland that when Christianity was first brought to Ireland it was 'protestant' in nature; the Roman claims were a later, novel addition. That ordinary members of the D.P.O.A. believed this interpretation is evident from remarks made at one of the association's meetings by a Mr Jones, who claimed that the catholics were the intruders in Ireland; the Church of Ireland bishops represented the true, unbroken tradition of episcopal authority.[3] The D.P.O.A., then, was attached to Ireland and Irish traditions, with the kind of devotion which Young Ireland was trying to foster among Irishmen of all creeds and races, but the Ireland they loved was a protestant Ireland. They saw themselves as belonging to 'the protestant nation of Ireland': catholics might be in the majority, but protestants had truth and divine approval on their side.[4] The future they looked forward to was one in which Ireland was regenerated through protestantism. For the D.P.O.A., the political relations between Ireland and England were satisfactory, and true patriotism required protestants not to join the repeal movement but to strive for the enactment of true Christian (i.e. protestant) laws. 'Then will your country be exalted and en-

---

[1] *Free thoughts on protestant matters*, pp 273, 275.

[2] *Warder*, 12 Sept. 1846.

[3] *Warder*, 1 June 1844. This was also Gregg's view: *Free thoughts on protestant matters*, chs 9, 12.

[4] 'Manifesto of the protestant operatives' in *Warder*, 6 May 1848.

riched; then will Ireland at last be a nation.'[1] So, as Patrick O'Farrell has pointed out, in view of the radical differences between protestants' and catholics' interpretation of Irish traditions, emphasis on these traditions was likely to produce not cooperation but a heightened awareness of religious divisions.[2]

As well as being deeply attached to Ireland, members of the D.P.O.A. were also equivocal about their relationship with England. Although England was often referred to in glowing terms (the land of 'integrity, holiness, purity, truth and liberty')[3] the D.P.O.A. always made it clear even on the eve of the rising in 1848,[4] that their allegiance to England was not unconditional. They owed allegiance to the queen, they believed, in so far as she upheld protestant principles. Rumours that the queen was a secret admirer of Edward Pusey's high-church views (which in the eyes of many evangelical protestants amounted to virtual acceptance of catholic principles) caused the D.P.O.A. much anxiety about the nature of their loyalty during the 1840s.[5] The same conditional attitude was adopted towards the queen's ministers. The period of Sir Robert Peel's government from 1841 to 1846 was a particularly trying time for the D.P.O.A., because under Peel's leadership a section of the conservative party had accepted catholic emancipation and was prepared to initiate reforms which would remove some catholic grievances, and also perhaps reduce support for repeal. But in the eyes of the D.P.O.A., which had not even accepted catholic emancipation, any concession to catholics was anathema. Again and again the association had to express its view that the state had compromised disgracefully with popery.[6] Peel himself came in for the lion's share of their fury; his failure to justify his policies in religious

---

[1] *Warder*, 12 Sept. 1846.

[2] Patrick O'Farrell, *Ireland's English question* (London, 1971), p. 133.

[3] *Warder*, 27 Mar. 1841.

[4] 'Manifesto of the protestant operatives' in *Warder*, 6 May 1848.

[5] See Memorial and Letters from the D.P.O.A. & R.S. to the lord lieutenant, July 1843 (S.P.O. Ireland, C.S.O., R.P. Z10352).

[6] *Warder*, 1 June 1844; *Two addresses to the protestants of Ireland*, no. II (24 Aug. 1843), p. 10.

or moral terms had made him suspect to the association well before he increased the grant to Maynooth.[1] It was the policy of conciliation towards catholics which prompted this warning from the D.P.O.A. to British statesmen in 1843: 'Foolish and contemptible men! Why, what signifies their "British supremacy" if it be not identified with the ascendancy of protestantism? Who cares one fig for the "integrity of the British empire" if it be not the empire of immortal truth?'[2] If England abandoned protestantism, the warning continued, she would deserve to be defeated, even by the Irish repealers.

There was one other way in which repealers could try to win the cooperation of protestants such as the members of the D.P.O.A. If it could be shown that substantial numbers of protestants supported repeal, this could be used both as a means of reassurance and also as an implicit warning or threat. Protestant support would mean that constitutional change was more likely: other protestants should recognise this possibility and make their terms with the repealers.[3] In the first three years of the movement the few protestants who had joined the repeal association were made much of, in an effort to remove the impression that repeal was a catholic movement for sectarian ends. There was certainly a need to try to remove such impressions: the D.P.O.A. was convinced that the repeal movement aimed at the overthrow of the established church in Ireland and the ascendancy of popery, and believed that sincere repealers openly avowed their aim, 'the extirpation of protestants'.[4]

In 1844 there did seem to be a possibility that a considerable number of liberal protestants would join forces with the repealers to seek constitutional change, perhaps on federal lines. Throughout the summer and autumn of that year Young Irelanders were optimistic that such a move would occur, and in this climate of expectation there came reports that some northern presbyterians

---

[1] *Warder*, 8 June 1844.
[2] *Two addresses to the protestants of Ireland*, no. II (24 Aug. 1843), p. 10.
[3] See 'Repeal—Ireland' in *Pilot*, 21 June 1844.
[4] *Two addresses to the protestants of Ireland*, no. I (17 Aug. 1843), p. 8.

were contributing to repeal funds.[1] At the climax of this period of expectation the *Warder*, champion of working-class protestant interests, noted with regret that 'protestant contributions are flowing into the coffers of Conciliation Hall'.[2] The *Warder*, which had hitherto adopted a consistently hostile attitude towards repeal, evidently believed that if the liberals and the repealers did join forces Ireland might soon be granted a measure of independence. The editor made his usual plea for protestants to stand together, but went on to indulge in a novel speculation—that the Irish protestants might at some future time decide to cooperate with the repeal party, in which case they should ensure that they made good terms for themselves. The entire article was notable for its lack of crude abuse of catholics and the repeal association.

However, if the *Warder* could bring itself to speculate about possible future cooperation between protestants and catholics, there is no sign that the D.P.O.A. was influenced by this mood. The account of its previous meeting showed that members continued to emphasise the need for protestant unity, but the 'no popery' language continued unabated, and no reference to cooperation with repealers was mentioned.[3] At the following meeting, the Schomberg orange lodge congratulated the association on its firm stand. Mr Rogers moved a resolution to the effect that the members saw no essential difference between federalism and repeal; under O'Connell's leadership either solution would tend to the overthrow of the established church and establishment of popery. In fact, repeal was the lesser of the two evils, because it would remove from the imperial parliament its powerful catholic minority. Once purged of this catholic element, Britain would rediscover her commitment to true protestant principles, and would begin to work for the over-throw of 'idolatry' in Ireland. With such arguments—tortuous, but consistent with its own interpretation of current events—did the D.P.O.A. reject the idea of cooperation with the repealers.[4]

In 1848 the climate of expectation of political change in the after-

---

[1] *Warder*, 12 Oct. 1844.   [2] *Warder*, 19 Oct. 1844.
[3] Ibid.   [4] *Warder*, 26 Oct. 1844.

math of the French revolution was even higher than in 1844. While support for repeal in the country as a whole had declined, as the population struggled with the effects of the famine, repeal still received enthusiastic support from the Dublin confederate clubs, whose members were chiefly catholic tradesmen. In this situation, it was decided to make another bid for protestant support by setting up a protestant repeal association.[1] The intention was to enroll the existing protestant repealers (chiefly Young Irelanders) in the new association, together with additional supporters who were expected to join in view of the safeguards for protestant interests that such a body could offer. Like the Irish Confederation, it was expected to form popular branches (called lodges, rather than clubs, presumably to reassure the orangemen). At the end of April, when advertisements for the first meeting of the new association had already appeared, several protestant repealers attended a meeting of the D.P.O.A. to urge support for the prospective body. News of this initiative by the protestant repealers had spread, and the meeting was well attended; about 2000 people were present, according to the *Warder*.[2] In fact, this was to be the first and last occasion on which repealers were to put their case at a meeting of the D.P.O.A. itself, so it is worth considering the arguments which were put, for and against the measure.

The first anti-repeal resolution was put by a Mr T. H. Thompson, who argued that it was unChristian conduct and ignorance of the word of God which lay behind Ireland's troubles. Why, he asked, should protestants give up the privileges of the British connection for those of an independent Ireland? When this resolution was put it was carried by an immense majority, with not more than a dozen dissentients, according to the *Warder*'s reporter. Gregg then rose to speak. He said that he felt a deep sense of responsibility in speaking at such a time. If the repealers had reason and truth on their side, the protestants should support them. He referred to the benefits that

---

[1] The initiative apparently came from William Smith O'Brien. See note appended to the reports of the spy 'C.D.', T.C.D. MS S. 3. 5, p. 42.

[2] *Warder*, 29 Apr. 1848.

repeal would bring for protestants like themselves. Obviously great evils existed in Ireland, but they were of a social not a political nature, and what was needed was not legislative rearrangements but 'national regeneration'. He wished to propose a resolution that repeal would be a disaster to Ireland. He could not forget the differences which would exist between the old Irish parliament, which was protestant, and the new one, which would be dominated by catholics. Catholics would never return protestants to offices of any kind if they could appoint a catholic. He did not blame them for this; they naturally objected to the establishment of a church which protested against popery. In his view, if the union were to be repealed there would be a war between catholics and protestants, and England would step in with her superior power and divide the spoils. Gregg also repeated the previous speaker's point that imperial opportunities would be lost to Ireland if she became an independent country. Repealers, then, were narrow-minded and contemptible in spirit. If they dared to rebel, the protestants would unite with the authorities and punish them. In short, the protestants had right and justice on their side: no one should remove their liberties or resist their authority.

At this point the protestant repealers (Walter Thorpe, Gilbert O'Reilly and R. D. Ireland) were allowed to put their case. The point was made that Irishmen of all creeds should sink their differences in mutual love of country. When Ireland tried to speak, he complained that he could not be heard, and in the confusion some of his supporters were driven from the hall; Ireland himself left soon afterwards. Only about six members of the audience were found to support the repealers' resolution.

After the meeting an anonymous letter in the *Freeman's Journal* claimed that the repealers' case had been met with such hostility because the meeting had been packed. Gregg indignantly denied this charge at the following meeting as a 'gross untruth'; the only people who had been kept out were the catholics.[1] Indeed, there

---

[1] *P.W.*, 12 May 1848.

seems little foundation for the charge, for had there been any substance to it the repeal press would have exploited it to a much greater extent. It would appear that it was not the D.P.O.A. which was packed, but the Protestant Repeal Association, when it eventually began to hold meetings in May. There is formidable evidence from several different sources that the meetings of that body were usually swelled not with protestants but with members of the Dublin clubs, the great majority of whom were catholics.[1]

However, the D.P.O.A. was about to dissolve itself. As the clubs increased their preparations for a rising, the working-class protestants of Dublin were turning more and more to their traditional means of support, the orange institution, now no longer a clandestine body. The last meeting of the D.P.O.A. took place only a week after the one which the repealers had attended. A manifesto, addressed to the public in general, expressed the operatives' determination to maintain the protestantism of the throne and the constitution which their fathers had died for. The 'physical force' of the Irish protestants could not be overcome. 'In conclusion,' the manifesto ran, 'we determine to join the orange society, and, as our fathers did, to stand together to oppose revolution and popish aggression.'[2]

Why did members of Dublin's protestant working class display such intransigence towards cooperation with catholics? What must be borne in mind is that protestants from the middle and upper classes had property, education and influence to cushion the impact of catholic emancipation, and for decades after 1829 they were able to retain their vested interests in positions of status, power and

---

[1] The Dublin orangemen made this point (*P.W.*, 2 June 1848): see also W. Battersby's letter to the Dublin protestants (*P.W.*, 16 June 1848). The Castle spies' evidence also confirms it: see report of 'E.F. no. 2' for 26 June 1848, T.C.D., MS S. 3. 6. The Protestant Repeal Association's meetings were filled with clubmen because the anticipated formation of protestant lodges had come to almost nothing. See T.C.D., MS S. 3. 7., 22, 25 July 1848.

[2] *Warder*, 6 May 1848.

responsibility. But for the majority of the working class there was nothing to distinguish them from their more numerous catholic counterparts save the sense of superiority engendered simply by being protestant. Their only vested interest therefore lay in the superiority of protestantism itself. By the late 1830s this had come under attack on several fronts. In religious terms, the effect of the Oxford movement was to play down the differences between protestantism and Roman Catholicism, while in Dublin itself the more impartial Drummond administration, followed by municipal reform, undermined certain social and political aspects of protestant superiority. By 1842 Dublin was no longer a 'protestant city'. These dramatic changes were accompanied by severe economic depression which attacked the livelihood of many working-class protestants. Neglected by their social superiors, and with only the cold comfort of the new poor law from the state, these protestants experienced bewilderment, anxiety and isolation—the classic conditions among a working-class community for a millennial movement to arise. The Reverend Tresham Gregg was on the spot, with an apocalyptic, anti-catholic message ready made; social, economic and political conditions created his following.

The political significance of the D.P.O.A. did not lie merely in its opposition to repeal, for most protestants were apathetic or hostile towards that measure and still had the political weight to prevent its being achieved. What was most significant was the quality of its resistance, inspired by an alternative vision of Ireland's past and future. While there was much in the D.P.O.A.'s outlook that was negative and backward-looking, there were also positive elements. Notably, there was the vision of Ireland transformed, made happy and prosperous, through evangelical protestantism. No doubt such a vision was unrealistic; but the D.P.O.A. could claim with justice that neither the state nor the established church had ever given wholehearted support to this policy.[1]

It is evident that members of the D.P.O.A. were not straight-

---

[1] *Two addresses to the protestants of Ireland*, no. I (17 Aug. 1843), pp 6–7.

forward British nationalists. British governments did not share their vision of Ireland's future, and the D.P.O.A. was prepared to threaten to withdraw its allegiance from Britain if governments did not adhere more closely to evangelical policies. The limitations of their loyalty emerged at the time of the rising of 1848, when Gregg, on a lecture tour in England, met and apparently recognised the Young Irelander Michael Doheny (a wanted man) but failed to report him to the authorities;[1] the Dublin orangemen, too, refused to act as spies for Dublin Castle.[2] But this equivocal attitude towards Britain could provide little encouragement for nationalists, since these protestants' interpretation of Ireland's past and future ruled out cooperation with catholics for political ends. And at the heart of this intransigence lay an apocalyptic interpretation of events which gave them the confidence to stand out against the policies of their social superiors. They bombarded the authorities in church and state (even the catholic bishops)[3] with their memorials, petitions and manifestos, all hammering home the same theme: that Ireland's problems were due to popery, and that the repeal movement was essentially a religious movement for religious ends. In a period when compromise was in the air—in the form of federalism and of proposals (supported even by certain conservatives in Ireland) for sessions of the imperial parliament to be held in Dublin[4]—these protestants made plain their refusal to contemplate even the least concession to the repealers. The D.P.O.A. did not, of course, speak for all Irish protestants, as it sometimes claimed to do; but the fact that it represented the outlook of a substantial section of the protestant working class indicates how grossly Young Ireland underestimated the difficulties of achieving a genuine non-sectarian national movement.

How representative of the protestant working class in general

---

[1] Michael Doheny, *The felon's track* (Dublin, 1918), appendix I, p. 292.

[2] See the report of the Grand Orange Lodge, *Nation*, 8 Dec. 1849.

[3] *Annual report of the D.P.A. & R.S. . . . for . . . 1845*, p. 7.

[4] See *First general report of the society for promoting annual sessions of the imperial parliament in Dublin . . .* (Dublin, 1848), R.I.A., H.P., vol. 2033 (1848).

were the D.P.O.A.'s attitudes? A full examination of this question lies beyond the scope of the present discussion, but one or two points may be suggested. First, there were protestant operative associations in other Irish towns during the 1840s, notably in Cork, Bandon, Youghal and Belfast; these were all engaged in similar activities and fulfilled similar functions to the D.P.O.A. by helping sustain working-class protestant morale and conducting political agitation for a change of official policy towards catholics. However, it was the Dublin association which had taken the lead in organisation and had set the example for the others to follow.[1] In 1844 a representative from the Belfast protestant operative association remarked that the D.P.O.A. had displayed an overwhelming commitment to the protestant cause, beyond anything he had met with in the north.[2] In fact, the other associations in the south were also extremely active, but during the 1840s only Dublin experienced the unique combination of a still numerous protestant working class which had suffered severe hardship, together with the talents and energies of a clergyman like Gregg. Moreover, the working class in Dublin does not appear to have been much affected by disputes between anglicans and dissenters which were still occasionally a source of dissension in Belfast.[3]

In the longer term, the leadership of the working-class protestant cause would switch away from Dublin, for demographic trends in the capital (as elsewhere in the south) ensured that the protestant working class would dwindle to an insignificant size, and the middle and upper classes would never be sufficiently numerous to challenge

[1] *Free thoughts on protestant matters*, pp 29–30. Gregg helped to establish the one in Belfast (*A voice from the protestants of Ireland*, pp 36–7). See also Sybil E. Baker, 'Orange and green Belfast, 1832–1912' in H. J. Dyos and Michael Wolff (eds), *The Victorian city: images and realities* (2 vols, London, 1973), ii, 789–819 (795).

[2] Soirée of the D.P.O.A. & R.S., *Warder*, 6 July 1844.

[3] For disputes in the Belfast association, see *Warder*, 13 Jan and 1 June 1844. The absence of such disputes in Dublin may be explained by the relatively small numbers of dissenters there: less than 5000, including Jews (*Dublin Almanac and General Register of Ireland for . . . 1841*, p. 575).

the catholics for political control of the city. In Ulster, by contrast, and especially in Belfast, the protestant and catholic working-class communities were of a more even size, and municipal government remained in protestant hands.[1] It was there that the attitudes which have been discussed here continued to recur and to be politically significant down to the present day: the apocalyptic hopes and fears, the attachment to protestant ascendancy, and the intransigence towards cooperation with catholics.

[1] The social background to sectarian strife in Belfast is discussed in Baker, 'Orange and green Belfast, 1832–1912'.

Temperance and Irish nationalism

ELIZABETH MALCOLM

IN August 1796 Dr William Drennan, a Belfast United Irishman, wrote home to his sister of a dinner that he had witnessed at an inn in Bray, County Dublin. You would scarcely credit the quantity of ale and whiskey which was consumed in the course of two hours, said Drennan, and he went on to claim that

Sunday in the catholic part of this country is much the most sinful day of the week, for, on going home in the evening, I counted more than thirty who had certainly spent the earnings of eight days before. The abolition of Sunday would be a blessing here, and Ireland must continue as she is, while her lower orders are kept in a state of intoxication, perhaps designedly, for this keeps them beasts of burden; not strong, however, as they appear generally feeble, withered animals—a perfect contrast to the aristocratic cast of country and city; yet these will say, 'You see how Sunday is spent, the only idle day'. Will anything of a reforming cast remove the habits of this people, high and low, with the one-half wine the chief good, and with the other whiskey.[1]

Whiskey consumption certainly rose dramatically during the course of the eighteenth century, for, while 461,274 gallons paid excise duty in 1725, the number of gallons charged had leapt by 1777 to 3,413,055.[2] This trend was condemned severely and repeatedly by contemporaries, particularly by those in positions of authority, as

---

[1] D. A. Chart (ed.), *The Drennan letters: being a selection from the correspondence which passed between William Drennan, M.D., and his brother-in-law and sister, Samuel and Martha McTier, during the years 1776–1819* (Belfast, 1931), p. 238. I have to thank Mr Brian Cathcart for drawing my attention to this particular letter.

[2] E. B. McGuire, *Irish whiskey: a history of distilling in Ireland* (Dublin, 1973), pp 110, 119.

Drennan indicates.[1] Although Drennan has no real solution to offer, his views are nevertheless especially interesting in that he, as a critic of the existing political situation, is inclined to lay the blame for this growing intemperance at the door of government, rather than attributing it to moral flaws in the Irish population. Also, he castigates the upper classes for their wine drinking and finds their criticism of the lower classes' fondness for whiskey hypocritical. This is an early example of what could be termed a nationalist approach to the drink problem in Ireland. By this is meant the recognition of a particularly severe Irish drink problem, but its attribution to an external agency—generally the conquest of Ireland by the British and the maintenance of their rule—and the identification of Ireland's political liberation with a diminution in, if not the complete disappearance of, this drink problem.

The temperance movement,[2] which sought to remove the habits of which Drennan complained, reached Ireland from America in 1829, appearing almost simultaneously in Dublin and Belfast.[3] The temperance societies in these cities in the 1830s were composed principally of protestant clergymen, doctors, businessmen and lawyers, with a sprinkling of landed gentry.[4] Alarmed by the econo-

[1] See for example George Berkeley, *The querist, containing several queries, proposed to the consideration of the public* (Dublin, 1725), p. 31, and *Agricola's letters to the right hon. the chancellor of the exchequer, demonstrating the pernicious effects of the cheapness of spirituous liquors etc.* (Dublin, 1791).

[2] For convenience, the campaign against intoxicating liquor in nineteenth-century Ireland will be referred to throughout as the temperance movement, though, strictly speaking, from the late 1830s onwards it was primarily a total abstinence movement.

[3] For Dr John Edgar's letter, which led to the formation of the first anti-spirits societies, see *Belfast News-Letter*, 14 Aug. 1829; though for evidence of earlier temperance activities in Ireland see *The importance of sobriety, illustrated by the evils of intemperance* (Dublin, 1818); *Short essay on the grievous crime of drunkenness in prose and verse, by a Roman Catholic clergyman* (Dublin, 1823); James Coombes, 'Europe's first total abstinence society', in *Journal of the Cork Historical and Archaeological Society*, lxxxii, no. 215 (Jan.–June 1967), pp 52–7.

[4] For biographical sketches of the leaders of the Irish anti-spirits movement, see the standard nineteenth-century histories of the temperance movement, P. T. Winskill, *The temperance movement and its workers* (London, 1892), i, 48–57, and Dawson Burns, *Temperance history* (London, [1889]), i, 31–3.

mic and social disruption caused among the working classes by the consumption of spirits, they sought through sermons, lectures and the distribution of tracts to persuade their social inferiors to abandon the practice. 'The movement was not viewed primarily as self-reform but as reform of others below the status and economic level of the organisational adherents. . . . Temperance doctrine . . . made an appeal as a means of controlling subordinates.'[1] Although Joseph Gusfield is here describing the American temperance movement of the period, his words apply equally to Ireland. These societies did not seek to reclaim the lower-class drunkard; rather, they aimed at inducing moderate drinkers to abandon spirits totally and to control their consumption of wine and beer. But societies which permitted the wealthy to enjoy wine (which Drennan had complained they abused) and at the same time tried to prevent the poor from indulging in the form of alcohol most popular with them were not likely to commend themselves to the majority of the people. This was particularly so in Ireland, where the majority of the population was catholic and the temperance societies, with a few notable exceptions, were led by protestants.

The anti-spirits movement of the 1830s had recognisably political goals. It aimed to make Ireland more prosperous and more peaceful under the existing political system and by so doing to bolster that system. Generally, anti-spirits advocates did not consider that faults in the socio-economic or political *status quo* contributed to intemperance. The first resolution passed at the inaugural meeting of the Dublin-based Hibernian Temperance Society in April 1830 stated that the 'unhappy propensity of our countrymen to the use of ardent spirits is one of the chief causes of pauperism, disease and crime prevalent in Ireland'.[2] The responsibility for intemperance and the many social problems associated with it was laid unequivocally at the door of the individual Irishman, and especially the lower-

---

[1] J. R. Gusfield, *Symbolic crusade: status politics and the American temperance movement* (Urbana, Ill., 1963), pp 42–3.
[2] Hibernian Temperance Society, *Proceedings of the first annual meeting; held at the Rotunda, on 7 April 1830* (Dublin, 1830), p. 18.

class catholic Irishman. Anti-spirits advocates argued that farmers and tradesmen, who were the main consumers of spirits, impoverished themselves by this indulgence, and that without drink such groups would be prosperous. Far from poverty driving men to drink, good wages and prices tempted the weak, the foolish, and the irresponsible into excessive drinking. Dr John Edgar, founder and leader of the Ulster anti-spirits movement, told the 1834 select committee on drunkenness that poverty made many a man sober; generally speaking, he was of the opinion that 'those who receive most, drink most, and the families of those who make thirty shillings per week are very often indeed not so comfortable as those who receive eight or ten shillings.'[1]

Intemperance was also seen as being at the root of much of Ireland's political disaffection and chronic violence. Dr Edgar believed that public houses were the haunts of subversive societies and that here, while under the influence of drink, young men could be exposed to revolutionary doctrines and enticed into joining illegal organisations. He claimed that many of the worst atrocities committed by the insurgents in 1798 occurred while the perpetrators were under the influence of drink.[2] The anti-spirits movement believed that excessive consumption of spirits destroyed the individual's sense of right and wrong, robbed him of his reason and reduced him to the condition of a brute.[3] Thus, only barbarism could be expected from a population habitually addicted to spirits, and temperance men felt that this was particularly so in Ireland, given the character of the people. Dr Philip Crampton, a leading Dublin physician, told the first meeting of the Hibernian Temperance

---

[1] *Report from the select committee on inquiry into drunkenness*, p. 70, H.C. 1834 (559), viii, 396.

[2] Ibid.

[3] See the graphic description of drunkenness in perhaps the most influential of all anti-spirits tracts, Lyman Beecher, *Six sermons on the nature, occasions, signs, evils, and remedy of intemperance* (8th ed., Boston, 1829; reprint, with introduction by John Edgar, Belfast, 1830), pp 25–31.

Society that the chief feature of the Irish character was a 'morbid excitability', 'a promptness . . . to rush upon any action without due consideration of the consequences'.[1] At the same time he described the physiological effects of spirits as being to excite the 'animal' in the human brain while paralysing the moral and intellectual faculties. The effect of spirits upon an Irishman was therefore especially deleterious, often making him a 'willing instrument' in any act, however cruel or desperate. This propensity to excessive drinking was, according to Crampton, invariably transmitted to the offspring, 'until, the brute nature . . . prevailing over the human, the whole race scarcely exhibit any of the attributes of humanity except in the outward form, and are only to be governed—if indeed they can be governed—by the force of arms instead of the force of opinion'.[2] Crampton felt that this accurately described the state of large parts of Ireland at the time. In similar vein Dr William Urwick, a Dublin congregationalist minister, writing in 1829, claimed that without intemperate habits the 'antipathies of ancient clans, the bigotry of religious difference, and the spirit of dis-affection to the government, if not altogether allayed would be comparatively harmless'. For it was Dr Urwick's opinion that a population addicted to intemperance was ready to obey the call of every political incendiary who addressed their passions and that they would not be 'deterred from advancing in the career of rebellion though the gibbet or the scaffold be in view'.[3]

However, there was a least one anti-spirits activist who had grave doubts about the nature and appeal of the anti-spirits movement. This was Bishop James Doyle of Kildare and Leighlin, the most prominent catholic publicly supporting the cause. In a letter of

---

[1] H.T.S., *Proceedings of the first annual meeting*, p. 22.

[2] Ibid., p. 23. That drunkenness was a hereditary disorder was a widely held view at the time, supported by the best scientific and medical authorities; see for instance Erasmus Darwin, *Zoonomia; or, the laws of organic life* (3rd rev. ed., 4 vols, London, 1801).

[3] *Remarks on the evils, occasions, and cure of intemperance. By W.U.* (Dublin, 1829), p. 13.

December 1829 on the subject of temperance societies, he bemoaned the gulf existing in Ireland between the classes and

how small—how very small the moral influence is of those called the upper ranks over those called the lower orders of the people. Gentlemen therefore may unite and preach to the people a temperance which they themselves do not always practise, whilst the people, who have not before experienced their friendship and protection, will hear them without attention, or scoff at their advice.[1]

Like Dr Drennan, Bishop Doyle found the upper classes' advocacy of restraint for their social inferiors hypocritical, and for this reason he was not particularly optimistic about the ability of the anti-spirits societies to suppress intemperance. However, he felt that they could do some good, and that even 'a small good' was 'worth seeking after'. Personally he believed that the really 'great and insurmountable obstacle to the progress of temperance societies' was the revenue law. Unlike his loyal protestant co-workers, Doyle had little faith in the morality or the benevolence of the British government, which encouraged spirit drinking and ignored glaring abuses in order to raise revenue. Only a drastic change in its attitude would produce a significant improvement. Doyle suggested that one step in the right direction would be for the government to promote beer consumption in order to diminish that of whiskey. This was attempted for England and Wales with the beer act of 1830, but the results were so disastrous that the policy was not extended to Ireland. However, Bishop Doyle's pessimistic views were not typical of the anti-spirits movement, nor did it generally seek government intervention to solve the problem.

It is extremely ironic that the temperance movement, which in the early 1830s was so sectional in its composition and so conservative in its views and methods, should within ten years be transformed into a mass catholic crusade for moral regeneration under the leadership of a Capuchin monk. The story of Fr Mathew's

---

[1] *Two letters from the Right Rev. Dr Doyle, Roman Catholic bishop of Kildare and Leighlin, on temperance societies* (Dublin, n.d.), p. 5.

campaign for total abstinence in the 1840s has been told many times, seldom in a dispassionate fashion. Historians seem to have largely abandoned the saintly monk to the hagiographers.[1] This is a great pity, for such a remarkably successful moral crusade, even if its success was ultimately only transitory, certainly deserves serious detailed study. For our purposes, however, we must limit ourselves to an examination of the interaction between Fr Mathew's movement and the major nationalist campaigns of the time, notably O'Connell's repeal movement and Young Ireland.

Having drawn attention to the differences between the anti-spirits movement and Fr Mathew's total abstinence crusade, it is only fair to add that some of the differences were more apparent than real. Most of the leaders of the earlier movement willingly enrolled themselves under the total abstinence banner, the main exception being Dr Edgar of Belfast who chose to regard total abstinence as without scriptural foundation and therefore heretical.[2] Fr Mathew himself was at pains to stress his loyalty and that of his followers to the government. Although he was the provincial of the Capuchin order in Ireland, Fr Mathew had been brought up in, for the period, a surprisingly non-sectarian family. The aristocratic Mathews of Thomastown, County Tipperary, were to be found in both catholic and protestant churches, and this produced what Bishop David Mathew later termed 'a very neutral attitude in religious questions . . . as the port circulated in the dining room at Thomastown'.[3] This background made Fr Mathew eminently suited to lead a movement

---

[1] Perhaps the best biography available at present is Patrick Rogers, *Father Theobald Mathew: apostle of temperance* (Dublin, 1943); also of use is Fr Augustine, *Footprints of Father Theobald Mathew, O.F.M. Cap.: apostle of temperance* (Dublin, 1947); while J. F. Maguire, *Father Mathew: a biography* (London, 1863), despite its notorious inaccuracies, has by no means been totally superseded.

[2] John Edgar, *Scriptural temperance: a discourse, preached in Fisherwick-place church, Belfast, at the request of the committee of the Ulster Temperance Society* (Belfast, n.d.); W. D. Killen, *Memoir of John Edgar, D.D., LL.D., professor of systematic theology for the general assembly of the presbyterian church in Ireland* (rev. ed., Belfast, 1869), pp 92–6.

[3] Introduction to Rogers, *Father Theobald Mathew*, pp xx–xxi.

which had been begun by loyal protestants and which now sought catholic support, though not at the cost of alienating its original adherents. Fr Mathew tried, albeit not very successfully, to placate both religious groups,[1] and he was equally determined that the temperance cause should not founder upon the rock of political controversy. His own politics, in keeping with his aristocratic background and personal distaste for dispute, were essentially conservative. He severely condemned secret societies[2] and tried strenuously to prevent links forming between his total abstinence crusade and O'Connell's repeal movement. He ordered teetotallers not to meet in repeal rooms and not to allow their bands to provide music at repeal demonstrations. And, much to the annoyance of repeal wardens, he tried at times to convince teetotallers not to join the repeal movement.[3] But despite Fr Mathew's efforts the two organisations did overlap to a very considerable degree.[4] Reports from county magistrates and inspectors, ordered by Dublin Castle in March 1840, concerning the true nature of the temperance crusade, generally agreed that though Fr Mathew himself was promoting no political cause many people saw political connotations in his work. The sub-inspector at Enniscorthy, for instance, reported that ribbonmen were joining in large numbers, while from Arthurs-

---

[1] For Fr Mathew's difficulties with both protestants and catholics, see Fr Mathew to Mary Shackleton of Ballitore, 4 Aug. 1841 (N.L.I., MS 5,055); [James Haughton] to Fr Mathew, 21 Nov. 1845 (Capuchin friary, Raheny, Mathew correspondence, uncatalogued); Paul Cullen to Fr Mathew, 10 Oct. 1841, in Peadar MacSuibhne, *Paul Cullen and his contemporaries* (Naas, 1962), ii, 11.

[2] See extracts from his speech against ribbon societies at Lucan, County Dublin, in June 1842, quoted in Maguire, *Father Mathew*, pp 216–17.

[3] For a complaint from a repeal warden regarding Fr Mathew's attitude, see J. J. Cantillon of New Glanmire, County Cork, to T. M. Ray, 30 May 1843 (N.L.I., O'Connell papers, MS 13,625 (56)).

[4] See Maguire, *Father Mathew*, p. 230, who claims that nine-tenths of teetotallers were also repealers, and also Patrick Quinn of Emly, County Tipperary, to T. M. Ray, 1 Sept. 1841 (N.L.I., O'Connell papers, MS 13,622 (16)), who says that he and all his fellow repeal wardens in the area are tee-totallers. I have to thank Dr Jacqueline Hill for these references to the O'Connell papers.

town, another part of County Wexford with vivid memories of '98, the sub-inspector wrote: 'it is whispered about here that if the battle was to be fought over again it would not be lost in consequence of intemperance as before.'[1] The same theme was to be found in reports from as far afield as Cork and Kerry.[2] Even if Fr Mathew scrupulously avoided political controversy, many of his followers clearly saw sobriety as an important weapon in the renewed struggle against British government in Ireland. In this they were following their other great leader, Daniel O'Connell.

O'Connell sought to promote the connection between temperance and repeal. At Easter 1842 he insisted, as lord mayor of Dublin, on participating in a great temperance procession in Cork, though, according to J. F. Maguire's biography, Fr Mathew was opposed, fearing that O'Connell's involvement would compromise his reputation for political neutrality and lose him support in loyalist circles.[3] O'Connell himself had taken the total abstinence pledge in 1840, though he quickly joined the large numbers of those withdrawing for medical reasons. There is little doubt that O'Connell in his support for Fr Mathew was motivated by political expediency. Until the 1840s his personal and political records were anything but in line with an anti-drink philosophy. He was a man who enjoyed lively company, food in vast quantities and the drinking that inevitably accompanied such occasions. The large dinner parties and substantial meals of Derrynane were described by many an admiring visitor. Charles Gavan Duffy, writing to Thomas Davis from O'Connell's home in September 1844, and referring to his host's appetite, warned: 'let no puny nibblers of toast or sippers of tea pretend to resist a titan like this.'[4] This is not to say that

[1] Reports of temperance inquiry, 1840 (S.P.O., miscellaneous papers, 1799–1868, nos 2–10 [1799–1840], IA/76/3).

[2] See reports from Charleville, County Cork, and Kenmare, County Kerry, ibid.

[3] Maguire, *Father Mathew*, pp 233–7.

[4] Charles Gavan Duffy, *Young Ireland: a fragment of Irish history, 1840–5* (rev. ed., London, 1896), ii, 105.

O'Connell was a drunkard, nor even that he was, by the generous standards of his time, a heavy drinker, but merely that total abstinence was wholly out of keeping with his style of life. In the early 1830s he had along with one of his sons and his friend, P. V. Fitzpatrick, invested heavily in a Dublin brewery, called O'Connell's Brewery.[1] At the same time in parliament he was vigorously defending the interests of Irish spirit grocers and distillers against legislation which they considered detrimental. His lack of success in this latter activity led some of the spirits lobby to suspect that he was compromised by his brewing interests.[2] But he was never accused of supporting the temperance movement. O'Connell in fact considered brewing and distilling important Irish industries which had suffered unjustly under the union and whose only hope of recovery was in repeal.[3]

Despite his frequently expressed admiration for Fr Mathew, O'Connell did find some aspects of the Capuchin's teaching quite unacceptable. He told a Dublin meeting, called to honour Fr Mathew in January 1843, that he felt the temperance movement in extolling its own achievements passed 'too heavy a censure . . . on the former condition of the country'. And he went on:

It would appear as if, prior to the temperance movement, the Irish were a depraved people—emphatically a drunken population—and that it required some mighty apostle of the living God to rescue them from their depravity. Take notice that, in saying this, I do not mean in the slightest degree to detract from the great merits of what has been done by the Rev. Mr

[1] For letters between O'Connell and Fitzpatrick dealing with the brewery, which was not a success, see *Correspondence of Daniel O'Connell the Liberator*, ed. W. J. Fitzpatrick (London, 1888), i, 420–21, 462–3.

[2] Ibid., ii, 60–4. For the spirit grocers' attitude to O'Connell see *Most important to grocers and spirit retailers: the only full report of the interesting proceedings of two great meetings held on the 23rd and 26th of August, 1836, to protect the Irish grocers: with an exposure of Shaw's pernicious scheme* (Dublin, 1836), and for O'Connell's defence of them in parliament see *Hansard 3*, xliv, 846–7, 1000, 1017–18; xlix, 1274; l, 580; for his dealings with the Guinnesses particularly, see Patrick Lynch and John Vaizey, *Guinness's brewery in the Irish economy, 1759–1876* (Cambridge, 1960), pp 144–5.

[3] *Correspondence of Daniel O'Connell*, ed. Fitzpatrick, ii, 141–2.

Mathew. I admit that he has performed a mighty moral miracle; but at the same time utterly deny that the people of Ireland were at any time inferior to their neighbours, or to the people of any foreign country, in any part of the globe.[1]

O'Connell was at pains to demonstrate that prior to Fr Mathew's crusade the Irish did not consume more liquor than their neighbours, and referring to parliamentary returns he claimed that, for every pint of whiskey drunk by an Irishman, a Scotsman drank two. 'There is no country on the face of the earth', insisted O'Connell, 'where the moral and domestic virtues of the people exceed those of the people of Ireland.'[2] Here we see O'Connell as a nationalist, a man convinced of the good qualities of his own country, of its superiority to other countries, trying to come to terms with a movement which was based largely on dissatisfaction with, and criticism of, the state of the country. The anti-spirits and total abstinence movements, as they appeared in Ireland in the 1830s and 1840s, were in many respects the antithesis of nationalism; they were anxious to proclaim their loyalty to a government which was anathema to Irish patriotism, and unrelenting in their condemnation of many aspects of Irish character and society. O'Connell did not deal adequately with this dilemma. His solution was basically inconsistent; while he denied that there was a serious drink problem in Ireland, he lauded the achievements of Fr Mathew and his crusade.

O'Connell then, although he associated himself with teetotalism in the hope of strengthening his own repeal movement, remained basically ambivalent about the issue. He did not want to see brewing and distilling, two of the few remaining prosperous industries in Ireland, destroyed. Nor is it likely that the middle-class, protestant, puritanical aspects of the temperance movement appealed to him greatly. Certainly attacks on the Irish people for their drunkenness, coupled with calls for the restoration of law and order and frequent expressions of loyalty to the government, were not calculated to

---

[1] *Nation*, 28 Jan. 1843.   [2] Ibid.

endear temperance to O'Connell, whatever may have been the personal merits of Fr Mathew.

Yet by no means all nationalists were suspicious of Fr Mathew's crusade. If O'Connell embraced the movement with severe reservations and not a little cynically, the Young Irelanders took it up much more wholeheartedly. A strong personal link had been forged between Fr Mathew and Gavan Duffy, to the extent that Fr Mathew broke his pledge of political neutrality by acting as a character witness at Duffy's trial in 1849.[1] But on an ideological level, as well, Young Ireland had much sympathy for Fr Mathew's endeavour. To Thomas Davis and his colleagues, unlike O'Connell, reform of the country's political and economic grievances was inseparable from the moral elevation of the Irish people. Only by cleansing themselves of laziness, dissipation, ignorance and selfishness would the people be capable of winning and maintaining national independence. Personal regeneration was the indispensable precursor of national regeneration. A firm believer in the perfectibility of man, Davis preached an all-embracing heroic and romantic nationalist creed, strongly influenced by contemporary Italian and German nationalism.[2] Personal knowledge, self-reliance and restraint were at the core of this doctrine, and an essential precondition was sobriety. Thus Davis welcomed Fr Mathew's crusade as signifying the beginning of a new era for Ireland. 'Irish intoxication', he wrote in the *Nation* in January 1843,

was the luxury of despair—the saturnalia of slaves. Irish temperance is the first fruit of deep-sown hope, the offering of incipient freedom. The moment when political organisation, social action, and the rudiments of education had set the people thinking, hope came down upon them like dew, and the fever of their hearts abated.[3]

---

[1] Fr Mathew to Charles Gavan Duffy, 28 Sept. 1845 (N.L.I., Gavan Duffy papers, MS 5, 756) and 17 Nov. 1848 (N.L.I., Gavan Duffy papers, MS 5, 757).

[2] For a discussion of Davis's nationalism see T. W. Moody, *Thomas Davis, 1814–45: a centenary address delivered in Trinity College, Dublin, on 12 June 1945 at a public meeting of the College Historical Society* (Dublin, 1945).

[3] *Nation*, 28 Jan. 1843.

Fr Mathew's crusade seemed to prove that the Irish people could be roused to decisive and united action for the betterment of themselves and their country by a reasoned appeal, and this was exactly what the Young Irelanders were seeking to achieve. Thus the success of the Irish temperance movement under Fr Mathew's leadership offered hope not only to the people, but to Young Ireland.

Davis did not consider the 'past error' of the Irish people with regard to drink 'as proof of vicious character, nor their late change as the victory of mere genius over a multitude' for

whenever, in past times, any great call has been made upon their energies, when the rallying of multitudes gave them hope, and the teaching of leaders gave them intelligence, they became for the time temperate—witness their temperance during the progress of the United Irish system, and through parts of the emancipation struggle. But the excitement faded and the hope grew cold, and they returned to habitual despair, and its periodic alleviation, drunkenness.[1]

Davis was therefore able, again unlike O'Connell, to integrate the problem of Irish drunkenness into his overall nationalist interpretation of Irish affairs. He differed from the anti-spirits movement in believing that the Irish people were driven to drink by misery and despair, and thus that their drunkenness was unlike that of other nations. Many of the happiest, wealthiest and most moral peoples in Europe drank more man for man than the Irish, but, according to Davis, these people drank everyday as part of their normal sober diet. Very different was the Irish drinking pattern:

[The Irishman] drank nothing for some 350 days in the year; but once or maybe oftener in the month, he got roaring drunk. This occasional debauch was the Lethe-moment of all his sorrows. He then forgot all his wrongs. His cabin was warm, his belly full, his back covered—for an afternoon; but he woke in the morning penniless, broken-headed, guilty, conscience-sore. During his intoxication he had flung off his chains, and his duties too. He lost sight of his own miseries and the comfort of his wife and children also; and for this transient flush of intemperance he not only inflicted severer

[1] Ibid.

privations on himself, but the hearth of his bosom's wife was colder and the board of his young ones more scanty for months to come. Narrowed means, injured character, and sourest temper, with starvation and quarrels and degradation, were a fearful penalty for a short pleasure. Still the very greatness of his suffering was his excuse—his natural excuse for making it greater, in order to achieve liberty and luxury for an hour by the magic of intoxication.[1]

Davis felt no need to deny the drunkenness problem as an insult to Irish nationalism; rather, he turned it into an argument supporting the nationalist cause. Unlike conservative temperance advocates, who saw intemperance as a product of individual moral failing and as the cause of Ireland's poverty and disorder, Davis regarded Irish drunkenness as ultimately the result of Ireland's political subjugation. In his mind the relationship was cyclical: poverty and despair caused by political repression produced periodic drunken debauches which in turn fed poverty and despair. Only through education and self-discipline within a nationalist philosophy could this vicious circle be broken.

Davis demonstrated for the first time in Ireland that temperance could be transformed from being a conservative movement seeking to patch up the existing political and socio-economic structures, or at most seeking, as in Fr Mathew's crusade, to help catholics participate more fully in these structures, into a radical doctrine attacking the very basis of this system.[2] He took Drennan's complaints, reconciled them with Irish national aspirations, and pointed to a solution. This solution was in the final analysis the political liberation of Ireland, but again Davis's argument was by no means simple. He was not prepared to allow moral and social reform to wait upon political change, and in fact, as we have seen, he considered such reform an essential precondition for change. Fr Mathew's

[1] Ibid. For another article by Davis on Fr Mathew see ibid., 19 Nov. 1842; for articles by Gavan Duffy, ibid., 10 Dec. 1842, 31 Dec. 1842 and 19 Aug. 1843 and by John Blake Dillon, ibid., 19 Nov. 1842.

[2] For an analysis of the American temperance movement of this period and later in terms of the changing socio-economic status of groups within the society see Gusfield, *Symbolic crusade.*

crusade seemed to signal that the moral reformation which Davis desired was at hand; and in its wake, he thought, political change must come. However, Davis's reconciliation between temperance and nationalism was essentially an intellectual abstraction, and one which neither O'Connell nor Fr Mathew would have totally accepted. It was in fact to be another fifty years before this reconciliation was to find widespread support in Ireland and be translated into concrete action.

As the wide-ranging romantic nationalism of Thomas Davis gave way to the revolutionary conspiracy of fenianism and later still to the parliamentary campaign for home rule, so the mass evangelical crusade of Fr Mathew gave way after the famine to a largely protestant and highly professional campaign for coercive anti-drink legislation. The Irish temperance movement from the 1850s into the 1890s concentrated its energies on getting through parliament licensing legislation which would severely curb, if not totally destroy, the drink industry. Reasoned argument aimed at the middle classes had failed in the 1830s to secure any diminution of the drink problem, while Fr Mathew's emotional appeal to the catholic masses, though initially extraordinarily successful, had in the long term proved disappointingly transitory. Failure drove the Irish temperance movement into increasingly extreme and authoritarian paths. Following similar trends in Britain and America, the Irish movement by the 1850s had concluded that the only way to solve the problem of excessive drinking was simply to abolish drink. In 1851 the state of Maine passed a prohibitory law, and over the next ten years nearly a dozen other American states followed suit. Both the British and the Irish temperance movements swiftly adopted the goal of prohibition. In 1853 the United Kingdom Alliance was established, with strong Irish support, dedicated to securing total and immediate prohibition.[1] T. W. Russell, later the parliamentary

---

[1] For an account of the origins of the American prohibition movement up to 1851, see J. A. Krout, *The origins of prohibition* (New York, 1925); for the United Kingdom Alliance see Brian Harrison, *Drink and the Victorians: the temperance question in England, 1815–72* (London, 1971), pp 196–218.

champion of Ulster farmers, but then a rising young man in Irish temperance politics, accurately expressed the simplistic thinking of the prohibitionist party when he wrote in 1866, 'If the trade be a useful and beneficial one, let it be wholly free; if it be an injurious trade, producing great evils and no counteracting good, let it be, not licensed, but prohibited.'[1] However, while American state legislatures may have been prepared to pass prohibitory laws, it quickly became clear that the parliament at Westminster was not about to follow their example. Thus the Irish movement, again closely following the British pattern, was forced reluctantly to seek legislation short of total prohibition, while comforting itself with the belief that such legislation would ultimately lead to the desired goal. Russell, the prohibitionist of the 1860s, was by the 1870s secretary of associations fighting for both a permissive bill and Sunday closing in Ireland. The Irish vigorously backed Sir Wilfrid Lawson's futile campaign to secure a local veto over the retail drink trade through a permissive prohibitory act. However, they were more successful with Sunday closing and in 1878, after a long and bitter fight in parliament, a partial and temporary Irish Sunday-closing act was introduced. The 1880s saw the movement still struggling to amend the licensing laws, though losing ground in parliament to more pressing Irish problems like land reform and home rule.

The disparities between the sort of temperance movement just described and fenianism are fairly obvious. The latter, as a revolutionary conspiracy aimed at overthrowing the British government in Ireland by violent means, could hardly be expected to have much in common with a movement of middle-class protestants seeking to curb Irish drinking by repressive legislation. One of the most frequent charges levelled against the fenians was that they used public houses as meeting and recruiting places, seeking to entice young men into the organisation while they were under the influence of

[1] *Irish Temperance Star*, i, no. 10 (Oct. 1866), p. 145.

drink.[1] An examination of John Devoy's memoirs, *Recollections of an Irish rebel*, would seem to bear out this charge. Devoy's account of his activities as a fenian recruiter among the Dublin garrison in 1865–6 reads in places rather like a guide to the city's more squalid drink shops. We find Devoy meeting soldiers in 'a room over Hoey's public house in Bridgefoot Street, where the bartender, a man named Furey, was a member'[2] and in 'Fitzpatrick's little public house at the corner of Dame and George's Streets, where the bartender, John Hollowed (later a prosperous liquor dealer in Chicago), was one of our trusted men'.[3] But the many public houses and spirit-grocer shops along Thomas and James Streets, frequented by soldiers from the nearby Richmond barracks, were the fenian recruiters' favourite hunting grounds. Along these streets were also Dublin's main breweries and distilleries. In 1866 Thomas Street had two distilleries, one brewery and twenty-four public houses and spirit-grocer shops, while James Street had three breweries (including Guinness's) and fifteen drink shops. Doubtless there were also numerous unlicensed shops and rooms in which drink could be bought.[4] A glance at *Thom's directory* for the years 1865 and 1866 shows that the shops in these streets used by Devoy, like Pilsworth's, Parker's and Bergin's were generally spirit-grocer shops with low rating valuations.[5] It was just such shops that the Dublin temperance societies of the 1860s and 1870s were trying most strenuously to have suppressed. The report of the 1868 select committee on Irish Sunday closing is full of complaints from magistrates, police and

---

[1] See for instance the evidence of the magistrates Christopher de Gernon and E. F. Ryan, in *Report from the select committee on the Sale of Liquors on Sunday (Ireland) Bill*, pp 6–19, H.C. 1867–8 (280), xiv, 564–77.

[2] *Thom's directory, 1865*, p. 1366 and *1866*, p. 1398, does not list a Hoey's public house in Bridgefoot Street, though it does list two vintners with rating valuations of £19 and £16 respectively. Hoey's could have been a popular name for one of these, or the name of an illegal drinking shop.

[3] John Devoy, *Recollections of an Irish rebel* (New York, 1929), pp 63, 75.

[4] *Thom's directory, 1866*, pp 1466–7, 1533–4.

[5] See Patrick Pilsworth's evidence in *Report from the select committee on the Sale of Liquors on Sunday (Ireland) Bill*, pp 35–6, H.C. 1867–8 (280), xiv, 593–4.

clergy about the conduct of both spirit grocers and beer dealers. Richard Corr, a D.M.P. superintendent, told the committee that the 'majority of spirit grocers in Dublin violate the spirit of their licence', while the chief commissioner, John Lewis O'Ferrall, urged that reform of the licences issued to spirit grocers and beer dealers should be the first priority of those interested in promoting temperance.[1]

However, in his memoirs Devoy was anxious to deny the charge of drunkenness so frequently levelled against fenians.

Our men were the soberest lot of soldiers I ever saw. Having to meet in public houses, because there was no other place available, some drinks had to be called for as an excuse, but it was never whiskey, and the quantity of porter consumed was very small. During those four months of incessant activity, visiting public houses every night, with from ten to twenty soldiers always present, I did not see half a dozen of our men even slightly under the influence of drink.[2]

Devoy himself was certainly an austere and dedicated man, living a temperate life in perhaps all respects except where politics were concerned. His father had been deeply religious and an active supporter of Fr Mathew, though he and several other members of the family subsequently found long-term employment with Watkins' brewery in Dublin.[3] Devoy approved of the temperance movement, or at least the one 'led by an Irish catholic priest',[4] but he showed no inclination to marry temperance and nationalist principles in any systematic way. James Stephens and John O'Leary showed even less interest in the temperance cause, both believing, unlike Davis, that political liberation must come before the consideration of socio-economic grievances. O'Leary put this general attitude most succinctly when he wrote, with regard to the land question:

It was not that then as now I did not feel keenly the wretched condition of the Irish peasantry, and the too often cruel conduct of the Irish landlords; but then, as now, I believed that the full remedy for that wretchedness and

---

[1] Ibid., pp 82, 119–20, 147.   [2] Devoy, *Recollections*, p. 63.
[3] Ibid., pp 377–9.   [4] Ibid., p. 377.

these wrongs could only come from freedom. England and English rule, directly or indirectly, proximately or remotely, were at the bottom of the whole trouble. English rule remaining, I saw little chance of the satisfactory settlement of the land question, or, indeed, of any question; and to shake, if not to shatter, that rule, was then, as it is still, the great aim, or, if you will, dream of my life.[1]

These lines were written in the 1890s, and there is about them the air of justifying a position which was far from generally held. Certainly by that time the narrow political nationalism of the 1860s was under severe attack from a new generation of nationalists with much broader cultural, moral, economic and social concerns, in the Young Ireland tradition. However this is not to say that the fenians had no interest in the temperance issue, rather that their views were unsystematic and thus often contradictory. The generation of fenian leaders was also the generation of boys and young men who had flocked in such vast numbers to take the total abstinence pledge from Fr Mathew. Such diverse figures within fenianism as Charles Kickham, John Denvir and O'Donovan Rossa took the pledge in the 1840s, but, more interestingly, the former two maintained it throughout their lives.[2] And Rossa, though his enemies frequently put down his wilder actions to drunkenness, chose to point out in his memoirs that he had been a total abstainer from 1848 to about 1857 and for the seventeen or eighteen years prior to the time of writing in 1898.[3] The Phoenix Society, of which Rossa was a

[1] John O'Leary, *Recollections of fenians and fenianism* (2 vols, London, 1896; reprinted with introduction by Marcus Bourke, Shannon, 1969), i, 38.

[2] For a discussion of Kickham's attitude to temperance see R. V. Comerford, 'Charles J. Kickham, 1828–82' (M.A. thesis, St Patrick's College, Maynooth, 1972), p. 6; also John Denvir, *The life story of an old rebel* (Dublin, 1910; reprinted with introduction by Leon Ó Broin, Shannon, 1972), pp 12–16 and Jeremiah O'Donovan Rossa, *Rossa's recollections, 1838–98* (New York, 1898; reprinted with introduction by Seán Ó Lúing, Shannon, 1972), p. 151.

[3] See for instance Devoy's accusations in William O'Brien and Desmond Ryan (ed.), *Devoy's post bag, 1871–1928* (Dublin, 1948), i, 316–19 and Major Henri Le Caron [Thomas Beach], *Twenty-five years in the secret service: the recollections of a spy* (6th ed., London, 1892), pp 2, 103.

member, initially forbade its members to touch drink.[1] Although fenian recruiters frequently used public houses, 'Pagan' O'Leary, Devoy's eccentric predecessor as a military recruiter in Dublin, had been a staunch teetotaller who followed the administration of the fenian oath with a lecture on temperance. Devoy later said that the 'Pagan', who was so called because of his antipathy to catholicism, was the first Sinn Féiner in that he 'never used tobacco on which duty had been paid to England, and never drank liquor, tea or coffee for the same reason'.[2] This argument, that drinking simply contributed funds to the British exchequer and further impoverished Ireland, was to become widespread in both the temperance and nationalist movements by the end of the century.

The *Irish People*, the fenians' Dublin newspaper from November 1863 to September 1865, generally showed little interest in the temperance issue, though its front page long carried an advertisement for the Dublin Total Abstinence Association's coffee palace in Marlborough Street. This was the city's oldest total abstinence society, for long presided over by James Haughton, a unitarian merchant and philanthropist with strong nationalist sympathies.[3] Perhaps we can detect Haughton's hand in this rather unexpected decision by a temperance society to advertise in a fenian newspaper. But, like Devoy, the *Irish People* only took up the subject of drink in order to refute charges of intemperance made by the enemies of fenianism. In a leader, entitled 'Fenianism metamorphosed', on 17 June 1865 Kickham, while dismissing the 'sneers of British and west-British scribes' that fenianism 'usually turned up in a tap-room, and was invariably "under the influence"', conceded that men 'who

[1] Statement of Robert Cusack, undated (S.P.O., reports on secret societies, 1857–9), quoted in R. V. Comerford, 'Irish nationalist politics, 1858–70' (Ph.D. thesis, Trinity College, Dublin, 1976), p. 219.

[2] Devoy, *Recollections*, pp 137–9; for another account of this curious character see O'Leary, *Recollections*, ii, 229–30.

[3] Samuel Haughton, *Memoir of James Haughton, with extracts from his private and published letters* (London, 1877); E. MacDowel Cosgrave, *Incorporated Dublin Total Abstinence Society, diamond jubilee celebrations: brief history of the Society* (Dublin, 1897).

[88]

consider themselves patriots' were not above attacking fenianism on these grounds. In this Kickham detected a double standard: 'The sight of a "fenian" coming out of a public house has furnished the text of many a sermon to pious agitators who would not scruple to give an order for an unlimited supply of whiskey to "prime" the liberal candidate's bludgeon-men.'[1] But far from encouraging drunkenness, Kickham argued, fenianism was actually an important factor in its diminution. Drunkenness and faction fighting were disappearing and Ireland's young men becoming more 'intelligent', 'manly' and 'moral' every day, and this was occurring precisely in those areas where the *Irish People* was read and where fenianism was said most to abound. The *Irish People* thus dismissed charges of intemperance levelled against fenians as British propaganda and chose to see the movement as one tending to increase sobriety rather than the reverse. Similarly in his novels, Kickham invariably associated nationalist sympathies with sobriety, if not total abstinence, and viewed drunkenness with a very critical eye.[2]

For the fenians, as for O'Connell, Ireland was 'among the most, if not *the* most, industrious, peaceful, and intelligent of the nations of Europe', while the same could not be said for its 'assailants and accusers', the British government and its lackeys in Ireland. Fenianism, as we have seen, had in fact no overall, coherent attitude to temperance, though such a fierce and narrow nationalism generally did not admit of the sort of criticism implicit within the temperance ideology. The leadership tended to put the goal of political independence first and to dismiss social problems, like drunkenness, as either enemy propaganda or distinctly secondary to the primary goal. Though, at the same time, there were some among the leaders who were personally committed to total abstinence. At the local level, fenianism fulfilled an important social function, bringing together young men, mainly of the artisan classes with nationalist inclina-

[1] *Irish People*, 17 June 1865.
[2] See for example his major novel, *Knocknagow, or the homes of Tipperary* (Dublin, 1879).

tions, in the isolated towns and villages of Munster and Leinster and in the large cities of Belfast and Dublin. The spirit of fraternity was strong, even if political awareness was not always of a very high order. There are several examples, for instance, of fenian marches and picnics where the social function was paramount, to the detriment of the political.[1] The public house, with its warmth and conviviality, functioned as an important meeting and socialising centre for such groups. Support for fenianism was correspondingly strong among publicans. A survey of fenian prisoners in January 1870, conducted by Samuel Lee Anderson, a crown solicitor at Dublin Castle, showed that a disproportionate number were publicans,[2] while Michael Carey, president of the Dublin Licensed Vintners' Association, actually defended fenianism before the 1868 Sunday-closing select committee, declaring that, in his opinion, fenianism 'had a wholesome effect upon some people who were in the habit of taking more than was good for them'.[3] Thus, despite some strong individual support for temperance, 'the general consensus among the fenians was in favour of the public house in preference to the temperance reading room.'[4] Given its political preoccupations and its social characteristics, fenianism left little room for temperance. Though, at the same time, it has to be said that even if fenianism had shown any systematic interest in the anti-drink cause, the conservative Irish temperance movement of the period would doubtless have spurned the attentions of a revolutionary secret society. If there was to be a *rapprochement* between nationalism

[1] Comerford, 'Irish nationalist politics', pp 207–11.

[2] Out of 1077 prisoners whose occupations were recorded, 128 (11·9 per cent) were publicans and shopkeepers with their sons and assistants ('Summary of the occupations of the prisoners in custody under the lord lieutenant's warrant'; S.P.O., 'F' papers, 5477R, discussed in Comerford, 'Irish nationalist politics', pp 203–7).

[3] *Report from the select committee on the Sale of Liquors on Sunday (Ireland) Bill,* p. 76, H.C. 1867–8 (280), xiv, 634.

[4] Comerford, 'Irish nationalist politics', p. 219. I have to thank Dr Comerford for allowing me to make extensive use of his thesis, particularly with regard to the social aspects of fenianism.

and temperance in Ireland, both parties were going to have to undergo major realignments.

The Irish temperance movement in the 1870s and 1880s concentrated its energies on getting anti-drink legislation of various sorts through parliament. In the 1870s they had some important successes with support from both liberal and conservative M.P.s, such as Jonathan Pim and Sir Dominic Corrigan of Dublin city, Richard Smyth of Londonderry and the O'Conor Don of Roscommon; but the next twenty years were to prove a singularly barren period with regard to temperance legislation. The Irish parliamentary party, under Parnell's leadership, was not in the main sympathetic to this type of legislation. Some members, such as A. M. Sullivan, John A. Blake, John Redmond, Arthur O'Connor and J. G. Biggar, did speak in favour of and even sponsor bills which were promoted by temperance societies. But generally Irish liberal, and even conservative, M.P.s were more active on temperance issues than the home-rulers. Temperance legislation found favour especially among Ulster M.P.s. Liberals such as J. N. Richardson, Thomas Lea, Thomas Dickson and T. W. Russell, and conservatives such as Lord Arthur Hill, C. E. Lewis, Major E. J. Saunderson, and from Belfast, William Ewart, J. P. Corry, E. S. W. de Cobain and William Johnston, all sponsored temperance bills or spoke in their favour in the 1880s. This support was doubtless largely based on religious considerations, total abstinence from intoxicating liquors being widely practised within Ulster protestantism.[1] The most vocal opponents of temperance legislation among Parnell's home-rule party at the time were John O'Connor, W. H. O'Sullivan, Philip Callan and John Daly. Callan was a notorious drunkard, highly unpopular with his colleagues, who was driven out of

---

[1] For the links between the temperance movement and Ulster protestantism, see William Gibson, *The year of grace* (jubilee ed., Edinburgh and London, 1909); Frederick Sherlock (ed.), *Fifty years ago, or Erin's temperance jubilee* (Belfast, 1879); John M. Barkley, *St Enoch's congregation, 1872–1972* (Belfast, 1972); while the *Irish Temperance League Journal*, issued in Belfast from 1863, is also a rich source of information on the subject.

politics by Parnell.[1] 'Whiskey' O'Sullivan, as he was popularly known, was a publican and consistently represented the interests of the trade in parliament.[2] O'Connor and Daly were fenians; Daly represented Cork city, the main brewing and distilling centre in the country after Dublin. Home-rule M.P.s prevented the Sunday-closing act of 1878 being extended and made permanent in 1883, and a majority of the party consistently abstained or voted against local-veto and earlier Saturday-closing bills for Ireland.

Arguments expressed in debates against temperance legislation were similar in some respects to views put forward earlier by O'Connell and the fenians.[3] In a debate, ostensibly on Welsh Sunday closing in 1881, J. A. Blake declared unequivocally that 'drink was the greatest curse of Ireland', and he went on to argue the connection between drunkenness, distress and outrage. In 1879, said Blake, where 'the greatest distress occurred in Ireland there had not only been the greatest amount of drunkenness, but also the largest number of outrages'.[3] Like Dr Edgar, Blake believed that the perpetrators of outrages were usually well fortified with drink. Irish temperance M.P.s did their case no good among the more militant home-rulers by often emphasising that this type of legislation would improve law and order and so make the government's task easier. Benjamin Whitworth, liberal M.P. for Drogheda, approvingly quoted W. E. Forster as having said 'Unless the Sunday-closing act is re-newed, I would not be responsible for the government of Ireland'. Blake regretted that Cork, the home of Fr Mathew, was so drunken

---

[1] F. H. O'Donnell, *A history of the Irish parliamentary party* (London, 1910), i, 315–16, 429; for possible reasons behind Parnell's hostility to Callan, see F. S. L. Lyons, *Charles Stewart Parnell* (London, 1977), pp 306–7, 414.

[2] Alan O'Day, *The English face of Irish nationalism: Parnellite involvement in British politics, 1880–86* (Toronto and Dublin, 1977), p. 143.

[3] The speeches cited in the following pages are taken from *Hansard 3*, as follows: Blake, cclx, 1765–9; Whitworth, cclxxviii, 1339; Shaw, cclx, 1777; William O'Brien, cclxxxix, 1031–2; John Daly, cclxxviii, 1320–21; T. M. Healy, cclxxxix, 1021–2; Maurice Healy, cccxxv, 1772–3; Harrington, cclxxxix, 1030; and Parnell, ccciv, 694; cccxxv, 1786. The group of speeches by Redmond, Biggar, Harrington and O'Brien comes from cclxxxix, 1026–38.

a city, represented, in the person of John Daly, by a man strongly opposed to temperance legislation. This brought an angry response from the M.P. for County Cork, William Shaw, the former chairman of the party and an opponent of Parnell. He vigorously defended his fellow Corkmen, declaring that they were 'as sober a people as any in the world', and he extended this into a general defence of Irishmen against their temperance critics.

As Irishmen had not the habit of eating as well as Englishmen, a little drink affected them, and the moment an Irishman began to stagger a policeman took him up. Until recently they had nothing better to do; but just now, perhaps, they were better employed, and so there were fewer arrests for drunkenness.

Like O'Connell, many home-rulers saw attacks on Irish drinking habits as attacks on the Irish people, which no true nationalist could tolerate. They denied that the Sunday-closing act of 1878 had diminished drunkenness, feeling, like Shaw, that arrests for drunkenness were very much a function of the attitude of the police and not a true reflection of the extent of the problem. Moreover many felt that the act had been enforced in a discriminatory fashion. In 1884 William O'Brien opposed the extension of Sunday closing on the grounds that

the one great effect of it would be to divide the publicans into two classes—policemen's friends and policemen's enemies—and would result in this, that all the attention of the police would be devoted to watching the nationalist publican, while those publicans who in any way had commended themselves to the favour of the police would be allowed by them to carry on any amount of Sunday trading without interference.

To many home-rule nationalists, temperance advocates were, to quote O'Brien again, a 'sect of puritans, who wished to impose their own opinions forcibly on the Irish people, and who really desired to treat the Irish people as though they were dipsomaniacs, and required to be put under restraint'. In this view temperance legislation was coercive in both intent and practice. It aimed to restrict legitimate recreation, which the vast majority of Irishmen indulged in moderately, while in practice it fell most heavily upon the working classes, damaged much-needed industry and trade, and further, could be used by the government to persecute nationalists. In 1883 John Daly opposed local veto as being oppressive on the working classes particularly, for the public house was the only place where such people could procure refreshment and recreation, lacking as they did the private cellars and clubs of the upper classes. Daly argued that it was a 'simple question of supply and demand' because 'the number of pubs depended upon the custom they received, and if the custom was not sufficient they would soon close.' Daly was against government interference, preferring to leave the drink industry to the forces of the market. He felt that the temperance minority, instead of trying to force their ideas 'down the throats of other people', would do much more good if they campaigned for the introduction of alternate forms of recreation.

Home-rule opponents of temperance also claimed that it was not a major issue in Ireland and that too much parliamentary time was being devoted to it at the expense of far more pressing issues. T. M. Healy berated the government in 1884 for consulting temperance lobbyists such as T. W. Russell, then secretary of the Irish Association for the Prevention of Intemperance, while ignoring the views of the Irish parliamentary party on the subject. He urged the government to bring forward 'non-contentious measures', like the land purchase scheme, the education bill and the endowed schools bill. The fact that temperance legislation was a contentious issue within home-rule ranks was amply demonstrated in the debate which followed Healy's remarks. Four leading home-rulers were among those who rose to speak; two, John Redmond and J. G. Biggar, were in favour of Irish Sunday closing, while the other two, Timothy Harrington and William O'Brien, were opposed. Even Healy's own brother, Maurice, differed from him in generally supporting temperance legislation. Harrington refused to believe that the 'stigma of intemperance, which some honourable members had endeavoured to fasten on the people of Ireland, could be justified', while O'Brien argued that instead of drunkenness causing pauperism . . . it was to a very large extent that poverty and misery were the cause of drunkenness. The lives of the Irish people were sufficiently joyless already; and he thought that the legislators of that house would be far better employed in doing something which would substantially improve the condition of the Irish people than by assisting in debarring them of one of the few enjoyments they had.

Parnell thus found his followers at odds on the temperance question, though with a majority either opposed or indifferent. Consequently, he was somewhat reluctant himself to take a firm stand on the issue. In 1886, for instance, he informed the mover of a bill dealing with the sale of liquor to children that a majority of his colleagues wanted Ireland excluded from the scope of the measure because they were not able to reach agreement as a party whether to support it or not. And he went on to inform the house that he had 'always attempted to keep clear of these temperance questions' and had 'never voted on any of them', because he believed that 'the question of temperance and of the control of the liquor trade is one which, of all others, could most suitably and properly be left to an Irish legislature to deal with.' This argument, that the drink question should be left to an Irish legislature, was common currency in the home-rule party, particularly during the latter part of the 1880s when it was given added impetus by the prospect of the establishment of local government authorities in Ireland within the foreseeable future. It was left to Maurice Healy, however, to point out the glaring inconsistency in arguing that the drink question be left to Irish local or national governing bodies, while demanding that the parliament at Westminster legislate on 'all kinds of topics, social and political, covering the whole field of social life'. But Healy, although he was sympathetic to temperance legislation, could see one strong argument for deferring it. This was that the 'question of closing public houses was of so angering and embittering a nature that it was inexpedient to raise it at the present time because of the effect it would have on the party . . . destroying amongst them the union which then existed'. He told the house that he understood that this was Parnell's own view. This is certainly consistent with Parnell's statement in 1886, where in effect he admitted that his party was so divided over the question of licensing legislation that he preferred to have Ireland excluded from the proposed legislation, and so avoid a damaging confrontation.

In 1888, in a debate on early Saturday closing for Ireland, Parnell made his most extended statement on the subject of temperance legislation. He said that he had watched, with the 'utmost interest', the parliamentary struggle over Irish Sunday closing for ten or twelve years. Originally he had supported the measure, but since 1878 he had come to the conclusion that it was not likely to serve the true interests of temperance, that in fact 'it was attended with greater evils than those which it sought to cure.' Parnell proclaimed himself a supporter of temperance:

I am, with perhaps a single exception, the largest employer of labour among the Irish members of all parties, and it has been brought constantly to my notice that the question of intemperance is undoubtedly a very great impediment to the progress of the industries of Ireland, and to the success of manufacturing and other operations as well as to the welfare and well-being of the people.

But, at the same time, he was 'firmly convinced' that measures proceeding from Westminster for the promotion of temperance would 'not have any chance of fair play in Ireland; that the backs of the people would be put up against them in advance; that there will be defects in the administration which will largely increase that disposition, and largely nullify the good intention of the legislature in passing such measures'. Parnell felt that the Irish would not accept such coercive legislation, and particularly if it was administered in a discriminatory fashion. He therefore advised delay, 'postponement, but not abandonment', and looked to the proposed local government bill, suggesting that licensing powers be vested in the new local authorities.

I believe that Irishmen acting at home, discussing this question amongst themselves, free from your interference, will decide this question much more advantageously and much more suitably and justly than you can ever hope to decide it here, and their decision will be attended with much better and happier results for the people.

While declaring himself in favour of temperance, Parnell was careful however to introduce the usual disclaimer with regard to the seriousness of the drink problem in Ireland. He could not admit, he said, for a 'single moment' that the Irish were a less temperate people than the English or the Scots; and, though remarking upon the odiousness of comparisons, he then went on to observe that 'certainly the balance is not against us, and may be in our favour.' Basically it would seem that Parnell was not greatly interested in the temperance issue, beyond a general desire to prevent drunkenness from damaging social and economic life, and he mainly aimed to prevent division in his party on the subject. His attitude was further illustrated by a remark he made in 1888 to Elizabeth Mathew, a descendant of Fr Mathew and later the wife of John Dillon. In her diary for 11 May of that year she recorded Parnell as having wished that there would be another apostle of temperance, since a crusade against whiskey would 'put the government in a difficulty, besides being good for the people, by diminishing an enormous source of revenue'.[1] To Parnell's pragmatic mind, temperance was an issue to be exploited or ignored depending upon the political advantages to be gained, and throughout the 1880s the balance was generally in favour of ignoring it.

Among Parnell's home-rulers, as among the fenians, there was no consistent policy on the temperance question, and in fact the deep divisions within the party on the issue only produced equivocation. The party was happy to accept financial support from the drink industry, as in the case of the Parnell tribute,[2] and also to make use of the local political power of the publican. Innkeepers and publicans, for instance, were vastly overrepresented among those arrested under the protection of person and property act of 1881. Of 845 arrested, 68 (8.1 per cent) were innkeepers or publicans, though

---

[1] Quoted in Lyons, *Parnell*, pp 385–6.
[2] O'Day, *The English face of Irish nationalism*, pp 143–4.

according to the 1881 census this group only composed 0.4 per cent of the labour force. Public houses were commonly used for land league meetings and for the posting of league placards.[1] At the same time, Parnell spoke in favour of temperance, though, like O'Connell, he was at pains to dismiss as totally unfounded any suggestion that, as a people, the Irish had a particular problem with drink. Like the Liberator, the Chief found it difficult to reconcile the claims of temperance and those of nationalism. Ultimately the results of this difficulty were empty and contradictory statements followed by an eloquent lack of action. In trying to avoid alienating either the drink industry or the temperance movement, and simultaneously to prevent his followers falling out too publicly over the question of licensing reform, Parnell attempted as much as possible to avoid the whole issue. As a result, between the Sunday-closing act of 1878 and the important licensing acts of 1902 and 1904, despite innumerable bills and several select committees, no significant Irish licensing legislation was passed at Westminster. The generally uncooperative, if not openly hostile, attitude of the home-rule party goes a long way towards explaining this situation.

If there was little cooperation in the period 1860 to 1900 between fenians and home-rulers, representing different strains of Irish nationalism, and the temperance societies seeking licensing reform, important developments were occurring during the 1860s and 1870s which were to help produce temperance organisations much more congenial to Irish nationalism. Specifically catholic temperance societies had been in existence in Britain and the United States in the 1830s and 1840s, though these had tended to wane with the swift decline of Fr Mathew's crusade in Ireland.[2] However, a resurgence of such organisations is apparent in England and America in the

---

[1] Sam Clark, 'The social composition of the land league' in *I.H.S.*, xvii, no. 68 (Sept. 1971), pp 447–69.

[2] Sheridan Gilley, 'Catholic faith of the Irish slums: London, 1840–70' in H. J. Dyos and Michael Wolff (ed.), *The Victorian city: images and reality* (London, 1973), ii, 837–53; Sister Joan Bland, *Hibernian crusade: the story of the Catholic Total Abstinence Union of America* (Washington, 1951), pp 8–18.

1860s, culminating in the establishment in 1872 of both the English League of the Cross and the Catholic Total Abstinence Union of America.[1] In 1867 Cardinal Manning had appeared on the platform at the annual meeting of the United Kingdom Alliance, marking a notable change in catholic policy towards temperance. Except for Fr Mathew's crusade, catholics in both Ireland and England had not been prominent in temperance work, generally fearing that the movement was a cloak for protestant proselytism. Cardinal Wiseman had not encouraged catholics to join in the 1850s, while Cardinal Cullen, except for the standard denunciation of drunkenness in lenten pastorals, showed little interest in the issue.[2] Manning, on the other hand, was anxious to improve the image of catholicism in England and to promote greater catholic participation in public life. As some eighty per cent of catholics in England were Irish, feared and hated by many Englishmen, Manning came to concentrate particularly on promoting sobriety, thrift, a respect for order and better education among his Irish flock. He feared the revolutionary potential latent in such an alienated section of the society and saw temperance as part of a campaign to integrate Irish catholics into English society, much as Fr Mathew had tried through temperance to help integrate them into Irish middle-class society.[3] Drink, wrote Manning, is the cause of

crime, of madness, of poverty; of ruined reputations, of strife, of murder; it empties churches, keeps souls from the sacraments; it leads to immorality, loss of faith, apostacy; it ruins homes, desolates families, brings scandal upon

---

[1] J. C. Gibbs, *History of the Catholic Total Abstinence Union of America* (Philadelphia, 1907); *The Catholic Total Abstinence Union of America: what it is, and why you should join it* (Pittsburgh, 1907); *The League of the Cross and crusade against intemperance: official report of the conventions of 1875 and 1876* (Manchester, n.d.).

[2] P. F. Moran (ed.), *The pastoral letters and other writings of Cardinal Cullen* (Dublin, 1882), i, 475.

[3] For a very useful discussion of Manning's views see A. E. Dingle and B. H. Harrison, 'Cardinal Manning as temperance reformer', in *Historical Journal*, xii, no. 3 (1969), pp 485–510.

the church; it makes bad husbands, bad wives, immoral children. Drink ruins body and soul. It is the stumbling block of the laity, the source of grief and care to the priest.[1]

The problem was most severe among the working and poorer classes, where catholics were disproportionately numerous. While he consistently supported the United Kingdom Alliance and favoured legislative measures against the drink trade, Manning also saw the need for an exclusively catholic temperance society. He wanted both to prevent the catholic faith being undermined in non-catholic organisations and to avoid Fr Mathew's mistake by establishing structures which would ensure the continuation of the work after his own departure from the scene. He aimed, he said, to create an organisation 'as strictly catholic as is the church from which it springs'.[2] Thus the rules of the League of the Cross, drawn up by Manning, laid down that only catholics could be members, that all members after they joined must 'live as good practical catholics' and that only a 'practical catholic' could hold any office in the league. The aim of the league, according to its constitution, was to unite catholics, both clergy and laity, in a 'holy war against intemperance' and thereby raise the 'religious, social and domestic state of our catholic people, especially of the working classes'.[3]

With its emphasis on the peculiar virtues of catholicism and the potential superiority of teetotal catholics, the League of the Cross obviously had its attractions for Irish catholic nationalists. The link between Irish nationalism and catholic temperance was actually forged quite early in England. John Denvir, a fenian agent in Liverpool and later the first general secretary of the Home Rule Confederation of Great Britain, had as a boy of nine taken the pledge three times from Fr Mathew, inspired by his mother's superstitious faith in the Capuchin's miraculous powers. But unlike many others

---

[1] *For private circulation: the League of the Cross* (Market Weighton, Yorks., 1890), pp 39–40.

[2] Dingle and Harrison, 'Cardinal Manning as temperance reformer', p. 495.

[3] Catholic Total Abstinence League of the Cross, *Constitution and rules* (London, 1888).

Denvir maintained his total abstinence from drink and also his faith in the temperance cause beyond the 1840s. He worked closely with Fr James Nugent, a nationalist priest, who ran the Liverpool *Catholic Times* and various catholic temperance societies in the city.[1] When Manning founded the League of the Cross, Nugent amalgamated his existing organisations with it. As his memoirs demonstrate, Denvir's nationalism ran in broad channels, taking in an appreciation of the Irish language and culture, as well as a deep concern for the plight of Irish slum-dwellers in British cities. Thus, early in the 1860s, Denvir was secretary of a boys' refuge in Liverpool, while at the same time smuggling arms to Ireland for the fenians. A few years later, with other young Liverpool Irishmen, he formed the 'Emerald minstrels' to perform songs, drama and poetry with nationalist themes for audiences in Dublin. He later wrote in his memoirs:

I must say without hesitation that we got our inspiration from the teaching of Young Ireland. . . . We started the 'Emerald minstrels' at a time when there was a lull in Irish politics; our objects being the cultivation of Irish music, poetry and the drama; Irish literature generally, Irish pastimes and customs; and, above all, Irish nationality.[2]

In 1870 Denvir established a printing and publishing business in Liverpool and 'commenced to realise what I had long projected as a useful work for Ireland'. This was the issuing of an Irish library of histories, biographies, stories and songs, which ultimately sold over a million copies.[3] In Denvir's combination of revolutionary nationalism with literary endeavour and a social conscience, we can see a forerunner of the cultural nationalism which was to flower in Ireland from the 1890s. It is hardly surprising then to find Denvir at this later period (while working in London as an organiser for the Irish National League and later the United Irish League) an active supporter of the Gaelic League and the Irish Literary Society, with a special interest in the new Irish drama.[4] Denvir's involvement in

---

[1] John Bennet, *Father Nugent of Liverpool* (Liverpool, 1949).
[2] Denvir, *The life story of an old rebel*, pp 117–18.
[3] Ibid., pp vii, 137.   [4] Ibid., pp 256–67.

Liverpool, during the 1860s and 1870s, with Nugent and Manning's explicitly catholic temperance movement went hand in hand with his efforts in other fields to educate the Irish, particularly along nationalist lines, and to elevate their moral character.

If the link between Irish nationalism and the catholic temperance movement could be seen clearly in England, in people like Denvir and Nugent, it was even more apparent in America. In 1882 Bishop John Ireland of St Paul, Minnesota, told the Catholic Total Abstinence Union of America that

the time is propitious; it is an era of Irish patriotism. The virtues and the sufferings of the Irish people have awakened universal interest. The day in the designs of providence is manifestly dawning, when the tears of centuries shall be dried, and their hearts throb at last under the influence of unalloyed joy. To hasten their deliverance, friends and patriots are on hand in numbers, each one with his remedy for the ills of the Irish people. I HAVE MY REMEDY, AND I WILL PUBLISH IT TO THE WORLD—TOTAL ABSTINENCE.[1]

Bishop Ireland argued that, though the Irish did not drink more alcohol than the English or the Scots, alcohol did more harm among the Irish people 'because the warm nature of the Irish people yields more readily to its flames, and, in the wreck which follows, they have more virtues to sacrifice'. And he went on to dwell upon these virtues:

The picture of their virtues entrances. They are the most liberty-loving people on the earth. Eight hundred years of oppression have left no mark in their freeman hearts. Generous—the will is ever beyond the means; selfishness melts and vanishes beneath their soft skies. Brave and spirited—battlefields tell their valour, as the counsels of nations speak their wisdom. Pure in morals—the gem of purity nothing can snatch away from the coronet of the isle of virgins and martyrs. Such are the children of Erin. But in an evil hour, hell—whoever may have been its agents—distilled alcohol through their plains and over their mountains, and, despite their grand qualities, a

---

[1] *How fare the Irish people? An address delivered by the Right Rev. Bishop Ireland, in the Roman Catholic cathedral of St Paul, Minnesota, U.S., August 2nd, 1882* (Dublin, 1883), p. 7.

sad story of misery has to be told. . . . This has been Ireland's curse, and he who still loves alcohol joins hands with Ireland's most bitter foe.[1]

If nationalists in the past had found it impossible to accept the seriousness of the Irish drink problem, Bishop Ireland's solution was to attribute it to Satan himself, as the only agent powerful enough to overcome this virtuous people. One could hardly wish for a clearer expression of temperance nationalism. For Bishop Ireland, the Irish people were superior to other nations, though corrupted by drink and oppressed by British rule, and he was confident that their liberation from both forms of oppression was near at hand.

While temperance organisations with a strong Irish and catholic identity were appearing in England and the United States in the 1870s, a similar trend was apparent in Ireland itself, though at a slightly later date. After the collapse of Fr Mathew's crusade, temperance had been discredited within the Irish catholic church, and for many years its propagation depended on the enthusiasm of individual clerics. Archbishops Leahy and Croke of Cashel[2] and Bishops Furlong and Warren of Ferns[3] had been keen supporters of the cause in their own dioceses, and by the 1880s their efforts were finding more widespread support within the Irish church. To some extent this was a result of the developments in England and America. While Manning was encouraged to join the temperance movement by clerical efforts in Ferns and Cashel to enforce Sunday closing,[4] the League of the Cross in turn quickly extended its work to Ireland.[5] Similarly Bishop Ireland and other leaders of the Catholic Total Abstinence Union of America visited the home country in the

---

[1] Ibid., pp 7–8.
[2] Christopher O'Dwyer, 'The life of Dr Leahy, 1806–75' (M.A. thesis, St Patrick's College, Maynooth, 1970), pp 648–77; Mark Tierney, *Croke of Cashel: the life of Archbishop Thomas William Croke, 1832–1902* (Dublin, 1976), p. 189.
[3] Lambert McKenna, *Life and work of Rev. James Aloysius Cullen, S.J.* (London, 1924), pp 306–7, 314.
[4] Dingle and Harrison, 'Cardinal Manning as temperance reformer', p. 488.
[5] *The League of the Cross: a year's work in Cork,* . . . . (Cork, 1886).

1880s, seeking to promote the catholic temperance cause.[1] Of considerable importance also was a letter sent to Bishop Ireland by the pope in 1887, in which he endorsed the controversial total abstinence pledge as 'the proper and the truly efficacious remedy for this very great evil', and generally gave papal blessing to the new movement.[2] Any fears that total abstinence and the pledge were protestant practices, unacceptable to catholic theology, were thus dispelled. But, as well, the growing support for temperance within the Irish church reflected important changes in that church. While Cardinal Cullen had virtually ignored the issue, and Cardinal McCabe had been at best equivocal,[3] Archbishop Walsh was much more wholehearted in his support, using the occasion of the centenary of Fr Mathew's birth in 1890 to order the establishment of temperance societies in every parish throughout Leinster. In this scheme Walsh was advised by both Manning and Croke.[4] Temperance was closely associated with the new emphasis on piety and devotions which was apparent in the Irish church in the latter part of the century.[5] Temperance societies and sodalities were usually dedicated to the Sacred Thirst or the Sacred Heart, and many of their activities consisted of devotional exercises aimed at strengthening the faith.

[1] *An address to the Father Mathew, O.S.F.C., Total Abstinence League of the Sacred Thirst in connection with the Church of Our Lady of Angels, Church Street, Dublin, delivered by the Rev. Thomas J. Conaty, D.D. (of Worcester, Mass., U.S.A.), president of the Catholic Total Abstinence Union of America* (Liverpool, 1889).

[2] *For private circulation: the League of the Cross*, pp 40–42.

[3] See for instance McCabe's evidence in 1868, when he opposed Sunday closing, in *Report from the select committee on the Sale of Liquors on Sunday (Ireland) Bill*, pp 105–13, H.C. 1867–8 (280), xiv, 663–71, and also his rather unsympathetic remarks regarding total abstinence at a temperance meeting in 1882, as reported in the *Freeman's Journal*, 14 Feb. 1882.

[4] *Pastoral letter of the archbishop of Dublin, and the bishops of Kildare and Leighlin, Ferns and Ossory, to the clergy and laity of their dioceses* (Dublin, 1890); Croke to Walsh, 3 Feb., 11 Mar. 1890; Manning to Walsh, 14 Mar., 17 Mar. 1890 (Dublin diocesan archives, Walsh papers, 404/4).

[5] For a discussion of this trend see Emmet Larkin, 'The devotional revolution in Ireland, 1850–75', in *American Historical Review*, lxxvii, no. 3 (June 1972), pp 625–52.

As with the League of the Cross, such organisations did not aim to convert the masses to total abstinence; rather were they elitist, seeking to involve only the most devoted catholics. Militant and ascetic catholicism was the hallmark of these new temperance societies. The sense of being a vanguard, of setting an example and making a sacrifice for the sins of others, was strong. Mass success was seen as a long-term objective, to be achieved by imposing total abstinence upon children. The practice of taking the pledge of total abstinence at confirmation, to last till the age of twenty-one, was introduced at this time. The catholic temperance movement, unlike its predecessors, did not expect to convert the existing generation (except the most ardent catholics) to abstinence; it looked rather to successive generations brought up without the taste of alcohol.[1]

The diocese of Ferns had been a temperance stronghold in Ireland from the 1850s into the 1880s, and it provided a training ground for several of the leaders of this new catholic temperance movement. The two most notable were Fr James A. Cullen, founder of the Pioneer Total Abstinence Association of the Sacred Heart, and Fr Michael Kelly, rector of the Irish college in Rome and later archbishop of Sydney.[2] Both men spent the early years of their priesthoods in the House of Missions established at Enniscorthy, County Wexford, by Bishop Furlong in 1866, and both conducted numerous temperance missions. Kelly's removal to Rome in 1891 and later to Sydney cut short his career as a leader of the Irish catholic temperance movement, but not before he had published two long and revealing articles on the subject in the *Irish Ecclesiastical Record*. The first article, entitled 'The suppression of intemperance', appeared in three parts in 1889 and provided an important summary of the

---

[1] *Pastoral letter*, 1890, pp 21–4.

[2] Kelly's papers are held in the diocesan archives, St Mary's Cathedral, Sydney. They include a collection of newspaper clippings, pamphlets and lecture notes, catalogued by this writer, dealing with the Irish temperance movement from 1865 to 1916; for a discussion of Kelly's personality and views see Patrick O'Farrell, *The catholic church in Australia: a short history, 1788–1967* (Melbourne, 1968), pp 205–9.

thought behind the new movement. In essence, it outlined the problem, describing the history of intemperance in Ireland and previous efforts to suppress it, and concluded by listing the principles upon which a successful temperance organisation needed to be founded. These principles were later to form the basis for Cullen's Pioneer Association.

While fully recognising the many problems which beset Ireland, Kelly was nevertheless unequivocal in his view that intemperance was Ireland's 'greatest national evil'.[1] Yet, at the same time, he argued that this evil was of relatively recent origin. Pre-Christian Ireland had been 'unstained by intemperance, or sensualism of any kind' and the coming of Christianity had ushered in an age of 'sanctity and learning'. The viking invasions did bring 'turbulence and bloodshed among kings and chieftains', but 'there was no intemperance', for the hospitality of the Celt was 'simple, cordial and abundant'. 'If hate was wrathful and affection warm, Christian virtue reigned in Ireland, and the usages that prevailed in regard of food itself were stamped by the very rigorous austerity which in part came down nearly to our own time.' While intemperance was rife in England from the fifth century, Ireland knew nothing of it before the twelfth, when the 'Anglo-Normans . . . of course, brought with them their characteristic vices; and at once we find "works of the flesh", intemperance included, "manifest in Ireland"'.[2] Still, intemperance mainly prevailed among the rulers while the people were largely uncorrupted. 'By divine favour, faith, hope and charity, and patriotism, were indestructible in Irish hearts . . . and the pastors of the flock, however persecuted and diminished, opposed this all-devouring wolf with saintly zeal and no small success.'[3] However, in the late seventeenth century for the first time Kelly found evidence of drunkenness among the general catholic population. This spread, 'canker-like', and by the latter part of the

[1] Michael Kelly, 'The suppression of intemperance', in *Irish Ecclesiastical Record*, 3rd ser., x, no. 3 (Mar. 1889), p. 245.

[2] Ibid., no. 7 (July 1889), pp 623–4.

[3] Ibid., p. 625.

eighteenth century intemperance had become 'general'. Nor was Kelly in any doubt as to why, after resisting for so long, the Irish people finally succumbed to this 'debasing vice'.

Competent writers ascribe this to the enforced idleness and wretchedness of the people. Confiscations, imprisonments, tortures, etc., had ceased; but legal disabilities debarred Irish youth from the learned professions; industries were suppressed; wholesome education impeded; and the peasantry were held in absolute thraldom and in desperate misery. The poor turned to drink, as the one earthly comfort within their reach. The rich sought in drink a pastime and a pleasure.[1]

This passage bears a striking resemblance to the views of Dr Drennan and Thomas Davis, already quoted, for here again is what could only be called a nationalistic view of Irish intemperance. Like Davis, Kelly saw the people as driven to drink by oppression, and he went further in laying the responsibility for the original introduction of drunkenness to Ireland at the door of the Normans and their heirs, the English rulers of Ireland. Irish history was falsified in order to produce a history of intemperance which would conform to nationalist principles. So, where Bishop Ireland had looked to the devil to find the true culprit for Irish intemperance, Fr Kelly looked no further than the English. Either way, responsibility was lifted from the shoulders of the Irish people, where the protestant temperance movement had sought to place it, and transferred to an external agency. Thus were the demands of nationalism satisfied. The gravity of the problem could now be emphasised without fear of offending nationalist sensibilities. So the argument ran that the English had brought intemperance to Ireland, had driven the Irish to excessive drinking by oppression, and continued to encourage it in order to raise revenue and also to keep the people servile.

According to Kelly, Fr Mathew's crusade had demonstrated that intemperance could be rapidly rooted out, but for this to prove lasting the active support of the whole church was required. 'The evil', he wrote, 'though radical, is not ancient, and it has been dealt

[1] Ibid., p. 626.

with effectively for a season—more than once. The general remedy—at home and abroad—is RELIGION.'[1] The work of Fr Mathew needed to be stamped with 'perpetuity and catholicity': the latter invariably producing the former. Kelly urged the Irish bishops to launch a crusade against intemperance. Acknowledging that 'practical men' might think a time of 'political excitement is inopportune, and fatally so, for the crusade proposed', Kelly then proceeded to turn this argument on its head by claiming that a 'favourable settlement of the most important political questions, and the successful use of the chief political agencies, must be promoted, and even ensured by the suppression of intemperance'.[2] The motto, 'Ireland sober, Ireland free', which was coming into use in the temperance movement in the 1880s, clearly expressed Kelly's approach to nationalist politics. But, while an end to Irish drunkenness might facilitate the solution of the country's political problems, the reverse did not apply. Political action alone would not solve the problem of intemperance. As he had rejected the efforts of protestant gentlemen in the 1830s and criticised Fr Mathew's one-man crusade of the 1840s, so Kelly denied the effectiveness of the temperance legislation which had been passed in the 1870s:

Civil legislation [he wrote] is inadequate to deal with moral vices. It can punish evildoers; it can deal with external agencies. In this sphere it can afford valuable assistance; but it cannot reform. The charge of social as of private virtue rests mainly with the church; and for all moral reformation we must look to her.[3]

While intemperance was a serious social problem and a barrier to the moral and political elevation of the Irish people, to Kelly it was, above all else, a sin. The church, therefore, and not parliament, was the proper agency to deal with it.

However, while emphasising the religious nature of the temperance question and the importance of the church in the war against drunkenness, many leaders of the catholic temperance movement were still very conscious of the political dimension. Some, following

---

[1] Ibid., p. 643.   [2] Ibid., no. 12 (Dec. 1889), p. 1106.   [3] Ibid., p. 1105.

Manning's example, still hoped for reformist legislation from Westminster, but the more militant nationalists were increasingly thinking in terms of an Irish parliament. For if Britain had a vested interest in Irish drunkenness, as many of them believed, then there was little chance that the temperance movement would receive aid from the British parliament. Before 1890 the triumph of temperance was being increasingly identified with the triumph of home rule. A meeting of the Father Mathew Total Abstinence Society in Dublin in October 1888, after hearing from J. G. Biggar how the publicans had tried to get M.P.s sympathetic to the trade on to the select committee which was then examining Irish Sunday-closing legislation, resolved that, 'by the encouragement of habits of temperance among their people they would also advance the home-rule cause'.[1] Similarly, in 1889 John Redmond expressed the view that, though the opponents of temperance

might succeed in preventing temperance legislation being carried for the present ... the more they tried to prevent it now, the more certainly will there follow, immediately on the concession of an Irish parliament, a system of restrictive legislation which would far exceed that which was asked by temperance reformers of the present day.[2]

But with the fall of Parnell, the resulting divisions in the home-rule party and that party's consistent failure to support temperance legislation, nationalists in the catholic temperance movement began to join the growing numbers of those turning their backs on the parliamentary arena. Fr Jeremiah Murphy of Rathkeale, County Limerick, summed up this criticism of parliament when he wrote:

I am not in a position to state how many of the six hundred and odd members of the house of commons are either actual owners of bars or drinking saloons, or have some direct personal interest in the welfare of some or other brewery or distillery, or owe their membership of the house to the powerful help of the licensed vote; but I am quite satisfied there is a number large

[1] *Irish Catholic*, 20 Oct. 1888.
[2] Quoted in Very Rev. Fr Aloysius, *Temperance legislation for Ireland* (Dublin, 1912), p. 8.

enough of that interested class to save the spirit-traders from all adverse legislation.[1]

The Irish parliamentary party's links with the drink trade were dramatically highlighted during the crisis over Lloyd George's 1909 budget, when the party's reluctance to accede to higher duties on liquor licences and spirits for a time threatened the alliance with the liberals and thus the prospect of securing home rule for Ireland.[2]

The emerging cultural nationalism, with its emphasis on the moral qualities of the individual and of the nation, seemed to some a more appropriate ally for the temperance movement than the divided and discredited parliamentary party. In 1903, at a temperance meeting in St Patrick's College, Maynooth, Fr Patrick Coffey declared that

the Irish revival . . . has caused many deep heart-searchings and drawn forth many resolves to amend our common faults and shortcomings. It sees the futility of hoping for economic or social reform without sobriety and self-respect. It has openly recommended to all Irishmen the work of temperance reform.[3]

This progression, from faith in legislation and the parliamentary party to an identification of temperance with more extreme forms of nationalism, can also be seen in the career of Fr James Cullen. Though Cullen strove principally to develop a highly structured temperance organisation with strong links to the church, he was also preoccupied as a nationalist with political aspects of the drink problem. In the 1890s he had endorsed campaigns for both local veto and the Gothenburg system,[4] but as parliament failed to produce significant temperance legislation so his mind came to dwell on more extreme forms of action. In 1911 he told a large temperance meeting, held significantly on Vinegar Hill, above Enniscorthy:

---

[1] Jeremiah Murphy, 'A plan for temperance reform' in *Irish Ecclesiastical Record*, 4th ser., ix, no. 4 (Apr. 1901), p. 302.

[2] F. S. L. Lyons, *John Dillon: a biography* (London, 1968), pp 308–11.

[3] Patrick Coffey, 'Students and temperance reform' in *Irish Ecclesiastical Record*, 4th ser., xiv, no. 2 (Aug. 1903), p. 119.

[4] J. A. Cullen, *Temperance catechism and total abstinence manual for the use of colleges, schools, and educational establishments* (Dublin, 1891), p. 23.

Vinegar Hill, on which we stand, has its warnings for us. In these very fields your fathers fought and fell—fell not so much beneath the fire of the north Cork militia and the orange yeomanry as by the treachery of drink. Drink lost the battle at Ross, lost the battle at Wexford, and helped to the disaster of Vinegar Hill. . . . Ireland lost all her fights through drink.[1]

The conclusion to be drawn was obvious: if Ireland was to resort to arms again in order to win its freedom, temperance would be vital in ensuring the success of the enterprise. Cullen then went on to conjure up for his audience the vision of a new, redeemed and liberated Ireland which would resume its old role as a champion of catholicism in Europe. He saw the Scandinavian countries struggling to rid themselves of the drink curse and felt that Irish missionaries, 'holding in one hand the torch of faith and in the other the torch of temperance . . . will help them to regain the faith that has been wrested from them'.[2] In Cullen's mixture of militant catholicism and revolutionary nationalism, temperance was a vital tool. It was the means by which the socio-economic ills of the country would be cured, the way prepared for eventual political liberation and Ireland ultimately set on the road to regaining its rightful place as a leader among the nations, renowned once again for its piety and learning.

If the catholic temperance movement felt an affinity with the new cultural and revolutionary nationalism, this latter movement in turn found much to admire in the temperance cause. The Gaelic Athletic Association, at the urging of Archbishop Croke, was quick to exclude drink from its meetings and to refuse sponsorship by publicans.[3] Arthur Griffith's Sinn Féin spoke in favour of temperance and found itself battling the 'whiskey ring', which dominated the Dublin

[1] Quoted in McKenna, *Life and work of J. A. Cullen*, pp 346–7; see also *Father Mathew Record*, vi, no. 7 (July 1911), pp 178–9.

[2] Ibid., p. 347. For a stimulating discussion of the nationalism of Cullen and his fellow leaders of the catholic temperance movement see Patrick O'Farrell, *Ireland's English question: Anglo-Irish relations, 1534–1970* (London, 1971), pp 223–7.

[3] T. F. O'Sullivan, *Story of the G.A.A.* (Dublin, 1916), pp 63, 78, 87.

corporation.[1] Similarly, Jim Larkin, a lifelong teetotaller, was anxious to encourage his union members to take the pledge, telling them on one occasion that it was 'the duty of everyone who had at heart the welfare of Ireland to call upon the national representatives to put in the forefront of their programme legislation to crush the curse of intemperance'.[2] In the north Bulmer Hobson and Denis McCullough reformed the Belfast Irish Republican Brotherhood and decided to accept only members who did not drink.[3] Like Larkin and Hobson, Patrick Pearse was also an enthusiastic teetotaller, refusing either to smoke or drink from an early age and lecturing his friends, as well as public meetings, on the evils of drink.[4]

Throughout most of the nineteenth century, as we have seen, Irish nationalism and the temperance movement were at odds. Temperance began as, and for long remained, the exclusive preserve of middle-class, pro-British protestants, who used it to bolster their own position while at the same time denigrating the customs and habits of their catholic social inferiors. It was strongest in Ulster, particularly among that province's presbyterians and methodists, and it was closely linked to developments in both the British and American temperance movements. Even Fr Mathew's crusade only permitted a temporary and fairly uneasy reconciling of these conflicting forces. He and his leading supporters may have aimed to improve the lot of catholics by elevating them into the sober, educated and industrious world of the middle classes. There were

---

[1] Richard Davis, *Arthur Griffith and non-violent Sinn Fein* (Dublin, 1974), p. 51; see also Arthur Griffith, *The resurrection of Hungary: a parallel for Ireland* (Dublin, 1904), pp 79–80, in which he shows how the Austrians foisted a reputation for drunkenness upon the Hungarians and implies that the English have done the same to the Irish.

[2] Emmet Larkin, *James Larkin: Irish labour leader, 1876–1947* (London, 1968), pp 6, 48–9, 126–7.

[3] Bulmer Hobson, *Ireland yesterday and tomorrow* (Tralee, 1968), pp 35, 98; Davis, *Arthur Griffith*, pp 25–6.

[4] Ruth Dudley Edwards, *Patrick Pearse: the triumph of failure* (London, 1977), pp 24, 120, 165.

nationalists, however, who saw in his movement the means of creating, not a law-abiding middle class, but a sober and disciplined people, dedicated to nationalist ideals and prepared to fight for the destruction of the union. Temperance certainly made a contribution in this latter sense, for it both facilitated O'Connell's organisation of mass meetings and gave encouragement to the more idealistic aims of the Young Irelanders. But, though temperance in the form of Fr Mathew's crusade was used by nationalists of different types and for different ends, temperance leaders remained generally hostile to the aspirations of Irish nationalism. We saw the difficulties O'Connell faced in trying to marry the two concepts at an abstract level. Davis's mind, which was more wide-ranging and flexible, could devise a theoretical reconcilation between temperance and nationalism, but lesser minds failed to do so. The revolutionaries and parliamentarians who succeeded Davis generally looked askance at temperance, viewing it as a favourite hobby-horse of Ulster evangelicals or as a weapon used by the British in their campaign to discredit the Irish people. At the same time, they found in the publican an important socio-economic, as well as a political, ally.

By the 1870s and 1880s, however, in the United States and England, as well as in Ireland, a temperance movement was emerging, as part of a general popular religious revival, which was implicitly and often explicitly sympathetic to Irish nationalism. This catholic temperance movement, and the priests who were its main leaders, saw British rule as the ultimate cause of Ireland's drink problem, and the British government as the main beneficiary of it, in respect both of taxes and of keeping the Irish demoralised and subdued. They did not feel a need, therefore, to deny or underplay the problem as some previous nationalists had done; in fact they highlighted it, by ascribing to drunkenness most of the evils with which the country was beset. Poverty, crime, insanity, emigration, poor health, bad housing and neglect of religion—all were ascribed to the infatuation with liquor, as was Ireland's failure to free herself from British rule. Drunkenness was seen as the real reason behind the failure of '98, while discontent with the home-rule party took the form of accusations that it was under the thumb of the drink trade. In the eyes of the catholic temperance movement a truly devout catholic and a truly patriotic Irishman could not fail but be a total abstainer. Convinced that Ireland was soon to achieve her independence, the catholic temperance movement and particularly the Pioneer Total Abstinence Association, which was its main institutionalised expression in Ireland, set about creating an élite of ardent catholic nationalists from among the existing generation, while at the same time working to ensure that Ireland's future generations would grow up in the practice of strict total abstinence. By the early years of the twentieth century the priests who led the movement were identifying temperance not just with Irish nationalism in a general sense, but with the most extreme elements in the nationalist movement of the time. Thus was temperance in Ireland over a period of some seventy years transformed from a largely conservative and protestant doctrine into one preached by catholic nationalists, often with markedly revolutionary overtones.

In aid of the civil power, 1868–90

DAVID N. HAIRE

THE attempts to gain home rule for Ireland, allied to the efforts to bring about a revolutionary land settlement, mark out the period between 1868 and 1890 as an unusual one in Irish history. The scope, the methods and the men of this era's politics, plus the near success of the nationalist programme, were sufficient in themselves to make it so, but it was the working alliance forged between the constitutional and agrarian forces which truly gave it an exceptional aspect. Such abnormal public activity created an air of tension and generated great excess of energy which frequently assumed a violent character, so that the period was marked by a high level of violence, and agitation leading to violence. The level of violence, at a peak in the early and middle eighties, became a grave embarrassment for the Royal Irish Constabulary, whose lack of numbers prevented it from carrying out peace-keeping measures unaided; and it was in order to correct this disadvantage that the Irish government constantly employed the Irish garrison of the British army throughout the period. It was a role which, by the very nature of its training and organisation, the army was wholly unsuited for, yet one which it would appear to have carried out with reasonable success in military terms.

By the latter years of the nineteenth century the British army had forged a long tradition of service in Ireland, which can be tentatively traced back to the days of Henry VIII. The Tudors' deep-rooted feeling of insecurity, coupled with a desire to expand their dominion, led them to attempt through armed invasion the permanent elimination of a possible source of danger. However, continuing Irish opposition to English rule, the rebellion of 1798, the union and the Napoleonic wars forced successive British governments to occupy

Ireland permanently with an army of garrison strength. There seemed to be every truth in the statement that 'there [was] no land in the world of so continual war within himself, nor of so great shedding of Christian blood, nor of so great robbing, spoiling, preying and burning, nor of so great wrongful extortions continually as Ireland'.[1] Had Ireland formed an integrated and vital part of the United Kingdom, the precaution of an oversize garrison would have been unnecessary and the Irish force smaller and less influential in consequence.[2]

Between 1792 and 1822 the army in Ireland doubled in strength, from 11,113 to 22,331.[3] The national and international crises of the period necessitated this rise, and the establishment's continuing fear of unrest, for example over the issue of catholic emancipation, probably accounts for the latter relatively high figure, at a time when the army as a whole was being somewhat reduced after the Napoleonic struggles. During the rest of the century its strength fluctuated, at times rather wildly, between extremes of 15,000 and 30,000 men. On average the garrison was housed in some fifty barracks and forts, although in all 112 barracks and fifty-three towers and batteries had been constructed to allow expansion of the garrison in emergencies.[4]

During the period 1868–90 the law-and-order situation in Ireland

---

[1] 'State of Ireland, and plan for its reformation' (1515), quoted in Neville Williams, *Elizabeth, queen of England* (London, 1967), p. 332.

[2] On the whole the Irish garrison was proportionately larger than the army maintained in England and Wales. In Ireland in 1871 the army stood at a ratio of 1 to 194·79 persons; in England and Wales it was only 1 to 304·17 persons. While they are not entirely responsible for this difference, Irish political disaffection and agrarian agitation must be seen as the major factors behind it.

[3] *Return of the number of commissioned and non-commissioned officers and men employed in the public service in Great Britain and Ireland and in the colonies (exclusive of India) on 1 January in the years 1792, 1822, 1828, 1830, 1835 and 1842*, pp 2–3, H.C. 1843 (140), xxxi, 146–7.

[4] *Return of the number of barracks in the United Kingdom now fit for the reception of troops; stating the place, the number of men and officers each barrack is calculated to hold; distinguishing the barracks for infantry, cavalry and artillery, and the number of men and officers now quartered in each barrack*, pp 1–6, H.C. 1831–2 (227), xxvii, 177–82.

was to place a heavy demand upon the manpower of the army, at a time when its commitments overseas were equally onerous. In addition to this strain the army underwent a period of unprecedented reform and change. The reforms were introduced by Edward Cardwell, secretary of state for war in Gladstone's first ministry, and were to alter the whole character of the army, at last turning its face away from the Napoleonic era of long service, purchase and unrelenting hardship. The army changed from one of long-service veterans, all too inclined to heavy drinking, slacking and indiscipline, to an army of youths, less excessive in their habits, though perhaps less readily fit for the active service conditions of Ireland.[1]

In 1868 the military authorities in Dublin Castle were keenly interested in the question of fenian infiltration of the army. The after-effects of the fenian rising of 1867 were still very much in evidence, and the attempts by Stephens and other fenians to seduce Irishmen in the army from their allegiance had illuminated a weak spot which the military authorities were busily repairing. These attempts did not end with the failure of the rising or the capture of the ringleaders behind the design to infiltrate the army. Though the immediate danger of a mutiny was past, and although that danger never assumed desperate and pressing proportions, the occasional attempt to win over soldiers to fenianism worried the military authorities, who gave the problem close and continuous attention. Lord Strathnairn, commander of the forces in Ireland, writing to Lord Spencer in December 1869, showed that the danger to military discipline and good order in certain regiments had been a real one and that care had still to be taken.

---

[1] The non-commissioned officers and privates were still, in 1868, the long-service soldiers of bygone days. Only as recently as 1847 had men ceased to enlist for life. The greater part of a soldier's career was spent abroad; this position was only radically altered by Cardwell's short service act, 1870, which reduced the term of enlistment to twelve years, half of it being spent in the reserve. Thereafter, young men slowly made up the bulk of each regiment. Their youth and inexperience were disadvantageous in Ireland, considering the nature of the duties carried out.

My predecessor Sir George Brown was a very fine gallant old soldier, but was under the same delusion as several Indian generals who to the last maintained that it was impossible that the British uniform could cover a traitor.

He therefore would not listen to numerous proofs, brought to him by commanding officers, of fenians in their regiment, and I therefore had a hard card to play when I took the command. But I soon became aware of the extent and danger of Stephen's [*sic*] intrigues in the army, and of the necessity of counteracting as vigorously as he plotted them.

But it required no less than 150 courts martial to accomplish this object; and it is still necessary to watch this dangerous crime, and to punish it when it shows itself.[1]

Clearly the fenian defeat in 1867 had fallen short of being total in the absolute sense and had merely resulted in the movement going to ground, as Strathnairn pointed out when he wrote to the duke of Cambridge, the commander-in-chief, in April 1870: 'However much military and constabulary movements have checked outrages and disorders, I regret to say that there is no diminution of the general disaffection, or elements of anarchy. They only wait a *better opportunity*.'[2] However, Strathnairn's assessment of the fenian threat in the army was that it could be eliminated if closely watched and dealt with when and where necessary. In the final analysis he did not believe the movement posed any greater threat at that time. 'I . . . *did not* and *do not* think', he assured the duke in December 1869, 'that any collective or insurrectionary movement will occur. I had the honour to give your royal highness my reasons for this opinion in London, a principal one being a split among the disaffected.'[3]

In the fenian threat Strathnairn had faced one of the more difficult problems of his time as commander of the forces in Ireland. While he felt that the threat of violence in the country had not been permanently eradicated, his prompt action within the Irish garrison

---

[1] Strathnairn to Lord Spencer, 26 Dec. 1869 (B.M., papers of Sir Hugh Rose, Lord Strathnairn, lv, MS 42826, p. 116).

[2] Strathnairn to duke of Cambridge, 27 Apr. 1870 (ibid., p. 216).

[3] Strathnairn to duke of Cambridge, 14 Dec. 1869 (ibid., p. 104).

had removed any threat of mutiny on the part of sympathising soldiers.

A second serious problem faced the army between 1868 and 1872, that of military presence at local and parliamentary elections. This practice, thoroughly disliked by the army itself, was by no means a new one, but reached a critical point during these years. Through long practice, military participation at elections, essentially in a peacekeeping role, had become part and parcel of such occasions. The scarcity of polling places, the absence of the secret ballot, the often critical issues at stake, and the influence of both landlords and the Roman Catholic church had all frequently contributed towards making the Irish election a violent affair. In direct contrast to the practice prevailing in the rest of the British Isles, the army was used in a leading role at elections: a role injurious to the army, since the nature of the tasks carried out by it during the elections often deprived it of any chance of remaining impartial in the eyes of the bulk of the community, and more often than not the army came to be seen as the guardian of landlordism and of the privileges landlords claimed to possess. The British army provided the conservative Englishman with proof that the Irish were incapable of governing themselves, and the nationalist with proof that democratic rights were being flouted in the opposition's favour. However unfortunate army participation was at elections, the fact remains that, given the unavoidable side-effects of existing electoral procedure, the army was until 1872 a necessary part of Irish politics. With the increase in the number of polling places and the introduction of secret voting in that year, the two most important reasons for the army's use at elections disappeared, and it ceased to play an active and odious part in them.

The question of military presence at elections was extremely controversial, if only for the fact that it was a peculiarly Irish phenomenon, which at first glance seemed particularly undemocratic. The dangers of undue military influence at election time were well known and were rightly recognised as being the reverse of the free and unhindered right to vote as one saw fit. It had long been the case in the rest of the British Isles that the army remained in barracks during polling day, or remained a fixed number of miles from a polling place, but this practice had not been extended to Ireland. Two duties were carried out by the Irish garrison at election time: it kept the peace at polling stations and escorted voters to and from the poll. The first duty required the dispersal of the garrison all over the country, in imitation almost of a military occupation, and frequently resulted in the army's involvement in street riots. Though there was nothing unusual in the nature of such a task, the fact that it took place during election time laid the army open to accusations of partisanship. The second duty, that of escorting voters to the poll, was extremely damaging to the army's reputation, as it presented the populace with all the proof they needed that the army was siding with the minority party of the district.

The general election of 1868 was the last such election held in Ireland under the old system of the open ballot and a restricted number of polling places. Due to the political issues at stake, both the Roman Catholic church and the landlord class recognised the crucial importance of winning, and threw their full weight into pre-election canvassing. As a result of the tension created by these forces, the army was involved in two events which again focused public and parliamentary attention upon its role during elections.

Prior to the polling day on 30 November 1868, both the police and army were active in escorting voters in the county of Sligo. Between 22 and 29 November seven applications were made to the high sheriff, nine to the army and seventeen to the resident magistrates for escorts of police and/or soldiers, and some 300 voters were brought in to the polling places, a number of whom were brought in nearly a week before the polling day.[1] Clearly the landlords were using the R.I.C. and the army as vote-collectors. The army itself escorted 112 voters to the polling places between 25 and 29 Novem-

[1] *Return of applications for escorts made to resident magistrates employed on election duty at the late election for the county of Sligo*, p. 10, H.C. 1868–9 (180), l, 222.

ber, ostensibly for their own protection, and public anger was quickly roused by what was obviously incorrect use of the forces of law and order.[1] The O'Connor Don, raising the matter with the Irish government, described the proceedings as follows:

> The Sligo election is now over, and the conduct of the authorities can have no further influence on it; but the course of proceeding all over the country for some weeks before the polling day, cannot be allowed to remain without inquiry. . . . All over the country, for eight or ten days before the election, the civil and military forces were impressed into the service of the conservative proprietors, and were sent out to bring in voters into the polling-places, not on sworn informations made by the voters themselves, but on those made by the bailiffs, underagents, or others, who in these informations did not state the names, residences, or even number of those voters, who they swore wished to go into the towns, and who required an escort, but who, in most cases when the escort went out, either hid themselves or openly declared that they did not desire to leave their homes.
>
> These proceedings I believed to be highly unconstitutional. I know they produced great irritation in the country, and therefore I believed it my duty to bring them under the notice of the government.[2]

Allowing for possible inaccuracies, these accusations were essentially correct and the army was powerless to refute them, as, indeed, it had been incapable of avoiding the duty itself. As has been mentioned, the army had to act upon receiving the signed requisition form from a magistrate, and though the latter's motive for calling for a military escort might be suspect, the army was unable to refuse aid unless ordered to do so by the government. In this way the landlord class in County Sligo was able to use the army for its own ends while still remaining within the law. The Sligo case was strong support for the view, current among nationalists and the liberal party, that the conservative party was using the army for its own

---

[1] *Return of applications made to military officers during the fourteen days preceding the day of election for the county of Sligo, for the aid of the military in collecting or escorting voters in that county; with certain particulars respecting each application*, p. 14, H.C. 1868–9 (180), l, 226.

[2] *The O'Connor Don to the under secretary, 21 Dec. 1868*, pp 5–6, H.C. 1868–9 (180), l, 217–18.

purposes. This argument was raised by the Hartington committee of inquiry into parliamentary and municipal elections in 1869, but was stoutly refuted by Lord Strathnairn. When asked if there was any truth in the suggestion that a difference was made, with regard to the use of troops, when a tory administration was in power, he replied: 'Not the slightest in the world. We have no power whatever to do it; and anything so unworthy never entered into an officer's head.'[1]

The evidence of the Reverend J. McDermot, a priest from County Sligo, took, however, a rather different line. Some of the voters had been escorted for quite long distances to the polling places, and McDermot was asked why he thought the army had escorted them over such distances. He answered:

It was done for display, and the people were convinced that it was to indicate that government intimidation was combining with landlord intimidation and that the one was made use of to supplement the other, and hence a great deal of evil accrued. The people believed that the government were so far supplementing the landlord intimidation, and they came to the conclusion then that their experience was correct in imagining that the government was as a matter of course, against them, and labouring in the interest of the landlords and the gentry.[2]

Though McDermot would not go so far as to accuse the government of bias himself, he did accuse the magistrates and the high sheriff of Sligo of exercising partiality. To this extent he was in agreement with Strathnairn, who considered the magistrates' handling of this situation and of subsequent riots in Sligo to have been badly at fault.

On 29 November 1868 a detachment of the 2nd battalion of the Norfolk regiment, in company with some troopers of the 14th Hussars, was escorting a party of conservative voters from the station to the voting booth in Drogheda. They were attacked by a mob some 1500 to 2000 strong who threw stones, sticks and bottles

---

[1] *Select committee on parliamentary and municipal elections, 1869,* p. 494, H.C. 1868–9 (352), viii, 516; hereafter referred to as *Committee of inquiry into elections, 1869.*

[2] Ibid., p. 353.

at the party, and some hand-to-hand fighting ensued. Four officers and fourteen men were injured, some severely, and the riot act was read a number of times. The officer in command of the escort was knocked out by a stone, and while he was incapacitated two soldiers opened fire without orders, killing one civilian. At the subsequent inquest the coroner's jury returned a verdict of manslaughter against one of the two privates, but could not say which one. Eventually the two men were tried for murder in Dublin, but were acquitted for lack of definite evidence as to which had fired the fatal shot. The Drogheda riot was far from being a unique example of an Irish election and of the part which the army was forced to play in them. It did, however, illustrate the dangers of using the army to escort voters, and further, it showed how ill-equipped the army was, as then organised and armed, to deal with street rioting. Strathnairn described the results of the Drogheda riot to the commander-in-chief, the duke of Cambridge, as follows:

The elections at Drogheda are a fresh and painful proof of the great evil resulting from the employment of troops at elections. The voters and the troops had to endure the greatest and wanton outrage, the former simply because they were discharging a right conferred on them by the constitution, and the latter because they were obeying orders and performing an unpopular duty.[1]

The use of the army at elections was clearly fraught with dangers; not only that, but the escorting of voters, a task distinct from simply keeping the peace, could in certain circumstances be called unconstitutional and an undue interference with democratic rights. It was a task thoroughly disliked by both the army and the civilian population, and one which in the end benefited no one but the landlords who chose to abuse it, if indeed even they gained anything. Election duty was for the army a costly and expensive business, involving a widespread and complicated dispersal of forces. It was not uncommon for regiments to be split up, and the two or more

---

[1] Strathnairn to duke of Cambridge, 21 Nov. 1868 (B.M., papers of Sir Hugh Rose, Lord Strathnairn, vol. liv, MS 42825, p. 177).

sections posted to different parts of the country. This ludicrous situation was experienced by the 14th Hussars in 1868, when one troop was posted to Belfast and the other to Kinsale. Among many others, Strathnairn detested the part the army was being forced to play in this respect and firmly believed that an increase in the number of polling places would remove the necessity for its use. He expressed such an opinion to the duke of Cambridge in July 1868:

Sir, I venture to state to your royal highness that today will be brought forward the second reading of the Irish registracy bill, when an opportunity will occur of expressing an opinion as to the deplorable results of Mr Gladstone and others having thrown out the measure proposed by the government of 'increased number of polling places', with a view of preventing the system of outrage and intimidation which places the troops employed, invariably at contested elections in Ireland, in a false and as disadvantageous position as it does freedom of opinion and the right of constitutional election of members of parliament.[1]

The events of the 1868 general election obviously influenced the duke in the same way, as is shown in a letter Strathnairn wrote to him in December 1868:

I entirely share your royal highness's opinion that some measure should be devised for obviating the necessity of employing troops at elections . . . The whole army of Ireland have now for the last three weeks been employed, as if it were for a campaign, all over, and in the remotest part of, Ireland.[2]

Though Strathnairn did not believe that the introduction of the secret ballot would help, feeling that the Roman Catholic clergy would use their influence in such a way as to negate its use, he had supported the increase in the number of polling places when he spoke in the house of lords on the registration (Ireland) bill in July 1868, and he continued to do so when he gave evidence before the Hartington committee in July 1869.

Military participation at elections in Ireland continued until

[1] Strathnairn to duke of Cambridge, 24 July 1868 (ibid.).
[2] Strathnairn to duke of Cambridge, 5 Dec. 1868 (ibid., p. 202).

February 1872. Escorts for voters were still supplied during these years and remained a common sight at local elections. Trouble continued to affect the army on this duty, resulting, for example, in the troops being forced to fire on a crowd in Granard on 3 January 1870. The passing of the ballot act in 1872, by providing for an increase in the number of polling places and by introducing the secret ballot, removed the necessity for using the army in its former role at elections. The situation was, therefore markedly different when the next general election occurred in 1874, and a circular sent out by Thomas Henry Burke, under-secretary for Ireland, to magistrates in January of that year, reflected the change:

Under the old system of open voting, with a small number of polling places, the government found it often hardly possible to comply, even in a very limited degree, with the requisitions of the sheriffs. It is obvious that if this difficulty existed when there were only 155 polling places in Ireland, it has been immensely increased now when there are 640 polling places; and his excellency deems it therefore right frankly to state that while willing to afford you all reasonable assistance within his power, it is manifestly impossible for him to hold out the hope that he will be able to continue the old system . . .[1]

Special instructions were also sent to the resident magistrates and the R.I.C. to induce magistrates to rely solely on the police to keep order and to ask for the barest military force, and that only if absolutely required. Though troops were used to keep order at this election on a few occasions, the old system of granting extensive military aid and of providing soldiers for escort duty was not repeated. The position was to change in some degree with time, however, in that the authorities did not so emphatically inhibit local authorities from calling on police and troops during the election of 1880.

The years between 1868 and 1871 formed a bleak period for the Irish garrison: the activities of the fenians, election duty, and a sharp

[1] Circular to R.Ms and magistrates, Dublin Castle, 28 Jan. 1874 (N.L.I., Kilmainham papers, lxvii, MS 1067, p. 19).

rise in the agrarian crime rate kept the army in a state of constant movement all over the island. To cope with the heavy demands made upon the garrison at this time, its average annual strength rose from 21,557 in 1868 to 27,653 in 1871. The duties carried out by the force included riot control, the escorting of prisoners, judges and voters, and patrolling. Guard duty at all barracks was greatly increased in anticipation of fenian attacks or arms raids, and, though never used at this time, flying columns were organised between December 1869 and the middle of 1870.[1] Similarly, general peace-keeping duties with the R.I.C. were heavier, especially after the passing of the peace preservation act in the early months of 1870. Having reached a peak in 1870, agrarian outrages fell quickly, and as the duties of the army decreased it entered a period of relative calm. Between 1871 and 1879 Ireland experienced a decline in the level of agrarian and political outrage and the annual average strength of the garrison reflected the change, falling from 27,653 in 1871 to 18,684 in 1879. Though the greater part of Ireland enjoyed quiet and peaceful times during this period, sundry outbreaks of violence continued and Belfast was shaken by severe rioting in 1872 and 1873.

The Irishtown meeting on 20 April 1879 heralded the end of this shaky peace, and with the foundation of the Irish National Land League at the Imperial Hotel, Dublin, on 21 October of the same year, Irishmen stepped out on the road of mass agitation of a new and striking kind.[2] The period of the land war, between 1879 and 1882, produced the terrible weapon of total social ostracism—the

[1] In theory in 1881 a flying column consisted of one troop of cavalry, one division of artillery, a section of Royal Engineers, Army Service Corps and Army Hospital Corps, plus four companies of infantry; in all some 300 men. The column was so organised as to enable it to act swiftly, independently and in all situations. Its purpose was to utilise its speed and strength to stem trouble quickly in any part of the country.

[2] The general principles of which Michael Davitt was author and which were to underline the ensuing land agitation were first enunciated at the Irishtown meeting in County Mayo. The meeting itself was held to protest against the actions of a local landlord.

boycott—, mass evictions, and Captain Moonlight, and the level of violence in all its forms rose far above that experienced in 1869–70. Sir John Michel, commander of the forces in Ireland since 1875, wrote to the duke of Cambridge in August 1880, describing the depths to which Ireland had fallen and the fears he held for the future.

The feeling in the disturbed districts can hardly be worse, thanks to the seditious and inflammatory preaching of Parnell and Co., apparently acquiesced in by the liberal chief [Gladstone] in England.

It will take years to eradicate the radically seditious immolation [*sic*] of the past nine months.

The Irishman of 1880 is an article sadly changed for the worse: in many districts, his kindly, generous nature is apparently gone, he is a rebellious Americanised Irishman without the good qualities of either.

We are much in the dark as to what will be the conduct of the people for the next three months: but it is believed in police quarters that in September, or before, if evictions are attempted, or legal rights [illegible], that partial serious outbreaks and perhaps nocturnal outrages are not unlikely.

Nothing, I think, will more tend to encourage outrage, and has already weakened the civil power more, than the non-renewal of the peace preservation act. The very hands of the police are tied—and their valuable espionage crippled—whilst arms may be found in any number.[1]

By 1881 agrarian outrage was endemic over much of Ireland and the situation had deteriorated to such an extent that the R.I.C. was incapable of dealing with it single-handed. The army, having already aided the civil power to a great degree, was then forced to assume an even greater share of the police's duties. Lack of manpower in the R.I.C. made it impossible for the army to continue in a supporting role, and for a time it aided the R.I.C. on a totally different basis, though it must be noted that the government did not go so far as to confer the legal powers of the police upon the troops. The period between 1879 and 1882 thus saw the duties of the army immeasurably increased; detachment duty, riot control, personal protection duty, patrolling, process-serving and eviciton duty were among the heavier

[1] Sir John Michel to the duke of Cambridge, 17 Aug. 1880 (N.L.I., Kilmainham papers, ccciv, MS 1304, pp 219–20).

and more obvious tasks carried out, and flying columns were again organised, as in 1869–70.

Agrarian outrages, between 1883 and 1890, continued to run at a very high level, though they fell greatly from the critical point reached in 1881. The annual average strength of the army again closely follows this pattern, never falling below some 24,600. The army continued to be fully occupied during these years, though it was permitted to relax somewhat from the feverish activity it had experienced at the height of the land war. With the demise of the land league and its replacement by the Irish National League in October 1882, the duties of the army entered another phase. Eviction duty continued to form a large part of the army's work, as did riot control, detachment duty and patrolling, and during this period it was increasingly used to prevent league meetings which the government had proclaimed. The most serious political-sectarian riots of the whole period under study occurred in Belfast in 1886, and occupied the attention of some 3500 troops as well as some 2500 police.

With the exception of election duty and special duties carried out in 1882, therefore, the army's duties in aid of the civil power remained essentially the same throughout the 1870s and 1880s. These duties were the control of street riots; the patrolling of disturbed districts; the protection of sheriffs and of the R.I.C. at evictions; the prevention of proclaimed meetings; guard duty at military and civilian installations; the protection of judges and witnesses at assizes; keeping the peace during mass processions; and searching for arms. With the exception of guard duty and the provision of certain patrols, all duties were carried out in company with a representative or representatives of the civil police force.

The duty of aiding the civil power during riots was heavy during this troubled period. It remains, however, a point in question as to the good or bad effects of using troops on such occasions. Dealing with civil riots was primarily the task of the R.I.C., a task it successfully carried out at most small confrontations. No two riots were the same, however, and the government's answer to them had to be as variable as possible. However, these variations were far from infinitesimal, and were in fact severely limited by the organisation of the police and army, and by the weapons available to both. The police were restricted to hand-to-hand fighting, the baton charge, the bayonet charge, and the use of mounted police in small numbers, and finally of the rifle, firing buckshot or ball ammunition. At all times the police were aware that they might not be able to contain a riot should it get out of hand, even after the drastic course of firing on the crowd had been taken. To cater for such a possibility the government was forced to introduce the army, if possible before such a point was reached, or after it if a military force was not immediately available. Such a course obviously aggravated the situation. However, the army was in precisely the same position as the R.I.C. to the extent that its ability to contain a riot without bloodshed was weakened by its having lethal weapons. It might have the advantage of much greater numbers, but in the end it was similarly faced with the choice of using its weapons or not. Since firing upon a crowd was to be avoided if at all possible, both the army and police were forced to experience a great deal of punishment during severe urban and country riots, the Drogheda election riot of 1868 being such a case.

Major-General M. McMurdo, commanding the Dublin infantry brigade, gave evidence before the Hartington committee on parliamentary and municipal elections in 1869, and pinpointed what he considered was the main defect in the system of employing troops at riots.

Anyone who reflects upon the deplorable occurrences at the late election at Drogheda ought to be convinced of the necessity that exists for remedying one of the worst defects that a military system can be subject to in its relations with the people, viz. the habitual and reckless employment of troops armed solely with deadly weapons; the provocation to outrage, on the part of an excited populace, being stimulated by the fact (well known to all) that soldiers dare not use their weapons; and are, therefore, at [the crowd's] mercy till the extremity of violence has been reached and the magistrate orders them to act; and then there being but one course open to the officer, he has only to obey his orders and to fire on the people, who, after all, are only rioting. . . . In short, the effectiveness of the armed soldier at [a riot] suffers inversion of its normal state, while his liabilities are increased in alarming proportion to the immunity enjoyed by the citizen.[1]

Stating the essence of his argument against the use only of armed soldiers at riots, McMurdo said:

The existence of the defect is therefore beyond dispute; and it is equally apparent that this defect is owing to the absence of a due gradation in the employment of physical force; in other words, because no other form of organised force is brought to bear at [a riot] between the defeated efforts of the police and the fatal action of the military.[2]

McMurdo's solution to this problem was to arm two-thirds of the soldiers present at a riot with batons, keeping the remainder armed with rifles in case of an emergency. If this were done he felt the danger of civilian fatalities would be much reduced, and the army, instead of being forced to take a great deal of punishment, would be enabled to act in a positive way to prevent a riot reaching the stage where firing on the mob remained the sole solution. Though a lot of practical experience and sound common sense stood behind this suggestion, it was quickly opposed by a later witness, Major John W. Percy, resident magistrate for part of Counties Galway and Tipperary, who described it as 'absurd', and said that 'there would be a dreadful wattling match [i.e. riot] . . . if there was anything of that sort done.'[3] The flippancy of Percy's evidence hardly refutes McMurdo's suggestion completely, but it does point to a factor which the latter appears to have underestimated.

The great advantage which the army possessed over the R.I.C. was the ease with which large numbers of soldiers could be supplied in a comparatively short time. The R.I.C. was better suited in organisation for providing many small parties of men, but large bodies of police could not be assembled without detriment to routine police duties. Experience had taught the military authorities that the

---

[1] *Committee of inquiry into elections, 1869*, pp 312–13.
[2] Ibid., p. 313.   [3] Ibid., pp 491–2.

success of the army in the face of a disturbed or rioting crowd depended very largely upon the size of the detachment and upon the crowd's knowledge that if things were pushed too far the soldiers would open fire. Bernard Becker, special commissioner of the *Daily News*, who witnessed the operation of the army on Captain Boycott's estate in November 1880, described how the people there were 'undoubtedly cowed by the overwhelming display of military force'.[1] Later on he summarised his views on the use of the army in such disturbed areas. 'A small force, insufficient to overawe the countryside, only provokes the resistance it is unable to overcome, but a strong detachment of redcoats thoroughly cows the adventurous spirits of the most mutinous districts.'[2] However, what was probably the vital element in the successful use of the army on these occasions was the fact that the crowd knew that the army could, and would if necessary, open fire. If, as McMurdo suggested, two-thirds of any group operating in a riot had their rifles replaced by batons, it was possible that this fear would have been removed or certainly that their deterrent effect would have been greatly weakened. In such a situation the mob could conceivably have defeated the baton-carrying soldiers, leaving the army in a worse position than before.

The reaction of a disturbed crowd to the appearance of the army cannot be categorised as being always either A or B. Major-General McMurdo was asked, 'Do you think that the presence of the military acts like a red rag to a bull?' He replied, 'Exactly. The people know very well that the soldiers dare not use their arms, and therefore they are all the more audacious.'[3] Major-General H. J. Warre was conscious of the same defect, and he expressed to General Lord Sandhurst, Strathnairn's successor, in July 1873, the fear that the troops would be prematurely brought on to the streets in Belfast to keep the peace during the 12 July celebrations, as they had been the previous year. Therefore, he said, he was going to keep them

---

[1] B. H. Becker, *Disturbed Ireland: being the letters written during the winter of 1880–81* (London, 1881), p. 132.

[2] Ibid., p. 200.

[3] *Committee of inquiry into elections, 1869*, p. 318.

out of sight till 'their services were actually required, as their employment in the streets till so required inflames the feelings of the populace and collects mobs'.[1]

At the other extreme, Colonel Alfred Turner, a soldier exercising magisterial powers as special commissioner of police for Clare, Kerry, Limerick and Cork, was quite convinced that the use of troops prevented violence:

Many people decry the use of troops to aid the civil power, but probably such persons have had no experience of the great difficulties and responsibilities of those who are charged with this unpleasant duty. The presence of the military has a most salutary effect even upon the most unruly spirits, who would not shirk a tussle with the police.[2]

He had already pointed out that during the six years he held the post of special commissioner, not one civilian death had resulted from police or army action 'owing to the precautions taken, and the forbearance and discipline of the troops and police'.[3] In other words, the tragedy of civilian deaths had been avoided by calling out large units of troops on all occasions when the slightest possibility of violence existed. The policy did have its detrimental side effect during these years, however, in that the use of large forces created the impression of the law's weakness. The author of *The annals of the King's Royal Rifle Corps* described the effect of a detachment of three officers and one hundred men of the 2nd battalion, the Rifle Brigade, on the local inhabitants of Dunfanaghy, between February 1888 and January 1890:

The detachment at Dunfanaghy had some very hard work and rough living during their stay in north Donegal. They were constantly being called out at all hours and in any weather, in aid of the civil power, to support the Royal Irish Constabulary at evictions, arrests of offenders and trials. It was very noticeable that although the police frequently met with resistance of

---

[1] Major-General H. J. Warre to Sandhurst, 7 July 1873 (N.L.I., Kilmainham papers, lxvii, MS 1067, p. 121).

[2] Major-General A. E. Turner, *Sixty years of a soldier's life* (London, 1912), p. 230.

[3] Ibid., p. 207.

the most violent type, whenever the troops were asked to take action the resistance immediately ceased. On several occasions the officer in command of the detachment was given an order by the magistrate present to fire. On each occasion the threat to do so was sufficient and resistance ceased. The explanation of this is said to have been that the people knew that the police never would shoot under any circumstances, because they knew that if they did so they would probably be let down by the authorities afterwards; and secondly, that they had to go on living in the country and would be marked men. On the other hand, the people believed that when an officer in command of troops said he was going to shoot he meant what he said.[1]

Strathnairn, however, recognised that the size and firepower of any infantry group facing a mob, though very often sufficient in themselves to restore order, could be very advantageously supplemented by the use of cavalry. The military authorities had quickly discovered that a company of cavalry was a most useful weapon against a rioting crowd, since few rioters chose to stand and face a cavalry charge. Although Strathnairn recognised that the employment of cavalry was subject to the nature of the terrain, he wrote to the under-secretary in October 1869:

After a very long experience of the preservation of the public peace in this troubled country, he has found that nothing prevents disturbances of the peace so effectually as a force which inspires respect amongst the people by its composition [i.e. one which included cavalry if possible], no less than by its numbers . . .[2]

It is evident that by 1873 practical experience had taught the army the best way to tackle riots and to disperse antagonistic crowds, given the organisation and weaponry it then possessed. The experiences of the Drogheda election riot of 1868 had shown the dangers of using a small armed detachment in the face of a larger mob, and the failure of the efforts to bring a large mob quickly

[1] S. Hare, *The annals of the King's Royal Rifle Corps* (London, 1913), iv, 157. Note that while the passage quoted here is corroborated by R.I.C. documents in the Balfour papers, these do not suggest that the action attributed to the police at Dunfanaghy was typical.

[2] Strathnairn to under-secretary, 1 Oct. 1869 (N.L.I., Kilmainham papers, lxiii, MS 1063, p. 133).

under control in the 1872 Belfast riots had shown the dangers of involving the military too early, and the problems which naturally arose from the absence of a unified civil and military command group. The army had also learned, for example throughout the disturbances of 1870, that success not only in controlling riots, but also in patrolling disturbed districts, in escorting, at evictions and in the general prevention of outrage, lay in a combination whenever possible of numbers, firepower and cavalry. That the army had learnt its lesson well can be seen in its correct response to the problems posed by the violence of the early years of the land war, and in the calming effect it had when introduced into Belfast during the severe riots of 1886.

The following description of the activities of the 27th Royal Inniskilling Fusiliers, during the Belfast riots, forms a sharp contrast to the reception experienced by the army during the riots there in 1872:

During July and August there were serious riots in the city and the troops were repeatedly called out in aid of the civil powers. The presence of the 27th regiment and of the depot of its linked battalion, the 108th, materially assisted the police in restoring order. For many days detachments of the Inniskillings occupied strategic positions in the town, from which they moved, as occasion required, to prevent collision between the faction mobs which filled the streets. The steadiness and discipline of the 27th were exposed to a great strain in the discharge of this, the most disagreeable duty which soldiers can be called upon to perform, and their good temper, their patience and their admirable solidity won praise from all classes of society. So much so indeed were the lower orders attached to the Inniskillings, that, when the mob were stoning their antagonists in the streets, the cry was often raised 'Don't touch the soldiers, but aim over them', i.e., at the police or the opposite faction. No greater proof of the popularity of the corps can be adduced than the fact that between April and October 292 recruits joined headquarters, of whom Belfast itself furnished a large proportion.[1]

Though such goodwill was seldom shown towards soldiers on duty, the more reasoned, mature and better organised approach to riots in

---

[1] Compiled by a regimental historical records committee, *The Royal Inniskilling Fusiliers* (London, 1934), p. 340.

1886, compared to the army's disorganised approach fourteen years earlier, had largely made it possible.[1] That the army's change in approach to the problem was a correct one can be seen in the fact that a very small number of civilians lost their lives after 1873 through army action. This is in direct contrast to the greater number of civilians fatally wounded by the R.I.C., a force which would appear to have continued to rely too heavily upon the rifle as its ultimate weapon. This error contributed to the deaths of several civilians in Belfast in 1886 and two in Mitchelstown in 1887.

The consideration that the police were more frequently engaged in peacekeeping duties than the army and were likely, statistically speaking, to injure more civilians, is to a large extent irrelevant when discussing the numbers killed by both forces. The very fact that the army became involved in a riot only when that riot had reached the point where the police were unable to contain it, meant that the army was being brought in at precisely the moment of highest tension. It seems logical to assume that at that moment the chances of the army being forced to fire were at their greatest. That the army managed on nearly all occasions to avoid using firearms at this point, or even subsequently, perhaps illustrates the success of the efforts taken by the military authorities to develop the best possible approach to the problem of riot control. However, an additional interpretation lies in the reluctance of the army to open fire unless presented with a written order by a magistrate, for fear of legal consequences; whereas the R.I.C. could be ordered verbally, and also possibly had less fear of subsequent prosecution.

In complete contrast to the army's use of large detachments of infantry and cavalry when aiding the civil power at riots, or in disturbed districts, was the part it played on special duties between

---

[1] It should be noted that the 27th regiment, having been recruited largely from Belfast and the rest of Ulster, had strong local ties with the very people it was opposing, and, therefore, could be seen to have been in a special position. However, it would appear that the 5th Dragoon Guards, a regiment with no special ties with Belfast, experienced a similarly warm reception by the rioters. On this occasion the real enemies of the rioters were the police.

6 January 1882 and 27 December 1882.[1] At this stage in the land war, the army was already heavily engaged in aiding the R.I.C.; for example, in patrolling disturbed districts. The widespread nature of the agitation and of outrage had by then overstretched the R.I.C. and it was suffering from a dangerous shortage of men. At this time no less than 735 policemen were stationed at some 235 posts on personal protection duty aimed at guarding threatened individuals from assassination and their farms or houses from attack. To relieve the R.I.C. from this necessary but rather unproductive duty, the government advertised for first-class army reservists and others to act as temporary auxiliary policemen in December 1881. However, such a solution would have taken too long to implement, and at the suggestion of Clifford Lloyd, special resident magistrate for Limerick and Clare, arrangements were made to replace the police with regular soldiers. The first of these, fifty-two non-commissioned officers and men of the Coldstream Guards and forty-five non-commissioned officers and men of the Scots Guards, left Dublin for posts in Lloyd's district on 6 January 1882.

Initially the war office sanctioned the employment of only 600 soldiers for three months on this duty and on duty 'in aid of the police'. This second duty, again suggested by Clifford Lloyd, was carried out by the army simultaneously with personal protection duty, and involved troops being placed in police huts or barracks to aid the police on all police duties. However, the continuing bad state of the country and continuing pressure on the police, plus the fact that only a small number of army reservists answered the government's advertisement, made it necessary to retain the services of the army for much longer than was at first expected and to increase the number of soldiers involved to 700 in July. One ex-

---

[1] A large part of the information on the subject of the army on special duty in 1882 has been obtained from John Ross's 'Memorandum on the military in aid of the civil power in Ireland, 1881–2' (S.P.O., C.S.O., R.P., 1883/2214); hereafter referred to as John Ross's memorandum, 1881–2. An edited version of the memorandum, with introduction and notes by Richard Hawkins, can be found in *Irish Sword*, xi, no. 43 (winter 1973), pp 75–117.

tension of three months was granted in early April, and in July Hugh Childers, the secretary of state for war, gave permission for the extension of the time limit to 31 December 1882. Both he and the duke of Cambridge were, however, reluctant to do this and Childers informed the chief secretary that it was to be clearly understood that the troops on these special duties were to return to their regiments by that date at the latest. By the end of June, 575 soldiers were involved in special duties, and during July more than 100 extra men were sent to Lloyd's district, making the total 700. After July the number of soldiers on special duties fell, to 648 on 1 September and to 621 in the middle of October, and continued to fall till by 27 December all soldiers had returned to their regiments.[1]

The nature of the special duties which the army was called on to perform in 1882 had automatically raised certain questions: first, what kind of men would the army supply; second, who would pay them and the costs of the whole enterprise; third, who should command the troops in so many detached pockets? In January 1882 the adjutant-general wrote to the general officer commanding Cork district, outlining the kind of soldier to be sent on special duties: 'The men to be employed on this duty should be of good character and steady habits, and should be selected from men of long service, and also, as far as can be, from those who are now applying to go to the reserve.'[2]

This policy whereby 700, not only of the steadiest but also of the most experienced, soldiers were withdrawn from their units must have placed an additional stress upon the regiments serving in Ireland, which were by then suffering from a scarcity of such men. The question of who should pay was solved after a certain amount of difficulty, it being agreed that the cost should be borne by the army votes and that the men should be paid an extra two shillings a day. The third question was a great deal more difficult, for by

[1] John Ross's memorandum, 1881–2, pp 20–21.
[2] Adjutant-general, Dublin, to G.O.C., Cork district, 14 Jan. 1882 (S.P.O., C.S.O., R.P., 1882/2584).

military law soldiers could not take orders from civilians. It was solved, however, by the soldiers retaining their separate identity, by placing troops under N.C.O.s who acted as their local superiors, and by arranging for the regular inspection of posts and barracks by officers.

Lieutenant John Ross, acting as an adviser on military matters to the chief secretary, summed up the results of the use of the army on special duties:

Although the plan of employing soldiers on special services has proved a success, in that an efficient force was at hand to aid the police very materially during a great emergency, yet it is scarcely likely that it will again be adopted; there are many objections to it both from a civil and a military point of view. It is true that the soldiers employed behaved well and got on with the constabulary; but they owed a divided allegiance and were so to speak under a dual control. Special service by soldiers is liable to demoralise them and to upset the susceptibilities of the Irish constabulary; also the want of police training might have led soldiers to commit illegal acts while endeavouring to do their duty. Even although a success, this plan of employ-ing soldiers showed the Irish people that they had for a time exhausted the physical power of the civil authorities.[1]

Steele echoed Ross's conclusion that the use of the troops in this situation, though successful, was unsatisfactory from a military point of view. In a note written at the bottom of a letter sent by Clifford Lloyd to the chief secretary's office on 20 November 1882, in which Lloyd stated that all the troops in his district had returned to their regiments, Sir Thomas Steele had scribbled 'Very satis-factory. I trust it may be a long time before soldiers are again used on such a duty.'[2]

In all, 1081 soldiers were involved on special duties during 1882. What these men thought themselves about such duties is somewhat obscure. They were not particularly dangerous duties since only

---

[1] John Ross's memorandum, 1881–2, p. 23.
[2] Steele's note on a letter from Clifford Lloyd to chief secretary, 20 Nov. 1882 (S.P.O., C.S.O., R.P., 1883/2214).

one man, Corporal Wallace, lost his life on personal protection duty. One can assume that when good quarters and good food were secured, and when they were earning the very welcome extra pay of two shillings a day, the tedium of continuous watchfulness was more easily overcome. However, it speaks well for the discipline of these men when one considers that they were for long periods isolated in small groups among a hostile populace, and were also largely free from the strict regimental discipline under which they normally existed. In 1886 a landlord's agent, who was possibly the first to be given protection by soldiers, wrote the following description of his experiences:

In the first week of January 1882, I got a notice to say that a corporal and four men of the 1st Royal Dragoons would arrive on the rest day [Sunday], and be placed in my house for protection duty. This to people living quietly in their houses in England must seem almost incredible. However, the next day the men appeared and at once entered on their duties. The inconvenience to me was not so great as might be imagined, as the house was very large and there was plenty of first-rate accommodation for them. I could give them a sitting-room and bedroom on the ground floor without in any way interfering with the rest of the household.

The men were much pleased with their quarters; and as they were all selected for their steadiness and good conduct I never had the least trouble with them. I found them most obliging, ready to turn their hands to anything they were asked to do, and most attentive to their duties. The corporal ... showed me his orders, which amounted to this: that two of the men were to accompany me wherever I went, never to be more than ten yards from me, and on no account to lose sight of me when out of the house for a moment; the other men to be constantly patrolling the premises night and day, and make frequent search of all out-buildings, shrubberies, etc. . . . No one who has not undergone this incessant watch can conceive what it is. At breakfast a man stationed a few yards from the window; at church to have them sitting behind you with their rifles; not to walk in the garden or sit outside your window on a summer's evening to smoke your pipe without hearing the click of the rifle or seeing a redcoat somewhere in the bushes close to you! Sometimes even this protection was thought insufficient; and often, when starting for the office, I found constables waiting to escort me as well. It formed a regular procession—first two constables, one on one side of the road and one on the other, every few yards looking over walls or fences to make sure no one was lurking behind. Then I came, and the two dragoons a few steps behind, all armed.[1]

The use of troops in small groups of eight or less was the exact opposite of normal practice while on most duties in aid of the civil power in Ireland. As already mentioned, troops generally acted in larger groups with the primary aim of preventing trouble by a show of force. This practice was used at riots and was one of the major principles behind the formation of the flying columns; it was also the practice whenever troops were employed at evictions or process-servings, when they were employed to stop meetings, and, as far as possible, while they were patrolling disturbed districts in daylight.

Troops were extensively employed in aiding the civil authorities at evictions, thereby reinforcing the viewpoint that the government was firmly on the landlord's side. This duty was particularly intense during the land war and for the remainder of that decade. At times this duty could prove difficult and dangerous if the tenants and their friends decided to make a fight of it. An example of such a defence which the army and the police were expected to overcome, occurred on Lord Ashbrooke's estate near Shannon Bridge in September 1881. All roads leading to the tenant's dwellings were ripped up and blocked by trees, while fires were lit among the barricades, and bee-hives were spread around them ready to be opened at a moment's notice. Military participation in evictions was necessary in order to protect the sheriff and the R.I.C. in such an event, and to prevent the outbreak of trouble by a show of strength on the spot. This did not mean that the army was to help in the actual process of physically ejecting a tenant, something it was legally barred from doing. This task was left to the sheriff, or bailiff, the R.I.C. and emergency men.

The great bulk of evictions passed without any disturbance large enough to warrant the intervention of the military, if indeed there was any disturbance at all. This, however, did not mean that the R.I.C. had a similarly easy time, since it was the police who had to

[1] Anon., 'The way we live now in Ireland', in *The Irish question*, I.L.P.U. tracts (Dublin, 1886), pp 15–16.

force an entrance to the house. In January 1889 the chief secretary, Arthur Balfour, who felt that the troops had not been doing enough to protect the R.I.C., ordered that 'in future the soldiery were to be used not just to "overawe the crowd", but to aid the police and bailiffs whenever they stood in danger of violence either from the besieged or from the throngs of spectators.'[1]

The eviction scene is one which even today remains charged with emotion, and it is understandable that feelings ran high on the subject among contemporaries. Evictions gave nationalists the opportunity to vent their scorn on the government and on the army as its agent. At a meeting to protest against the wholesale evictions at Bodyke in June 1887, Michael Davitt had the following to say on the part played by the army:

Had the masses of the people in England, Scotland and Wales—had it been possible for them to be here today—what would they have witnessed? English soldiers, English uniforms, English weapons in the hands of English mercenaries, making war upon whom? Not upon a government or nation at war with the English people, but making war on a child three years old in the first house where an eviction took place . . .[2]

This was understandably the view taken by the evicted and their supporters. Was the view taken by the army similar in essence, if not in tone, or did it carry out eviction duty without regret? Unfortunately no record has been discovered of what the ordinary soldier felt about the subject. However, it is highly likely that their sympathies lay with the tenant rather than with the landlord, considering the misery evictions produced. Such sympathy would have been deepened by the rank and file's affinities with the class being evicted and the general hardship the soldiers often experienced on the duty itself. A degree of feeling for evicted tenants is reflected by the historian of the 9th Norfolk regiment, who wrote about the work of the 1st battalion around Templemore in 1881:

[1] L. P. Curtis, Jr, *Coercion and conciliation in Ireland, 1881–1892: a study in conservative unionism* (London, 1963), p. 244.

[2] *The Times*, 4 June 1887.

The battalion took its full share in the hard and unpleasant work of those troubled times, in guarding against threatened disturbances, protecting evicting parties and the like. Such work weighs heavily on soldiers, who generally find it an uncongenial and thankless task.[1]

Fortunately General Sir Redvers Buller and Colonel Alfred Turner, who as successive special commissioners of police in the south of Ireland personally controlled a large number of eviction parties, have left their opinions on the subject on record. Both of them, perhaps as a result of their experiences, became at times outspokenly anti-landlord and both did their best to ensure that if an eviction had to take place it did so with the minimum of hardship possible.

Turner, who commanded the evicting party of 170 soldiers and 120 R.I.C. on the Vandeleur estate near Kilrush, west Clare, in the summer of 1887, wrote 'we all loathed the work, and most of us deeply sympathised with the poor ejected ones.'[2] Buller was even more emphatic: 'For 120 years British bayonets have backed up landlords in extracting excessive rents, and have supported them in grossly neglecting their tenants.'[3] Such a statement can hardly have pleased the landlords, who, in common with the nationalists, had fully expected Buller to quell the disturbances with brute force. Of evictions in general Turner had this to say:

No landlord should have had the power of ejecting tenants wholesale, and devastating the homes of large numbers of people; while no government should be bound to furnish the forces of the crown to protect those who commit arbitrary acts of oppression. It was by no means agreeable to the government to aid in such measures, and whatever may have been said by the nationalists in their natural wrath at the scenes which were being enacted, Mr Balfour, Sir Redvers Buller (a large landlord himself), and Sir West Ridgeway ... were, one and all, impartial, and by no means eager to give assistance to unjust and grasping landlords; and where any pressure

---

[1] F. Petre, *The history of the Norfolk regiment, 1685–1918* (Norwich, 1924), i, 349.

[2] Turner, *Sixty years of a soldier's life*, p. 252.

[3] Ibid., p. 314.

could be brought to bear to stay their hands from evicting, it was done, and done with success in some cases.[1]

Whether these views were the views of the officers as a whole or not must remain in doubt. However, considering the strong associations of that body with the landlords, it is more probable that Turner and Buller only represented a more radical group among the officers, rather than all of them.

The patrolling of disturbed districts, whether in company with the police or alone, occupied a great deal of the army's time and manpower especially in the early seventies and during the eighties. The duty took many forms: patrolling in large combined army-and-police parties, or in parties of soldiers alone, with a view to showing the government's strength to as many people as possible—a duty not often carried out till the eighties and usually performed in daylight; patrolling in small groups with the R.I.C. at night with a view to detecting and preventing crime; and finally, forming a patrol while on route or training marches. All the above duties were carried out on foot, horseback or in cars. After 1882 it was normal practice for patrolling to be in complete coordination with the movements and plans of the R.I.C. This had not necessarily been the case in previous years, but early during the land war it was discovered that both the size of the military contingent and the regularity or predictability of its movements were quickly ascertained by the local population, thus negating the whole purpose of the duty. In January 1882, therefore, new rules were issued. Three main points were made: first, the strength of the patrols, usually twenty or above, could be altered by the local authorities; second, the hours for patrolling and the directions to be taken were to be arranged by the local commanding officer in consultation with the police, and were to be kept secret; third, the patrols were to be equipped with cars whenever necessary in order to increase their range.[2] These rules, by increasing military and police cooperation on the spot, by

---

[1] Ibid., p. 258.
[2] John Ross's memorandum, 1881–2, p. 7.

increasing the surprise element in the patrols and by increasing their range and number, made the military-and-police patrol a very useful weapon against the nocturnal activities of Captain Moonlight. Night patrolling at any given station could, and did, become a complicated business. A detachment of fifty could usually furnish about four patrols a week, varying from six to ten men, or even in some less disturbed areas to twenty. The patrol would often split up into smaller groups, each with their own police officer, in order to cover a larger area and rendezvous later. Patrols sent from neighbouring barracks often planned their routes so as to meet somewhere along the way. The task of ambushing, however (lying in wait at a suspect dwelling or a crossroads), was left strictly to the police.

The duty of dispersing land league or national league meetings was consistent with most of the duties the army carried out in company with the police. Parties involved on this duty were usually large, composed of both army and police, often backed up by a force of cavalry. This duty became particularly severe after the suppression of the national league in 1887, and was frequently carried out in the face of resistance; as, for example, occurred during proclaimed meetings at Ennis on 9 April 1887, and at Mitchelstown in the same year. Colonel Turner, looking for examples to reinforce his argument that a show of force, in the shape of the army and the R.I.C., preserved law and order and prevented rioting, cited the occasion of a proclaimed national league meeting at Ballycoree, near Ennis, County Clare, on 4 September 1887. Turner's force comprised three companies of the Leinster regiment, a squadron of hussars from Limerick and 250 police.

As it was, the constant demonstration of a large force, and the loyal carrying out of orders that no roughness or violence of any kind was to be displayed by the police, unless they were attacked, to which I must add the prudence and self-command of the national leaders and their English friends, combined to falsify the dire anticipations which had been formed by the government and many others as to what the day at the Ballycoree meeting would bring forth.[1]

[1] Turner, *Sixty years of a soldier's life*, pp 235-6.

Two further duties carried out by the army in aid of the civil power deserve mention: procession duty and anniversary duty, both closely connected. The latter was an annual duty in Ulster throughout the period under study, and one which only in the years 1879, 1881, 1883, 1888 and 1890 did not require the sending of troop reinforcements to the north of Ireland. It could prove an arduous duty, and did so especially in 1872 and 1886, involving the troops in bitter sectarian riots. The possibility of riots always meant that an appreciable military force had to be stationed in Ulster as a precaution. As an example, the orange celebrations of 12 July 1869 held down a force of 666 cavalry and 1951 infantry, distributed among the following towns: Armagh, Banbridge, Belfast, Belturbet, Carrickfergus, Dundalk, Dungannon, Enniskillen, Londonderry, Monaghan, Newry, Newtownards and Portadown.[1]

Keeping the peace at all kinds of processions was almost a full-time occupation for the R.I.C. at certain times of the year. The list of marchers was long and included orangemen, home-rulers, tenant-righters, ribbonmen and even representatives of the Roman Catholic Temperance Society. Between 1872, when the party processions act was repealed, and 1880, when the available records cease, 1730 processions of all sorts were held in Ireland, 1601 in Ulster and only 129 in the rest of the country.[2] The army, however, was only called out to assist the police at nineteen of them, a very good illustration of the extent to which the army was allowed to remain in the

---

[1] List of stations to be occupied in the north of Ireland, 10 July 1869, with the number of troops at each station (S.P.O., crime and police records, VIC/11/23, 1869/9907).

[2] *Return, as far as practicable, of all party processions, whether orange, nationalist, amnesty, 'martyr', or other, specifying those which did not suffer molestation, which have taken place in Ireland since the repeal of the party processions act in 1872; of all homicides, outrages, or injuries to life and property arising out of such processions; of the number of military and police drafted to the scenes of such processions on each occasion on special duty; and of the total cost to the country occasioned by movement of such forces*, pp 1–38 [380, sess. 2], H.C. 1880, lx, 395–432; hereafter referred to as *Return of processions, 1872–9.*

Returns in continuation up to 30 August 1880, of the return ordered on 9 May 1879, showing, as far as practicable, all party processions, whether orange, nationalist,

background during the seventies. All the processions at which the army was present took place in Ulster (six in Belfast, five in Armagh, four in Down, two in County Londonderry, one each in Cavan and Tyrone), and violence broke out at only six of them.[1] As far as the army was concerned, procession duty was infrequent and of minor importance, and was regarded as being part of anniversary duty since the processions which it did cover all took place while it was carrying out that duty.

These, then, were the main duties carried out by the army in aid of the civil power in Ireland between 1868 and 1890. Law and order were frequently subverted by fluctuating violence which was on a scale hitherto unknown; and it was the widespread endemic nature of that agitation, its occasional callous disregard for human and animal life, and the inability of the police force to cope with its extent, which drew the garrison deep into Irish problems. For the army it was an unusual experience for which it was by training and organisation largely unprepared. While Edward Cardwell had begun the process of turning the army away from the disasters of the Crimea in terms of structure and conditions of service, Tommy Atkins still thought of war in terms of cavalry charges and pitched battles. Captain Moonlight's activities, the urban riot and the boycott were brands of violence unfamiliar to him and demanded novel approaches from his superiors.

As the Curragh mutiny was to illustrate some years later, service in Ireland also placed unique strains upon the individual British soldier. It was, after all, to serve in a part of the United Kingdom which, for many, meant service at home. An additional source of

---

amnesty, 'martyr', or other, specifying those which did not suffer molestation, which have taken place in Ireland since the repeal of the party processions act in 1872; of all homicides, outrages, or injuries to life and property arising out of such processions; of the number of military and police drafted to the scenes of such processions on each occasion on special duty; and of the total cost to the country occasioned by movement of such forces, pp 3–13 [389, sess. 2], H.C. 1880, lx, 437–47; hereafter referred to as *Return of processions, 1879–80.*

[1] *Return of processions, 1872–9. Return of processions, 1879–80.*

stress lay in the near-active-service conditions which many experienced on their tours of duty there. The high command of the army was similarly placed in the awkward position of often having to bow to civilian political direction in military matters, since the solution to Ireland's ills was seen to be a political and not a purely military one. Poor living quarters, long hours of duty, a damp climate and a scarcity of social amenities among a partially hostile population, all added to the soldier's discomfort and gave the phrase 'duties in aid of the civil power' a distinctly unwelcome connotation.[1]

[1] A more detailed study of the army in Ireland can be found in D. N. Haire, 'The British army in Ireland, 1868–90' (M.Litt. thesis, Trinity College, Dublin, 1973).

Anglo-French tension and the origins of fenianism

RICHARD V. COMERFORD

A CERTAIN mystique envelops many aspects of fenianism and especially its beginning, mention of which regularly evokes the image of the
phoenix arising from its own ashes. One of the best-informed
historians of Irish separatism, P. S. O'Hegarty, captured the sense of
mystery (and unconsciously pushed aside the question of causes)
when he wrote of a personified Ireland being 'again about to stir
herself' in the late 1850s.[1] Such descriptions convey a feeling of
inexorability, and underpin the belief that fenianism was an inevitable (or at least predictable) resort to a policy of physical force by
a nation disappointed in constitutionalism. Undoubtedly the Irish
Republican Brotherhood (otherwise the Irish Revolutionary Brotherhood, or I.R.B.)[2] did meet the needs—political and social—experienced by a section of the Irish population,[3] and to that extent it can
be seen as a product of contemporary Irish conditions. However, it
was not launched because of any particular development in Ireland:
although they subsequently permitted the fact to be forgotten,
Stephens and his collaborators were responding not to a domestic
but to an external (and fortuitous) stimulus—a crisis in Anglo-French
relations. The purpose of this article is to demonstrate the influence
of the international factor in the early stages of fenianism and to

[1] P. S. O'Hegarty, *A history of Ireland under the union, 1801–1922* (London,
1952), p. 423.
[2] Fenian nomenclature is complicated; it is convenient to use the terms
'fenians' and 'I.R.B.', interchangeably and with effect from 1858, in reference
to the anonymous organisation founded in that year by James Stephens and
later named by others.
[3] This and other topics are examined in R. V. Comerford, 'Irish nationalist
politics, 1858–70' (Ph.D. thesis, Trinity College, Dublin, 1977).

[149]

touch on some consequent questions about the place of France in Irish political thought and feeling.

The centuries-old concept of Ireland as a strategic pawn between Britain and France was not abandoned after 1815, at least not by Irish nationalists or British statesmen. During the political turbulence of the 1820s those responsible for ruling Ireland kept a wary eye on developments in France.[1] The popular slogan equating England's difficulty with Ireland's opportunity could be reiterated with convenient ambiguity about how the opportunity should be exploited, but everybody understood that France was the expected source of the difficulty. Although the Crimean war (1854–6) was grievously troublesome for Britain, it caused little anticipation of imminent advantage among Irish nationalists because France was Britain's ally. A handful of Irish-American extremists in New York calling themselves the Emmet Monument Association made resolutions about taking advantage of the crisis, but their enthusiasm ran far ahead of practical possibilities. They planned (or, rather, promised) for September 1855 a rebellion in Ireland spearheaded by a force of returned emigrants.[2] A Kilkenny exile in New York, Joseph Denieffe, was sent some months in advance to make preparations among the Irish at home. Even if the New Yorkers had been capable of fulfilling their promises, the project would have been doomed for lack of preparation in Ireland. Denieffe's account of his mission is a story of very limited success.[3] Britain might be in difficulty, but in Irish thinking on international strategy Russia was no substitute for France.

In the aftermath of the Crimean war the security of Britain came to appear more, rather than less, vulnerable as the French alliance gave way to a menacing rivalry. Despite the conclusion of hostilities Louis Napoleon continued to maintain a very large standing army.

[1] J. A. Reynolds, *The catholic emancipation crisis in Ireland, 1823–9* (New Haven, 1954), pp 128–9, 143–5.
[2] Joseph Denieffe, *A personal narrative of the Irish Revolutionary Brotherhood* (New York, 1906), p. 3.
[3] Ibid., pp 8–12.

Then, in 1857, imperial France touched one of the most sensitive nerves in the British body politic—as imperial Germany was to do just fifty years later—by embarking on a programme of shipbuilding that threatened the naval supremacy on which British power and security were based. The threat appeared particularly severe because France was pressing ahead with technological changes which could revolutionise naval warfare. The newly-developed ironclad ships being built on Napoleon's instructions might radically alter the balance of naval power; they might even permit the landing of an invasion force on the south coast of England.[1]

The impact of the rising Anglo-French tension on Irish thinking was greatly increased by the news of the Indian mutiny which began in May 1857. The *Nation*, the mouthpiece of Irish nationalism, made no secret of its hopes for a sepoy victory and it was clearly motivated by something other than disinterested sympathy for the natives of India.[2] The prime minister, Lord Palmerston, was keenly aware of Irish disaffection and opportunism:

Young Ireland, the catholic party and its newspaper organs in Dublin are trying to do all the mischief they can. They are praising the mutineers and calling upon the Irish to follow their example. I think it will be advisable to call out and embody 5000 more militia, making 20,000 in all, and it would be best to bring over to England all the Irish regiments belonging to the catholic counties . . .[3]

In the version of history inculcated by Daniel O'Connell (and by most of the Young Irelanders) the volunteer movement of 1778 and following years featured as a glorious and memorable instance of Irish patriots taking advantage of English difficulties. By the autumn of 1857 it was possible for an optimistic Irish nationalist to discern

---

[1] P. M. Kennedy, *The rise and fall of British naval mastery* (London, 1976), pp 172–3.

[2] See e.g. *Nation*, 23 Jan. 1858.

[3] Lord Palmerston to Lord Panmure, 28 Sept. 1857 (Sir George Douglas and Sir G. D. Ramsay (eds), *The Panmure papers, being a selection from the correspondence of Fox Maule, second baron Panmure, afterwards eleventh earl of Dalhousie, K.T., G.C.B.* (2 vols, London, 1908), ii, 436).

the pattern of nearly eighty years earlier being repeated: England was struggling with rebellion in the empire (North America in 1778, India in 1857) and France appeared ready and eager to strike at her traditional rival. This was the context in which the fenian organisation was launched.

Despite the failure of 1855, the remaining members of the Emmet Monument Association felt by late 1857 that conditions justified another attempt at fomenting conspiratorial organisation in Ireland. This time they invited James Stephens to take the initiative. Stephens was a veteran of the abortive Young Ireland rebellion of 1848, following which he fled to Paris where he spent almost seven years before returning to Ireland. Around mid-December 1857 he received by messenger from John O'Mahony and Michael Doheny (fellow fugitives of 1848) and other Irish activists in New York an offer of substantial assistance from America if he would undertake to set up an organisation in Ireland.[1] His decision to take up the offer was the effective beginning of fenianism. In his reply Stephens promised that, given adequate financial support on his own terms, he could organise an underground force of ten thousand men within three months.[2] That is an instance of Stephen's characteristic braggadocio, but it also throws light on the thinking of all concerned. They were not envisaging a conspiratorial society with inexhaustible stamina; instead they were preparing a necessarily swift response to an imminent crisis.

While Stephens waited for confirmation that O'Mahony and the others in New York would accept his stipulations, especially those concerning financial support, Anglo-French tension heightened dramatically. On 14 January 1858 the Orsini plot against Louis Napoleon's life came dangerously near to success and gave rise to an immediate outburst of French recriminations against England, where the conspiracy had been hatched among a group of exiled

---

[1] Denieffe, *Narrative*, p. 17; Thomas Clarke Luby's recollections of early fenian events communicated to John O'Leary, 1890–91 (N.L.I., MS 331, p. 7).
[2] Ibid., p. 8; Denieffe, *Narrative*, pp 17, 159–60.

continental revolutionaries.[1] Palmerston's attempt to placate French opinion misfired disastrously. His conspiracy to murder bill, which proposed to curb the activities of foreign conspirators in Britain, was met in the commons by a rising tide of resentment against French dictation of English law. The debate provided an occasion for the airing of much anti-French sentiment and concluded with the defeat of the conciliatory legislation and the overthrow of the prime minister who had dared to introduce it.[2]

The urgency and feasibility of Stephens's project now appeared greater than ever, but final approval from America was slow in coming because it had to be accompanied by money. The I.R.B. was formally inaugurated in Dublin on the evening of 17 March 1858, but the date was not chosen for its national significance: it was determined by the arrival from America that morning of Joseph Denieffe with a substantial sum of money for the eager and impatient Stephens.[3]

Although we have very little knowledge of the thought processes of those who joined the ranks of Stephens's organisation during 1858, there is ample evidence of widespread awareness that the current international diplomatic and military situation gave meaning to conspiracy in Ireland just then. Needless to say, many other factors contributed to the appeal of fenianism, and the rank and file would not have been as well informed as Stephens about international affairs. Even so, there are indications in the comments of well-placed observers that expectation of an Anglo-French conflict was in the air. A constable in Kilgarvan, County Kerry, received information that the people of the area joining the new secret society were being sworn not just to oppose the government but 'to aid a foreign foe if any should land'.[4] A police spy in the Kenmare area discovered

---

[1] See R. E. Zegger, 'Victorians in arms: the invasion scare of 1859', in *History Today*, xxiii, no. 10 (Oct. 1973), pp 705–14.

[2] *Hansard 3*, cxlviii, 1844–7 (19 Feb. 1858).

[3] Denieffe, *Narrative*, p. 25.

[4] Constabulary report, Kilgarvan, 5 Oct. 1858 (S.P.O., police and crime records, reports on secret societies, 1857–9).

that the local conspirators expected to be supplied with arms from France within a few weeks.[1] In October 1858 the parish priest of Kenmare, in the course of a pulpit denunciation of the new secret society well known to exist in the locality, made the dramatic announcement that it was under the leadership of Louis Napoleon himself. After denouncing it on moral grounds he argued against the expediency of its political implications by showing that, however unjust some existing laws might be, French law would be even more oppressive.[2] That keen observer of rural Ireland, William Steuart Trench, was similarly aware of the French dimension when he wrote to Dublin Castle on 4 October 1858:

My own impression of the whole matter is that it is a movement of certain emissaries of France, whether authorised or not it is impossible for me to say, who have come to ascertain the feeling of the people in this part of the country (I mean the whole south-west) in the event of a war between France and England; and I grieve to say I fear they would find many who would by no means be unfavourable to their views.[3]

It is clear that at this stage the brotherhood had a strong sense of urgency about its work, action being anticipated by the end of 1858 at latest.[4] Before that deadline was reached the authorities had moved against the conspirators, arresting a handful of prominent members in Counties Cork and Kerry in early December. However, for as long as James Stephens remained in charge, fenianism never lost the sense of imminent action. There was constant girding of loins in anticipation of some threatening crisis or of some initiative promised by Stephens. The fenianism of indefatigable ideologues, prepared to wait patiently through years of frustration, was a later development.

Military and diplomatic developments during 1858 moderated

---

[1] Constabulary report, Kenmare, 7 Nov. 1858 (ibid.).

[2] Constabulary report, Kenmare, 4 Oct. 1958 (ibid.).

[3] Quoted in Seán Ó Lúing, 'The Phoenix Society in Kerry, 1858-9', in *Kerry Archaeological Society Journal*, ii (1969), p. 7.

[4] Constabulary reports, Kenmare, 3, 7 Nov. 1858 and Skibbereen, 27 Dec. 1858; statement of Robert Cusack, undated [evidently late 1858] (S.P.O., reports on secret societies, 1857-9).

the immediate threat to British security: the crisis of the Orsini affair passed, and British authority was reestablished in India. At the same time a new fluidity became apparent in European affairs, and by the year's end a major war was being widely predicted. (It had indeed been decided upon by Napoleon and Cavour at Plombières in July.)[1] By February 1859 the *Nation* and a new, more extreme, nationalist weekly, the *Irishman*, were forecasting a great war involving Britain, to be followed by a revision of the Vienna settlement of 1815 in line with the principles of nationality.[2] The imminent 'quarrel' in Europe, the *Irishman* argued, would end inevitably in war between England and France.[3]

James Stephens had gone to America in the autumn of 1858 to secure renewed support from that quarter. When he left in March 1859 after a less than fully successful mission but with about six hundred pounds sterling to his credit, he made his way to Paris as to the capital of a country that would soon be at war with England. From there he controlled his Irish organisation through emissaries while he waited for the deterioration of Anglo-French relations that would enable him to present himself to the French government as a useful ally, and advance the prospects of an invasion of Ireland.[4] Of the first three years of the I.R.B.'s existence Stephens spent just over six months in Ireland, just under six months in America and almost two years in Paris.

The apparent good sense of Stephens's residence in Paris during these years was endorsed in most convincing fashion by one of the patriarchs of Irish republicanism, John Mitchel, who never lost the prestige acquired on his conviction for treason-felony in 1848. He had been approached by Stephens in America in late 1858 and after some hesitation had decided to withhold his support and approval

---

[1] A. J. P. Taylor, *The struggle for mastery in Europe, 1848–1918* (Oxford, 1954), p. 103.

[2] *Nation*, 5 Feb. 1859; *Irishman*, 12, 19, 26 Feb. 1859.

[3] *Irishman*, 19 Feb. 1859.

[4] Desmond Ryan, *The fenian chief: a biography of James Stephens* (Dublin and Melbourne, 1967), pp 161–2.

from fenianism, thereby depriving Stephens's organisation of what would have been a most valuable propaganda boost. Quite independently of Stephens, he abandoned his American affairs in the summer of 1859 and moved to Paris, convinced that, as the capital of a country about to engage Britain in mortal combat, it was the place where a devoted advocate of Irish independence could most effectively advance his objectives[1] (apart, perhaps, from Ireland itself, where Mitchel would have been liable to immediate arrest as an unpardoned felon—he had absconded from penal detention in Van Diemen's Land in 1853). As with every other stage of his career, this sojourn of Mitchel's in Paris (he remained until September 1862, apart from one eight-month interval) had literary rather than practical results. In the role of Paris correspondent of the *Irishman* he tossed off a series of weekly commentaries on Irish and European affairs, some of them in his most brilliant and pungent Carlylean style.[2]

Joseph Denieffe, who was one of those with James Stephens in the French capital in the summer of 1859, recalled years later that 'Paris at this time was in its halcyon days. We saw the army depart for Italy, and return, covered with glory. Magenta and Solferino were victories the nation was proud of.'[3] In Ireland, too, Magenta and Solferino were hailed. From the beginning of the campaign nationalist opinion had been strongly on Napoleon's side. He was going, the *Nation* proclaimed, to vindicate the popular will of Lombardy, and in the same way he might at another time come to the aid of another oppressed people.[4] The sudden and unexpected conclusion of hostilities by the peace of Villafranca in July, before a wider war could develop, might have dampened the optimism of those hoping for an Anglo-French war, but such was not the case. Its inevitability was still accepted and proclaimed.[5]

[1] William Dillon, *Life of John Mitchel* (2 vols, London, 1888), ii, 132.
[2] *Irishman* (Dublin), 22 Oct. 1859 and ff.
[3] Denieffe, *Narrative*, p. 48.
[4] *Nation*, 14 May 1859.
[5] *Irishman*, 30 July 1859; *Nation*, 6 Aug. 1859.

This analysis of international prospects was endorsed in most convincing fashion by British opinion. The summer of 1859 witnessed the rise of a mass volunteer movement throughout Great Britain called into being by the spectre of French invasion. Hundreds of thousands of civilians who could afford the price of a rifle armed themselves, joined their local volunteer corps, and devoted their spare time to drill and arms practice.[1] Not since the era of the first Napoleon had Englishmen been so fearful of war on their own soil. Even the most extreme hopes of Irish francophiles were supported by corresponding English alarms: at the end of June the London *Morning Advertiser* was predicting that Napoleon would begin his assault on the United Kingdom with an invasion of Ireland.[2]

How, it might be asked, was public opinion in Ireland responding to the prospect of invasion? The thesis that the I.R.B. was launched in response to an international crisis must prompt the question of why nobody else in Ireland should have reacted to the same stimulus. Was everyone unmoved apart from Stephens's few thousand supporters? The answer is that Irish political life in the period 1858–61 witnessed a number of developments provoked by an awareness of fluidity in international relations, including two clearly identifiable movements that attracted far greater popular support than the contemporary I.R.B. Through the accident of survival, fenianism is remembered while the others are almost forgotten.

While volunteering fever was reaching its height in Britain during the summer of 1859 Irish nationalists were launching the MacMahon sword movement. The MacMahon in question was Marie Edmé Patrice Maurice de MacMahon, scion of a family long established in France, but, as the patronymic indicated, of Irish stock. MacMahon achieved fame and glory as commander of the victorious army in northern Italy in May and June 1859, being raised in recognition of his success to the dignities of marshal of France and duke of Magenta. Sentimental Irish nationalists rejoiced in this exaltation of a member

[1] *Annual Register, 1860*, pp 27–8.
[2] Cited in *Nation*, 2 July 1859.

of 'the Milesian race': Magenta was hailed as a 'celtic' victory.[1] The occurrence of such a name, in connection with a triumph that would have been so warmly welcomed in any case, gave rise to immense excitement. The *Nation* featured MacMahon in one of its rare lithographic portraits,[2] and the *Irishman* filled four of its closely-printed pages with genealogical reports on his family.[3] Descended from the 'wild geese', he was now represented as the personification of the legendary Franco-Irish amity, and of the high hopes of optimistic Irish nationalists. The *Irishman* of 2 July 1859 summarised a letter from a correspondent suggesting that Ireland might need a prince 'one of these days', as Belgium did in 1830–31 after its successful struggle for independence, and that MacMahon would be an ideal choice. On the same day both the *Nation* and *Irishman* proposed in editorial articles that money should be collected in Ireland to make a presentation to the marshal, the latter journal specifying that the gift should be a sword of honour. Under the circumstances the proposal was laden with political symbolism.

The public response was immediate and each of the two sponsoring journals received subscriptions and held them pending the formation of a committee.[4] Then the precaution was taken of securing MacMahon's consent. He was approached through J. P. Leonard, an Irishman resident in Paris, and he replied on 19 August 1859 that he was willing to accept the sword, but that the emperor's permission would have to be obtained beforehand. This was eventually forthcoming.[5] The MacMahon Sword Committee was formed in Dublin during August 1859 and held its first meeting at the beginning of September. The chairman was The O'Donoghue, M.P. in the popular interest for County Tipperary, while Patrick Mac-Mahon, M.P. for County Wexford, was vice-chairman.[6] Two honorary secretaries were appointed, T. D. Sullivan of the *Nation* and P. J. Smyth of the *Irishman*.[7]

---

[1] *Nation*, 11 June 1859. [2] *Nation*, 30 July 1859.
[3] *Irishman*, 23 July 1859. [4] *Irishman*, 9 July 1859; *Nation*, 6 Aug. 1859.
[5] *Nation*, 3 Mar. 1860. [6] *Irishman*, 3 Sept. 1859.
[7] *Nation*, 22 Sept. 1860.

With subscriptions pouring in from the enthusiastic public, the committee advertised for designs for the sword from Irish artists. Design and manufacture took many months, the completed artefact eventually going on display during the last week of August in the window of a Dublin bookshop, where it attracted considerable attention and admiration. The hilt was of bog oak, while the steel blade and precious sheath carried fulsome inscriptions interspersed with elaborate tracery of celtic design.[1]

A deputation charged with making the presentation left Dublin on 2 September 1860; the members were The O'Donoghue, T. D. Sullivan and Dr George Sigerson.[2] In Paris they were joined by J. P. Leonard and John Mitchel, and on 9 September all five proceeded to the military camp at Châlons where they were received by MacMahon with all due propriety and, it seems, with quite warm hospitality.[3] He accepted the sword most graciously, but, in his reply to the deputation's formal address, he was careful to confine the significance of the occasion to the sentimental recall of ancient family links.[4]

That was a bland ending to a movement dealing in such menacing symbolism. From the start the MacMahon sword had the advantage of vagueness: it could signify as much or as little as the inclination of the individual or the vagaries of the international situation required. By the time the business had come to its decorous conclusion at Châlons, a far more sophisticated scheme to express and publicise the Irish national will was being prepared.

If the cause of Irish nationality was to take advantage of any great international upheaval, it would be highly desirable to convince the European powers, and France above all, that the country wished for and desired self-government. Writing from Paris on 18 October 1859 John Mitchell had reminded his readers that in France the case of Ireland as a suppressed nation was not accepted and that, under the

---

[1] *Nation*, 1 Sept. 1860.
[2] *Nation*, 8 Sept. 1860.
[3] *Nation*, 15, 22 Sept. 1860; *Irishman*, 15 Sept. 1860.
[4] Quoted in *Nation*, 15 Sept. 1860.

circumstances, it was crucial to let Napoleon know that he would be welcome in Ireland if he should decide to intervene there.[1] In contemporary Europe the plebiscite was in vogue as a means of ascertaining and demonstrating the national allegiance of peoples. During the spring of 1860 the expansion of the Sardinian kingdom in the direction of an Italian nation state was given legitimacy by the holding of plebiscites in Tuscany, Parma, Emilia, Modena and the Romagna. Liberal English statesmen had little option but to approve of this development, and their enthusiasm for 'a vote of the population' increased when the future of the papal territories came to the forefront of discussion. Irish propagandists subsequently compiled anthologies of statements made by English statesmen and leader-writers at this time in support of the right of every nation to dismiss its rulers if dissatisfied with them, and generally to direct its own affairs in accordance with the popular will and untrammelled by any outside interference, however introduced.[2]

Not surprisingly, Irish nationalists soon thought of challenging the British government to apply to Ireland the principles which they supported in the case of Italy. In a leading article entitled 'Taking England at her word', the *Nation* of 14 April 1860 proposed that a petition should be presented to the queen or to parliament asking for a popular vote in Ireland on whether the people would prefer to be ruled by London or by an Irish parliament. Three weeks later the paper reported that the suggestion had been approved in a large number of letters received by the editor and that the type of movement envisaged was already in being in one part of the country.[3] The promoters at no time expected the request for a plebiscite to be granted, though they hoped that the inevitable refusal would make its own point. They really intended that the petition itself should be an informal plebiscite.[4] The *Nation* insisted that it would be highly desirable to have the government's reply in advance of a French

[1] *Irishman*, 22 Oct. 1859.
[2] E.g., *Nation*, 11 Jan. 1868, and A. M. Sullivan, *New Ireland* (popular ed., London, 1878), pp 241–4.
[3] *Nation*, 5 May 1860.   [4] *Nation*, 14 Apr., 5 May 1860.

invasion. For, it went on, if both the British and the French were on Irish soil, the natives, being unable to expel both, might have to side with one against the other.[1] The following excerpts give the essentials of the formula eventually adopted:

To the queen's most excellent majesty. May it please your majesty, the petition of the undersigned natives of Ireland humbly sheweth: that petitioners have seen with deep interest the recognition of the right of every people to change or choose their rulers and form of government which is contained in the speech delivered by your majesty at the opening of the present session of parliament, also in a speech delivered on a recent occasion at Aberdeen by your majesty's foreign secretary, as well as in the speeches of many other statesmen and persons of high position in England, and in the writings of the most influential English newspapers ...

Your petitioners, therefore, pray that your majesty may be pleased to direct and authorise a public vote by ballot and universal suffrage in Ireland to make known the wishes of the people whether for a native government and legislative independence, or for the existing system of government by the imperial parliament. Petitioners trust that their request will be stronger, not weaker, in your majesty's estimation, for being made respectfully, peacefully, and without violence, instead of being marked by such proceedings as have occurred during the recent political changes in Italy which have been so largely approved by your majesty's ministers.[2]

A campaign to collect signatures from males over the age of fifteen was launched during the summer of 1860, and soon claims of spectacular success were being reported from various places.[3] The year's efforts were crowned by a large public meeting in Dublin on 4 December at which the speakers included The O'Donoghue, M.P., J. F. Maguire, M.P., W. J. O'Neill Daunt, John Martin and A. M. Sullivan. A letter of support was received from Archbishop Mac-Hale of Tuam.[4] The gathering was informed that the number of signatures to date was about 200,000, and the meeting itself aroused new interest in the petition. Waves of new signatures were forthcoming in subsequent weeks and months, and when the final dead-

---

[1] *Nation*, 23 June 1860.   [2] *Nation*, 1 Sept. 1860.
[3] *Irishman*, 30 June, 7 July 1860.   [4] *Irishman*, 8 Dec. 1860.

line was reached on 16 April 1861, 423,026 were said to have signed.[1] That number fell considerably short of a majority even of catholic males over fifteen, of whom there were almost one and a half million in the country according to the returns of the 1861 census;[2] and, of course, we must allow for the possibility that the number was swollen by fraud and intimidation. Nevertheless, the national petition constituted a very considerable vote for self-determination.

The failure of the petition to attract fuller support reflected a division of long standing within Irish catholicism on the subject of French aid, and of loyalty to the British crown. It was a division that had been painfully open in the 1790s, and finding a formula to bridge it had been one of the keys to Daniel O'Connell's success. By 1860 it was a division not between loyalists and nationalists but between on one hand those catholic nationalists who from principle or prudence would never appeal to a foreign power against the British government (notably most of the bishops and clergy), and on the other hand nationalists who felt justified in exploiting any available pressure on London. The latter group propagated the national petition, but the petitioners were divided among themselves on how they hoped their strategy would develop. Most of them (A. M. Sullivan is an example), while prepared to welcome a French invasion, would have preferred to advance the nationalist cause by gaining constitutional concessions in a peaceful way and without actual outside interference. Like the English volunteers, they were convinced of the seriousness of the external threat. They hoped to use it as a lever. By contrast a small but very active group within the petition movement fervently desired the threat of foreign intervention to become a reality; many of these subsequently joined the I.R.B.

The seriousness with which the topic of French invasion was regarded at this time is demonstrated by the controversy which

---

[1] *Irishman*, 11 May 1861.
[2] *Census Ire., 1861, pt V: general report*, pp xiv, xvii, xxvii, 464 [3204-IV], H.C. 1863, lxi.

William Smith O'Brien dre w upon himself when he questioned its desirability. Although he shunned active political involvements, O'Brien was a regular commentator on Irish national affairs in the five or six years before his death in 1864, and his opinions and support were sought by a wide range of nationalist politicians; nationalist journals vied with one another for the opportunity to publish anything he might have to say on the past, present or future of Irish politics. He commented critically on the prospect of French invasion in a letter in the *Tablet* (Dublin) of 5 June 1858. Reactions to this included an anonymous letter from an 'old repealer' protesting that Irishmen would rather be governed by France any day than live in slavery.[1] The controversy was renewed at a much higher pitch of intensity in 1860 after O'Brien had referred to the subject in a letter to the *Irish American* (New York).[2] In subsequent exchanges he elaborated on his objections to the policy of the 'French party', and they reduced essentially to three. Firstly, there was no point in replacing one foreign ruler by another;[3] secondly, the French imperial system involved unacceptable elements of dictatorship;[4] thirdly and most important of all, civil war would ensue among the inhabitants of Ireland.[5] Catholics with nothing to lose would, he believed, support the invasion, it would be opposed by protestants and by some catholics, and would end like 'the war of 1641',[6] by which he meant the years of politico-religious conflict that preceded the Cromwellian conquest of Ireland. Protestants, O'Brien said, saw in the 'French policy' the threat of the imposition of an intolerant catholic regime.[7]

---

[1] Anonymous to O'Brien, 8 June 1858 (N.L.I., W. S. O'Brien papers, MS 446, no. 3042).

[2] Referred to in *Nation*, 8 Dec. 1860.   [3] *Nation*, 26 Jan. 1861.

[4] Draft of O'Brien to David White, 12 Oct. 1860 (N.L.I., W. S. O'Brien papers, MS 447, no. 3186).

[5] Draft of O'Brien to secretary of Cork National Reading Room, 20 Oct. 1860 (N.L.I., W. S. O'Brien papers, MS 447, no. 3189).

[6] *Irishman* and *Nation*, 8 Dec. 1860.

[7] Draft of O'Brien to secretary of Cork National Reading Room, 20 Oct. 1860 (N.L.I., W. S. O'Brien papers, MS 447, no. 3189).

Objective and far-seeing analysis of this kind cut very little ice with O'Brien's fellow-nationalists, and it brought much vituperation down upon the head of its well-meaning and inoffensive author. The *Irishman* published the insinuation that he was motivated by jealousy of Marshal MacMahon who, as the representative of the senior line of Brian Boru's descendants, would have a better claim than O'Brien himself to the throne of an independent Ireland![1] There was also righteous indignation at the idea that the catholic majority in a free Ireland would countenance the slightest impairment of the civil and religious liberty of protestants.[2] The response which interested him most came in a letter to the papers from John Martin, another protestant survivor of the heyday of Young Ireland, who argued, among other points, that since the institution of standing armies no country had freed itself without foreign assistance.[3] Martin's arguments prompted O'Brien to restate his own case and publish it in pamphlet form.[4] But, despite his able argumentation and his high reputation, he had to confess that his opposition to the idea of French intervention isolated him from his political friends.[5]

The ability of O'Brien to examine critically and reject something that appealed instinctively to other advanced nationalists is symptomatic of his thoughtful approach to all political questions. By the late 1850s he was immersed in the study of European politics, so that it was easy for him to appreciate the shortcomings of political life under the second French empire. By contrast the generality of Irish francophiles did not care whether France was royalist, republican or Bonapartist, because they had no occasion to reflect on the differences. In particular Irish popular opinion was largely insensitive to

[1] *Irishman*, 8 Dec. 1860.
[2] J. E. Pigot to O'Brien, 27 Dec. 1860 (N.L.I., O'Brien papers, MS 447, no. 3202).
[3] *Irishman* and *Nation*, 5 Jan. 1861.
[4] John Martin and W. S. O'Brien, *Correspondence between John Martin and Smith O'Brien relative to a French invasion* (Dublin, 1861).
[5] *Irishman*, 13 Apr. 1861.

the full meaning of the revolution of 1789, and in this respect the situation in 1858 may not have changed greatly since General Humbert's forces had been welcomed at Killala in August 1798 as champions of 'France and the Blessed Virgin'.[1] The fenians were strongly conscious of France as a traditional friend and (for a time) as a potential ally, but even among the fenians only a handful of leaders and intellectuals appreciated or sympathised with the French revolutionary heritage.

While Irishmen may have been justified in foreseeing important consequences for their country arising from an Anglo-French war, they tended to make assumptions about the extent of French concern for Ireland which were blatantly unjustified; it was easy to make the mistake of imagining that their affection for France was reciprocated. A young man who involved himself enthusiastically in advanced Irish politics in the late 1850s and early 1860s quickly became disillusioned about French feeling for Ireland when he settled in Paris a few years later; writing home he vehemently denounced 'the ridiculous illusion that the French like [us]'.[2] John Mitchel had issued an implicit warning on the same subject in 1859 when he wrote in a dispatch to the *Irishman* that in the event of war Napoleon would consider an invasion of Ireland only if it appeared to serve French interests.[3] But even Mitchel gave way to euphoria about foreign interest in Ireland when continental journals began to notice the country in the late autumn of 1859.[4] One of the first in the field was the pro-government *Constitutionnel* (Paris) of 23 October. Then the Brussels *Revue Trimestrielle* published what Mitchel thought was the first Belgian notice of Ireland since 1844.[5] About the same time a new paper, *L'Espérance*, devoted to the principles of nationality, was launched in Geneva; it soon carried an article on Ireland by Mitchel

---

[1] Thomas Pakenham, *The year of liberty: the bloody story of the great Irish rebellion of 1798* (paperback ed., London, 1972), p. 351.

[2] John Augustus O'Shea, writing as 'Irishman in Paris', in *Irishman*, 3 Aug. 1867.

[3] *Irishman*, 22 Oct. 1859.   [4] *Irishman*, 29 Oct., 5 Nov. 1859.

[5] *Irishman*, 5 Nov. 1859.

himself.[1] During 1860 Dublin papers reported discussion of Irish affairs in *Le Monde* (Paris), *La Presse* (Paris), *L'Ami de la Religion* (Paris), *L'Univers* (Brussels), *Le Nord* (Brussels) and in a number of pamphlets including *La question irlandaise*, and *MacMahon, roi d'Irlande?*[2] And this period saw the production of Perraud's *Études sur l'Irlande contemporaine*[3] which remains unsurpassed as an apologia for Irish catholic nationalism in the nineteenth century.

This phase of continental interest in Ireland passed as quickly as the serious likelihood of an Anglo-French war. Even while the English volunteers were arming, statesmen on both sides of the channel were working quietly to ensure a future of peaceful coexistence. The Cobden–Chevalier free-trade treaty of January 1860 was an indication of what lay ahead, and by 1861 the prospect of a conflict was disappearing. In Ireland the 'French party' persisted in the belief that Anglo-French war was inevitable whatever the short-term indications might be. In March 1861 John Mitchel admitted that Napoleon had no intention of provoking a war either sooner or later, if he could avoid it; but, he argued, events might leave the emperor without any choice in the matter.[4] A year later Mitchel was exhorting the Irish at home to 'keep the fire burning' in anticipation of the inevitable conflict between England and France, in 'a year, two years or ten years'.[5]

By the end of 1861 Anglo-American tension had taken over as the dominant international influence on Irish nationalist politics, and it remained so until well after the ending of the American civil war. Nevertheless, any development on the continent that appeared to offer the prospect of trouble for Britain was eagerly noted in Ireland. So, with the crisis over Schleswig and Holstein assuming major proportions in January 1864, the *Nation* speculated at length on the prospect of a widespread European war, and urged that Ireland

[1] *Irishman*, 5, 12 Nov. 1859.
[2] *Nation*, 19 May 1860; *Irishman*, 21, 28 July 1860.
[3] Adolphe Perraud, *Études sur l'Irlande contemporaine* (2 vols, Paris, 1862).
[4] *Irishman*, 9 Mar. 1861.
[5] *Irishman*, 8 Mar. 1862.

should make sure to count for as much in it as Venice or Hungary.[1] When the Austro-Prussian war was brewing, early in 1866, the *Irishman* envisaged the involvement of all the European powers.[2] In August 1867 the *Irishman* once again discerned 'war clouds and omens' over Europe, and declared that England would soon be involved in a great war, and that Ireland would consequently have its chance as in 1782.[3] However, when a decisive European war did come, in 1870, it finally shattered the dreams of the Irish francophiles.

Irish reaction to the Franco-Prussian war is exceptionally interesting. During the diplomatic crisis preceding the war the *Nation* —confident of British involvement and French victory in the anticipated conflict—warned the London government that it would be well advised to placate the people of Ireland by repeal of the act of union.[4] News of the French declaration of war against Prussia produced in Dublin a huge and apparently spontaneous popular demonstration centred on the residence of the French consul. Irish and French tricolours were intermingled and bands played alternately the martial airs of each country, while thousands of excited citizens milled about the streets.[5] There were shouts of 'cheers for France', 'cheers for the emperor', 'down with the Prussians', 'groans for the English' and 'God save Ireland'. The *Freeman's Journal* of the next morning affirmed that the demonstration was a true reflection of existing and historic Irish feeling.[6] More formal but equally enthusiastic pro-French demonstrations took place at many venues throughout the country in subsequent weeks.[7] When it became clear that France was threatened with disastrous defeat, plans were made and money was collected for an Irish ambulance corps which would bring medical relief to wounded French soldiers, as well as providing cover for the dispatch of Irishmen to fight for France.[8]

In rural County Cork, O'Neill Daunt observed and recorded local reaction: 'the country people here evince the strongest French

[1] *Nation*, 23, 30 Jan. 1864   [2] *Irishman*, 14 Apr. 1866.
[3] *Irishman*, 17 Aug. 1867.   [4] *Nation*, 16 July 1870.
[5] *Irishman*, *Nation*, 23 July 1870.   [6] *Freeman's Journal*, 20 July 1870.
[7] *Irishman*, 30 July, 6, 20, 27 Aug. 1870.   [8] *Irishman*, 24 Sept. 1860.

feeling. "If the French are beat, Ireland's beat", said one of them to me.'[1] And, a few weeks later, 'the low protestants of this locality crow loudly over the defeat of France which they interpret as the favour of providence to protestantism.'[2] Nothing could illustrate more succinctly the place of France in Irish political sentiment down to 1870.

Editorial control of the *Irishman* in 1870 was in the hands of a group of young I.R.B. men who were more doctrinaire than James Stephens and much less willing than he to suppress for tactical purposes the revolutionary's dislike of Louis Napoleon's regime. That, and the fear that if Britain entered the war it would probably be on the side of France, caused them to display just a little unease about the uncritical pro-French enthusiasm of the populace, though they did not dare to take a firm stand against the popular tide.[3] After the collapse of the empire and the proclamation of a republic in Paris the *Irishman* became unambiguously pro-French,[4] but by then France under any regime was incapable of evoking confident expectations.

Up to 1870 an Anglo-French war with all its potential consequences for Ireland might for much of the time be highly improbable but it could be envisaged quite plausibly in terms of the international balance of power. After 1870 all that was changed. French power had been humiliated; if it revived, France had Alsace and Lorraine to recover. Even the most deluded Irish nationalist could see that France's 'natural enemy' was no longer Great Britain but imperial Germany, and not even the accession of Marshal MacMahon to the presidency of France in 1873 could revive the old dreams. The Franco-Prussian war had finally silenced the traditional Irish refrain about the French being 'on the sea'.

The change was not confined to a loss of interest and awareness at the popular level. Like Smith O'Brien and James Stephens, almost

[1] Journal of William J. O'Neill Daunt, 12 Aug. 1870 (N.L.I., MS 3041).
[2] Ibid., 7 Sept. 1870.
[3] *Irishman*, 30 July, 6 Aug. 1870.
[4] *Irishman*, 10 Sept. 1870.

all the other leaders and would-be leaders of Irish nationalism for generations prior to 1870 (whether politicians, conspirators or journalists) appear to have taken a keen interest in internal French politics. The immediacy of the contact was amply demonstrated as late as 1869 when the nomination of the political prisoner Henri Rochefort (together with Victor Hugo and Louis Blanc) for the French assembly elections inspired the idea of putting forward the fenian convict Jeremiah O'Donovan Rossa for the celebrated Tipperary by-election in November.[1] While such matters are very difficult to measure, it seems clear that after 1870 there was a decline in the direct interest taken by leading Irish politicians in French political affairs.

The tradition of watching for the opportunity to ally with any potential antagonist of Great Britain was maintained by the I.R.B. In 1876 John Devoy and others met the Russian ambassador to Washington to point out the mutual advantages of an understanding in the event of a war between Britain and Russia.[2] In the following year a proposal for fenian and Spanish cooperation in a raid on Gibraltar was put to the government in Madrid.[3] The Clan-na-Gael/I.R.B. intrigue with Germany in 1914–16 was the application of a fenian principle of long standing. Indeed, only in 1914 did the great European conflict involving Britain, in expectation of which the I.R.B. had been founded fifty-six years earlier, eventually come to pass. Germany had replaced France as the natural ally of Irish extremists, but without inheriting very much of the traditional Irish popular affection for France.

In conclusion we have to consider the question why the memoirs and recollections of contemporary activists show so little awareness of international tension as an influence on the foundation of fenianism and on other developments in Irish politics in the years 1858–61. One reason is that, after 1870, it would have been highly embarrass-

[1] *Irishman*, 30 Oct., 13 Nov. 1869.
[2] William O'Brien and Desmond Ryan (ed.), *Devoy's post bag, 1871–1928* (2 vols, Dublin, 1948–53), i, 209.
[3] Ibid., i, 292–3.

ing to admit that great hopes had been reposed in the France of Louis Napoleon. Indeed, it seems likely that many people simply lost the memory of a fact that was at once inconvenient and easily forgotten. For fenians there was the consideration that a quickly-evolving mythology represented the I.R.B. as an automatic and necessary expression of the national spirit. Proclaiming the doctrine of awaiting England's difficulty (as the fenians did) was one thing, but it would have been quite another thing to admit that their movement was conceived in opportunism rather than as a spontaneous ignition of the phoenix flame.

Non-fenian nationalists had a different but even more compelling reason for quietly dropping all references to the 'international dimension'. We can take Alexander Martin Sullivan as an example. With his brother, Timothy Daniel, he was a prime instigator of the MacMahon sword movement and the national petition. Under his proprietorship and editorship the *Nation*, in 1858 and subsequent years, carried many leading articles considering and heartily welcoming the possibility of foreign intervention in Ireland. The following is an extract from an article headed 'The weak point of the British empire' which appeared as late as 1863.

Whenever and wherever the chances of war with England are discussed, then and there the disaffection of Ireland becomes an element in the calculation. The only question is the possibility of availing of it. Some of the powers would find it difficult to act effectively in this country—to others it would be an easy task. Russia felt her way here in 1855, but what Russia could not undertake to do would be possible to America and a facile work to France. A war with either of these powers implies, to a certainty, the dispatch from their shores of men, arms and money to Ireland, and an uprising of Irishmen for the independence of their country.[1]

Not even the most efficient faculty of disremembering could have obliterated from Sullivan's mind his long period of interest in outside interference. Yet one could read his well-known collection of reminiscences, *New Ireland* (first published in 1877), and never get

---

[1] *Nation*, 2 May 1863.

the impression that he had at any stage contemplated the intrusion of international factors on Anglo–Irish relations: the MacMahon sword movement and the national petition are recalled, but with their wider implications carefully trimmed.[1] Why?

By 1877 Sullivan was a propagandist and leading figure of the home-rule movement, which (whatever Isaac Butt might wish) could hope to unite Irish nationalists and work within the constitutional framework only if it maintained ambiguity on the question of support for Britain against all comers in the event of international war. Anything Sullivan might have published in 1877 in his popular history about comparatively recent interest in cooperation with a foreign power would have invited discussion of this divisive topic, one fraught with danger for Sullivan and his home-rule associates. It was indeed a formidable peril: in 1878 Butt lost what remained of his authority over the movement he had founded, when in the parliamentary debates on the Russo-Turkish war and the Afghan war he made it clear that he would support the empire without reservation against any foreign enemy.[2] Ambiguity, or at least ambivalence, on the subject of ultimate loyalty remained a feature of the central home-rule tradition until John Redmond in his Woodenbridge speech of 20 September 1914 unequivocally committed himself and his supporters to the war against Germany.[3] Long before that the international dimension to Irish politics in the period 1858–61 had been forgotten, as others followed A. M. Sullivan's example in suppressing memory and mention of the 'French party' of those years and what it represented.

[1] A. M. Sullivan, *New Ireland*, pp 206–8, 242–4; however, T. D. Sullivan, *A. M. Sullivan: a memoir* (Dublin, 1885), p. 33, has a hint of the suppressed factor.
[2] David Thornley, *Isaac Butt and home rule* (London, 1964), pp 360–63 and 373–4.
[3] F. S. L. Lyons, *Ireland since the famine* (London, 1971), p. 328.

An assessment of the economic performance of Irish landlords, 1851–81*

W. E. VAUGHAN

IN George Birmingham's novel, *The bad times*, the land agent Mr Manders tried to explain to one of his employers, Lord Daintree, the difficulties of managing several estates at the same time, when one of them, Stephen Butler's, was let at a lower rent than the others.

It's awkward for me having a property under-rented alongside of yours, Lord Daintree, and Snell's bit of land. I've told the trustees, Stephen Butler's trustees, you know, fifty times that the rents could be raised thirty per cent all round. The beggars could pay it if they had to. Your fellows pay all right, Lord Daintree, and so do Snell's, who really are a bit racked. But those Belfast quakers were as obstinate as mules. Not a penny more they'd allow to be put on the tenants. The result is that the man across the fence, your man, Lord Daintree, is for ever grumbling, because he sees the other fellow getting his land for less than its proper value.[1]

This passage, written thirty years after the events it describes, with its comparison of high and low rents, its implicit but vague assumption that such a thing as a 'proper' rent existed, and its silence on any method of determining the 'proper' level of rents except by reference to other rents, is as typical of any contemporary discussion of rents and estate management as many more verbose passages in the pages of parliamentary inquiries. In the period between the famine and the land act of 1881 practically every aspect of rural society and landlord and tenant relations was subjected to scrutiny, whether official or unofficial. While the period 1881–1914 may have produced a greater weight of comment, the volume and comprehen-

* I am grateful to the Public Record Office of Northern Ireland and the National Library of Ireland for permission to use material.

[1] George A. Birmingham, *The bad times* (4th ed., London, 1914), p. 40.

[173]

siveness of the pre-1881 material remains impressive. Detailed statistics of agricultural production were annually collected and published from 1847; agrarian crime and evictions were recorded in detail by the police; over a dozen parliamentary and other official inquiries examined landlord and tenant relations before 1881; numerous pamphlets were written and published; and the newspapers reported in detail the more lurid disputes between landlords and tenants.

In spite of the accumulation of all this information, some of the most important aspects of estate management and landlord and tenant relations remain obscure. Rents were discussed in practically every inquiry but there was no assessment of either the rental capacity of Irish land or of rents as a proportion of agricultural incomes.[1] Comments on rents were vague and the criteria applied to them were quasi-moral: 'good' landlords charged 'moderate' or 'reasonable' rents; 'bad' ones charged 'excessive' rents. Standards of fairness were implicitly applied, but a method of adjusting rents which was demonstrably fair and practicable was never defined. Contemporaries did not attempt to articulate a relationship between rents and agricultural output and prices, or to measure what that relationship should be in practice. The nearest that most descriptions came to a quantitative definition of rents was to compare them with the tenement valuation; but few were prepared to state precisely what the relationship between rents and valuation should be.[2] There seemed, in practice, to be no middle ground between 'rackrenting' and 'moderate' rents, and in both cases the basis of evaluation was

---

[1] For an exception see Léonce de Lavergne, *The rural economy of England, Scotland and Ireland* (Edinburgh, 1855), p. 351. De Lavergne estimated that the value of agricultural output in Ireland was £31·62 millions, rent £9·88 millions, profits £2·63 millions, wages £15·81 millions and taxes and incidentals £3·3 millions.

[2] George F. Trench, *Are the landlords worth preserving, or, forty years' management of an Irish estate* (London and Dublin, 1881), pp 30–31. Trench suggested that the letting value of farms out of lease should be ascertained by adding 25 per cent to the tenement valuation, adding 73 per cent to that for increased prices and then deducting 5s. 0d. per acre for increased costs of production.

entirely subjective. Rents, too, were almost always seen only from the viewpoint of those who paid them. How landlords disposed of their rents, how fair they thought they were, and what their disposable incomes were, were questions which were rarely asked or answered except in contemporary fiction.[1] Likewise, the amount of rents invested by landlords in the improvement of their estates was rarely quantified before the 1880s because most discussions of agricultural investment were concerned with the tenurial difficulties of tenants who invested in farms which they held on yearly tenancies.[2]

Although modern research has done much to modify the traditional picture of a rackrenting landlordism in the period before the land war,[3] little has been done to assess the effectiveness of landlords' management of their estates and its economic and social implications. So much attention has been given to the tenurial aspects of landlord and tenant relations and their connection with political and social developments that the economic aspects of landlord behaviour have been neglected. Irish landlords may have been transformed from predatory rackrenters into passive bystanders in complex social developments, but their economic position in rural society was too important to be assessed only in terms of innocuous passivity. First, landlords, even after the land act of 1870, managed their estates under a legal system which gave them complete freedom

[1] Anthony Trollope, *The Eustace diamonds* (London, 1873). One of Lady Eustace's suitors, Lord Fawn, had an estate in County Tipperary worth about £5000 a year, but his mother, who had inherited the estate in her own right, enjoyed half the income for her life.

[2] *Reports from poor law inspectors in Ireland as to the existing relations between landlord and tenant in respect of improvements on farms, etc.* [C 31], H.C. 1870, xiv, 37–192.

[3] See James S. Donnelly, Jr, *The land and the people of nineteenth-century Cork: the rural economy and the land question* (London, 1975), pp 173–218; B. L. Solow, *The land question and the Irish economy, 1870–1903* (Cambridge, Mass., 1971), pp 51–88; W. E. Vaughan, 'Landlord and tenant relations in Ireland between the famine and the land war, 1850–78', in *Comparative aspects of Scottish and Irish economic and social history 1600–1900*, ed. L. M. Cullen and T. C. Smout (Edinburgh, 1977), pp 216–26.

of contract. Most tenants held their farms by the year, and landlords could, in theory, increase their rents every year and evict them on only six months' notice to quit.[1] Secondly, rents, even 'moderate' ones, absorbed from 25 to 40 per cent of tenants' gross incomes. Rent increases, therefore, could have a considerable effect on the distribution of incomes in rural society. Thirdly, most of the land of Ireland was held in fairly large estates. In 1876, 66 per cent of the area of the country was owned by less than 2000 landlords whose estates were larger than 2000 acres. If this figure is broken down further, it appears that less than 800 landlords owned half of the country.[2] The effect of this was to concentrate in very few hands a large proportion of the rental of the country and to form considerable reservoirs of disposable capital. Landlords were, therefore, in a powerful position in rural society: they could in theory exploit their estates to the full, they could influence drastically the distribution of incomes in rural society, and many of them could channel large sums into agricultural investment. Their behaviour, whether passive, vigorous or violent, could not be without its consequences for rural society as a whole. On the one hand, landlords could have, in theory, cleared their estates of tenants and turned the countryside over to large cattle ranches and sheep farms.[3] On the other hand, they could leave sitting tenants to their own devices as long as they paid existing rents. Most landlords tried to steer a course between these extremes, avoiding socially disruptive clearances while trying to increase the returns from their estates.

Within these limits a wide variety of options was open to landlords who wished to increase their rentals or to invest in the improvement of their estates. An examination of the rentals and accounts of

---

[1] *Returns showing the number of agricultural holdings in Ireland and the tenure by which they are held by the occupiers* [C 32], H.C. 1870, lvi, 737–56.

[2] *Summary of the returns of owners of land in Ireland*, H.C. 1876 (422), lxxx, 35–60.

[3] For an example of landlords clearing land for sheep, see letters, memoranda and newscuttings concerning the state of the county of Donegal; compiled by Sir Thomas Larcom, 1856–66 (N.L.I., MS 7633).

individual estates showed that landlords' behaviour varied considerably. On some estates rent increases between 1851 and 1881 were negligible. On the Le Fanu estate in County Cavan, for example, rents were stable for the whole period covered by its rentals.[1] On other estates, rents were increased by small amounts. On the Pratt estate in County Cavan, for example, rents were increased, on average, by only 14 per cent between 1851 and 1881. Similarly, rents were increased by only 18 per cent on the Ranfurly estate in County Tyrone, by 20 per cent on the Knox estate in County Roscommon, by 22 per cent on the Erne estate in Fermanagh and by 23 per cent on the duke of Manchester's estate in Armagh.[2] On other estates, rent increases were rather higher: 26 per cent on the Hodson estate in County Wicklow, 28 per cent on the Butler estate at Castlecrine in County Clare, 29 per cent on the Deane estate in Kildare, 33 per cent on the Inchiquin estate in Clare and 36 per cent on the Archdale estates in Fermanagh and Tyrone.[3] Average rent increases of over 40 per cent were rare. An increase of 44 per cent occurred on the Hall estates in Armagh and Down, and dramatic increases of 50 and 60 per cent occurred on the

[1] Rentals and accounts of the estate of Joseph Le Fanu in County Cavan, 1847–75 (P.R.O.I., M 5634/1–27).

[2] Rentals of the Pratt estate in County Cavan, 1850–97 (N.L.I., MSS 3122, 5088–91); rentals and accounts of the Ranfurly estate in County Tyrone, 1858–85 (P.R.O.N.I., D 1932/1/1–2, 2/1–12, 3/1–12, 4/1–16); rentals of the estate of the Knox family in County Roscommon, 1849–86 (N.L.I., MS 3178); rentals of the estates of the earl of Erne in the counties of Donegal, Fermanagh, Sligo and Mayo, 1848–86 (P.R.O.N.I., D 1939/4/2–15, 8/2–3, 9/9, 10/2–3); rentals of the estate of the duke of Manchester in County Armagh, 1850–80 (P.R.O.N.I., D 1248/R/15–43).

[3] Rentals, accounts and agents' reports of the estates of Sir George Hodson, bt, in the counties of Cavan and Wicklow, 1841–88 (N.L.I., MSS 16,393–6, 16,404–6, 16,419); rent ledgers and rentals of the estate of the Butler family at Castlecrine, County Clare, 1848–81 (N.L.I., MSS 5410–14, 5422); rentals of the estate of J. W. Deane at Timolin and Portersize, County Kildare, 1845–81 (N.L.I., MSS 14,281–2); rentals and accounts of the estate of Sir Lucius O'Brien, 13th baron of Inchiquin, in County Clare, 1850–80 (N.L.I., MSS 14,522–53); rentals and accounts of the Archdale estates in the counties of Fermanagh and Tyrone, 1849–85 (P.R.O.N.I., D 704/10–82).

estates of the third earl of Leitrim in the counties of Leitrim and Donegal.[1]

While average rent increases show the variety of practice from estate to estate, an examination of the individual rent increases on which the averages were based reveals considerable differences even within the same estate. On Lord Erne's estate in Fermanagh, for example, where the average rent increase was 22 per cent, some rents were increased by as much as 50 per cent while others were not increased at all. Comparisons of the rents of individual holdings with the tenement valuation shows that the level of rents varied considerably from holding to holding. The timing of rent increases, too, was erratic. On a handful of estates there were general increases of rents in the 1850s, followed by stability until the 1880s. Occasionally, rents were increased when a holding changed hands or when a tenant was succeeded by his son, but generally the timing of rent increases was so arbitrary and unpredictable as to excuse the tenant who told the Bessborough commission that rents were increased just as 'the landlord or his agent take the whim into their heads'.[2]

The management of rents on individual estates presents a contradictory picture. On the one hand, there was the essential moderation of rent increases as a whole. Allowing for estates whose rents were not increased and for holdings whose rents were not increased, average increases on a group of over fifty estates between 1851 and

[1] Rent ledgers of the estates of the Hall family in the counties of Armagh and Down, 1846–74 (P.R.O.N.I., D 2090/2/2–3, 3/1, 7–28); rentals and rent rolls of the estates of the earl of Leitrim in the counties of Donegal and Leitrim, 1844–69 (N.L.I., MSS 179–80, 3803–12, 5175–8, 5794–800).

[2] *Report of her majesty's commissioners of inquiry into the working of the Landlord and Tenant (Ireland) Act, 1870, and the acts amending the same*, vol. ii: *minutes of evidence*, pt i, p. 212 [2779–1], H.C. 1881, xviii, 430. This tenant was complaining particularly about Lord Gosford, whose agent, William Wann, seems to have been scrupulous to the point of fussiness in his dealings with tenants. See letters from William Wann to Lord Gosford, 1848–78 (P.R.O.N.I., D 1606/5A/1–4).

1881 were about 20 per cent.[1] Most individual rents, furthermore, were increased only once in twenty or thirty years. But, on the other hand, there were landlords whose rent increases were relatively dramatic, and on most estates rent increases were unpredictable and apparently inconsistent. The fact that the fortunes of individual tenants on the same estate varied considerably probably explains many of the complaints of anomalies heard by parliamentary inquiries. The fact, too, that the principles on which rents were adjusted were obscure added to the confusion which fuelled the fires of discontent. Although an examination of the rentals of individual estates reveals more accurately the movement and level of rents than much of contemporary comment, it sheds little extra light on the principles on which rents were adjusted. Some landlords tried to introduce an element of objectivity into the levying of rents by employing professional valuators to survey and revalue their estates. But the principles on which the valuators worked were obscure, and some agents even prided themselves on not giving the valuators instructions about the size of rent increases expected.[2] One landlord who was understandably curious about the methods used by the valuator he employed received a rather tart reply to his inquiries:

In reply to yours of yesterday's date asking to see the basis of my valuation of your estates, I beg to inform you that the basis on which I make a valuation is the knowledge which I have acquired after five and twenty years of practice and experience in every county in Ireland. I have never tabulated it and cannot therefore comply with your request.[3]

---

[1] W. E. Vaughan, 'A study of landlord and tenant relations in Ireland between the famine and the land war, 1850–78' (Ph.D. thesis, T.C.D., 1974), pp 47–65; Solow, *Land question*, pp 57–77; Donnelly, *Land and people of Cork*, pp 187–200.

[2] William Wann to W. C. Kyle, 23 Oct. 1861 in copy letter book of William Wann, 1854–70 (P.R.O.N.I., D 1606/5/4). For an example of a valuation, see valuation of the estate of Lord Powerscourt in the counties of Dublin and Wicklow by Brassington and Gale, 1853 (N.L.I., 2740).

[3] Thomas Fitzgerald to Sir Charles Domvile, 9 May 1872 (N.L.I., Domvile papers, MS 11,305).

The general impression created by examining the movement and level of rents on individual estates is that the management of rent was not conducted on clearly enunciated principles, and that rent increases were unpredictable and, on most estates, relatively low. The average rent increases given above demonstrate not only the variety of practice from estate to estate, but the failure of some landlords to make the most of their opportunities. The earl of Erne, for example, fared much worse than the earl of Leitrim in terms of increasing income. Even the contrast between the Erne and Archdale estates which were within fifteen miles of each other in the same county was noticeable—increases of 22 per cent compared with increases of 36 per cent.

A more vigorous policy of exploitation, pursued more predictably and within clearly defined limits, might have created less friction between landlords and tenants, caused fewer demonstrable grievances and increased rents at the same time. The period between the early 1850s and the mid-1870s was one of remarkable prosperity for Irish agriculture and was, in many ways, suited to innovations in estate management. Calculations of the value of agricultural output show a strongly pronounced upward trend from the poor years of the early 1850s to the boom years of the early and middle 1870s.[1]

Annual average value of agricultural output (excluding potatoes) 1851–80

period	£ millions	period	£ millions
1851–5	28·80	1866–70	37·04
1856–60	33·20	1871–5	40·64
1861–5	31·92	1876–80	39·10

Although the trend was subject to cyclical movements—the peak years of 1855, 1865–6 and 1876 corresponding with the poor years of 1851–2, 1861–3 and 1879–80—rising prices for livestock and

[1] W. E. Vaughan, op. cit., pp 336–58.

livestock products, especially store cattle and butter, more than compensated for the decline in cereal prices that occurred after the boom year of 1855. By the mid-1870s, the value of output was double what it had been in 1851–2, and a comparison of the five-year periods 1851–5 and 1871–5 shows an increase of over 40 per cent. During a period of such substantial increases in agricultural prosperity, rent increases of at least 40 per cent over a period of twenty years would have been necessary to have given landlords a proportionate share in the increased wealth of agriculture. Given the strong legal and economic position of landlords and the fact that much of the increase in the value of agricultural output was generated by products which were not labour intensive, landlords should have expected average rent increases in excess of 40 per cent. Average rent increases of 20 per cent, therefore, whether measured by the yardstick of changes in the value of agricultural output or by the performances of the most vigorous landlords, fell short of the potential rental capacity of Irish land. Even under a system of land tenure which maintained freedom of contract, most Irish landlords failed to exploit their estates and allowed their rents to fall behind the real letting value of land. It is arguable that landlords would have been better off under alternative systems of regulating rent, even if that meant sacrificing the theoretical freedom of contract which they enjoyed. If, for instance, a system of state-regulated rents modelled on the Trinity College, Dublin, leasing powers act of 1851[1] had been established in the 1850s, giving tenants security of tenure and landlords the benefit of flexible rents, the landlords would have been much better off by the 1870s. Under the T.C.D. leasing powers act, the rents paid by the college's middleman tenants were regulated by taking one or other of the government valuations as the basis of letting value and adjusting rents upwards or downwards as the prices of certain agricultural products deviated from those on which the government valuations were based. In practice this method of adjusting rents would have favoured the tenants after the mid-1850s,

[1] 14 & 15 Vic., c. cxxviii.

because the commodities whose prices had the most weight in its operation—wheat and oats—were either falling or steady in price from the mid-1850s. In spite of this, however, the application of the T.C.D. leasing powers act to the management of Irish estates in the 1850s would have given landlords immediate increases of about 36 per cent and subsequent increases of over 20 per cent after the mid-1860s, making a total increase of over 60 per cent between the mid-1850s and the mid-1870s.[1]

The weakness of this sytem, as the college discovered in the 1880s, was that the rents appropriate to one decade were paid in another, because the rents paid in each decade were determined by the agricultural prices of the previous one. When prices were rising as in the 1860s and 1870s, this favoured the tenants, but when prices began to fall in the 1880s, rents based on the 1870s became burden-some.[2] The advantages of the system, nevertheless, were consider-able because rent increases occurred at predictable intervals and rents moved upwards and downwards according to principles which were clearly enunciated in advance and which bore some systematic relationship to agricultural prices. If the working of the system led to difficulties, it was amenable to adjustment by negotiation within a framework of clearly definable alternatives. The equity of the system, conceived initially as suitable for regulating the rents payable by tenants who were in effect landlords in their own right, was un-deniable because it allowed both landlords and tenants to share in increases in agricultural incomes generated by rising prices.

The system of regulating rents established by the T.C.D. leasing powers act was only one of several methods of regulating rents put forward in the 1850s. In the same year as the passing of the act, the second edition of Henry Stephens's *Book of the farm* was published.

---

[1] These estimates are based on the provisions of the act itself combined with the tenement valuation and the index of agricultural prices in Thomas Barrington, 'A review of Irish agricultural prices' in *Journal of the Statistical and Social Inquiry Society of Ireland*, xv (1927), pp 251–2.

[2] W. J. Lowe, 'Landlord and tenant on the estate of Trinity College, Dublin, 1851–1903', in *Hermathena*, cxx (summer 1976), pp 5–24.

Stephens, looking back at the changes which had taken place in agricultural prices since 1815 and fearing future changes as a result of the repeal of the corn laws, recommended a system of fluctuating rents for leaseholders and yearly tenants.[1] Recognizing that fluctuations in agricultural prices, taken on their own, did not necessarily reflect fluctuations in farmers' gross incomes, he suggested that changes in rents should be based not only on prices but on the average acreable value of certain commodities.[2] The only difficulty, according to Stephens, in establishing such a system was that of 'determining the statistical facts of the annual average acreable produce of grain and stock-feeding crops in each country'. Such statistics were not available in England and Wales until 1867, in spite of the agitation of agricultural experts like James Caird.[3] But in Ireland very detailed statistics of agricultural production had been annually collected and published since 1847. In addition, the tenement valuation, begun in the 1850s under the supervision of Sir Richard Griffith, provided a starting point for the adjusting of rent on every holding in the country. By combining statistics of agricultural production with current agricultural prices and the tenement valuation, landlords and agents had all the information necessary for operating a sophisticated system of carefully regulated rents from the 1850s.

The hypothetical application of either the T.C.D. leasing powers act of 1851 or a system of annually fluctuating rents, based on Stephens' ideas, to the actual rental of Ireland in the period 1856–75 gives a measure of the extent to which most Irish landlords failed to exploit their estates. The following table is an attempt to estimate the effects of different methods of increasing rents on the amount of gross rents yielded over a twenty-year period.

---

[1] Henry Stephens, *The book of the farm* (2nd ed., Edinburgh and London, 1851), ii, 498–510.

[2] Ibid., p. 501.

[3] B. R. Mitchell and Phyllis Deane, *Abstract of British historical statistics* (Cambridge, 1962), p. 76.

Actual and hypothetical rents, 1856–75[1]

The figures in square brackets show the percentage by which the increased rents exceeded the assumed pre-1856 annual gross rental of £10 millions.

Method of adjusting rents	Total rents 1856–75 (£ millions)	Annual average rents (£ millions)
Actual rents		
Sporadic increases	220	11·00 [10]
General increases	240	12·00 [20]
Fluctuating rents		
Method A	256	12·80 [28]
Method B	292	14·60 [46]
T.C.D. system	297	14·86 [49]

Of the various methods of increasing rents, the one used most by landlords—sporadic increases of about 20 per cent over twenty years—yielded less than any other method. Even general increases of 20 per cent imposed in 1856 would have yielded an extra £20 millions over the next twenty years. Any of the methods of fluctuating rents would have yielded much higher incomes—anything from 16 to 35 per cent more than that yielded by sporadic increases of 20 per cent. Even the first method of fluctuating rents yielded £36

[1] The estimates of actual rents are based on the assumption that the total rental of agricultural land (excluding buildings) was £10 millions in 1856, i.e. about 10 per cent above the tenement valuation; see *Report from the select committee on general valuation, etc. (Ireland); together with the proceedings of the committee, minutes of evidence, and appendix*, pp 213–19, H.C. 1868–9 (362), ix, 225–31. The sporadic increases were assumed to be 20 per cent on all holdings between 1856 and 1875 and the general increases to be 20 per cent on all holdings in 1856 followed by twenty years' stability. The estimates of fluctuating rents are based on the assumption that a gross rental equal to the tenement valuation (£9 millions, excluding buildings) fluctuated annually with the value of agricultural output. Method A took the value of £25 millions as the starting point for agricultural output and method B took £22 millions. The latter figure is the approximate value of agricultural output based on the price scale used in the tenement valuation. The estimates based on the T.C.D. system assumed that rents were adjusted every five years and that the tenement valuation was the basis of the letting value. The prices used were taken from Barrington's index; see above p. 182, note 1.

millions more than actual rents, and this was the equivalent of sporadic increases of 50 per cent spread over twenty years. But the effect on the tenants of annually fluctuating rents was much less immediately burdensome than once-and-for-all increases of 50 per cent. The main disadvantage of sporadic increases was that they suddenly reduced farmers' net incomes. For example, a tenant whose rent was £11 probably enjoyed a net income of £20 after he had paid his rent. A rent increase of 50 per cent would have immediately diminished his net income by £5·50 or over 25 per cent. But under a system of fluctuating rents, this increase would have been spread over twenty years. Under method A of the system of fluctuating rents, there would have been increases of 20 per cent between 1856 and 1860, rents would then have been reduced almost to their pre-1856 level between 1861 and 1863, and from 1864 to 1875 they would have increased again by 40 per cent. By 1876 rents would have been 50 per cent above the pre-1856 level.

Some of the advantages of a system of fluctuating rents were obvious. Not only would they have given landlords and tenants proportionate shares in the profits and losses of agriculture, but they would have done it 'without influencing the gain or loss due to the tenant for his peculiarly good or bad management'.[1] Much of the unpredictability of the existing system of sporadic rent increases would have disappeared under a system of fluctuating rents. It is true that the majority of tenants would have paid more in the long run, but they would, at least, have paid the extra rent gradually and predictably as their incomes improved. Tenants would have received relief in bad years not as a matter of favour but as a matter of course. Downward adjustments of rents would have occurred, for example, in the early 1860s and in the late 1870s according to a well-tried scale of values. Many of the criticisms of landlords in the 1850s and 1860s would have been irrelevant if rents had been adjusted rationally. The argument, for example, that tenants did not improve their farms because they feared rent increases—an argument without

[1] Stephens, *Book of the farm*, ii, 501.

much substance in practice—would have had no weight at all under a system which guaranteed the individual tenant the full return on his good management. Above all, a system of rent adjustments based on explicit principles and working according to objective criteria would have transformed the debate on rents by replacing qualitative and quasi-moral criteria with quantitative and empirical ones.

Although the advantages of fluctuating rents are obvious in the context of a growing demand for the legislative regulation of land-lord and tenant relations, the disadvantages of the existing styles of estate management were not so obvious. Since land was under-rented, for example, it found its true value only when it changed hands in tenant-right transactions: in other words, when tenants bought and sold the tenant right of farms, they were buying and selling part of the true rental value of their land. Once this process became established it created vested interests whose real value was obscured by the general vagueness about rents. By the late 1860s and early 1870s, many tenants had a strong interest in keeping rents low, or at least lower than they should have been; and it is not surprising that demands for fair rents and free sale were voiced strongly at the very time when rents were slipping behind the real value of land. It is arguable, too, that land which was let below its full value was inefficiently used. There is no doubt that the productivity of Irish agriculture, as distinct from its value, did not increase much between the 1850s and the 1870s. Whether properly adjusted rents would have spurred tenants into farming more intensively and more profitably is by no means certain. But the belief that 'smart' (i.e. high) rents would have this effect was as plausible a tenet of con-temporary wisdom as the belief that security of tenure would en-courage tenants to invest in their farms.[1]

[1] See Solow, *Land question*, p. 80. Calculations of the value of agricultural output at constant prices show only slight increases between the 1850s and the 1870s. Calculations of the value of agricultural output on farms of different sizes in the 1870s suggest that if all farms had been as intensively cultivated as farms in the 15–30 and 30–50 acre categories, total agricultural output would have been 25 per cent higher.

The most important consequence of landlords' policies of rent management was the fact that the share of agricultural output which rents absorbed declined between the 1850s and the 1870s. The following table shows the effects on agricultural incomes of rent increases in that period.

Agricultural output, rents and cost of labour and gross farming profits, 1854–74[1]
The amounts are £ millions.

Years	Agricultural output	Rents	Cost of labour	Gross farming profits
1852–4	28·7	10·0	9·00	9·70
1872–4	40·5	12·0	11·35	17·15
% increase	41	20	26	77

This table shows that rents lagged behind not only increases in the value of agricultural output but gross farming profits as well. In the 1850s rents and profits were almost the same, but by the 1870s profits exceeded rents by 43 per cent. The most remarkable development between 1854 and 1874 was that profits increased by 77 per cent while rents increased by only 20 per cent. If rents had been increased by 50 per cent between the 1850s and the 1870s profits would still have increased by 46 per cent—slightly in excess of increases in the value of output. In the 1870s some landlords and agents were becoming aware of their failure to exploit their estates to the full. A survey, for example, of an estate in County Clare, made in the 1870s, suggested that the rents of some holdings could be increased

---

[1] The figures for agricultural output are averages for three years. Costs of labour are based on information derived from Richard Barrington, 'The prices of some agricultural produce and the cost of farm labour for the last fifty years' in *Journal of the Statistical and Social Inquiry Society of Ireland*, ix (1887), pp 148–9, Sir Richard Griffith, *Instructions to valuators and surveyors . . .* (Dublin, 1853), pp 32–3, and *Second report by Mr Wilson Fox on the wages, earnings, and conditions of employment of agricultural labourers in the United Kingdom . . .*, p. 137, [Cd. 2376], H.C. 1905, xcvii, 489.

by 100 per cent.[1] In the same county the Butlers of Castlecrine, whose rents had been increased by 28 per cent in the 1850s, planned a general increase of rents in the 1870s of, on average, 24 per cent. But their plans were overtaken by the events of the late 1870s, and the rents were not increased.[2]

Although the rents paid by tenants aroused the interest of contemporaries, the costs of estate management and its effects on the disposable incomes of the landlords who received the rents received little attention. In 1874 the governor-general of Canada, Lord Dufferin, an experienced commentator on the problems of managing Irish estates, wrote to the duke of Argyll declaring that he intended to sell his Irish estate.

I shall have to leave something like £150,000 behind me in the shape of improvements, from which I have had time to reap no other advantage than the ameliorated condition of the farmers themselves; but an Irish estate is like a sponge, and an Irish landlord is never so rich as when he is rid of his property.[3]

A superficial examination of surviving estate accounts and correspondence certainly confirms the notion that tenants regarded their landlords as sponges which could be squeezed at will, but a detailed examination of estate expenditure suggests that their efforts were not always attended with the effects experienced by Lord Dufferin.[4] Surviving estate accounts show that the net incomes of Irish landlords were much smaller than their gross rentals. From the rents collected by the agent, a number of demands had to be settled before the landlords received what was their disposable income. Taxes and

[1] Survey of the estate of the Westropp family in the counties of Clare and Limerick, 1871–7, Robert L. Brown, agent (N.L.I., MS 5397).

[2] Rent ledgers and rentals of the estate of the Butler family at Castlecrine, County Clare, 1848–81 (N.L.I., MSS 5410–14, 5422).

[3] Dufferin to the duke of Argyll, 7 May 1874 (P.R.O.N.I., D 1071H/H7/1–). I am indebted to Mr Andrew Harrison of the Public Record Office of Northern Ireland for this reference. Dufferin owned 18,238 acres in County Down in 1876.

[4] See, for example, the minute books of tenants' requests submitted to the guardians of Lord Powerscourt, 1847–57 (N.L.I., MSS 16,376–9).

fixed charges, such as head-rents, the costs of management, improvements, allowances to tenants, subscriptions, and the interest on encumbrances, usually consumed a fair proportion of the gross rental. The following table shows how the rent receipts of Lord Inchiquin were disbursed during the period 1851–80.

Disbursements of rent receipts on the Inchiquin estate in County Clare, 1851–80[1]
The figures give each item as a percentage of total rent receipts.

Items of expenditure	1851–60	1861–70	1871–80
Fixed charges and taxation	17	14	15
Management	4	4	4
Improvements	2	3	3
Allowances	5	2	2
Interest	29	22	28
Net income	43	55	48

The net income of Lord Inchiquin during the thirty-year period covered by the table ranged from 43 to 55 per cent of his rent receipts. Out of total annual rent receipts of about £12,000 in the 1850s and of £14,000 in the 1870s, he received about £5000 and £7000 a year. From this sum came the money to run his house at Dromoland and to pay allowances to members of his family. The main burdens on the estate were the payment of interest on encumbrances, closely followed by fixed charges and taxation. The combined expenditure on improvements and allowances accounted for only 5 to 7 per cent of rent receipts. The actual amount spent on improvements and allowances between 1851 and 1880 was about £23,000. During the same period, over £100,000 was spent on interest payments and over £60,000 on taxes and fixed charges. While it is true that Lord Inchiquin was not as rich as the size of his estate or the amount of his rental would suggest, the main beneficiaries of his estate were not his tenants but a small group of

---

[1] Rentals and accounts of the estate of Lord Inchiquin in County Clare, 1851–80 (N.L.I., MSS 14,523–53).

encumbrancers and the bodies to whom he paid tithe rent charge, poor-law rates, head rents and quit rents.

While it is dangerous to generalise from one case, a comparison of the Inchiquin estate with other estates whose accounts are available suggests that the pattern of expenditure on the Inchiquin estate was not exceptional. The amounts spent on taxation and fixed charges, for example, were rather high but they were paralleled on the Archdale estates in Fermanagh and Tyrone, the Crofton estate in Roscommon, the Ranfurly estate in Tyrone and the Murray Stewart estate in Donegal. The amounts spent on management were slightly smaller than on other comparable estates, but the differences were not great and may have been caused by different methods of accounting. The amounts spent on improvements and on allowances to tenants were rather smaller on the Inchiquin estate than on the Erne estate in Fermanagh, the London companies' estates in Londonderry or the Murray Stewart estate in Donegal, but the practice on the Inchiquin estate was probably more typical of Irish estates as a whole than was that of these estates.[1] The size of the interest payments on the Inchiquin estate was larger than on some other estates, but it was not exceptionally large. The estates of Lord Gosford, for example, were encumbered by debts whose interest payments consumed 40 per cent of the annual rental in the 1870s.[2]

Although the Inchiquin estate is not in all respects typical of other estates whose accounts have survived, its pattern of expenditure suggests several things about the financial management of Irish estates. First, while something was spent on improvements, the amounts spent were small. Secondly, the net incomes of landlords, while strongly influenced by the presence or absence of encum-

[1] For a penetrating analysis of landlords' investiment in agricultural improvements, see Cormac Ó Gráda, 'The investment behaviour of Irish landlords 1850–75: some preliminary findings' in *Agricultural History Review*, xxiii (1975), pp 139–55. See also O. Robinson, 'The London companies as progressive landlords in nineteenth-century Ireland' in *Economic History Review*, 2nd ser., xv (1962–3), pp 103–18.

[2] Letters from William Wann to Lord Gosford, 1875–8 (P.R.O.N.I., D 1606/5A/4, p. 76).

brances, were considerably less than the gross rentals of their estates. Lord Inchiquin's disposable income was about 50 per cent of his rent receipts, but even if his estate had been free of encumbrances his disposable income would rarely have exceeded 75 per cent. Since payments to his immediate family and the upkeep of Dromoland had to be met from his net income, his real disposable income would have been a good deal less than 50 per cent of his rent receipts. The financial burdens to which an estate was subject were fixed, or, at least, not easily changed in the short term. A fall in rent receipts, therefore, had a drastic effect on landlords' disposable incomes. A fall of 20 per cent, for example, in rent receipts would have reduced Lord Inchiquin's net income by 40 per cent. Even if his estate had been free of encumbrances, a fall of 20 per cent would have reduced his net income by 27 per cent. Since landlords were the pivot around which a complicated series of transactions involving the redistribution of rents took place, stability of income was probably their most pressing need. This may partly explain not only their reluctance to give abatements of rent in bad years but also their failure to experiment with more flexible methods of rent management. Rents which were well below the real value of land had at least the merit of being punctually paid.[1] The doubtful wisdom of this unadventurous policy was summed up by one experienced agent: 'I honestly feel it is better for a landlord to let his lands at a moderate rent and be paid than subject them to a sharper figure and render the payments uncertain.'[2] The implementation of more adventurous rent policies would have required far-reaching changes in estate management, including the emergence of flexible burdens to correspond with flexible rents. Indeed it is possible that more flexible rents, which would have increased income dramatically between the 1850s and the 1870s, would have only encouraged landlords to plunge into more onerous commitments. The burden of interest

---

[1] See Vaughan, op. cit., pp 88–9.
[2] William Wann to Francis Meade, 13 Apr. 1855 in copy letter book of William Wann, 1854–70 (P.R.O.N.I., D 1606/5/4).

payments on the Inchiquin estate, for example, kept pace with increasing rent receipts.

On the Inchiquin estate, about 3 per cent of rent receipts were spent on improvements, and amounts ranging from 2 to 5 per cent were allowed to tenants for various purposes. This seems to represent the total investment by Lord Inchiquin in agricultural improvements in the thirty years before 1881. Although this contradicts the idea that Irish landlords spent little or nothing on the improvement of their estates, it explains why Irish landlords were often unfavourably compared with English and Scottish landlords, who spent large amounts on improvements.[1] Some comparisons, of course, were unfair because many English landlords were able to draw on incomes from outside agriculture. The duke of Bedford, for example, spent 33 per cent of his rents from his Thorney estate on repairs and permanent improvements between 1856 and 1875, and his net income was only 23 per cent of his gross rental.[2] But the duke was able to manage his estates in this extravagant manner because his property in London yielded about £100,000 a year.[3] More realistic estimates of English landlords' investment put it at about 20 per cent of rent receipts.[4] The contrast between Irish and English landlords, nevertheless, was considerable, and even a great landlord like Lord Inchiquin spent less on improvements than many English landlords of the same standing.

---

[1] Solow, *Land question*, p. 77.

[2] The duke of Bedford, *The story of a great agricultural estate* (London, 1897), pp 234–5; David Spring, *The English landed estate in the nineteenth century* (Baltimore, 1963).

[3] John Bateman, *The great landowners of Great Britain and Ireland* (4th ed., London, 1883; reprinted with introduction by David Spring, Leicester, 1971), p. 19.

[4] See R. J. Thompson, 'An inquiry into the rent of agricultural land in England and Wales during the nineteenth century' in *Journal of the Royal Statistical Society*, lxx (Dec. 1907), p. 603, Richard Perren, 'The landlords and agricultural transformation, 1870–1900' in *Agricultural History Review*, xviii (1970), pp 41–2; and *Particulars of expenditure and outgoings on certain estates in Great Britain and farm accounts reprinted from the reports of the assistant commissioners*, pp 54–60 [c. 8125], H.C. 1896, xvi, 522–8.

The reasons for the relatively poor performance of Irish landlords in agricultural investment can be guessed at but cannot be either documented precisely or quantified.[1] But two factors, at least, seem to have been important: the smallness of agricultural holdings and the character of agricultural production. Agricultural holdings were on average much smaller in Ireland than in England and the south of Scotland. A comparison of the Scottish and Irish estates of Horatio Granville Murray Stewart, for example, illustrates this vividly. Although both estates were about the same size, in 1858 Murray Stewart received rents of over £13,000 from his estates in Wigton and Kirkcudbright, and £7000 from his estate in Donegal.[2] But while only 99 tenants on the Scottish estates paid the £13,000, the £7000 from the Donegal estate was paid by over 1500 tenants. It was argued that Irish landlords could not possibly build houses and out-offices for their tenants because there were so many of them.[3] Irish landlords could not spend on the same scale as English landlords without at the same time spending ruinously. Instead they were content to supply tenants with timber and slates to improve their houses. Irish landlords were, therefore, excluded from one of the most expensive outlets for estate improvement—the house and cottage building which was the pride of English landlords—, and their improving impulses had to find cheaper outlets.

At first sight this is a sound argument, but it is one which on closer examination seems less convincing. No Irish landlord could have

---

[1] See Solow, *Land question*, pp 80–84 for an assessment of the impediments to landlord investment which relies heavily on the argument that holdings were small.

[2] Rental of the Scottish estate of H. G. Murray Stewart, 1857–8 (N.L.I., MS 5477) and rental and account of the estate of H. G. Murray Stewart in County Donegal, 1857–8 (N.L.I., MS 5896). In 1876, the Scottish estate had over 47,000 acres and the Irish one 51,000. See Bateman, *Great landowners*, p. 423.

[3] Solow, *Land question*, p. 80: 'after all, no English landlord would have provided houses and offices for his tenants if he had had to build a few dozen houses on 200 or 300 acres.' Even on the Murray Stewart estate, the landlord would have had to build only three houses per 100 acres.

contemplated building on any of his farms the elaborate miniature imitations of Balmoral fashionable as farm houses in England in the 1850s. At Thorney, for example, the duke of Bedford spent £3500 on buildings for a farm of 500 acres.[1] Although such buildings were as unnecessary as they were impossible on most Irish farms, the more humble cottage-building carried on in England would not have been inappropriate in Ireland. Bailey Denton, the great English authority on farm buildings, produced designs for large cottages with three bedrooms which could be built for £150.[2] Such cottages, the equivalent of second-class houses as defined by the census authorities in Ireland, were superior to the majority of houses in rural Ireland where, even in 1881, only 45 per cent of houses on farms were classified as first or second-class.[3] If Irish landlords had devoted £1 million a year to house-building between 1851 and 1881, they could have built 200,000 commodious houses for their tenants. If they had chosen to build the rather less commodious houses designed by Henry Stephens and costing about £70 each, they could have built 400,000. In other words, less than 10 per cent of the gross rental of Ireland, spent over thirty years, would have built houses for anything from 50 to 80 per cent of the tenants. Any of the alternative methods of managing rents described above would have yielded enough extra income to have renewed most of the houses in rural Ireland between 1851 and 1881.

Although an examination of more economical forms of house-building weakens the argument that landlords could not afford to build houses on a multitude of small farms, the real weakness of the argument lies in a misconception about the structure of land occupation in Ireland. It is true that, on estates like the Murray Stewart estate in Donegal, only an enormous expenditure, equivalent to the purchase price of the estate itself, would have been enough to have built houses on all the holdings between 1851 and 1881. But not all

---

[1] J. Bailey Denton, *The farm home steads of England* (London, 1854), pp 12–14.
[2] Ibid., p. 119; see also Stephens, *Book of the farm*, ii, 546, for labourers' cottages which cost about £68 each.
[3] *Census Ire., 1881, general report*, p. 166.

estates, even in the west of Ireland, were as fragmented as the Murray Stewart estate. Lord Inchiquin, for example, had less than 500 tenants on his estate of over 20,000 acres. An expenditure of £150 on each of these would have consumed only 19 per cent of his rent receipts of over £400,000 between 1851 and 1880. Although Ireland was a country of small farmers it was not predominantly a country of small farms. Small farmers holding less than 30 acres accounted for the majority of farmers—74 per cent in 1854—but much of the actual land was held by farmers with larger holdings. Farmers with holdings of more than 50 acres, of which there were just less than 90,000 in 1854, occupied 60 per cent of the land in 1854.[1] Even landlords conscious of Bailie Denton's advice that 'no farm should be so small that it cannot support a house above the pretensions of a bailiff's cottage' had plenty of outlets for investment in these larger farms. An annual expenditure of £2 millions, less than 20 per cent of rent receipts, would have allowed landlords to have spent about £700 on each of these larger farms between 1851 and 1881.

A more substantial explanation for the relatively low rate of expenditure on improvements on Irish estates may lie in the character of Irish agriculture, whose underdeveloped state offered many outlets for cheap improvements while not offering many for expensive ones. Ireland's mild winters and superb grassland meant that Irish farmers did not usually house-feed their livestock. Landlords, therefore, were relieved of one of the most expensive forms of estate investment: the provision of out-offices suitable for feeding livestock. At the same time, the inferior quality of Irish livestock, the careless cultivation methods of many farmers, and the prevalence of weeds,[2] bad fences and ruinous gates, gave landlords many cheap outlets for improving agriculture by keeping pedigree bulls, and encouraging better farming by means of prizes. This explanation

[1] *Returns of agricultural produce in Ireland, in the year 1854*, pp x–xi (2017), H.C. 1856, liii, 10–11.

[2] Ibid., p. 223. A survey of farms in 1854 found that on 50 per cent of farms the extirpation of weeds was either wholly or largely neglected.

may have some substance, but it is not entirely convincing because there were some expensive forms of improvement, such as thorough drainage, which were quite appropriate to Irish conditions. Only 270,000 acres were drained between 1847 and 1880, at an average cost of £7 per acre.[1] If Irish landlords had spent £500,000 a year between 1851 and 1881—less than 5 per cent of rent receipts—,over two million acres, or 10 per cent of the land, would have been drained in a generation.

The efforts of landlords to improve their estates, though commendable, useful and gratifying to themselves, seem to have been erratic and transient, often amounting to little more than a few gates here and a few slates there. Exhortations about weeds and crop rotation went hand-in-hand with uneasiness about the expense of keeping pedigree bulls with enormous appetites for oil cakes. Few agents seem to have worked to any plan for the systematic improvement of the estates which they managed. It is difficult to generalise about the training of agents, but it seems unlikely that many of them had any agricultural experience beyond some dilettante farming.[2] Estate management was not primarily an agricultural pursuit but one which combined rent collection, the settlement of disputes among the tenants, and a general duty to represent and further the landlords' social and political interests. The typical agent was more a rustic statesman with proconsular functions than the manager of a vast agricultural enterprise. In the hands of some agents, expenditure on agricultural improvements was more a form of largesse than a form of investment.[3]

Although it was plausible enough to argue that Irish landlords

[1] Ó Gráda, 'The investment behaviour of Irish landlords 1850–75: some preliminary findings' in *Agricultural History Review*, xxiii (1975), pp 146–7.

[2] For a surprising exception, see W. S. Trench, *Realities of Irish life* (reprint, London, 1966). Trench was awarded a gold medal by the Royal Agricultural Society of Ireland for his work of reclamation at Cardtown, Queen's County.

[3] See, for example, William Wann to W. C. Kyle, 24 Apr. 1863 in copy letter book of William Wann, 1854–70 (P.R.O.N.I., D 1606/5/4): 'In giving lime and seeds and such like I have always tried to assist in the *first* place the *honest industrious tenant who punctually settles his accounts.*'

interested in improving their estates could not easily discover, in the peculiar tenurial structures of those estates, outlets for sound investments of the kind common in England and Scotland, their inability to create suitable outlets was due to lack of enterprise or determination rather than to the absence of actual opportunities. What was needed in Ireland was not the mere imitation of the techniques appropriate to the high farming of England, but the adapting of the general principles of English estate management to Irish conditions. There were outlets in Ireland for investments which were neither trivial nor piecemeal, and whose usefulness was not dependent on the size of farms. Thorough drainage is a good example of this. But landlords could have most usefully invested in schemes to mitigate the shortcomings of small-farm production. They could have financed and supervised the grading and transport of butter, for example; or they could have bought machinery and become agricultural contractors on a large scale.[1] Such an approach to estate investment, anticipating the cooperative movement of later decades, would have been novel by English standards and would have required qualities of management possessed by few landlords and agents in Ireland.

The failure of Irish landlords to invest vigorously in the improvement of their estates was not without its consequences, social as well as economic. The economic consequences are not easy to assess except in terms of fields not drained, dwelling houses not built and farm roads not constructed. It is much more difficult to assess the positive contribution that any of these would have made to increasing either the value of agricultural output or the prosperity of rural society—except in the case of the provision of better dwelling houses.[2] But the social consequences of landlords' failure to invest

[1] For a description of farm machinery see Denton, *Farm home steads of England*, p. 89.

[2] The economic benefits of landlord investment may not have been as great as some contemporaries believed. For differing opinions on returns on agricultural investment, see Robert E. Brown, *The book of the landed estate* (Edinburgh and London, 1869), p. 40; J. D. Chambers and G. E. Mingay, *The*

in their estates was probably more important than the economic ones. By investing in their estates, landlords would have improved their relations with their tenants. Expenditure, if carefully planned, could have eased tenants through bad years, helped them to adjust to changing market conditions and encouraged them to invest on their own account. Even if the return on such investments was small, the fact that rents absorbed such a large portion of agricultural output created the expectation that it was the duty of landlords to put something back into the land. By failing to indulge generously in what may well have been conspicuous waste, landlords missed an opportunity to make their continued existence as a class indispensable to their tenants, or to render their demise regrettable. Such investment would have complicated landlord and tenant relations by mitigating their most obvious characteristic—the starkly simple one-way flow of money from tenants to landlords. Any modification of the prevailing pattern of the distribution of the proceeds of agriculture could only have relieved the conspicuously isolated position of the landlords as a social class. Estate investment, by complicating and obscuring the relationship between landlords and tenants, would have made it more difficult for the tenants to alter that relationship without financial loss.

By the mid-1870s the characteristics of landlords' management of their estates in the generation after the famine were clearly defined. They had failed to exploit rationally the rental capacity of their estates, and they had failed to invest significantly in improvements. Although the landlords had missed many opportunities to exploit their estates more rationally and, at the same time, to bind their tenants more closely to themselves, it is difficult to see how their estate management, fundamentally moderate as it was, could have caused the land war of the late 1870s. Indeed, in the mid-1870s, the possibility of any major conflict in rural society seemed remote.

---

agricultural revolution, 1750–1880 (London, 1966), pp 163–4, and O. Robinson, 'The London companies as progressive landlords in nineteenth-century Ireland', in *Economic History Review*, 2nd ser., xv (1962–3), p. 117.

Statistics of evictions and agrarian outrages were low,[1] and agricultural prices and the value of agricultural output were both high. Only a massive, concerted and clumsy attempt by the landlords to redress the balance of agricultural incomes in their favour by making large increases of rent could, it seemed, disturb the calm of rural society. Although few landlords attempted to do this, the sharp falls in the value of agricultural output in the late 1870s had the same effect on tenants' incomes as drastic increases in rent.[2] In such a crisis, it was almost inevitable that tenants would seek a solution to their problems at the expense of the landlords, and it was at this point that the patterns of estate management of the last thirty years became important. First, the failure of landlords to invest in improvements made it unlikely that tenants would look to such investments to help them to adjust to new market conditions. Secondly, the fact that rents had been the subject of almost endless discussion for the last thirty years meant that attention would concentrate on rents and that the argument would be carried on along the same vague, quasi-moral lines. Thirdly, the simplicity of the existing economic bonds between landlords and tenants left the landlords in a weak bargaining position. If rents had been more flexibly adjusted in the past thirty years, if the principles on which they had been adjusted had been more clearly enunciated and understood, and if a fair proportion of the rents had habitually found their way back into tenants' pockets, a more rational economic approach to the agricultural depression of the 1870s might have taken place.

[1] *Return 'by provinces and counties (compiled from returns made to the inspector general, Royal Irish Constabulary), of cases of evictions which have come to the knowledge of the constabulary in each of the years from 1849 to 1880, inclusive'*, p. 3, H.C. 1881 (185), lxxvii, 727; Irish crime records, 1848–83 (S.P.O., viiib wp, 2/1–2).

[2] In 1879 the value of agricultural output fell to £35·5 millions—a fall of £8 millions from 1876, or the equivalent of a rent increase of 66 per cent.

Origins and development of the land war in mid-Ulster, 1879-85

R. W. KIRKPATRICK

I

MANY factors contributed to the depressed economic and agricultural state of Ireland in 1879. The exceptionally wet weather led to the widespread failure of crops; prices for agricultural produce fell sharply as American competition took its toll; hunger once again began to stalk the Irish peasant as his staple foods became scarce, and the spectre of famine and disease seemed once more to threaten thousands of tenant farmers.

While it is true that the areas worst affected in times of extreme hardship tended to be principally in the west of Ireland, distress was certainly not limited to the western seaboard counties. It is often assumed, incorrectly, that famine, like land agitation, was foreign to other parts of Ireland, and particularly to Ulster. The assumption that Ulster escaped the effects of distress and disturbance is often made on the basis that the 'Ulster custom' insulated the landlords and tenants of that province. In the 1870s and 1880s, however, the 'Ulster custom' was at the root of rapidly developing tenant dissatisfaction, and definition of that nebulous formula was a most controversial issue, particularly in the years immediately preceding the land war of 1879-85. It is surprising to discover that in some respects the Ulster tenants fared worse than their counterparts in the other provinces in the 1870s and early 1880s. While never facing the worst extremes of deprivation experienced in the most westerly areas of Ireland, the tenants of Ulster were in the 1870s paying rents which were often as high as, if not higher than, in the other three provinces. In the early 1880s evictions were actually more frequent in Ulster than elsewhere. It is because agrarian outrages were consistently fewer in number and less serious in nature that Ulster is often dismissed when examining the land war.

Because tenants were often of the same religious persuasion as their landlords in mid-Ulster, it is all too easy to assume that the land league, predominantly catholic in membership elsewhere in Ireland, had little influence in Ulster. This is substantially untrue; moreover, the membership of the league in mid-Ulster was multi-denominational in several areas, and several branches, particularly in County Fermanagh, boasted protestant leaders. The league was most emphatic in advocating a class war, not a denominational or sectarian struggle, in mid-Ulster. The seeds of class antagonism had already been sown in the 1870s after Gladstone's first land act, and the strong tenant-right movement bore witness to the divisions which were widening in the 1870s between landlord and tenant. As early as 1881 this situation was acknowledged to exist; on 2 August in that year the lord chancellor in a parliamentary speech made it quite clear that he regarded Ulster as the cradle of the land agitation of the 1870s:

It was in Ulster if anywhere that this land movement began. It is the greatest error in the world to say that this state of things was due to the land league. The land league was its effect, not its cause. The land league would never have had the power which it acquired if it had had no materials to work upon: the previous state of feeling and opinion; the previous demand for legislative change which existed before the land league, and nowhere more prominently than in Ulster. The significance and importance of this fact are that if any part of Ireland can be called prosperous it is Ulster; if any part is loyal it is Ulster; if any part is more difficult to draw into the vortex of disaffection it is Ulster. Yet in Ulster this desire for change was strongest because of the feeling that the landlord's power to raise the rents might be exercised so as to transfer to the landlord the rights of the tenant.[1]

By 1879 the tenant-right movement was also strong in parts of County Mayo, and it was there that the land league was launched.

---

[1] These remarks were reported and commented upon in *The Times*, 3 Aug. 1881.

The league however took several months—almost a year, in fact—before it had much impact in Ulster, but it was in mid-Ulster that the movement first took root in that province.

It was also in mid-Ulster that the first clashes between the Orange Order and the land league took place in 1880. This development complicated the progress and operation of the land league's campaign in Ulster, and was to broaden and deepen into sectarian and political divisions later in the 1880s. The nature of the land war in Ulster therefore became very different in character to the campaigns which occurred in other parts of the country.

It would however be an over-simplistic interpretation of events to suggest that the tenant-right movement gravitated towards the land league position, or that the campaign of the 1870s simply developed into the land war of 1879–82. The fact is that the areas which most strongly supported the tenant-right movement, particularly County Antrim, were never deeply affected by the land league campaign. The existence of the tenant-right movement, the dissatisfaction with the operation and interpretation of the 'Ulster custom', and the very different proportions of the numerical strength of the various religious denominations, gave the land war in mid-Ulster a unique and none the less positive character, embodying the beginnings of later political and social developments. The origins, escalation and consequences of the land war in mid-Ulster will be examined in detail below.

2

It is almost impossible to define the Ulster custom satisfactorily; and it was this difficulty of definition and interpretation which made the custom so controversial in the 1870s and 1880s. Far from insulating Ulster against agrarian troubles, the custom, in the decade following the 1870 land act, had become the main source of dissatisfaction among Ulster tenant farmers. This dissatisfaction had made itself manifest in the various tenants'-defence and tenant-right associations throughout the province. Admittedly the tenant-right movement was strongest in County Antrim, but it had firmly taken root in mid-Ulster by the end of the 1870s.

Inevitably, with an unwritten custom, local interpretations played a major part in adding to the confusion which attended all discussions on tenant-right, and no two landlords, or for that matter tenants, could be found who could agree on precisely the same definition of the custom. The reason for the controversy in the 1870s was that the 1870 land act had attempted to give the force of law to the Ulster custom; and one major result of the act, in the eyes of the tenant farmers, was that landlords had begun to encroach on the benefits of the custom as practised before 1870. The application of the Ulster custom had always depended heavily on local tradition and the attitude of individual landlords. Now that landlords felt that their rights had been interfered with by Gladstone's land act, they were more inclined to stand by those rights left to them. The tenant-right associations claimed that the consequence of this was greater interference by the landlords in the practice of the custom and an ever-increasing number of 'office rules' or 'estate rules' which limited the value of the custom on many estates. The confusion over the subject was all the more acute when one considers that interpretations of the Ulster custom ranged from one extreme, where landlords insisted that it was no more than a limited payment made by an incoming to an outgoing tenant for his interest in the farm, to the other, where tenants claimed that the custom guaranteed them the 'three Fs': fair rent, fixity of tenure and free sale of their improvements on the holding. To understand fully the seriousness of the controversy which was erupting in Ulster in the 1870s it is necessary to take a closer look at some widely differing but fairly representative views of the problem.

Thomas Shillington, chairman of the Antrim Tenant Farmers Association, was one of the first to voice strong opinions on the Ulster custom in the 1870s, and from his association sprang many others throughout the province. He had a clear definition of what he believed the Ulster custom ought to be: 'continued occupancy at an easy and unrestricted right of disposal'.[1] He felt that any dilution of this formula was automatically an encroachment on the rights of the tenant; as far as he could see, his definition of the Ulster custom was simply not in operation on any estate, and this was the root cause of the dissatisfaction which his organisation ought to articulate. He summarised the situation as follows.

The relations of landlord and tenant as they exist in the north of Ireland are strained and unsatisfactory as far as the tenants are concerned; ... the tenant under the present law is entirely under the control of his landlord ... He cannot bargain freely as to the conditions of his holding ... and there is great misapprehension and uncertainty as to the character of a future land-lord in the case of a change of landlords.[2]

Samuel McElroy, of the Antrim Central Tenants' Rights Association, had explained the situation in much the same way as Shillington but had gone further in alleging that resolutions passed by tenant-right conferences in 1870, 1874 and 1880 had been ignored by the landlords. He was forthright in his condemnation of the encroachment on the value of the Ulster custom by the implementation of arbitrary office rules by many landlords in Ulster.[3]

For the majority of Ulster tenant farmers in the 1870s rents and evictions had not been a major grievance, for rents were not generally high and evictions were few in comparison to other provinces. Was it, then, that the spokesmen of the tenant-right organisations were justified in their accusations? The answer to this question is as difficult to find as a clear definition of the Ulster custom. As with the practice of the custom, the abuses were just as localised and as hard to define. The fact was that conditions varied not simply from county to county, or barony to barony, but from estate to estate. The custom, going back as it did to the seventeenth century, had altered with political and social conditions and necessi-

---

[1] *Report of the commission of inquiry into the working of the Landlord and Tenant (Ireland) Act, 1870, and the amending acts: minutes of evidence*, 1881 [C 2779], H.C. 1881, xix. This report is hereafter referred to as *Bessborough commission*, and page references are to the printed pagination of the minutes of evidence.
[2] *Bessborough commission*, p. 186.   [3] Ibid., pp 159–62.

ties. James Morton, a Belfast solicitor, defined the origins and difficulties of interpretation as follows:

I conceive that it consists of the right of the tenant to sell subject to the approval of the landlord. I also consider that it consists of an implied contract that the tenant is not to be rackrented, and not to be disturbed as long as he pays a fair rent. I conceive the origin of it to have been the equity of certain landlords, denoting that those men were planted there for a particular purpose—I think it arose in that way, I have read a great deal on the subject and I have never regarded it as having any other origin . . .

I think it is at present very unsatisfactory. I regard the custom as involving, if it is worth anything, fixity of tenure at a fair rent. It is either that or it is nothing. I regard it as unsatisfactory inasmuch as there is no means of ascertaining what that fair rent is or ought to be.[1]

One of the factors which had altered the practice and value of the Ulster custom was the development, following the 1870 land act, of lapsed leases. Many tenants, fearing with some justification that landlords might exclude them from the benefits of the act by a clause in a renewed lease, opted instead to let their option on a new lease lapse and become tenants-at-will. W. D. Henderson, in a lecture delivered to the National Reform Union, Manchester, in 1877, underlined the importance of this trend. He explained that Ulster tenant-right had predominated for centuries, and while it had, in the eighteenth century, applied almost exclusively to leaseholders, its application by the second half of the nineteenth century had changed radically. As fifty-year leases ran out, many not being renewed, three-quarters of the tenants in Ulster enjoyed tenant-right but were not leaseholders. By the 1870s, Henderson claimed, most of these tenants, while nominally secure, were really tenants-at-will. By this change, he suggested, the whole nature of the Ulster custom had been altered.[2]

At almost the same time as Henderson delivered his lecture, the

---

[1] Ibid., p. 175.

[2] Henderson's lecture was later published as part of a pamphlet on the Irish land acts and the Ulster custom by the Ulster Tenants' Defence Association (Belfast, 1898).

Ulster Tenants' Defence Association gave their definition of the Ulster custom, differentiating clearly between tenant-right and the custom:

Tenant-right: the sum paid to an outgoing tenant for the value of his good-will and improvements, temporary and permanent, on a farm.

Ulster custom: the practice of allowing a tenant to sell his tenant-right to the highest bidder—to levy no more rent than the original value of the land before tenant improvements, that is, to allow the value of the improvements to go to the improver while the landlord may have no claim in rent on them from the next tenant, or pre-empt from the outgoing tenant at the lowest-bid price for the tenant-right. If the landlord should want the farm back, he must bid for it in the open market.[1]

Many landlords disagreed with this definition in that it virtually granted the 'three Fs' to the tenants and greatly diminished the land-owner's powers. In practice the Ulster custom, especially in mid-Ulster, meant little more than the payment of tenant-right at the vacation of a holding. The divergence of opinion over the interpretation left many tenants unsure of their rights under the custom; after 1870 the situation became more rather than less ambiguous. This point was made later in the speech of the lord chancellor (referred to above) when he replied to the leader of the opposition (Sir Stafford Northcote):

I was very much struck by what ... the leader of the opposition ... said yesterday ... that in the case of the Ulster custom there was always the absolute power of the landlord in the background to raise the rent. But that is the very thing which is causing irritation. The people have felt that by the legislation of 1870 you had recognised their rights and not defined them but left them to be indefinitely taken away from them whether by en-croachment or otherwise; ... they felt that they were liable to have their rights diminished and encroached upon by the exercise, unlimited and un-controlled, of the landlord's power to raise the rent which, consistently with the Ulster custom, he was not entitled to do ... There is now in Ulster, whether or not the landlords have used that power unjustly, the greatest amount of uneasiness, dissatisfaction and sense of insecurity.[2]

[1] Ibid.   [2] *The Times*, 3 Aug. 1881.

The 'sense of insecurity' referred to was born of two weaknesses in the practice of the Ulster custom. The first was that although security for the tenant existed, to the extent that he was certain to receive compensation for improvements made to his farm, he was not guaranteed freedom from eviction. This did not matter greatly while evictions remained low during the 1860s and 1870s; but when the rate of eviction suddenly increased, to the point where Ulster had the highest number of evictions for any province in 1880, the tenant suddenly realised his vulnerability. The second weakness lay in the practice of deducting arrears from the money received for his tenant-right when an evicted tenant vacated his holding. This left him unable to bid for another farm and little better off than his counterparts in Munster and Connacht. Added to this the landlords in some areas sought to pre-empt the tenants' interests by forcibly buying them out when they fell into arrears. This payment of tenant-right did not take place at auction but as a method of avoiding eviction and all the legal processes involved. In these ways the Ulster custom had become abused by the late 1870s and early 1880s.

Even the more liberal landlords in mid-Ulster (for instance, Hugh de Fellenburg Montgomery, Sir Victor Brooke, Lord Erne, Lord Belmore and the duke of Abercorn) saw serious disadvantages in the system of payment of tenant-right, although they allowed the practice of the Ulster custom to take place quite freely on their estates. They maintained that unfettered bargaining and uncontrolled prices for tenant-right were actually disadvantageous to the tenant farmer in that he had to encumber himself with a substantial bank loan at the start of his tenancy to enable him to pay tenant-right to the outgoing occupier. Montgomery in particular argued that very often the loan repayment would be higher than the annual rent paid by the tenants; in bad seasons, therefore, the bank would have to be paid but the landlord was made to wait for his rent. These landlords were however perceptive enough to realise that the advantages of the Ulster custom outweighed the difficulties and made their tenants, in general, more prosperous and secure.

Even the duke of Abercorn, whose liberality as a landlord was legendary, attempted to limit the amount paid for tenant-right on his estate, although he was aware that private deals often took place. He tried to protect tenants from excessive bank loans by placing a limit of five or ten years' purchase on all transactions, but his rent-books show that in reality anything between eighteen and fifty-four years' purchase was paid.[1] Any fault that tenants had to find with the duke lay in this limitation; he was never a landlord to pre-empt or to raise rents arbitrarily at the change of tenancy, so little dissatisfaction was found on his estates in Londonderry, Donegal and Tyrone.

Two of the most experienced land agents in mid-Ulster, Richard Brush and Frederick Wrench, giving evidence before the Bessborough commission, insisted that the Ulster custom was practised on most large estates in their areas (Tyrone and Fermanagh), and that only minor office rules interfered with the operation of the custom. They both agreed that it would be in the tenants' interests to restrict the amount of tenant-right paid, but realised that it was impractical to attempt to impose any such rule. Brush however admitted that on Lord Belmore's estates no auction was permitted. Arbitrators could be appointed but the landlord had to approve of the incoming tenant. There had been no complaints under this system, and arrears rarely occurred on the estates. Apart from approving the incoming tenant, Brush maintained that the estate office was really only interested in securing the annual rent and was not interested in restricting the practice of the Ulster custom beyond the points mentioned.[2] All the mid-Ulster land agents who gave evidence insisted that they never charged tenants for their own improvements, and that where this practice occurred it was usually on smaller estates and those purchased under the encumbered estates act.

[1] Evidence of limitations on tenant-right is found in *Bessborough commission*, p, 587; information on secret deals and extent of tenant-right purchases comes from *The Times*, 28 Jan. 1881, and Abercorn estate papers, rentals, P.R.O.N.I., D 2400/21/1.
[2] *Bessborough commission*, p. 241.

Frederick Wrench, however, made the point that although the Ulster custom was practised, in his experience, in Tyrone, Fermanagh, Armagh, Cavan, Monaghan and in some parts of Louth, the practices varied from estate to estate. In particular he explained that on Sir Victor Brooke's Fermanagh estates no payment was permitted for the goodwill of the tenant farmer, only the tenant-right on improvements. Auctions were not permitted on Sir Victor's estates, but a system of arbitration was in force. This, he claimed, gave no cause for complaint, as the landlord was generous and the tenants had great security. Moreover, the tenant-right paid on these estates tended to be almost double that realised by public auction, which he described as a 'lottery'.[1]

While tenants on estates such as Lord Belmore's and Sir Victor Brooke's were virtually guaranteed security and relative prosperity as long as they paid their rent, there were tenants whose situation was not nearly as fortunate. The Reverend Charles Quin, parish priest of Camlough, County Armagh, and president of Camlough Tenant-right Association, complained of serious and deliberate invasions of the rights of tenants over forty years, culminating in a critical erosion of the fabric of the Ulster custom since the 1870 land act. He maintained that although the custom was practised in most areas of Tyrone and Armagh there were widespread abuses, particularly on the smaller and mountain farms. While defining the Ulster custom as 'the right from time immemorial of Ulster tenants to their farms and improvements thereon, subject to the proprietary rights of the landlords',[2] he recognised that landlords had specific rights such as the fee simple rental and the rights to mines and quarries. He found fault not only with landlords who over-extended their rights to the detriment of tenants but also with the land act, which failed to define the very custom which was at the basis of unrest in Ulster: 'the Ulster custom in its integrity has not been defined in the land act, and I have never seen a definition of it yet.'[3]

According to Fr Quin there were several flagrant violations of the

---

[1] Ibid., p. 199.   [2] Ibid., p. 205.   [3] Ibid.

spirit of the Ulster custom in the mid-Ulster area. These violations were not limited to any one type of landlord, but the majority of serious cases arose on smaller estates purchased after 1850. The earl of Castlestuart had only recently sullied the long-standing good name of his family by increasing rents in a new valuation by up to 500 per cent. This had wiped out the value of Ulster custom at a single stroke, claimed Fr Quin, and the increase had affected not only the catholic tenants on smaller upland Tyrone farms but also the relatively more prosperous protestant tenant-farmers on the more fertile lowland holdings. Tenant-right, goodwill and tenant improvements had been set at naught by this move. Sir John Stewart, also of Tyrone, had been equally guilty, in Fr Quin's opinion, of raising rents to the detriment of the Ulster custom. Tenants had however resisted a second attempt at rent-raising in the 1870s, and Sir John's efforts to increase the rents proved fruitless. Nevertheless one result of poor landlord-tenant relations on the estate was one of the highest levels of arrears anywhere in Ulster by the end of the 1870s and up to the mid-1880s.[1]

Thomas Shillington, whose opinions on the Ulster custom are cited above, bears out a substantial part of Fr Quin's argument in detailing a trip through Armagh in the late 1870s. Limitation of prices paid for tenant-right, say to £5 per acre, was only symptomatic of the ills endured by tenants on the estates where these limitations were imposed. Shillington claimed that on at least four estates in Armagh—those of Mrs Bacon of Richhill, Major Blacker, the duke of Manchester and Lord Lurgan—not only was tenant-right limited but rent-raising and office rules further restricted the rights and freedom of the tenantry. Where landlords allowed full practice of tenant-right, argued Shillington, farms were neat, orderly, well-cultivated and prosperous. Where restrictions were in force the holdings were slovenly and neglected; the tenants were

[1] Ibid., p. 206 and Stewart estate papers, rentals, P.R.O.N.I., D 1716/3/A and B. It is interesting to note that Sir John Stewart's estate in Carrickmore was let at a much higher rent than his Ballygawley property, where leases were more common and arrears lower in the period 1876–83.

apprehensive of rent increases and postponed improvements in fear of revaluations.[1] Shillington singled out the Carrickblacker estate for criticism, for its very high rents and restrictions on the practice of the Ulster custom. Although Major Blacker's rents were somewhat above Griffith's valuation,[2] no serious difficulties were reflected in the estate rentals; moreover definite records of up to sixteen years' purchase as a price for tenant-right exist in those rentals.[3] Shillington in this instance may have been generalising from a particular case or overstating his complaints; his general comments, however, regarding rent-raising and revaluations, office rules and restrictions are for the most part borne out by the facts.

In his evidence Shillington cited another important grievance which had arisen during the 1870s and which was also connected with the dissatisfaction over the practice of the Ulster custom. On the duke of Manchester's Armagh estates, tenants were forbidden to make improvements on their farms and tenant-right was strictly limited to £5 an acre. Improvements where necessitated would be carried out by the duke's agent; but no such improvements had been made in twenty years since the rule had first been implemented (it was revived in the 1870s). This situation again led to a deterioration of farms, illicit tenant-right deals and dissatisfaction on the estate. Judging by the amount of arrears and non-payment on that estate, Shillington's claim may have had more than a little substance.[4]

The grumbling which had grown common in the 1870s might have remained at that level had it not been for the disastrous harvest of 1879–80. Hugh de Fellenburg Montgomery, who recognised the value of the Ulster custom and its advantages for the tenants on the well-run estates of Tyrone and Fermanagh, foresaw two developments at the end of the 1870s. His great fear was that, in the long-term, escalating tenant right transactions, whether legitimate or

---

[1] *Bessborough commission*, p. 187.
[2] See below, p. 219.
[3] Blacker estate papers, rentals, P.R.O.N.I., D 1252/14/1 and 2.
[4] *Bessborough commission*, p. 187; Manchester estate papers, rentals, P.R.O.N.I. D 1248/R38–50.

not, would precipitate an economic crisis whereby the running of the country would pass into the hands of financiers who would be less benevolent and tolerant than the existing class of landlords. Secondly, Montgomery foresaw further unrest developing into the 1880s.

Some landlords who had been tolerably considerate before the land act . . . seem to have considered that, law having taken the place of custom and mutual confidence, they were at liberty to get all the law allowed them out of the tenants. These extortions were suffered by the few, and feared by the many, with a moderate amount of grumbling as long as the fine seasons and high prices lasted, but when the late series of bad harvests and low prices arrived the victims saw themselves threatened with ruin; in the south with eviction for non-payment of rent, without compensation; in the north with the reduction to little or nothing of the value of their tenant-right.[1]

3

Towards the end of September 1879 it was obvious in many parts of Ireland that the disastrous harvest and the abnormally wet weather were going to cause widespread distress during the winter. Traditionally the Atlantic seaboard counties had always suffered worst in times of famine or hardship and at first 1879 seemed to be no different. Distress, however, was by no means universal, and press and politicians of the establishment saw no undue cause for alarm. Their view, backed up by the opinion of many landlords, was that a difficult winter might be experienced in the poorest and most remote areas of Ireland but that the degree of hardship was being greatly exaggerated for political purposes by the propagandists of the home-rule party.

As the winter progressed and the extent of distress became apparent it was finally admitted that 1879 had been the worst season since the great famine. Local reports from boards of guardians, local government inspectors and provincial newspapers made it plain that

[1] Hugh de F. Montgomery, *Irish land and Irish rights* (London, 1881), pp 10–11.

certain areas were experiencing severe distress and that those regions were not confined to the west coast. Even mid-Ulster, which traditionally had escaped the worst excesses of bad seasons, was badly hit. The widespread flooding of the Erne basin, particularly in Cavan and Fermanagh, the failure of the potato and fruit crops in most of mid-Ulster, the floods in Armagh and the general effect of poor crop yields in all the mid-Ulster counties were beginning to take their toll. The greatest problems in Tyrone, for example, were lack of employment, scarcity of fuel and increasing instances of hunger, especially on the hill and mountain farms. Fermanagh and Armagh had many instances of farms under feet of water which temporarily deprived hundreds of tenant farmers of both shelter and food. With the rent due on most farms on 1 November and 1 May, the anxiety among tenants became greater as the gale day approached. In February 1880 two fairly typical petitions from tenants in mid-Ulster were made to the lord lieutenant. The first was from the parish of Ballygawley in County Tyrone:

Our district in conjunction with the rest of Ireland has severely suffered by reason of the wet summer of last year, the bad harvests of the last three years and the low price of stock. Our turf is still in the bog—our potatoes at the best were a missed crop, and the few we kept for seed the exigencies of our families compelled us to eat. Our corn too was far below the average, the consequence being that there is a greal deal of suffering amongst us. We are unable, without borrowing to meet our rents, and the credit with our shops is collapsed.[1]

In the latter paragraphs of the petition the tenants (whose plea was written by the local rector, the Reverend Thomas Adderley) argued that the situation was now beyond their own power to remedy as their landlords were absentees and there was no employment available. As they were reluctant to give up their holdings to enter workhouses or to beg, they pleaded with the lord lieutenant to order

---

[1] Petition from the tenant farmers of Ballygawley to the duke of Marlborough, lord lieutenant of Ireland, 13 Feb. 1880 (S.P.O., C.S.O., R.P. 1880 10176/3922).

relief works for the area to protect them from ruin and starvation. The second petition, from Findrum, County Tryone, was in a similar vein but made a practical suggestion for relief works:

We suffer great inconvenience through there being no road through our land—nothing better than mere paths—and we are so situated that we obtain very little benefit from existing public roads . . . there is scarcely any other part of our district so ill off for a road . . . The present distress is acutely felt by us and it is with the utmost difficulty that we shall be enabled to retain our holdings or to preserve our lives. Therefore we pray your excellency to direct a road to be made . . . at the same time it will give employment to the distressed in this place.[1]

The problem was exacerbated by agricultural and economic trends in Ireland in the late 1870s. Not only was the acreage under crops diminishing at this time but the yield per acre was gradually declining towards its lowest point, which was reached in 1879. Prices were falling rapidly, a trend which was accelerated and then aggravated by the influx of cheap American grain and abundant harvests in America in the late 1870s. The butter market had become severely restricted by the backwardness of methods in Ireland and the advance of other European countries in marketing dairy produce. In Ulster the decrease in area under crops and the yield per acre of both cereals and root-crops had been sharper than in the other provinces. The sharp decline, particularly in the potato crop, had brought a substantial degree of hardship to farmers, but most notably to small tenant farmers, in Ulster.[2]

[1] Petition from the tenant farmers of Findrum, County Tyrone, to the duke of Marlborough, lord lieutenant of Ireland, 13 Feb. 1880 (S.P.O., C.S.O., R.P. 1880 10176/3883).

[2] Observations on crops and yields per acre for the late 1870s are derived from the parliamentary papers and official reports for the period, in particular the following. *Agricultural statistics for Ireland for 1879: tables showing the extent in statute acres and the produce of the crops*, pp 2 ff [C 3068], H.C. 1881, xciii, 825; *Agricultural statistics of Ireland for 1879*, pp 2 ff [C 2534], H.C. 1880, lxxvi, 815; *Preliminary reports of the returns of agricultural produce in Ireland*, pp 2 ff [C 2495], 1880, H.C. lxxvi, table V, 899. Interesting comments on the state of agriculture in Ireland at the time, which have been taken into account in my

During the next few months distress became more common in mid-Ulster, with cases of extreme hardship and poverty being reported in parts of Donegal, Fermanagh, Tyrone, Cavan and Armagh. As the situation deteriorated the reactions of landlords became extremely important to the condition of tenants all over the country, not only in mid-Ulster. The reactions varied from an immediate granting of substantial rent abatements and the distribution of food and clothing to a refusal to assist tenants who had benefited in good seasons and who must now accept the hardship which accompanied a less productive season. The earl of Erne, Hugh de Fellenburg Montgomery, J. G. V. Porter, and Captain Collum, all holding estates in Fermanagh and Tyrone, granted abatements and assistance to their tenants without being first petitioned.

As the spring of 1880 approached and rent abatement petitions proliferated, many other landlords reacted favourably, although many of them found themselves in financial difficulties in so doing. The earl of Enniskillen (Fermanagh), the earl of Charlemont (Armagh and Tyrone) and James Price (Down) all fell into the second category of landlords, those who believed that tenants should have provided for bad seasons when prices and harvests were good. Their main argument stemmed from the complaint that landlords had not sought to levy additional rent when seasons were favourable but were now expected to reduce the rent in harder times. It was in the conditions which prevailed in 1879–80 that the controversy over the Ulster custom reached its height, as those landlords who refused abatements often maintained that they were losing their rents while the banks were receiving their repayments on loans advanced for tenant-right purchases. It was also at this juncture that leaseholders felt most discriminated against, as they were usually excluded from rent abatements on the grounds that they had contracted to pay a fixed

---

observations, can be found in Michael Davitt, *The fall of feudalism in Ireland* (London and New York, 1904), p. 187; N. D. Palmer, *The Irish land league crisis* (New Haven and London, 1940), p. 64; the *Lisbellaw Gazette, Tyrone Constitution, Fermanagh Impartial Reporter, The Times, Irish Times* and other local and national newspapers.

rent for a fixed period and should therefore be in a more advantageous position than the yearly tenant.

It is worth examining some of the developments in Fermanagh and Tyrone at this time to acquire a clearer picture of why the land war developed in mid-Ulster from 1880 on. Among the most generous landlords of the area it was assumed automatically that their duty was to assist their tenants in every possible way. The earl of Erne not only granted rent abatements and gave free seed and fuel but gave detailed instructions to his tenants on how to improve the making of butter so that it could compete with foreign imports and yield some much-needed income.[1] He was also one of the leading lights in promoting the Erne drainage scheme, which would not only improve the land but should prevent future flooding. In this plan he was joined by the earl of Belmore, J. G. V. Porter, Sir Victor Brooke, Captain Collum, Captain Archdale and John Porter Porter; between them the drainage project was instituted and carried out with great success and benefit to all in the area.[2] J. G. V. Porter wrote a series of articles in the *Lisbellaw Gazette* with a view to helping tenants and promoting understanding throughout the local community on social and economic issues.[3]

Despite the genuine efforts of these landlords, and the many others whose generosity was regularly reported in local and national journals, the severity of the 1879–80 season brought great difficulties for landlord and tenant alike. Rents, despite abatements, often went unpaid and arrears mounted alarmingly. Tenants feared eviction and the income of many landlords was severely reduced, making further acts of generosity even more difficult. It was in response to this situation that the land league gradually spread in mid-Ulster; as arrears mounted, evictions increased to unprecedented heights and fear of the land league among landlords led to further threats of eviction. Many local newspapers condemned Parnell, home rule

[1] Erne estate papers, P.R.O.N.I., D 1939/4; *Tyrone Constitution*, 9 Jan. 1880.
[2] *Irish Times*, 4 Aug. and 25 Oct. 1879.
[3] *Lisbellaw Gazette*, 1 Mar., 1 Aug. 1879; 17 Feb., 16 Mar., 4 May, 7 Sept. 1880.

and the 'communistic' land league; while some of them had openly espoused the tenants' cause throughout the crisis, none of them openly advocated support of the league or Parnell, with the occasional exception of the *Fermanagh Impartial Reporter*. Agents began to worry over the extent of landlord generosity as 1880 progressed, and often felt that tenants were being intimidated into non-payment of rent by the league. Even on one of mid-Ulster's best-managed estates the agent Frederick Wrench wrote to a neighbour: 'If you once begin giving an allowance on an estate it is so hard to draw the line—if I suggested an allowance I should be more inclined to recommend help being given in the spring in the shape of seed to those who pay up all the rent due now by a certain date.'[1]

Once the question of arrears and evictions is raised, of course, the whole subject of the level of rents, Griffith's valuation, manner of payment, rent raising and the economic situation of the tenant demands to be analysed. While it is not possible to elaborate at length on this intricate topic, a brief examination at least must be undertaken to understand what lay at the basis of the land war in mid-Ulster.

Definition of a 'fair rent' is notoriously difficult; the problems start to arise when an adequate criterion is sought. In the late nineteenth century the search for such a criterion bedevilled all discussions on the nature and levels of rents. Inevitably such discussions went deeper to the very fundamentals of land ownership and the nature of tenancy, not to mention the political undertones which could be brought to any debate on the matter. Michael Davitt, for example, believing in the theory of land nationalisation but subordinating it for the duration of the land war to the land league's policy of peasant proprietary, felt that the state should own all land and let it out to farmers at perhaps ten per cent of its annual value in crop yields. Montgomery, the Fermanagh landlord, also influenced by Mill in his approach to land, felt that the theory of

[1] Wrench to Bailie, 22 Dec. 1880; Brooke estate papers, out-letter books, P.R.O.N.I., D 998/6/1.

'political economy' was not irreconcilable with a system of benevolent landlordism where the land should be made to produce its maximum to the benefit of both landlord and tenant, and where neither should be penalised by an unfair rent system. More conservative landlords, such as Lords Charlemont and Annesley, believed in the immutability of the fundamental laws governing the rights of landlords to charge, more or less, what they pleased for their land and to change tenants rather than levels of rent. In between, the vast majority of landlords and tenants seemed to refer regularly to Griffith's valuation as the only trustworthy criterion for arriving at a fair rent—the landlords accepting 30 per cent above the valuation as the optimum rent level and the tenants holding fast to the valuation as it stood.

Given that there were several irreconcilable points of view on rent levels it is not surprising therefore that arguments should have centred around Griffith's valuation, controversial though it might have been. In reality most of the medium and large estates in mid-Ulster were rented at a figure not all that much at variance with Griffith: most of them fell into the region of 10 per cent below to 20 per cent above his figures. Arguments about rent were, naturally, complicated by the widely-held belief among landlords that Griffith's valuation, made in the 1850s, was out of date and at variance with current prices for agricultural produce, and moreover was never intended to be a direct guide to rent levels. Despite all these shortcomings, however, the valuation was the criterion most cited by all parties in discussions on rent. While most landlords regarded 30 per cent above Griffith as a 'fair rent' the earl of Erne, seeking to clarify the situation, was informed by Griffith himself that, not taking tenants' improvements into consideration, the rent he would regard as fair should be between 10 and 15 per cent above his valuation.[1] Even this information was largely irrelevant in the 1870s, when prices were between 25 and 90 per cent above the 1850s

---

[1] Sir Richard Griffith to Lord Erne, 22 Nov. 1858, quoted in *Lisbellaw Gazette*, 20 Feb. 1882.

figures. When prices began to fall in the late 1870s and early 1880s the whole discussion became even more confused, and each side to the argument tended to use Griffith and to interpret his findings exactly as it pleased. The extent of the divergence can be observed when one considers that Davitt regarded rents at the level of Griffith's valuation to be '50 per cent rackrents', while landlords such as Lord Lifford believed them to be extremely favourable to the tenants when set at 25 per cent above the valuation.[1]

It was clear therefore that other criteria had to be employed to find the elusive 'fair rent'. These included ability to pay, weather, crop yields, agricultural prices and output, allowances and gifts from landlords, and many others. As rents in Ireland were levied on the land at a fixed rate and not as in England where the farm including buildings was rented, or in Scotland where half the annual rent was calculated on crop prices, arguments over rents tended, as with the Ulster custom, to vary from area to area and estate to estate as conditions differed.

Statistically the landlords and the Irish land committee, which often voiced their viewpoint through pamphlets and articles, could prove that prices in the 1870s and 1880s were not all that far behind the best years of the 1850s and in certain seasons were in excess of them. Spasmodic depressions did however hit the market in 1879–80 and in several seasons in the 1880s.[2] The ability of the tenant to pay rents, therefore, should not have been seriously impaired by a few bad seasons. One Ulster landlord, who preferred to remain anonymous, argued that tenants had for years been putting 35 per cent of his income in their pockets and were now complaining because their profit had been cut back. While these statistical arguments may be true in general, they do not, of course, allow for extreme individual cases. It is beyond dispute that in 1879–80 large numbers of tenants in mid-Ulster simply could not pay their rent at all. This occurred

---

[1] Davitt, speech in Belfast, 15 Nov. 1882 (S.P.O., R.I.C. reports 1882–4, carton 1/c) and Lord Lifford to editor, *The Times*, 10 Nov. 1879.
[2] Mulhall, *History of prices* (London, 1885), p. 123.

on the smaller holdings in Cavan, where the earl of Annesley could collect virtually no rent from his estate in the wretchedly poor Glangevlin area; it was also true of the flooded farms in Fermanagh and Armagh, not to mention the hill-farms in Tyrone where starvation stared many poorer tenants in the face and disease became rife. Inability to pay in the 1879–80 season was recognised in their 10 to 20 per cent abatements by Montgomery, Brooke, Lord Erne and others who foresaw disaster if some allowance were not immediately made. Later on, it is true, agitators encouraged rent abatement petitions and witholding of rents; but as the first reductions were made by resident landlords who had not been petitioned, the situation of the poorer tenantry was undoubtedly giving cause for concern even in the autumn of 1879.

In general tenants admitted that rents were not too high to pay in average seasons but where landlords had ordered revaluations or increases at the fall of leases then poverty was a real prospect. At first, in fact, there was no great unwillingness to pay rents, but from 1880 onward a definite reluctance was shown on many estates. The spontaneous pleas for rent abatements in 1879–80 became a weapon in the arsenal of land agitators from mid-1880 onwards, and landlords began to complain that their often unsolicited generosity in 1879 was being repaid by unwarranted demands for reductions in the 1880 and 1881 seasons when harvests were much better. The agents of the earl of Annesley, the earl of Charlemont and Sir William Verner found it very difficult to extract rents from unwilling tenants whom they deemed to be perfectly capable of paying in 1880 and 1881. Arrears had certainly mounted in 1879–80 and threatened to worsen in 1880. Landlords who could not understand why they were being deprived of their income for a second year were less reluctant to evict recalcitrant tenants, and, coupled with apprehension and the spreading land agitation, this may explain the veritable explosion in evictions in Ulster in 1880–1.

On the other hand, it is of great interest to note that those landlords who had been most sympathetic to their tenants in 1879–80 and who had met them, discussed their difficulties and advised against using the land league as a vehicle for their grievances were generally left undisturbed during the land war. The land league in mid-Ulster tended to direct its campaign against landlords who were absentees, had not given abatements or had raised rents in the late 1870s. It is to this matter of how the land war developed in mid-Ulster that we must now turn.

4

Evictions, non-payment of rent, arrears, agrarian outrages, land meetings and the growth in membership and activities of the land league comprise the elements of the land war most closely ex-amined by historians and considered most likely to yield statistical correlations. Such an analysis of the mid-Ulster situation provides some interesting and perhaps unexpected results. It has already been mentioned that Ulster had a disproportionately high number of evictions in 1880–81. It is less surprising but no less significant that Ulster consistently exhibited the lowest figures for agrarian crime throughout the land war period.

The real crux of the matter lies in the statistics for the years 1879–83. With the exception of 1876 Ulster had experienced fewer evictions than the other provinces for many years. It might be assumed that Munster and Connacht had the greatest number of evictions once the land war started; but, rather surprisingly, this was not so, particularly in the early stages. Between 1879 and 1880 evictions of families in Ulster almost trebled, whereas the increase elsewhere was more gradual. By 1881 Ulster had the greatest num-ber of evicted families, 1219, which was between 70 and 80 per cent above the other provinces. Again, Ulster preceded (and perhaps anticipated) the national trend by having fewer evictions in 1882; by 1883 the statistical pattern had returned to what had become normal prior to 1879. More curious still, it was not in the worst hit western areas of Ulster that evictions were most frequent; neither was it in the areas where the land league became strongest; rather it was Tyrone that led the statistical trend, followed by Donegal, Monaghan and Armagh respectively. On the other hand, up to 87 per cent of evicted families in Ulster were reinstated as caretakers with perhaps six months or a year to redeem themselves, whereas it was unusual to find more than a 50 per cent reinstatement rate in Munster or Connacht.[1]

This latter trend of course raises the question of why landlords evicted tenants in Ulster. The answer is not as readily available as the figures for evictions. It would appear that many landlords did not evict simply for non-payment of rent, although this was almost always the stated cause (when such explanation was given). As many landowners had tolerated relatively high levels of arrears in the 1870s the reason for eviction must have been deeper. It is probable that several factors combined to cause such numerous ejectments. Firstly, arrears had not only mounted for two seasons but showed no signs of diminishing, and landlords feared for their own financial position which had also been made difficult by the bad seasons. Secondly, there appears to have been an attempt made to prevent tenants from joining the land league by using the weapon of eject-ment process, not necessarily with the intention of depriving the tenant permanently of his holding. This policy was certainly carried out on the estates of the earls of Charlemont, Annesley and Gosford in various parts of mid-Ulster, and their agents admitted as much in the correspondence. The third reason was that many landlords feared the forthcoming land legislation and the degree to which rents might be reduced: faced, therefore, with the permanent loss of the unpaid rents, they sought to recover what they could before it was too late. Interestingly, it appears that few evictions were executed simply for membership of the league or as reprisal for sympathy with it. The fact that the eviction weapon was used to

---

[1] Figures for evictions and reinstatements are quoted or calculated from parliamentary papers for the years 1880 to 1887, e.g. *Returns of cases of evictions in Ireland . . . showing the number of families and persons evicted in each county and the number readmitted as tenants and as caretakers, 1880*, p. 3, H.C. 1881 (2), lxxvii, 713.

discourage membership could well account for the sudden increase in evictions in Ulster before the other provinces. As the league took longer to spread in Ulster the landlords could see what was happening in the west and south and wished to forestall such developments in their province. More correctly it was more often the agents who foresaw developments and advised the landlords, many of whom were unwilling to be harsh, to take a sterner line in their own interests.

Agrarian outrages in Ulster, and particularly mid-Ulster, were comparatively low, and although the statistics show that the other three provinces always experienced higher numbers of such crimes there is still a coincidental rise and fall in the figures as the land war progressed. More important, perhaps, is the fact that violent agrarian outrages occurred only rarely in mid-Ulster. Tyrone, with the highest eviction figures, never had a wave of violent crime during the period. Perhaps one thorny problem can, however, be at least partially solved: the correlation between evictions and outrages. With the length of time taken to serve ejectment notices, evictions normally followed their causes by an interval of at least a year; as outrages tended to increase in Ulster approximately one year after a rise in evictions this possible correlation can be virtually discounted. It appears rather that outrages followed the agitation which resulted from widespread evictions, and the majority of these outrages were classed as 'intimidation'. There is however another side to agrarian disturbances in Ulster during the land war: as urban outrages were not included in agrarian crime figures, much of the violence which

Agrarian outrages in Ireland, 1879–87, by provinces

	1879	1880	1881	1882	1883	1884	1885	1886	1887
Ulster	111	259	414	320	89	76	67	88	61
Leinster	147	351	833	732	184	140	156	114	108
Munster	136	1019	1957	1500	446	429	568	631	493
Connacht	476	961	1235	881	151	117	153	223	221
Total	870	2590	4439	3433	870	762	944	1056	883

Agrarian outrages in Ulster, 1879–87

	1879	1880	1881	1882	1883	1884	1885	1886	1887
Homicide	3	1	0	0	0	0	0	0	1
Assault	18	12	9	15	6	2	2	5	12
Arson	8	21	0	22	15	14	9	10	9
Intimidation*	70	179	247	206	45	36	40	34	24
Other	13	46	158	77	23	24	16	39	15

* Includes intimidation by threatening letter or notice.

Agrarian outrages in Ulster, by counties, 1879–87, with corresponding figures for Kerry and Galway

	1879	1880	1881	1882	1883	1884	1885	1886	1887
Antrim	1	15	16	13	7	2	3	2	1
Armagh	8	39	18	20	8	4	1	2	5
Cavan	37	73	95	92	23	16	19	14	4
Donegal	25	52	119	58	10	22	7	9	8
Down	10	20	22	14	3	4	6	5	4
Fermanagh	4	6	28	22	10	8	8	9	6
Londonderry	7	14	24	20	6	6	12	13	15
Monaghan	8	19	52	22	19	9	8	12	7
Tyrone	11	21	40	59	3	5	3	22	11
Ulster	111	259	414	320	89	76	67	88	61
Kerry	14	298	401	347	146	117	180	209	108
Galway	180	402	487	349	56	43	79	116	110
Ireland	870	2590	4439	3433	870	762	944	1056	883

All figures in these tables and in the text derive from reports published in parliamentary papers. Figures for 1879 are taken from *Return of all agrarian outrages which have been reported by the Royal Irish Constabulary between the 1st day of January 1879 and the 31st day of January 1880, giving particulars of crime, arrests, and results of proceedings . . .*, H.C. 1880 (131), lx, 199–290. Figures for 1880–87 are taken from reports in parliamentary papers for the sessions 1881–7 inclusive, under the title *Agrarian outrages and offences (Ireland): returns of the number of agrarian outrages committed in Ireland which were reported to the Royal Irish Constabulary*, and include the sequence from *Agrarian outrages . . . Ireland*, 1881, p. 3, H.C. (121), lxxvii, 643, to *Agrarian outrages . . . Ireland*, Oct. to Dec. 1887, 3 [C 4955], H.C. 1887, lxviii, 33.

occurred, particularly in mid-Ulster, during the land war did not appear in the official statistics at all. This seemingly trifling point is of importance in mid-Ulster because the Orange Order and the land league regularly clashed as the land war intensified. The trouble usually stemmed from orange counter-meetings organised to prevent the land league from holding unopposed demonstrations in rural towns. The resulting disturbances, which on occasion led to serious injury and even death, were not recorded as agrarian outrages but were nevertheless an offshoot of the land war.

The land war in mid-Ulster can be said to have started not with the land league but with the tenant-right movement. Although the league had established itself in a small way in Fermanagh late in 1879, it was the various organisations supporting the tenant-right cause which sought to voice their opinions most loudly, especially with the imminence of the 1880 general election. In that election campaign the tenant-right issue figured prominently: at one time or another the cause was supported by liberal and conservative candidates, catholic and protestant tenants, the Orange Order, some landlords and many townspeople. The Fermanagh farmers association was fairly typical of the organisations which sprang up to put forward the cause of the tenant righters. Interestingly it was in Armagh that the Orange Order offered official support to candidates adopting the tenant-right issue, and in that county most of the aspiring M.P.s embraced the cause.[1] In Fermanagh, however, it appeared that, although individual orangemen supported tenant-right and criticised their (frequently orange) landlords, the order itself was reluctant to lend its support, led as it was by the very landlords who were being brought to book, particularly William Archdale.[2] Eventually the association found a landlord, J. G. Vesey Porter, to stand on their behalf in the election. Standing as a liberal and espousing the cause of land reform and non-sectarian cooperation,

[1] Orange Order election poster, scrapbook collection, Atkinson papers, P.R.O.N.I., D 1382/2.
[2] *Lisbellaw Gazette*, 16 Mar. 1880.

he gained over 1800 votes but was beaten into third place by Archdale and Crichton.[1] The association's star waned thereafter, but many of its supporters were to reappear in other organisations, notably Jeremiah Jordan in the land league.

In Armagh the issue of tenant-right had also been in the forefront of the election campaign, and although Sir William Verner, a local landlord, had embraced tenant-right the Orange Order refused to endorse his candidature and between that and personal animosities he lost the seat. What is perhaps more interesting is that the order had already begun to take different attitudes in different counties and to link people and movements which had little in common. Whereas in Fermanagh the official orange view was that while land reform was necessary the tenant-right farmers' movement was 'green' and should be avoided, its attitude in Armagh was less predictable and not a little confusing. 'We have never lost sight of your and our interests as tenant farmers, seeking a more secure tenure of the land we occupy, and protection from bad landlords, who without just cause increased the rents, the leaders of which class in this county belong to the liberal school of politics. . . . We are threatened with a union of liberals and home-rulers.'[2]

In Tyrone the election was also closely fought with frequent reference to the tenant-right issue. McCartney, who headed the poll, was proposing a tenant-right bill, while Litton, narrowly beaten into second place, was later in the year appointed a land commissioner by the Gladstone administration. Ironically the vacancy created by Litton's appointment created the by-election which split the land league in mid-Ulster. The land question had certainly come to the forefront by 1880 and Montgomery's agent Pomeroy reported: 'Nobody here I am afraid cares a button for anything except the three Fs . . .'[3] With the impending by-election in view, Thomas Dickson, who subsequently won the seat, made a speech at a

[1] *Irish Times*, 16 Mar. 1880.
[2] Orange Order manifesto, P.R.O.N.I., D 1382/2.
[3] Pomeroy to Montgomery, 3 Apr. 1880, Montgomery correspondence, P.R.O.N.I., D 627/294.

banquet in Litton's honour declaring himself as a tenant-righter who advocated the three Fs and peasant proprietary. As the by-election witnessed the first major electoral clash between the league and the liberals, Dickson was forced to condemn a movement almost all of whose policies he supported as a tenant-righter.[1]

The major difference between the strong but now declining tenant-right movement and the land league in mid-Ulster was the issue of home rule. Those who wished to foil the plans of both organisations were not slow to label tenant-righters as loyalists, and leaguers as communists or nationalists. The tenant-righters themselves often demonstrated just how close and how far they were from league aspirations. An example of this can be seen when 'orange tenant-righters' petitioned Lord Gosford in Armagh for rent reductions. While upholding the aims of the tenant-right movement and demanding a rent abatement, they 'reaffirmed that if landlords were fair and just then they were ready to fight for queen and constitution'.[2]

The land league was in fact only just beginning to make headway in mid-Ulster. It had been established in west Fermanagh late in 1879 and had held its first public meetings early in 1880. Jeremiah Jordan was immediately drawn to the league's programme and became one of its principal organisers and speakers in Fermanagh and Tyrone. From the start the league attracted not only catholics but many protestants as well in Fermanagh, in which county multi-denominational membership remained a feature.

By autumn 1880 the land league had arrived in Down, Armagh, Tyrone and Londonderry as well as Fermanagh, and its first serious membership drives took place. The police feared disturbances would ensue, but none occurred.[3] On 17 October in Armagh, however, a development which bore sinister overtones accompanied the league's inaugural meeting there. Once the league had an-

---

[1] *Irish Times*, 3 Nov. 1880.

[2] Ibid., 26 Nov. 1880.

[3] R.I.C. report to chief secretary, 2 Aug. 1880 (S.P.O., C.S.O. R.P. 1880/18473).

nounced its meeting, the Orange Order organised and advertised a counter-meeting which threatened to drive out or kill the Parnellites.[1] Before the league had had its opportunity to state its case another orange meeting in Lurgan was told that 'protestants must arm themselves and keep their powder dry. Ulster will oppose murder and intimidation and crime . . . and will agree to abolish trial by jury.'[2] The league found itself very soon taking on not only the landlords and government but the Orange Order as well, and although the anti-league campaign was well orchestrated its intensity depended on the attitude of local orangemen in the various counties. By November 1880 the orange campaign was made official at national and county grand lodge level; in Fermanagh the resolution was quite specific:

That in the event of any land league meeting being held in the county of Fermanagh, the district in which such a meeting is held should, when practicable, announce a counter-meeting for the same day, and that the cooperation of the neighbouring districts be invited.[3]

Captain Mervyn Archdale was instructed in December to prepare Fermanagh orangemen by acquiring firearms and organising drilling.[4]

Clearly the order in Fermanagh was anxious to prevent the spread of the league. Already in November a large meeting had been held in Belleek when Parnell and Dillon had been the principal speakers. The chief league organisers were protestants and many protestant members had been enrolled, a development which particularly alarmed the orange leaders. Parnell stressed the non-sectarian policy of the league and played down home rule; the next day, 10 November, an orange counter-meeting was planned to coincide with a further league meeting in Enniskillen. In the event no trouble

---

[1] *Irish Times*, 18 Oct. 1880.

[2] Ibid.

[3] Fermanagh Grand Orange Lodge minutes, 20 Nov. 1880, P.R.O.N.I., D 1402/1.

[4] Ibid., 9 Dec. 1880.

occurred, but the pattern was set and the sides drawn up for a long campaign which well outlived the land league.

Further counter-demonstrations were planned for December and the tactic was clearly to have both meetings proclaimed as a means of silencing the land league. The league generally persevered with its meeting and complained bitterly to the authorities in Dublin that landlords and agents who were also magistrates and orangemen were using their official positions for partisan purposes and deliberately subverting the right of free speech by one-sided actions. Further league meetings took place in Brookeborough, County Fermanagh; Pomeroy, County Tyrone; Castlewellan, County Down; and Derrygonnelly, County Fermanagh. On the occasion of the latter meeting Captain Archdale (who was a J.P. of the county) not only sought to have the league meeting banned but actively organised a violent orange counter-demonstration after the main meetings had ended. Harvey, the R.M. in charge, had reported to Dublin that the day had passed off peacefully,[1] but was apparently unaware of Archdale's intention to lead his followers from the far shore of the lake over to the town. Troops had been despatched to Derrygonnelly to prevent any disturbance, but they had to be recalled later in the evening when Archdale's orangemen attacked the leaguers with a variety of weapons. Peace was restored later that night but a serious disturbance had nevertheless taken place. The important points arising from this incident were that as many protestants appeared to attend the league meeting as joined Archdale, and secondly that, despite protests, Archdale did not lose his magistracy on account of his behaviour. Montgomery angrily attacked Archdale and pro- tested to the chief secretary but to no avail; a split between Fer- managh landlords had now opened up.[2]

Jordan shrewdly concentrated on presenting the league as a

---

[1] R.I.C. report, 10 Dec. 1880 (S.P.O., I.L.L. papers C/1); *Irish Times*, 23 Dec. 1880; Harvey to C.S.O., 22 Dec. 1880 (S.P.O., C.S.O. R.P. 1880/ 33079).

[2] Montgomery to Forster, 13 Mar. 1881 (S.P.O., C.S.O. R.P. 1880/33079).

peaceful and loyal organisation petitioning her majesty's government for a favourable land-reform bill in the coming year. On the other hand retaliation was taking place in the blacking of orangemen's merchandise at local markets. Davitt addressed a league meeting in Downpatrick where the local parish priest and the unitarian minister (the Reverend Harold Rylett) shared the platform. Ten thousand reputedly attended that meeting in January 1881, and as the months passed the league's progress appeared to be substantial. The earl of Charlemont complained that if all protestants did not become orangemen there was always the danger of their joining the league. Also in Armagh, Verner's agent Crossle wrote that the league was not confined to catholics, while the earl of Gosford's agent found it almost impossible to collect rents. The earl of Annesley's agents in Castlewellan, County Down, and Glangevlin, County Cavan, had to fight the league on two fronts. Interestingly, it was absentee landlords such as Annesley and Gosford who had most trouble with the league. Few serious outrages occurred following league meetings, but intimidation and encouragement to withhold rents were becoming widespread by the spring of 1881.

When Parnell paid his second visit to Ulster in April 1881 he congratulated the league for its remarkable progress in the province and the fact that the membership was non-sectarian, a feature epitomised by the chairman of the meeting, to whom Parnell referred as an orange tenant farmer. Certainly league branches were multiplying and seemed to be thriving despite the close attentions of the Orange Order, but a cloud appeared on the horizon just as the league had become self-confident in mid-Ulster. The Tyrone by-election split the league's ranks and did irreparable harm: the Reverend Harold Rylett was not universally popular as a league candidate and many supporters of the league preferred Thomas Dickson, the tenant-right liberal. Parnell was horrified that the representative of the 'coercionist' Gladstone government should attract league support, but despite his exhortations to the electorate Dickson swept to victory over Knox, the conservative, and Rylett.

[231]

The campaign clearly had a divisive effect on the league in mid-Ulster; and although the league had begun to gather strength again by the time of its suppression in October 1881, it was severely damaged by the controversy.

5

The land war in mid-Ulster underwent three fundamental changes in 1881–2. Firstly, the land act was enthusiastically greeted by the majority of tenants, who thronged the land courts and had judicial rents fixed in numbers exceeding those of the other provinces. Secondly, the tenant-righters who had supported the league in some instances took little interest in it following the land act, and a large number of its protestant members, satisfied for the time being with the act, ceased to take much part in its activities thereafter. And thirdly, the divisions which had stemmed from the Tyrone by-election, although healed by October 1881, had given the Orange Order its opportunity to take the initiative in its counter-attack on the league.

The order had taken the unprecedented step of expelling not only members but lodges which had lent support to the league in 1881; and when it seemed to be struggling, the league was proclaimed and the tide turned in the orangemen's favour. In fact the landlords of Fermanagh formed a defence association which drew together protestant landlords and tenants in October 1881 and which began to undo the work of the league in concentrating on a multi-denominational organisation. Following the failure of the no-rent manifesto, the negligible impact of the ladies' land league on Ulster, the upsurge in violence elsewhere in Ireland, and finally the Kilmainham 'treaty', the whole basis on which the land league had developed in Ulster changed. The shift to political issues which took place with the formation of the Irish National League did not augur well for the old leaguers in mid-Ulster. Now that the home-rule issue took precedence it was almost impossible even for Davitt and

Jordan to convice their Ulster audiences that the national league wanted a non-denominational land and national organisation in their province. On the other hand it became much easier for the Orange Order to convince the protestants of Ulster that the land league had after all been but a wolf in sheep's clothing, and that now the wolf was emerging in the form of the national league. Parnell's efforts to establish the new organisation in Ulster and to reorganise the old league on an election-oriented basis were soon styled 'the nationalist invasion' by the orangemen.

Nevertheless the land issue in Ulster was far from dead. Although the land act had at first been enthusiastically received by tenants and some liberal landlords, the economic difficulties which reappeared in 1882, the exclusion of leaseholders, the arrears problem and the bleak outlook for landlords after 1882 all led to renewed campaigning and complaints from both sides. Landlords argued that despite the land act tenants were not paying up rent or arrears; they themselves had been dispossessed and yet in the intervening years of tenant purchase they were not even to receive the compensation guaranteed to them by the act. A brief revival of the tenant-right movement, particularly in Fermanagh, campaigned for an arrears bill. Once it was passed many landlords began to settle purchase terms with their tenants outside the land courts, and many agreements were made in this fashion. A bad harvest in 1884 again proved that the land question was not yet satisfactorily resolved, and even landlords like Montgomery began to despair of ever seeing the problem solved.

Davitt had launched the national league in Ulster at a Belfast meeting in November 1882, where he had outlined his personal views on settling the land question. He had stressed the continued non-sectarian nature of the new league, and although he was well received in the city the message he imparted had little chance of success in mid-Ulster. It was September 1883 before the national league got under way in mid-Ulster. By this time the orangemen were well prepared to oppose, if not break up, every meeting planned by the league. Meetings at Aughnacloy and Dungannon in

September were attacked by orange crowds who had turned up to hear the speeches of the counter-meetings. League supporters alleged that labourers were bribed with money and drink to harass their meetings, while orange leaders complained that the national league's campaign represented a wanton attack on the loyalist province by traitorous nationalists. The war between them worsened considerably when trouble broke out at Rosslea, County Fermanagh, on 16 October. Viscount Crichton (heir to Lord Erne) addressed the orange counter-demonstration, accusing the Parnellites of invading their province and announcing that 'the orangemen are ready for them'. Lord Rossmore led a body of orangemen dangerously close to the league meeting despite the warning of the R.M., Captain Hugh McTernan. As a result of the fracas Rossmore was dismissed and the indignation of the orangemen was expressed in further demonstrations, now supported by a very large number of mid-Ulster landlords. Trouble erupted in Londonderry and Newry but came to a head in December at Dromore. A pro-Rossmore demonstration was organised to clash with a scheduled league meeting; hundreds of orangemen were transported to the scene by train at the expense of the landlords who had been asked to contribute funds for the purpose. The army kept the peace, although one orange supporter died from injuries received in a police bayonet charge, but no dismissals followed on this occasion. Early in 1884 meetings at Blacklion and Castlewellan were banned simply as a result of the orangemen's announcing a counter-demonstration. Despite league efforts to concentrate on the land issue, sectarianism had begun to take over, and the aims of the land league and the tenant-righters were largely forgotten as the sectarian divisions deepened. Of the landlords who had hoped to keep both sides together and to prevent sectarian trouble, only Montgomery and Porter made their voices heard above the orange-national clamouring which reached a crescendo after the 1885 general election. Eventually even they went with the current, Montgomery becoming a unionist M.P. and Porter a reluctant nationalist.

Even the earls of Erne and Belmore and the duke of Abercorn

began strongly to resent the government's land policy after 1883. The land war had eventually yielded reductions of up to 25 per cent to mid-Ulster tenants who were now buying out their holdings, but in bad seasons, which recurred in 1884 and 1886, the landlords claimed they had lost everything. Even when they accepted peasant proprietary these landlords complained that non-payment persisted, eviction was almost impossible and financial ruin was a real prospect. In 1880 the earl of Charlemont, the most conservative of landlords and not a little eccentric in his declining years, had declared that all concessions to tenants had been a mistake and that landlords would rue the day they were generous to tenants in distress. By 1885 even the most liberal landlords were beginning to believe this line. While the Plan of Campaign scarcely touched mid-Ulster, there was still plenty of dissatisfaction among tenants, who were finding it difficult to maintain even reduced judicial rents when faced with an economic depression and the return of bad seasons. Landlords were beginning to realise that an agrarian revolution had overtaken them, while for many tenants it seemed that the system of gradual change in ownership of the land had changed little for them in their annual struggle to pay the rent. By 1885 the land war as such was virtually over in mid-Ulster, but the seeds of renewed sectarianism had been sown; one form of tension had been replaced by another, which was potentially more dangerous and far-reaching than the campaign which had started with the tenant-right associations and the land league.

To the Northern Counties station:
Lord Randolph Churchill
and the prelude to the orange card*

R. F. FOSTER

I

A CONSIDERATION of Lord Randolph Churchill's involvement with Irish affairs usually culminates in his historic visit to Ulster in February 1886 (where he did not say 'Ulster will fight and Ulster will be right');[1] which is usually presented in a way to bear out the currently favoured interpretation of his extraordinary career, being seen most recently as a temporary aberration on the part of a home-ruler *manqué*, whose primary intention was to defuse Ulster emotions.[2] However, to recapture an essential contemporary dimension, it is necessary to consider both the experiences and contacts represented by his Irish connection over the previous decade, and what was generally expected of him by 1886; in which light both the visit and what it represented may appear from an unexpected angle.

And to consider the development towards the triumphal progress from the Northern Counties station to the Ulster Hall on 22 February 1886, it is necessary to go back nine years, to the arrival of Churchill's father, the seventh duke of Marlborough, in Ireland as viceroy,

* For grants towards the research involved in writing this paper I am grateful to the Central Research Fund of the University of London; and for permission to quote from collections of papers I owe thanks to Mr Winston Churchill, M.P., Mr Peregrine Churchill, the duke of Marlborough, Earl St Aldwyn, and Mr Gerald FitzGibbon, M.A.I.

[1] The phrase occurred in a public letter written some time later; see W. S. Churchill, *Lord Randolph Churchill* (London, 1906), ii, 64–5.

[2] See A. B. Cooke and J. R. Vincent, *The governing passion: cabinet government and party politics in Britain, 1885–6* (Hassocks, 1971).

following the involvement of both his sons in a celebrated Victorian scandal.[1] The strangeness of the Castle world, an admixture of Gilbert and Sullivan with Mr Pooter, must have struck the Marlboroughs forcibly: on the one hand public jeers at their financial embarrassments,[2] on the other an extraordinary avalanche of private letters bitterly contesting questions of personal politics and social precedence, still incongruously preserved in Blenheim Palace.[3] But for the majority of their tenure, the Marlboroughs made a remarkable public success of the viceroyalty. Duly warned, the duke kept social life up to expectations; and he adroitly followed an 'Irish' line in policy most untypical of Disraeli's last administration. He travelled widely in the country, opposed coercion, called for religious toleration in the north,[4] supported land purchase for small farmers,[5] and cultivated a public image far removed from the hauteur of predecessors like the duke of Abercorn.[6] Most of all, he strongly identified himself with the catholic side in schemes for intermediate and higher education, working closely with Hicks Beach, his chief secretary, and enthusiastically corresponding with

[1] See Randolph S. Churchill, *Winston S. Churchill, 1874–1965, 1: youth, 1874–1900* (London, 1960), pp 25–34.

[2] For the question of Marlborough's finances see *Weekly Irish Times*, 13 Jan. 1877; the duke's worried correspondence with his comptroller, Colonel Caulfield, in Marlborough family papers at Blenheim palace (hereafter 'Blenheim MSS'), D/1/3; and R. B. McDowell and W. B. Stanford, *Mahaffy: a portrait of an Anglo-Irishman* (London, 1971), p. 99.

[3] It comprises exhortations not to patronise the Belfast Linen Company for political reasons, calls for martial law from the country gentry, ascendancy sneers about the Dublin bourgeoisie, and frenzied denunciations of the social antecedents of Castle guests, written anonymously by those who had not received invitations. See letters in Blenheim MSS, D/1/2.

[4] See memorandum dated 28 May 1877, Blenheim MSS, D/1/29, and speeches on Belfast visit reported in *Weekly Irish Times*, 31 Aug. 1878.

[5] See for instance report of speech at agricultural banquet, 6 Aug. 1878, in *Weekly Irish Times*, 10 Aug. 1878.

[6] On Abercorn's viceroyalty see Lord George Hamilton, *Parliamentary reminiscences and reflections, 1868–85* (London, 1917), pp 112–14; Lord Ernest Hamilton, *Old days and new* (London, 1923), p. 123; and Sir John Ross, *The years of my pilgrimage* (London, 1924), pp 43–4.

the hierarchy from the beginning.[1] The outcome, a cautious intermediate scheme introduced by Lowther in 1878, was disappointing,
as was the eventual abandonment by the government of the
university scheme worked out by Butt and the O'Conor Don, and
warmly supported by Marlborough; the substituted plan for the
royal university only indirectly subsidised the catholic university.[2]
There was talk of the viceroy resigning over this. He and Beach had
been assured by their clerical contacts that 'in Irish politics the education question has practically displaced even the home-rule question
and the land question',[3] an analysis in which they devoutly believed.
They were bombarded by Butt with letters telling them that
catholic opinion was more favourable to a conservative than a
liberal government,[4] and they took this seriously, though under no
illusions about Butt's own increasingly eroded position. In education
above all, the viceroy and other conservatives in Ireland backed an
approach which was essentially alien to the government's approach
in England.

At the same time an almost equally important initiative was

[1] See letters from Marlborough to Beach in Blenheim MSS, D/1/2 and
Glos. R.O., St Aldwyn papers (hereafter D2455), PCC/64–5; also D. A.
Thornley, *Isaac Butt and home rule* (London, 1964), pp 350–54, and Lady
Victoria Hicks Beach, *Life of Sir Michael Hicks Beach (earl St Aldwyn)* (London,
1932), i, 26–7, 467.

[2] See especially Marlborough to Beach, 18 Nov. 1879 (Glos. R.O., D2455,
PCC/65); also Sir William Gregory to duchess of Marlborough, 13 Aug. 1879
(Blenheim MSS, D/1/7), and Beach's memorandum on Irish education,
Dec. 1877 (Glos. R.O., D2455, PCC/52). For the effect of the 1879 measure
see T. W. Moody, 'The Irish university question of the nineteenth century' in
History, xliii (1958), pp 90–109.

[3] Bishop Conway of Killala to Beach, 17 Jan. 1877 (Blenheim MSS,
D/1/19).

[4] See for instance Butt to Beach, 28 May 1878 (Glos. R.O., D2455, PCC/66):
'Since I returned to Ireland, I have been astonished at the number of communi-
cations which have been made to me by Roman Catholics in various positions
to the effect that a very general feeling is pervading the Roman Catholic body
that their true and natural alliance is with the conservative party, and a general
wish to be able to support them'. Also see Thornley, *Isaac Butt*, pp 350–51, 355,
367.

represented by the duchess, an energetic politician obsessed with the need for good publicity and famous for her dedication to 'feeding the press' at Castle receptions.[1] Besides the routine involvements of a viceroy's wife, she cultivated a network of Irish contacts, to which her correspondence bears witness, ranging from liberal landlords like Sir William Gregory to a phalanx of clerics from Cullen down.[2] Her late sister, the countess of Portarlington, had been converted to catholicism and entertained a stream of clerical admirers at Emo Park; here the duchess met men like Bishop Delany of Cork, Bishop Nulty of Meath, and Dr Molloy of the catholic university, who were duly invited to Blenheim.[3] Such men were firm conservatives, but put her in touch with coming men like Walsh. These contacts were invaluable in projects like her famine distress fund. And when she left Ireland the duchess was showered with addresses and poems from all over Ireland, many in Irish, and some no less fulsome in her praise for declaring parenthetically a pious wish to repeal 'the curse of union'.[4]

The initiatives and attitudes of the Marlboroughs gave their reign a characteristic identity, which was added to by the presence of their *déclassé* and socially disgraced son Lord Randolph, the hitherto undistinguished M.P. for Woodstock. His position at the Castle was anomalous; it was decided he could not occupy a paid private secretaryship, but the official private secretary had to give up his house to Lord Randolph, and pledge that he would defer to him behind the scenes.[5] And he figured largely in Castle life, accompanying his father on political tours (including a prophetic visit to Belfast

[1] Maud Wynne, *An Irishman and his family: Lord Morris and Killanin* (London, 1937), p. 98.

[2] See Sir Bernard Burke to duchess of Marlborough, 4 Mar. 1877 (Blenheim MSS, D/1/6), for the duchess's overtures to Cullen. Her lengthy correspondence with Delany and Molloy is in ibid., D/1/7, 9, 11.

[3] Blenheim MSS, D/1/8.   [4] Ibid.

[5] See W. S. Churchill, *Lord Randolph Churchill*, i, 75–6; also Beach to Marlborough, 28 Nov. 1876 (Blenheim MSS, D/1/3), and n.d. (ibid., D/1/6), and letters from Percy Barnard (the official private secretary), Oct.–Nov. 1876 (ibid., D/1/1).

in 1877), meeting his future friends at viceregal parties and in the Dublin Castle offices, and imbibing the political atmosphere at a time when the *Freeman* was still able to hold out hopes of the 'Irish catholic conservative' as a desirable political phenomenon;[1] Churchill worked at the Castle on the education schemes which had this very end in view. Given this, the fact that Butt dined regularly with him need not seem surprising.[2] Certainly, Churchill eschewed the great houses of the ascendancy in favour of cultivating Irish friends; but, despite biographers' comments about his 'close contact with intellectual home rulers',[3] these were not nationalists. Churchill cultivated an overwhelmingly 'Trinity' clique of professional men, educated tories, the products of an immensely distinguished university generation—David Plunket, Michael Morris, Edward Gibson, John Pentland Mahaffy, Gerald FitzGibbon.[4] They took him up, launched him on the College Historical Society in T.C.D. as his first Irish public appearance, and in many ways formed his thinking on Ireland.[5]

FitzGibbon was the most important of these. Law adviser and then solicitor-general in the Irish administration, he came from a robustly tory and protestant legal family.[6] Fourteen years older

---

[1] See editorial in *Weekly Freeman*, 22 Mar. 1879.

[2] Mrs G. Cornwallis-West, *The reminiscences of Lady Randolph Churchill* (London, 1908), p. 80.

[3] R. R. James, *Lord Randolph Churchill* (London, 1959), p. 62.

[4] On this group see Mahaffy's speech at the T.C.D. tercentenary, where he referred to Plunket, Gibson, FitzGibbon, Lecky and Thomas Dudley as 'the most brilliant group of men that ever came together in the [Historical] Society' (J. J. Auchmuty, *Lecky* (Dublin, 1945), p. 119); also Ross, *Years of my pilgrimage*, on his university days.

[5] See W. S. Churchill, *Lord Randolph Churchill*, i, 80–82; also an autobiographical memoir by Edward Gibson (Lord Ashbourne) in Ashbourne papers, H.L.R.O., quoted by A. B. Cooke, *The Ashbourne papers, 1869–1913: a calendar of the papers of Edward Gibson, 1st lord Ashbourne* (H.M.S.O., Belfast, 1974; P.R.O.N.I. in association with H.L.R.O.), p. 31.

[6] His father, a master in chancery also named Gerald FitzGibbon, had put himself through law school and produced a series of tracts on the Irish situation, such as *Ireland in 1868* (1868), an argument against disestablishment; also see J. G. Swift Macneill, *What I have seen and heard* (London, 1925), p. 132.

than Churchill, he was already well known for his success in nearly every 'heavy case' that came on in Dublin. His advancement to lord justice of appeal in 1878 need not have been due to viceregal favour, for he was conspicuously able; even the unenthusiastic Beach lamented his 'waste' in Dublin legal life.[1] FitzGibbon himself would probably have preferred politics, in which he was immersed behind the scenes, but the promised seat for Dublin University went to Gibson instead in 1875.[2] FitzGibbon was a realistic, decisive, superficially flexible but basically intractable unionist and protestant: an influential freemason, whose mother came from Belfast.[3] The fact that he had a wide circle of catholic friends and contacts was in no way incompatible with this, contemporary English ideas of Ireland notwithstanding.

FitzGibbon formally promised to keep Churchill informed on Irish politics; which he did, in a flow of marvellous letters, until the end of Churchill's life.[4] Despite his complaint that advising his mercurial friend was 'crying in the wilderness through the privacy of the penny post',[5] time and time again a public Irish initiative of Churchill's followed—in both senses—private advice from Fitz-Gibbon. His reiterated lesson to Churchill was that there were *other* Irish unionists than landowners to be considered; himself of the professional middle class, he deeply resented 'the identification of the union and of constitutional rule with the collection of rent'.[6]

---

[1] Beach to Gibson, 15 Nov. 1878 (H.L.R.O., Ashbourne papers, 77/130); for a contemporary comment on his ability see *Weekly Freeman*, 10 Nov. 1878.

[2] Swift Macneill, *Seen and heard*, pp 128–9.

[3] He referred disparagingly to the opinions of 'Gibson, Plunket and other *moderates*' (FitzGibbon to Churchill, n.d. [Christmas 1881]; Churchill College, Lord Randolph Churchill papers (hereafter R.C.P.), 1/i/62). For comments on his approach to legal questions see Ross, *Years of my pilgrimage*, p. 201.

[4] 'As regards Ireland, whenever and wherever and however it may seem possible I will do all in my power from time to time to keep you *au courant* with the floating notions of the locality; so far as you think anything I can say, do, or write can avail for any good, you have only to call on me.' FitzGibbon to Churchill, 27 July 1886 (R.C.P., 1/xiii/1581).

[5] Same to same, 23 Aug. 1887 (ibid., 1/xxi/2634).

[6] Same to same, 20 Nov. 1887 (ibid., 1/xxi/2735).

He pressed the claims of the denizens of Dublin's professional squares, and also of the northern brethren; time and again this theme recurs. His circle included no landowners. Plunket and Gibson were careerist lawyer-politicians, later sundered by politics; Gibson's success alienated most of his Irish associates, and Churchill, after briefly considering him Fourth Party material, came to dislike him intensely for his affiliation to Northcote. He could appear all things to all men, being suspected in 1886 of secret home-rule sympathies by authorities as varied as Lord Carnarvon, Wilfred Scawen Blunt, and the Kildare Street club.[1] Morris (later Lord Morris and Killanin and first catholic lord chief justice of common pleas in Ireland) was a Spartan pessimist from a Galway catholic background, though educated at an Erasmus Smith school, and a Trinity gold-medallist. He combined intransigent unionism with a dislike of most Englishmen, believing that the Irish question arose from a quick-witted race being governed by a slow-witted one. Like Plunket and Gibson, he had been a *protégé* of Disraeli's (an even more untypical Englishman than Churchill); like FitzGibbon, he left direct politics through lack of money. He advised Churchill closely, and became more relentlessly unionist as the years went by;[2] but he always disagreed with coercive legislation, seeing a

[1] See W. S. Blunt, *The land war in Ireland* (London, 1912), diary entry for 10 Jan. 1886, p. 18; Sir Arthur Hardinge, *Life of H. H. Molyneux Herbert, fourth earl of Carnarvon* (Oxford, 1925), iii, 175–6; A. B. Cooke and J. R. Vincent (ed.), *Lord Carlingford's journal: reflections of a cabinet minister, 1885* (Oxford, 1971), p. 128, n. 2. For a sensitive treatment of Gibson's career see A. B. Cooke's introduction to *Calendar of the Ashbourne papers*; also A. B. Cooke and J. R. Vincent (ed.), 'Ireland and party politics, 1885–7: an unpublished conservative memoir', part I, in *I.H.S.*, xvi, no. 63 (Mar. 1969), pp 330–33.

[2] He refused to dine with anyone who had broken bread with Parnell, and made a famous retort to Lady Aberdeen when she remarked on the large turnout of home-rulers at a Castle function during the Union of Hearts period: 'Not at all, your excellency; barring yourself and the waiters, there's not a home-ruler in the room.' None the less, his cynicism about the English administration of Ireland continued; a family pastime was poking fun at the earnest deputations who visited their home at Spiddal on tours of the congested districts (Wynne, *An Irishman and his family*, p. 90).

typically English lack of imagination in the government's inability to use the ordinary legal processes.

Churchill's single contact among the Irish landlords was made outside the FitzGibbon circle—his uncle, Lord Portarlington, who has been presented as a disapproving high tory,[1] but was in reality an extraordinarily liberal landlord who praised Archbishop Croke's pronouncements, believed in a peasant proprietary, and eulogised Gladstone's land bill of 1881 in the house of lords.[2] But generally, Churchill's friends were in the FitzGibbon set: Lord Chief Justice Ball, Ben Williamson of Trinity, the celebrated wit Dr Nedley, and the indefatigably socialite parish priest of Little Bray, Fr Healy. Healy, though no snob, was noted for his dining-out in grand houses (which he called 'my outdoor relief'). In no way a typical Irish priest, he regularly visited Trinity high table and the viceregal lodge, involved himself in conservative politics, and was close to tory politicians like Balfour and orange families like the Leslies, opposing Archbishop Walsh on national questions.[3] In England he was welcome at Blenheim and Hatfield, as well as at Gladstone's breakfasts; and both Churchill and his father dined often at his little house in Bray, where the fare was invariably boiled mutton, but the company could include, at one sitting, Monsignor Persico, Lord Powerscourt, Archbishop Walsh, Lord Morris, Chief Baron Palles, Prince Edward of Saxe-Weimar, and the ubiquitous Gibson.[4]

Against the background of his parents' initiatives and his friends' opinions, Churchill's celebrated speech at Woodstock in September

---

[1] W. S. Churchill, *Lord Randolph Churchill*, i, 82.

[2] For Portarlington's relations with his tenants, and his genial view of their land league activities, see *Weekly Irish Times*, 4 June 1881, and for his views on the land bill, a speech of 8 Aug. 1881 reported in ibid., 13 Aug. 1881.

[3] Healy's biographer described him as a 'strong conservative': *Memories of Father Healy of Little Bray* (anon., but actually W. J. Fitzpatrick; Dublin, 1896), p. 160. He was accused of exerting undue influence against Philip Callan in the 1874 Louth election. Also see Emmet Larkin, *The Roman Catholic church and the creation of the modern Irish state, 1878–86* (Dublin and Philadelphia, 1975), pp 271, 275.

[4] *Memories of Father Healy*, pp 152, 214.

1877, attacking the government's neglectful Irish policy as causing
the antics of the obstructionists at Westminster, need not be seen as
unduly surprising; it was no more than what educated Irish conservatives were saying in private, probably at viceregal dinners.[1]
The duke mollified Beach by the supposition that his unofficial
private secretary had been drunk,[2] but there are other aspects to
be considered. The speech can be seen as an attempt by Churchill to
put himself between parties, or to steal the thunder from Gladstone's coming visit to Ireland.[3] However, press opinion made much
of it; traduced by the *Morning Post* and treated with some embarrassment by the *Irish Times*, he was welcomed by the *Freeman's Journal*
as demonstrating *noblesse oblige* (a quality dear to the heart of the
editor, Edmund Dwyer Gray). Though Churchill rapidly mended
his fences in England,[4] the speech had a spectacular and lasting effect
in Ireland.[5] A friendly relationship began between the *Freeman* and

---

[1] 'He had no hesitation in saying that it was inattention to Irish legislation
that produced the obstruction to English legislation. There were great and
crying questions which the government had not attended to, did not seem
inclined to attend to, and perhaps did not intend to attend to. These were the
questions of intermediate and higher education, the assimilation of municipal
and parliamentary electoral privileges to English privileges, and other matters
which he would not go into . . .' (*Weekly Freeman*, 22 Sept. 1877; also see
W. S. Churchill, *Lord Randolph Churchill*, i, 90–94, and R. R. James, *Lord
Randolph Churchill*, op. cit., pp 63–4).

[2] Marlborough to Beach, 25 Sept. 1877 (W. S. Churchill, *Lord Randolph
Churchill*, i, 92).

[3] An unnecessary precaution; Gladstone confined himself to the country-
house circuit and the only sign of disturbance he noted was that somebody had
cut down a tree planted by the prince of Wales. See Morley, *Gladstone*, iii, 571,
and Agatha Ramm (ed.), *The political correspondence of Mr Gladstone and Lord
Granville, 1876–86* (Oxford, 1961), i, 54, 56.

[4] A letter to the *Post* described as 'impenitent' by his son (*Lord Randolph
Churchill*, i, 93–4) reads more like a denial of the charges presented, claiming
inaccurately that he 'never even mentioned' the obstructionists. (See copy in
R.C.P., 1/i/5.)

[5] T. P. O'Connor described it as 'moving the small world of Dublin to its
depths'; *Memories of an old parliamentarian* (London, 1929), i, 58. In March 1881
Churchill was still being attacked for having preached home rule while his
father was viceroy (see *Weekly Irish Times*, 19 Mar. 1881).

Churchill, who carefully referred to it in public as 'the best-written paper in Ireland';[1] Gray rewarded him by greeting even his defection over the Irish borough franchise in 1879 'more in sorrow than in anger'.[2]

Churchill was, moreover, determined to become a tory 'Irish expert'. From 1876 he had energetically followed the family interest in intermediate education; this culminated in his publication in early 1878 of a pamphlet which argued firmly in favour of denominational education, and condemned the organisation of protestant educational trusts. It pressed strongly for a restructured system, with the aid of the surplus fund of the disestablished church, to provide state intermediate schools catering for the catholic middle class; this fairly represented enlightened Castle thinking.[3] The scheme devised by Beach and passed in June 1878 resembled it in many points,[4] though not actually endowing catholic education and not reorganising the endowments monopolised by protestant schools. When Beach's measure was introduced, Churchill (who was actively involved in the negotiations preceding it)[5] called for a commission

[1] See a letter from 'a true liberal' to the *Freeman* deprecating its criticism of Churchill's view of the Irish franchise, reprinted in *Weekly Freeman*, 22 Feb. 1879.

[2] *Weekly Freeman*, 22 Feb. 1879.

[3] See *Intermediate education in Ireland: a letter to Sir Bernard Burke, C.B., Ulster, from Lord Randolph Churchill, M.P.* (Dublin: J. Charles and Co., 1878). (Burke had been closely involved in negotiations between the Castle and the hierarchy; see Glos. R.O., D2455 PCC/52, 64.) Churchill wanted the royal free grammar schools greatly extended into a state system of intermediate education, available to catholics, with the religion of the schoolmaster in charge of a school being dictated by that of 'the great proportion' of the surrounding population. The scheme also involved precautions like a conscience clause and competitive examinations for gratuitous instruction. In general, the embryonic state of organisation of endowed schools was to be rationalised. Inefficient and exclusive foundations like that of Erasmus Smith were to be taken over, and the commission for endowed schools appointed in 1854 dissolved: 'they have never understood the importance of the duties committed to them, and much of the deplorable deficiency in higher education in Ireland must be laid directly at their door' (p. 18).

[4] See Thornley, *Isaac Butt*, pp 350–54.

[5] See his letter in *F.J.*, 31 Dec. 1877; also letters to Morris, 14 and 18 Jan. 1878 (Wynne, *An Irishman and his family*, pp 103–4, 207).

of inquiry into endowed schools in Ireland, attracting the support
of Chamberlain and Forster, annoying Lowther,[1] and earning
grateful mention in the nationalist press.[2] A commission was
appointed, though with only limited advisory powers, and was
commandeered by Churchill, FitzGibbon and Mahaffy, under the
chairmanship of the earl of Rosse.[3] Such membership did not
encourage catholic opinion, and it was looked on in some quarters
as an attempt to preserve a protestant initiative in education; but
it compiled an interesting and effective report,[4] obediently following
the lines set out in Churchill's pamphlet. His own attendance at
sittings of the commission was regular, and his questioning highly
pertinent, as well as markedly hostile to administrators who had
contrived to make their endowments exclusive.[5] Unique among the
commissioners, his questioning was forensic and tendentious, trying
to draw out suggested remedies and alternatives, despite the commissioners' limited scope.[6] Churchill's questioning also concentrated

[1] As Churchill had anticipated; see letter to Morris, 18 Jan. 1878 (ibid.).

[2] Editorial in *Weekly Freeman*, 22 June 1878.

[3] For Mahaffy's experiences on the commission see Stanford and McDowell,
Mahaffy, pp 47–8.

[4] See *Reports from commissioners, inspectors and others, 1881, no. 21: endowed
schools (Ireland)* [c. 2831, 2831–1], H.C. Jan.–Aug. 1881, xxxv; hereafter cited
as *Report*.

[5] He was accused of wishing to convert the Erasmus Smith endowment into
a Roman Catholic charity (*Weekly Irish Times*, 12 Apr. 1879); and the whole
tenor of his questioning was to condemn the inefficiency and haphazard
approach of the 1854 commissioners (see *Report*, i, 118–19, and ii, 186–7),
especially in the management of estates (ibid., i, 22–3). Many catholic schools
were examined (though many held themselves as not coming under the
provenance of the commission); those investigated generally performed
impressively, and the thorough, utilitarian nature of the education provided by
several of the religious orders obviously appealed to the commissioners (ibid.,
i, 132); the work of social stabilising carried out by an institution like St
Stanislaus's, Tullamore, was greatly admired. However, the only endowed
school which occasioned an unsolicited favourable judgement from Churchill
was the quaker boarding-school at Newtown, Waterford: 'it would be fortunate for the Irish people if all their schools were as well managed as yours'
(ibid., ii, 449).

[6] See for instance his insistent questioning of Robert Russell Currie, a
catholic J.P., on education in Swords (*Report*, ii, 246) and his brutal interroga-

upon the management of landed estates; and his overall reactions indicated an impatience with rickety ascendancy institutions which had outlived their function. His prime consideration may have been to make a figure, but at the same time he learned a lot.

The same is true of his involvement in the duchess's famine relief fund, which she set up in December 1879 after taking lengthy soundings from her landlord and clerical friends,[1] and against the advice of Castle officials.[2] By mid-December her formidable publicity machine was in action, English politicians canvassed, and the mayor of London set to producing a steady flow of £2000 cheques from a parallel fund in Britain.[3] And almost at once the Dublin lord mayor, Dwyer Gray, began the Mansion House fund for a similar purpose; after initial amity, the two organisations were soon in violent opposition, the duchess having been warned early on that any cooperation with Gray would dry up the English contributions which made up the majority of her takings.[4] Sir William Gregory consoled her with the assurance that such vendettas were part of Dublin life,[5] but the war was soon prosecuted on a wider front; Disraeli's indolent attitude towards Ireland hardened into

---

tion of the dean of Limerick (ibid., ii, 751); he was similarly aggressive in his cross-questioning of estate agents, accusing one of 'ignorance' (ibid., ii, 439).

[1] See letters from Sir William Gregory and Colonel King Harman to duchess of Marlborough, Sept.–Dec. 1879 (Blenheim MSS, D/1/11).

[2] Who recommended nothing more radical than a ladies' charity; see memo of a correspondence between Sir Bernard Burke and Churchill, n.d. (ibid., D/1/9).

[3] See letters to press, 18 Dec. 1879; Gladstone to duchess of Marlborough, 19 Dec. 1879 (ibid., D/1/9); Northcote to same, 30 Jan. 1880 (ibid.).

[4] See letter from Dwyer Gray to *Weekly Irish Times*, 10 Jan. 1880, deploring 'anything in the shape of rivalry'; and T. C. Grimshaw (secretary of the fund) to duchess of Marlborough, n.d. (Blenheim MSS, D/1/11); also Lord Mayor Truscott to duchess of Marlborough, 4 Mar. 1880 (ibid., D/1/11). By March, £53,000 of the total £88,000 subscribed had come from England; and British organisations as far afield as St Petersburg and Hong Kong were involved. See correspondence in Blenheim MSS, D/1/14.

[5] Gregory to duchess of Marlborough, 14 Feb. 1880 (Blenheim MSS, D/1/7). For exchanges between the two funds see newspapers for April–May 1880.

intransigence with the land crisis, and on 8 March 1880 he sent the famous open letter to Marlborough about the 'pestilential' nature of the home-rule movement.[1] The duke had already boycotted the Mansion House, for the ironic reasons of Dwyer Gray's supposed support of extremists; after agonised tacking and veering Gray had to abandon attendance at the Castle, and neither he nor the *Freeman* ever forgave Marlborough.[2]

The duchess's fund carried on, a prodigy of organisation and financial productivity, attacked by English protestants for 'favouring catholics'[3] and by Irish nationalists for deliberately concealing the government's responsibility for the distress; and racked by internal crisis when an embezzling secretary threw himself into the canal in a drunken fit of remorse (a story which at all costs had to be kept from the Mansion House fund).[4] After the election defeat the duchess left Ireland with a *grande dame* circular letter in Irish and English addressed to the distressed districts, and her harassed trustees finally wound things up at the end of the year, receiving an abusive epitaph in the *Freeman*.[5]

In this involvement, Churchill was a moving spirit. He drew up for the duchess a cautious and considered memorandum on the extent of agricultural distress at an early stage, advising against hasty commitment and looking at the question almost entirely from the

[1] See W. F. Monypenny and G. E. Buckle, *The life of Benjamin Disraeli, earl of Beaconsfield* (6 vols, London, 1910–20), vi, 514–16.

[2] See *Weekly Freeman*, 31 Jan. 1880; T. M. Healy, *Letters and leaders of my day* (London, 1925), i, 79; William O'Brien, *Recollections* (London, 1905), p. 185.

[3] From the beginning, some protestant ladies had refused to collect for the fund, and the duchess was also inundated with acrimonious letters from English clergymen (Blenheim MSS, D/1/7, 9, 12).

[4] The episode remains preserved in a series of hysterical letters from J. C. Meredith, a trustee of the fund, to the duchess throughout May 1880 (Blenheim MSS, D/1/11).

[5] *Weekly Freeman*, 4 Dec. 1880. The fund had dispensed £125,000, and a residue was eventually made over to the duke of Bedford's emigration fund in 1883 (see letters from duchess to *The Times*, reprinted in *Weekly Freeman*, 17 Mar. 1883).

angle of political priorities.[1] When the fund was started, however, Churchill as honorary secretary worked incessantly: corresponding with bishops, organising liaison in London, arranging local distribution of seed and potatoes, advising about the feud with the Mansion House, and showing a tactless degree of impatience at the objections to 'favouring catholics'. At the end of it all he organised the dispersal of surplus funds in an emigration scheme.[2] It was, taken with his work on the endowed-schools commission, a baptism into Irish politics.

Meanwhile, the duke was increasingly alienated from public opinion in the transforming country under his nominal command. Long before the election, he announced his intention not to return;[3] he had even lost favour with the episcopacy;[4] and after leaving office he continually called for coercion in the house of lords.[5] The duchess, too, had hardened; she believed that in the winter of 1881 the Irish gentry would be living 'as in the dark days of the French revolution'.[6] When Marlborough died suddenly in 1883, the *Freeman* used the occasion to resurrect all the contentious issues it

---

[1] See a long memorandum in Churchill's writing (n.d., Blenheim MSS, D/1/4); sceptical of King-Harman's warnings, it called for more statistics, and warned his mother of the danger of seeming to corroborate the extremists' claims about the state of the country. For King-Harman's reaction, see his angry letter to the duchess, 15 Dec. 1879 (Blenheim MSS, D/1/11).

[2] For Churchill's involvement in organisation, see his correspondence with Archbishop Logue and Lord Mayor Truscott, Jan.–Feb. 1880 (Blenheim MSS, D/1/12), and reports in *Weekly Irish Times*, e.g. 7 Feb. 1880; for references to his cautious stance on the Mansion House fund see J. C. Meredith to the duchess, 14 May 1880 (Blenheim MSS, D/1/11); on his denunciation of protestant objections see Rev. Cardale of Uckfield to the duchess, 14 May 1880 (ibid., D/1/9); on his eventual assignment of the surplus to an emigration scheme see T. C. Grimshaw to the duchess, 24 Mar. 1881 (ibid., D/1/6), Sir A. Galt to *The Times*, 27 Mar. 1881, and Churchill to the duchess, 15 Dec. 1881 (Blenheim MSS, D/1/7).

[3] *Weekly Irish Times*, 13 Jan. 1880.

[4] See Larkin, *Roman Catholic church*, p. 32.

[5] See *Weekly Freeman*, 12 June 1880, for a bitter attack on Marlborough's 'mischievous and undignified behaviour'.

[6] See correspondence with Lord Lytton in Blenheim MSS, D/1/8.

could: a thankless end to all the duchess's unsparing efforts to feed the press.

Though their son cannot have been unaffected by this, he had also absorbed and retained a variety of progressive and activist attitudes towards Ireland. He had made a figure. Educated unionism was interested in him. Though someone of Gregory's orientation could rate him very highly indeed,[1] the normal Irish landlord interest thought him an enemy and told him so, in private letters[2] as well as in slightly ridiculous incidents like barring him from their meetings.[3] This, however, should not be identified with a 'green' orientation. Butt may have been a friend, but he was desperately courting the conservatives; Father Healy may have been an intimate, but his political opinions were 'unpalatable to the majority of his own cloth in the country'.[4] And antipathy to the landlords was a characteristic of the staunchly unionist FitzGibbon circle,[5] which kept Churchill in touch with Ireland, bringing him back nearly every year to FitzGibbon's famous Christmas house party at Howth. Here the faithful, arriving at the seaside house by train like Madame Ver-

[1] See for instance Gregory to duchess of Marlborough, 15 June 1880 (Blenheim MSS, D/1/11): 'He—Lord R.—is a very clever fellow, but I wish with all my heart that he would take a higher line than skirmishing. . . . Forgive my venturing to interfere, but you know how high is my opinion of his ability, and that opinion was not lightly formed. I like him so much moreover that I want the world to rightly estimate him and to see that he can act as well in heavy armour as in light.'

[2] See for instance Lord Castletown to Churchill, 10 May 1884, trying to enlist his help in a purchase clause amendment: 'I know you have little feeling or respect for Irish landlords . . .' (R.C.P., 1/iii/364).

[3] This occurred in January 1881; Churchill believed that Colonel A. L. Tottenham had claimed publicly that he had been refused entry to the meeting, and denied ever wanting to attend it; Gorst, however, who was with him, *had* wanted to be smuggled in. See correspondence in R.C.P., 1/i/63, 65, 66, 67.

[4] A remark of Wolseley's; *Memories of Father Healy*, p. 216.

[5] For a typical comment see FitzGibbon to Churchill, 20 July 1886 (Churchill College, R.C.P., 1/xiii/1568): 'The Irish landlords, as you well know, are neither personally nor politically worth the money or the labour which it would require to preserve them from the, I believe, inevitable operation of the economic laws which are crushing them.'

durin's 'little band', convened to talk, drink, play whist and cook their own suppers. Besides Plunket, Morris, Mahaffy, Gibson and Father Healy, the party could include stray English politicians, Archbishop Walsh or the viceroy. In later years John Morley became an incongruous regular. But the parties originated 'to enable Lord Randolph to meet many of his Irish friends'.[1] Winston Churchill, Ashbourne and others claimed that these gatherings were 'unpolitical'; given the personnel, this could hardly be so. Fitz-Gibbon sometimes called his annual gathering 'the feast of the holy innocents', but he also referred to it as 'the *haute école* of intelligent toryism',[2] and this was nearer the mark. Sometimes the company was eclectic enough to frighten off even Churchill;[3] but then he generally came for the new year instead. And, to anticipate, the Christmas of 1885 was just one of his returns to FitzGibbon's '*haute école*', when the intelligent tories introduced him to the unintelligent but potent toryism of Colonel Saunderson and the Ulster unionists.

2

When considering Churchill's behaviour in relation to Irish issues after he left the country in 1880, many of his actions must be seen in terms of fourth party politics: the running skirmish carried on against both front benches by Churchill, Gorst, Wolff and—at a slight distance—Balfour. The fact that the fourth party's policy (a loose term) was more often than not to place themselves between parties meant that they automatically seemed aligned with the Irish; the recurrent rumours of their breakup were generally seen as meaning a setback to the Irish cause.[4] The fourth party consolidated

---

[1] Wynne, *An Irishman and his family*, p. 97.

[2] FitzGibbon to Churchill, 23 Dec. 1888 (R.C.P., 1/xxiii/3032).

[3] As at Christmas 1889 when he went to Sandringham instead, possibly because Balfour was to be at Howth; see FitzGibbon to Churchill, 5 Jan. 1890 (R.C.P., 1/xxv/3359).

[4] As for instance in April 1883, over the debate on the criminal code; see 'Parliamentary progress' column in *Weekly Freeman*, 21 Apr. 1883.

this impression by presenting arguments which used the Irish case, on issues like the *clôture*.[1] However, many of the issues chosen by Churchill to differentiate himself from his leaders' low-key approach had to do with attacking the government for not proceeding firmly against the Irish malcontents.[2] Escalation of confrontation attitudes was in the fourth party's interests; Gorst proudly told Churchill that Charles Russell believed they were responsible for most of the threatening letters in Ireland.[3] Their priority was to use language so extreme that, for instance, Northcote wondered in November 1881 if the government might arrest Churchill on his next visit to Ireland.[4] The Irish appreciated the raising of the political temperature, and ignored the actual implication of what Churchill was saying.

At the same time, he continued to represent himself as an Irish expert, referring to his first-hand knowledge of the country on every possible occasion (his recurrent desire for the chief secretary-ship may have been manifesting itself early on). To an extent, he was successful; even the despised Northcote referred to him on Irish affairs.[5] But his line on Ireland was not as sympathetic to the nationalists as it sometimes seemed. In the fourth party, both Gorst and Wolff were far more radical on the issue of home rule. Gorst had his own Irish connections;[6] he visited the country on fact-

---

[1] Which Churchill denounced on 1 Nov. 1882 as 'an evil, abhorrent and intolerable conspiracy' between the two front benches; quoted in *Weekly Irish Times*, 14 Nov. 1882.

[2] He was prepared to call for Davitt's arrest in January 1881, to embarrass the government; see *Weekly Freeman*, 17 Feb. 1881.

[3] Gorst to Churchill, 2 Nov. 1880 (R.C.P. 1/i/19).

[4] Northcote to Gibson, 7 Nov. 1881 (H.L.R.O., Ashbourne papers, B/71/16).

[5] See Northcote to Churchill on Parnell's arrest, 3 Nov. 1881 (R.C.P. 1/i/54). In 1880 Disraeli mentioned to Wolff Churchill's 'ability and authority' regarding Irish affairs (Disraeli to Wolff, 11 Nov. 1880; H. D. Wolff, *Rambling recollections* (London, 1908), ii, 264).

[6] Including the murky Philip Callan, being involved in his court case against T. D. Sullivan; see Gorst to Churchill, 19 Sept. 1880 (R.C.P., 1/i/180) and 27 Nov. 1880 (ibid., 1/i/30).

finding tours; he disliked Ulster tories and southern landlords; and he dreamt of working home rule into an expansive imperial framework.[1] He wrote to Churchill about this, wondering if the fourth party should 'shadow out' such a scheme in parliament.[2] Wolff was nearly as adaptable. He too had Irish connections;[3] and, like Gorst, he could cheerfully accept the inevitability of Irish separation. He believed that whatever measure of home rule might arrive would make little enough difference in the end. Like Gorst, he was ready to anticipate the trend, in the conservative interest.[4]

But Churchill never committed himself thus far, at least on paper; maybe because such was not his practice (when he wrote at length and discursively there tended to be a motive of publicity in the background), or maybe because he did not believe in the idea. Nor did Balfour commit himself: possibly indicating the difference between Wolff and Gorst, 'scholarship boys' in politics, and their allies, who were born to inherit the political earth and expected— with good reason—to do so. The others never felt they could rely on Balfour, who in his turn suspected Churchill of too much Irish

---

[1] On the question of the Ulster tories see Gorst to W. H. Smith, quoted in A. Jones, *The politics of reform, 1884* (Cambridge, 1971), p. 81. For his more general ideas see a long letter to Churchill, 21 Oct. 1881 (R.C.P., 1/i/52) reporting enthusiastically on the chances for a conservative initiative in Ireland.

[2] See Gorst to Churchill, 29 Jan. 1883 (ibid., 1/i/105); in this letter he assumed that the home-rulers would get their way in the end, and should be anticipated, capitalising on the probable advantage to the conservative party in a scheme of federal devolution. He recurred to this later (Gorst to Churchill, 15 Aug. 1883, ibid., 1/i/157) and continued to cultivate his Irish contacts.

[3] Wolff was liked by the Irish members (*Rambling recollections*, ii, 116) and Parnell and O'Connor used him as a channel to Salisbury in August 1883 (Wolff to Churchill, 25 Aug. 1883; R.C.P., 1/i/160).

[4] See Wolff to Churchill, 28 May 1886 (ibid., 1/xii/1514); 'You will see that when the Irish get home rule they will split into two parties and the protestants will have the whip hand.' In October 1885 he sent Churchill (at the latter's request) a long memorandum urging that if home rule was taken up 'before it is forced on you, it might be carried out satisfactorily'. He pointed to the Hungarian experiment, and held no fears for the protestant interest (memorandum dated 9 Oct. 1885, ibid., 1/viii/961).

trafficking.[1] But it is interesting to speculate as to what extent he was learning from Churchill the decisive ideas on Irish policy which he, and not Churchill, would eventually have the opportunity to put into practice—if only after their time had gone by.

Even if Churchill avoided theoretical commitment in these years, his actions gave rise to widespread suppositions of a covert relationship with the Irish. He was capable of light references to the inevitability of home rule in private; and there was a considerable sympathy on the personal level, as well as identity of political interest, between the Parnellites and Churchill, especially in the early days of obstruction.[2] There was also a frivolous public camaraderie between them, which involved Churchill having long discussions with Justin McCarthy about recent novels during dull debates, and making Mrs Jeune sing 'The wearing of the green' at dinner parties attended by Northcote.[3] Churchill also got on remarkably well with Biggar,[4] and communicated closely with Healy;[5] he met Parnell at Mrs Jeune's, one of the few social waterholes frequented by the Irish leader,[6] and was often noticed sitting with him, Sexton, and Labouchere round the stove in the lower smoke-room of the house

[1] See Balfour to Churchill (n.d. [late 1880]; ibid., 1/i/21); in December, Churchill wanted to join with the Irish and radicals in reneging on the late government's Irish policy (Wolff to Churchill, 28 Dec. 1880; ibid., 1/i/34).

[2] For Churchill's remarks about home rule at this period see letter to Morris, 23 Oct. 1884 (Wynne, *An Irishman and his family*, p. 120), and, more seriously, Healy's statement that Churchill 'spoke vaguely about home rule' to his Irish contacts in 1885 (Algar Thorold, *The life of Henry Labouchere* (London, 1913), p. 231). F. H. O'Donnell refers to him as an 'ally' (*History of the Irish parliamentary party* (London, 1910), i, 486–7, ii, 186); and William O'Brien recalled the common ground between the fourth party and the Irish, and the inability of liberals to understand the warmth of their relationship, which did not follow the normal course of British party politics (*Evening memories* (London, 1920), pp 82–3).

[3] Justin McCarthy, *Reminiscences* (London, 1899), i, 433–4, 436.

[4] Henry Lucy, *A diary of two parliaments*, ii (London, 1886), 228–9, 299–300.

[5] Healy, *Letters and leaders*, i, 128, 130, 213.

[6] See S. E. M. Jeune, baroness St Helier, *Memories of fifty years* (London, 1909), p. 171.

of commons.[1] McCarthy emphasised how Churchill liked to create the *impression* of an alliance. Numerous conservative authorities have concluded with relief that no actual compact existed.[2] There certainly, however, seemed to be an 'understanding'. When Churchill brought an anti-Irish line into debate, it was as often as not simply in order to raise a contentious point at a juncture in the session which precluded any real discussion.[3] When he came round to supporting coercion in early 1881, it was in such an ambivalent way that he was thought to be abandoning the fourth party;[4] he continued to taunt Forster's policy as being at once draconian and inept,[5] and to be referred to by Gladstone as the Irish party's 'single English ally'. As the prime minister kept pointing out, Churchill's position in regard to the Irish was shared by no one else in the house.

But in many ways his idiosyncratic approach could be attributed to his particular Irish *unionist* bias. He disapproved of the liberal policy of coercion unaccompanied by remedial measures, as did FitzGibbon and Morris; and he railed against the government's inability to use the existing jury law more intelligently for the maintenance of order, again like any conservative Dublin lawyer. To attack the Errington mission, to call for grants to Irish fisheries, was also in this tradition. The exigencies of parliamentary tactics could lead onlookers to infer an alliance: when Churchill could, for instance, begin a speech on the land bill of 1881 by congratulating Parnell on it, then denounce it as an expropriating measure, and finally mount a campaign of amendments related to it, despite anguished requests from W. H. Smith to cease.[6] Over land pur-

---

[1] Healy, *Letters and leaders*, i, 155.

[2] Besides Churchill's biographers, see Lord George Hamilton, *Parliamentary reminiscences and reflections* (London, 1917), i, 179.

[3] As when he asked whether exceptional powers would be asked for to govern Ireland in August 1880; see *Weekly Irish Times*, 28 Aug. 1880.

[4] See report in *Weekly Irish Times*, 12 Feb. 1881.

[5] Asking, for instance, why he did not arrest Archbishop Croke as well as Father Sheehy; see *Weekly Irish Times*, 28 May 1881.

[6] See *Hansard 3*, cclxiv, 138–47, reporting debate of 29 July 1881; also W. H. Smith to Churchill, 27 July 1881 (R.C.P., 1/i/45). For Churchill's line

chase, too, Churchill combined extravagent public denunciation with sober private investigations.[1] On the issue of franchise extension in Ireland he changed front not once, but twice;[2] at a juncture when one can certainly see the pressures of English party politics far outweighing any actual analysis of the Irish situation.[3]

Whether or not this was always the case is difficult to say; but what one can establish is that Irish nationalist opinion held out great hopes for him, and usually gave him the benefit of the doubt. In England, his stand over the Irish franchise in 1884 was seen purely in terms of opportunism or power politics; in Ireland, the *Freeman* hailed him as '*the* man of his party'.[4] He was also seen as 'recognising the influence upon the Irish youth of education and the study of the past history and present political position of their country',[5] a reference to the fact that he was pursuing his continuing involvement in Irish educational schemes—principally through FitzGibbon and the duchess's old friend Dr Molloy (described by FitzGibbon as 'a colourless philomath who attends evening parties at Dublin castle

---

on Irish fisheries see 'In the house', *Weekly Freeman*, 8 Nov. 1884; and for the Errington mission, ibid., 2 May 1885.

[1] He was seen as a likely follower of Lord George Hamilton on this issue in July 1883. Also see George Fottrell to Churchill, 13 July 1885 (R.C.P., 1/vi/692), providing information in response to an initiative from Churchill.

[2] He had called for Irish franchise extension in his 1877 Woodstock speech, turned against the idea in 1879 (*Hansard 3*, ccxliii, 1231–6), and to the delight of the Irish opposed his leaders by supporting it once more in May 1884 (*Hansard 3*, cclxxxviii, 853–61).

[3] His opposition of Brodrick's motion to exclude the Irish from franchise extension was closely connected with his simultaneous dealings with Healy and Parnell over Beach's motion of censure on the Egyptian question (W. St John Brodrick, earl of Midleton, *Records and reactions* (London, 1934), p. 62; also see Jones, *Politics of reform*, pp 128–9). It was at this time, Churchill later told Henry James, that Parnell 'came several times to my house' and 'arranged many things . . . the most perfect confidence existing between us' (Cooke and Vincent, *Lord Carlingford's journal*, pp 129–30, n. 2). For further references to Churchill's constant negotiations with the Irish, see D. W. R. Bahlman (ed.), *The diary of Sir Edward Walter Hamilton* (Oxford, 1972), ii, 617, 712; and Cooke and Vincent, op. cit., p. 129, n. 2.

[4] See leader in *Weekly Freeman*, 24 May 1884.

[5] Ibid.

but is a gentleman').[1] Molloy and others believed that Churchill alone was reliable regarding catholic educational claims, and had dreams—which they shyly shared with him—of seeing him as chief secretary.[2] When the tories briefly entered power in 1885, they did do something for Irish education, in the educational endowments act, which went some way towards the kind of financial restructuring outlined by Churchill in his pamphlet and on the Rosse commission. This took place via a concerted effort by FitzGibbon, Holmes (conservative attorney-general for Ireland and a protégé of FitzGibbon), and Churchill himself.[3] Sexton was also involved and, at a later stage, Dwyer Gray—dealing directly with Churchill. The measure was passed on 14 August, the last day of the session.

When the constitution of the commission set up by this act ran into trouble with the Irish hierarchy, Churchill involved himself, at FitzGibbon's request sending a letter full of 'vigour and vertebra', in FitzGibbon's phrase, to bring the bishops to heel.[4] But when

---

[1] FitzGibbon to Churchill, 9 Sept. 1885 (R.C.P., 1/vii/883).

[2] In the house on 6 August 1884 Churchill condemned the queen's colleges and emphasised that Irish education must be made formally denominational. Molloy wrote thanking him for 'exposing the delusion about mixed education . . . I am quite satisfied that you have mastered the difficult question of Irish education, that you have cleared away the mists in which it has been too long enveloped, and that you are better able to deal with the subject in a thorough and reasonable way than any other statesman of the day'; he added that he held high hopes of Churchill as chief secretary (7 Aug. 1884; ibid., 1/v/466).

[3] Molloy had pressed the question on Churchill from late June (Molloy to Churchill, 26 June 1885; ibid., 1/v/651). For details of catholic organisation at the time see Larkin, *Roman Catholic church*, pp 304, 314–15; and for Holmes's part, Cooke and Vincent, 'Ireland and party politics', pt I, in *I.H.S.*, xvi, no. 62 (Sept. 1968), pp 154, 160–61. FitzGibbon had insisted on coming over at once, though Churchill had not been very receptive (see FitzGibbon to Churchill, 5 Aug. 1885, R.C.P., 1/vi/772). Dwyer Gray communicated catholic discontent to Churchill on 23 August, nine days after the measure passed (ibid., 1/vii/825); also Larkin, *Roman Catholic church*, 320–22).

[4] Walsh objected to the membership of the commission, which he felt under-represented the catholic interest. See Larkin, *Roman Catholic church*, pp 320–22; FitzGibbon to Churchill, 1 Sept. 1885 (R.C.P., 1/vii/853), 9 Sept. 1885 (ibid., 1/vii/883), 11 Oct. 1885 (ibid., 1/viii/967), 13 Sept. 1885 (ibid.,

FitzGibbon went on to drive a rift between the moderates, such as Delany and Molloy, and the increasingly intransigent figure of Archbishop Walsh, Churchill baulked. The story of education commission politics in 1885–6 has a symbolic interest; the clerics who had been so pleased to work with the Marlboroughs in the 1870s can be seen as crushed between the immovable presbyterian interest on one side, and the equally intractable Walsh on the other. There was a new dispensation at work. Churchill failed to see it; he pressed FitzGibbon not to play episcopal politics, telling him the bishops were the only bulwark between them and home rule, which 'they don't care a damn for'.[1] This may have held good in the 1870s, but by 1885 it was no longer true. Walsh was determined on an intransigent stance, and in December 1885 he formally boycotted the commission after all. Churchill did not give up; he asked Salisbury's permission to 'intrigue with Walsh' on his Irish trip in that month, believing that FitzGibbon had not understood him.[2]

But FitzGibbon had decided that Churchill's policy of winning over the bishops was no longer viable,[3] an assessment also reached by Carnarvon.[4] Churchill continued to back FitzGibbon in his parleys about catholic university education (and had drawn up plans for this in a sweeping remedial outline of Irish policy which he presented to Salisbury in November 1885).[5] However, on uni-

---

1/viii/971); also Carnarvon to Churchill, 16 Oct. 1885 (ibid., 1/viii/980), Larkin, p. 328, and Labouchere to Chamberlain, 23 Dec. 1885, in Thorold, *Labouchere*, p. 252.

[1] 'It is to the bishops entirely to whom [sic] I look in the future to turn, to mitigate, or to postpone the home rule onslaught . . .' (Churchill to FitzGibbon, 14 Oct. 1885; R.C.P., 1/viii/978. See also W. S. Churchill, *Lord Randolph Churchill*, ii, 4).

[2] See Cooke and Vincent, *Governing passion*, p. 296.

[3] Fitzgibbon to Churchill, 10 Nov. 1885 (R.C.P., 1/ix/1048).

[4] In a long memorandum of 7 December (see Larkin, *Roman Catholic church*, pp 346–9).

[5] For his outline on Irish policy to Salisbury see W. S. Churchill, *Lord Randolph Churchill*, ii, 8–14, and original in R.C.P., 1/x/1126. He wanted to transfer the Cork college to a catholic board of management, endow the catholic college in Dublin, establish a catholic college in Armagh, and transfer the college in Belfast to a presbyterian board of management.

versity education too Walsh stuck fast, after lengthy negotiations;[1] taking his ground on the point most impossible for Irish unionist opinion to accept, a demand for changes in the status of Trinity College, 'the citadel of ascendancy'.[2] This led to a series of letters from FitzGibbon to Churchill, remarkable for their uncharacteristically alarmist tone. The existence of non-landed Irish protestants, he wrote, depended upon Trinity; already an exodus of professional men had begun from Dublin, for the sake of their children's education.[3] Walsh's obstinacy and FitzGibbon's alarmism came at just the point when Churchill was switching to a confrontation policy. And he had visited Dublin twice that autumn and winter; he saw much of the Howth symposium; he ended by falling back on a violent unionist initiative. If there were objective Irish reasons as well as obviously expedient English ones, it seems logical to look at the suddenly embattled attitude of his Dublin contacts, and the breakdown of negotiations with the traditionally friendly Irish episcopacy.

There were also, of course, party manœuvres, which can provide reasons for this as for everything else. Intense negotiations between Churchill and the Irish during the summer were alleged by everyone from John Dillon to Herbert Gladstone,[4] and a home-rule undertaking was widely inferred; but others had heard that Churchill anticipated, early on, a policy which involved ditching the Irish by

---

[1] Principally between FitzGibbon and Molloy; see FitzGibbon to Churchill, 7 Dec. 1885 and 11 Dec. 1885 (R.C.P., 1/x/449, 461); also Carnarvon to Churchill, 16 Dec. 1885 (ibid., 1/x/1157) and A. B. Cooke and J. R. Vincent, 'Ireland and party politics', pt III, in *I.H.S.*, xvi, no. 63 (Sept. 1969), p. 452.

[2] FitzGibbon to Churchill, 16 Jan. 1886 (R.C.P., 1/xi/1354).

[3] 'The existence of the imperialists and protestants (other than landowners) of Ireland depends on the maintenance of the higher education now offered them in the University of Dublin' (FitzGibbon to Churchill, 16 Feb. 1886; ibid., 1/xii/1380). He went on to give instances of lawyers and other professional men leaving Dublin in order to ensure their children an education in England.

[4] See report in *Weekly Irish Times*, 21 Nov. 1885.

occupying a strong anti-home-rule platform.[1] A shadowy dimension is added to Churchill's dealings with the Irish by his links with less savoury members of the party like Callan and O'Shea. Callan, the contentious M.P. for Louth who was the first to raise in public the spectre of the O'Shea liaison against Parnell,[2] wrote to Churchill in 1885 making ominous allegations about the home-rule leader, asking for money to continue in politics, and later soliciting a job in India.[3] Cardinal Manning urgently asked Churchill to oblige; perhaps he knew Callan's secrets, and his proverbially loose tongue.[4] O'Shea, too, was on close terms with Churchill (he turns up in 1881 in the bizarre role of Churchill's second in a threatened duel with Hartington).[5] They themselves later crossed swords metaphorically on several occasions, Churchill at one point mischievously referring to O'Shea in public as 'repugnant politically *and from every point of view* to the Irish party.'[6] O'Shea took violent exception to this,[7] and it is likely that Churchill was throwing out a hint; Parnell's private life was stale gossip in Churchill's circle by 1886.[8] O'Shea later

---

[1] See Blunt, *Land war in Ireland*, p. 183, and Labouchere to Chamberlain, 1 Dec. 1885 (Thorold, *Labouchere*, p. 244).

[2] See F. S. L. Lyons, *Charles Stewart Parnell* (London, 1977), pp 306–7; on Callan's career, see references in Thornley, *Isaac Butt*, p. 329; Cooke and Vincent, *Lord Carlingford's journal*, p. 141, n. 3; Lucy, *Diary of two parliaments*, ii, 95–7; O'Donnell, *Irish parliamentary party*, i, 315. By 1885 most of the Irish party saw him as a pariah, but he was cultivated by politicians like Chamberlain (Viscount Milner, J. A. Spender and others, *Life of Joseph Chamberlain*, published by Associated Newspapers, London, n.d.). I owe this last reference to Professor J. R. Vincent.

[3] Callan to Churchill, 19 Nov. 1885 and 27 Nov. 1885 (R.C.P., 1/ix/1070, 1105). Of Parnell he wrote: '*He* has not a few secrets, and they are very well kept.'

[4] Manning to Churchill, 15 Jan. 1886 (ibid., 1/xi/1277).

[5] R. R. James, *Lord Randolph Churchill*, p. 107.

[6] This wording appeared in *The Times*, the *Freeman* leaving out the italicised clause.

[7] See O'Shea to Churchill, 15 Feb. 1886 (R.C.P., 1/xi/1387), also N.L.I., O'Shea MSS, MS 5732.

[8] See Labouchere to Churchill, 31 Dec. 1886 (R.C.P., 1/xviii/2274) and Alfred Rothschild to Churchill, 25 Sept. 1886 (ibid., 1/xvi/1842).

worked with Churchill over catholic education.[1] Possibly Churchill retained links with Callan and O'Shea because of the potential advantage to be derived from Parnell's personal position, though it could as well be put down to a bohemian love of slumming, or a congenital addiction to intrigue.

Not everyone, however, saw him in this light. The fourth party wrote derisively to each other about Wilfrid Scawen Blunt, who expected Churchill to be redeemed through Ireland and to assume the 'mantle of conscience' from Gladstone's shoulders, as well as that of Elijah from Salisbury's;[2] he took a long time to disembarrass himself from the conception. Blunt was not alone; W. H. Duignan, a radical interested in Ireland, also tried to enrol Churchill publicly on the side of the angels.[3] And from the opposite bias, chauvinist tory democrats worried desperately about Churchill's seduction by Irish issues,[4] which seemed to contradict their hopes of him. Similarly, the gimcrack iconography of the Primrose League had nothing to do with remedial ideas about Ireland.

It is a moot point how far all these expectations and fears would have been upheld if Churchill had ever become chief secretary. An

[1] See Churchill to Salisbury, 15 Nov. 1886, and O'Shea to Churchill, 22 Nov. 1886 (ibid., 1/xvii/2020, 2048).

[2] This conceit appears in a letter from Blunt to Churchill, 19 June 1884 (ibid., 1/iii/412). For a characteristic reference to Blunt's *naïveté* see Gorst to Churchill, 24 Dec. 1883 (ibid., 1/ii/230). Blunt was convinced that Churchill had unequivocally declared to him in 1885 his support for home rule. Up to January 1886 he believed—and was told by others—that Churchill's intention was to educate his party in this direction (*Land war in Ire.*, pp 1, 18, 20, 34, 140, 143). Blunt even believed Churchill had converted a group of Cambridge undergraduates to home rule (ibid., p. 24). When Winston Churchill's life of his father appeared in 1906, Blunt's chief criticism was that the book obscured Churchill's initial commitment to home rule (W. S. Blunt, *My diaries, being a personal narrative of events 1888–1914* (London, 1919–20), ii, 128).

[3] See Duignan to Churchill, 28 Dec. 1883 (R.C.P., 1/ii/235). For Duignan's connection with Ireland see C. H. D. Howard (ed.), '"The man on a tricycle"; W. H. Duignan and Ireland, 1881–5', in *I.H.S.*, xiv, no. 55 (Mar. 1965), pp 246–60.

[4] See A. B. Forwood to Churchill, 11 and 21 May 1884 (R.C.P., 1/iii/377, 395) asking him to stop cultivating Parnell and warning him that the anti-Irish conservative workingmen were being alienated.

ostensibly solid rumour of this reached Portarlington in June 1885, and delighted him.[1] Even though Churchill went to the India office instead, he still presented Salisbury with an enormous memorandum on Irish policy in November;[2] this took an impeccably anti-repeal line, which may or may not have been principally dictated by a wish to tell Salisbury what it was politic for him to hear. In January 1886 Churchill suggested himself as an alternative to Smith for the chief secretaryship, an idea that recurred in June, when Beach shuddered at it as 'an ideally bad appointment'.[3] Through 1885–6 Churchill was constantly receiving advice about Ireland, several tory contacts there advocating a constitutional alliance with Parnell and remedial legislation 'only short of a separate legislature';[4] even Morris suggested an above-party solution, incorporating Parnell.[5] Churchill sent a *non possumus* reply, in terms of strict ministerial piety: 'radical work must be done by radical artists', he chided Morris, who must have gulped.[6] But copies of such letters were simultaneously sent by him to an approving Salisbury,[7] self-presentation being as ever an urgent priority.

There was also a constant thread of advice from FitzGibbon, who

---

[1] 'Your appointment would be *such* a popular one in Ireland, especially with all the Roman Catholic party. . . . The fact is, *you* are the only conservative leader who understands this country. All the others are really in full ignorance of it. They have *never been* over here, and look at all Irish matters from a purely *English* point of view' (Portarlington to Churchill, 'June 1885' (ibid., 1/v/629)).

[2] See W. S. Churchill, *Lord Randolph Churchill*, ii, 8–14, and R.C.P., 1/x/1126.

[3] See Churchill to Salisbury, 16 Jan. 1886 (W. S. Churchill, *Lord Randolph Churchill*, ii, 36); also A. B. Cooke and J. R. Vincent, 'Ireland and party politics', pt II, in *I.H.S.*, xvi, no. 63 (Mar. 1969), p. 329.

[4] See G. Birdwood to Churchill, 5 Dec. 1885, and E. Wilmot to Churchill, 19 Dec. 1885 (R.C.P., 1/x/1138, 1189).

[5] See Morris to Churchill, 5 Dec. 1885 (ibid., 1/x/1137). Gibson agreed with such an idea (Hardinge, *Carnarvon*, iii, 204).

[6] Churchill to Morris, 7 Dec. 1885 (Wynne, *An Irishman and his family*, and R.C.P., 1/x/445).

[7] Salisbury wrote to Churchill that he 'could not say how heartily he agreed with the tone' of Churchill's letter to Morris (Salisbury to Churchill, 8 Dec. 1885; ibid., 1/x/1149a).

more and more emphatically urged Churchill 'not to touch the national question'; rumours had reached Dublin of a halting tory home-rule scheme in December 1885.[1] There is an implication in this and other letters that FitzGibbon was not sure of Churchill's reliability on the issue. This urgency heightened as the 'Hawarden kite' tugged at its moorings in mid-December; but Churchill was due at Howth for Christmas (he had already been there in September, as well as encountering FitzGibbon at Ashbourne's French holiday house in August). Pressure would be applied then. Nationalist opinion in Dublin continued to have hopes of a tory conversion under Churchill; in early 1886 reference was still being made to the chance of a settlement represented by the catholic conservative ethos.[2] Much attention had been paid earlier to Churchill's criticism of the Dublin Castle system published in the *Pall Mall Gazette*.[3] When he first entered office, the *Freeman*

---

[1] 'There remains only the national question—*for heaven's sake don't touch it!* It is red hot. If Parnell takes it up, he must either formulate a demand for total separation, on which whig and tory must join in giving him a facer, or by some recognition of a continuation of the English connection alienate his extreme followers, who even now are only with difficulty induced to put up with the constitutional method of promoting Irish independence. If Gladstone takes it up he must split with either the Irish or the whigs, whom the counties have returned in force—if an attempt is made to compel you to take it up you can meet it by requiring, as Gladstone did, those who have the mandate to formulate the demand, and at the worst you need only an inquiry, pending which the waste and disintegration which time brings with it will go on, and your university bill with your other measures move on in peace. . . .' (Fitz-Gibbon to Churchill, 7 Dec. 1885; ibid., 1/x/1149). A postscript warned Churchill against any thought of coalition. See also same to same, 11 Dec. 1885 (ibid., 1/x/1161).

[2] See for instance Gavan Duffy's article in the *National Review*, Jan. 1885, pp 721–40, urging the conservatives to take up the Irish question; a similar case was presented by Henry Bellingham in the *St Stephen's Review*, Jan. 1886. M.P.s such as Justin McCarthy were similarly inclined; and as late as October 1885 Davitt was telling Labouchere of an influential lobby within the Irish party who would prefer a conservative home-rule bill to a liberal one, largely because of the conservatives' record on denominational education (Thorold, *Labouchere*, p. 234).

[3] See a long and approving editorial in *Weekly Freeman*, 6 Dec. 1884. Churchill had referred to the Castle as 'a nest of political corruption'.

referred to him approvingly as 'a friend to Ireland';[1] a Unionist correspondent informed him 'you are popular to a surprising degree in Ireland.'[2]

The political shifts of 1885–6 have been microscopically dealt with elsewhere,[3] with careful attention to Churchill's part in them. Afterwards, he himself chose to see these bewildering months in terms of the realisation by the tories that they could not govern without coercion—despite the fact that he for one had made it clear he could not enter a government committed to such a policy. For this basic contradiction Churchill violently, and conveniently, blamed Ashbourne's erroneous and self-interested advice on the Irish situation to Salisbury.[4] Others did not see Churchill's progress towards advocacy of coercion in mid-January 1886 as a moral dilemma, but simply as trimming. He was in an impossible position; his genius for giving easy impressions out of office was called to account once power was gained. July 1885 had seen his celebrated challenge to his leaders in the Maamtrasna debate, when he went against prearranged conservative tactics by denouncing the Spencer regime and promising the Parnellites an inquiry into the Maamtrasna murders.[5] Salisbury was not particularly bothered,[6] but the

---

[1] When attacking Corrie Grant's opposition to Churchill's Woodstock candidature, June 1885; see *Weekly Freeman*, 4 July 1885.

[2] H. Rochfort to Churchill, 9 July 1885 (R.C.P., 1/vi/681).

[3] See Cooke and Vincent, *Governing passion.*

[4] See memorandum in R.C.P., 1/v/620. Churchill's theme was that Ashbourne, being anxious for office, a peerage and a pension, was prepared to advise anything that would expedite this; and the tories entering office, which was based on Ashbourne's advice that they could govern without coercion, forced Gladstone to go for home rule.

[5] This incident, so Spencer told many people, led him to accept home rule, as an alternative to Irish law and order becoming a party shuttlecock. See Brodrick, *Records and reactions*, p. 63, and Ross, *Years of my pilgrimage*, p. 177. In England, people assumed that it indicated a formal tory-Parnellite alliance; in Ireland, Carnarvon was inaccurately identified with the action (see Larkin, *Roman Catholic church*, p. 318).

[6] 'I do not think R. Churchill could have said much else, pledged as he was': Salisbury to Carnarvon, 22 July 1885 (Hardinge, *Carnarvon*, iii, 170).

Ulster tories were infuriated. Churchill attempted to mollify them with a speech at Sheffield, geared, not very convincingly, to ridiculing the very idea of a Parnellite alliance.[1] But the Ulstermen were not appeased; to Churchill's chagrin, Lord Claud Hamilton (a moving spirit in defence organisations in the province as well as a creator of the Ulster unionist base in parliament) refused to share a platform with him in Liverpool the next month.[2] Conservative candidates in November inundated him with requests to make it publicly clear that he had not sold his political soul to the Parnellites, though they also begged him for help with the Irish vote in their constituencies.[3] His Irish unionist contacts also emphasised the message.[4] Visiting Dublin in September and October, Churchill attempted to reassure them, informing Holmes that 'we must have nothing to do with home rule in any shape or form'.[5] Holmes, a flinty unionist lawyer with an Ulster background, hardly needed telling; the intention was primarily to clarify Churchill's own position, and provide reassurance. Christmas saw him once more at Howth. On this visit, Blunt believed Churchill was still talking home rule to select acquaintances,[6] though he had already made his position after the flight of the Hawarden kite clear to McCarthy and

[1] See *Weekly Freeman*, 12 Sept. 1885. Both Fitzgibbon and Gibson warmly approved of this speech (FitzGibbon to Churchill, 9 Sept. 1885; R.C.P., 1/vii/883).

[2] See Churchill to Forwood, n.d. (ibid., 1/vi/1737). Lord Claud's brother, Lord George Hamilton, who was closer to Churchill, spoke to him after the Maamtrasna debate, and was told that he was extremely perturbed by the die-hard reaction (Lord George Hamilton, *Parliamentary reminiscences and reflections*, i, 283).

[3] See for instance G. A. Jamieson to Churchill, 14 Nov. 1885, and H. R. Hughes to Churchill, 25 Nov. 1885 (R.C.P., 1/ix/1063, 1902).

[4] FitzGibbon to Churchill, 8 June 1886 (ibid., 1/xiii/1526).

[5] This is quoted in W. S. Churchill, *Lord Randolph Churchill*, i, 459–61, and probably came from a letter to the author by Holmes himself.

[6] Blunt, *Land war in Ire.*, pp 26, 45. His proposed 'intrigue' with Walsh, however, almost certainly concerned no more than the membership of the educational endowments commission (cf. Cooke and Vincent, *Governing passion*, pp 296–7).

to Blunt himself.[1] Back in London in January, he began his with-drawal from formal opposition to coercion, constantly bombarded by FitzGibbon, as he did so, with calls for firm measures.[2] Carnarvon, who had been led along by Churchill through a halcyon Irish summer of home-rule half-promises, where many of his contacts and ideas echoed Churchill's,[3] was scandalised to see his supposed ally a convert to draconian measures by mid-January. At this point Churchill floated the idea of proclaiming the national league and arresting prominent politicians and league leaders. There is a key

---

[1] 'His party thought they had no chance about home rule after Gladstone had taken it up, and they had therefore better drop it and take to the British philistine view' (Justin McCarthy to Mrs Praed, 'December 1885', in Justin McCarthy and Mrs Campbell Praed, *Our book of memories* (London, 1912), p. 28). Also Churchill to Blunt, 27 Dec. 1885: 'If you want home rule, you must go to Mr Gladstone. We cannot touch it.' (Blunt, *Land war in Ire.*, p. 9).

[2] Rather than 'spasms' or 'a dribbling crescendo', he wanted a measure 'unlimited in duration and such as will make trivial overt acts summarily punishable wherever committed and enable serious cases to be tried by special juries' (FitzGibbon to Churchill, 16 and 18 Jan. 1886; R.C.P., 1/xi/1354-5); essentially the view taken by Spencer and his associates a year earlier. At the same time Churchill was writing to Salisbury in much the same vein, but ended by accepting the 'orthodox coercion line' (see A. B. Cooke and J. R. Vincent, 'Ireland and party politics', pt III, in *I.H.S.*, xvi, no. 64 (Sept. 1969), p. 454). Having come round to Salisbury's way of thinking, Churchill brought pressure to bear on Beach too (see letters between Churchill and Salisbury, 16 Jan. 1886, R.C.P., 1/xi/1302a, 1302b; also Beach to Churchill, 17 Jan. 1886, ibid., 1/xi/1305). On 24 January Salisbury told the queen that Churchill had come round to open coercion 'under party pressure' (*Letters of Queen Victoria*, 3rd ser., i, 17); on 26 January, as soon as the government fell, Churchill offered himself to Saunderson for a Belfast trip.

[3] On Churchill's relations with Carnarvon see Cooke and Vincent, 'Ireland and party politics', pt III, pp 452-5, and *Governing passion*. Churchill's correspondence for autumn 1885 shows them in close agreement over Irish educa-tion, the hierarchy, and the ignorance of the English press on Irish issues; Carnarvon visited Churchill's uncle, Portarlington, and hoped for a *rappro-chement* between Ashbourne and Churchill. But by December, Churchill was frightening Carnarvon badly; and for his part, Churchill wanted Carnarvon dropped from early December, and knew from mid-December that he would be. Churchill's draconian ideas of mid-January alientated Carnarvon at once, since he felt that war on the national league was ruled out because of the clergy's close identification with it.

in the fact that, as outlined initially to Holmes, this scheme was part of a plan which involved—yet again—Churchill going to Ireland as chief secretary.[1] But Carnarvon could only take refuge in the comforting assumption that Churchill was mad.[2]

This was not, in fact, the case. But Churchill had heard, via Henry James and Labouchere, that Parnell would not be fobbed off with remedial measures;[3] he wanted a powerful initiative, probably led by himself, in Ireland; he had been apprised by FitzGibbon of the significance of the hierarchy's new hard line; and he had to allay suspicions of his own reliability on the home-rule question. As for Carnarvonism and Carnarvon, Churchill had never been committed to the viceroy, who was brutally categorised by the FitzGibbon circle as a 'gusher';[4] Holmes thought him 'weak, vain, and emotional',[5] and Churchill followed this line too. Later, he magnanimously described Carnarvon to McCarthy as 'a Don Quixote', adding unnecessarily 'I am not that kind of man at all'.[6] Nevertheless, by this point, he was engaging himself to go adventuring in Ulster, where windmills tilted at rhetorically could turn out to be giants after all.

[1] See Cooke and Vincent, 'Ireland and party politics', pt I, pp 168–9. Churchill had already scandalised Holmes with the notion of arresting the Irish members on the charge of high treason, and Sir Algernon Bourke had relayed similar ideas to an equally horrified W. S. Blunt five days before the cabinet of 15 January (Blunt, *Land war in Ire.*, p. 18). For Carnarvon's reactions to Churchill's 'extraordinary proposals' at the cabinet meeting, see Hardinge, *Carnarvon*, iii, 211–12.

[2] Carnarvon's diary, 29 July 1886 (Hardinge, *Carnarvon*, iii, 232).

[3] James to Churchill, 30 Jan. 1886 (R.C.P., 1/xi/1349).

[4] FitzGibbon kept Churchill caustically informed of Carnarvon's doings in 1885 (see, for instance, ibid., 1/x/1196).

[5] Cooke and Vincent, 'Ireland and party politics', pt I, p. 163.

[6] McCarthy, *Reminiscences*, i, 437.

3

Immediately following these shifts in emphasis, Churchill publicly identified himself with hardline Ulster unionism in February 1886, a *rapprochement* begun before the tories left office, though he would have seemed the most unlikely of candidates a year before. But besides the events of the moment, there were some inner strands of logic in the development. One might go back as far as his mother's Ulster background, and both the Marlboroughs' disenchantment with Ireland after 1880, as well as his own observation of the Irish political situation in the late 1870s and early 1880s, when activity in the north was beginning to escalate.[1] In 1880 he had vague thoughts of making an 'inflammatory' tour in Ulster, but confided to Gibson that he 'feared Kane'.[2] Dr R. R. Kane was a grand master of the Belfast orangemen, who suspected Churchill of secret commitment to nationalism; Churchill did not enlarge on why he feared him in 1880, and one might wonder in what direction the inflammation was intended. Certainly his references to Ulster members at this time tended to be hostile. FitzGibbon thought Churchill cared too little for Ulster, warning him in October 1883 (apropos of North-cote's visit) that he ignored the real and deserving unionism of the Ulstermen: 'no doubt the orange flag is given to frightening otherwise steady horses, but it is the only one which gathers any rank and file together in Ireland who would not cut all your Britishers adrift tomorrow if they could, and cut all *our* throats the day after'.[3]

---

[1] See D. C. Savage, 'The origins of the Ulster unionist party, 1885–6' in *I.H.S.*, xii, no. 47 (Mar. 1961), pp 185–208. Contemporary Irish newspapers gave much space to discussing the political implications of religious disturbances and demonstrations in the north (see for instance editorials in *Weekly Freeman*, 31 Aug. 1878 and 21 Aug. 1880).

[2] H.L.R.O., Ashbourne papers, B/32/1.

[3] 'You always will ignore the fact that more than two-thirds the education and *all* the love of England and of law and order, not to mention three-quarters of the property not yet relegated to the laws of Jupiter and Saturn, though probably *en route* thither, belonging to Ireland, is not included in the average Englishman's definition of "the Irish" . . .' (FitzGibbon to Churchill, 11 Oct. 1883; R.C.P., 1/ii/181). Later he argued for a 'local orange university'

This points up the fact that FitzGibbon's advice, despite his network of catholic contacts and his support of denominational education, all tended towards unflinching, Ulster-oriented unionism. And shortly after this letter came the celebrated Rosslea incident, giving Churchill the opportunity to play a small orange card in late 1883, which he did with gusto.[1] Just after this, a speech at Edinburgh in December 1883 also shows him bringing out the theme of the indivisible union, in an extreme formulation.[2] However, his line on Irish franchise the following year was seen as a direct threat by the Ulster unionists;[3] and it is only when Churchill had to mend his fences after the Maamtrasna debate that we find him again referring, in a speech at Sheffield, to the wisdom and probity of the Ulster M.P.s.[4]

In the same month, September 1885, Carnarvon had visited the north of Ireland; Hicks Beach, who gloomily expected little good from his journey, hoped that Churchill would soon do likewise.[5] Such ventures were a stock in trade for conservative politicians: Northcote, for instance, had sent Gibson off there with Colonel Taylor in 1880,[6] and made his own tentative visit in 1883.[7] The

---

for Belfast to make her 'the capital of culture, as she claims to be of loyalty' (same to same, 7 Dec. 1885; ibid., 1/x/1149).

[1] See below, pp 274–5.

[2] He declared that the home-rulers' demand was for total separation, 'made more loudly, determinedly and unanimously than it was even in the days of Elizabeth, Cromwell, or William III'. The liberals wanted to give Parnell control of the island by lowering the franchise, reforming county government and dividing up the land—all of which Churchill himself advocated at one time or another. See *Weekly Freeman*, 29 Dec. 1883.

[3] See above, p. 257.

[4] 'In the house of commons the representatives of Ulster, with a rare and exalted patriotism and a singular discrimination and knowledge of this [*sic*] country, almost without exception supported the policies of the government . . .' (*Weekly Freeman*, 12 Sept. 1885).

[5] Beach to Churchill, 25 Sept. 1885 (R.C.P., 1/viii/919).

[6] Northcote to Gibson, 17 Oct. 1880 (H.L.R.O., Ashbourne papers, B/71/7).

[7] See A. B. Cooke, 'A conservative party leader in Ulster: Sir Stafford Northcote's diary of a visit to the province, October 1883' in *Proceedings of the Royal Irish Academy*, lxxv, sect. C, no. 4 (1975), pp 61–84.

heightened political activity in the province over this period[1] made tories like Northcote worry whether the party really ought to be identified with orangeism;[2] but Irish conservatives paid more attention to orange cries from 1884 on, including Churchill's friends Plunket and Gibson.[3] At the same time, nationalist opinion adhered to the comfortable belief that orange intransigents in the north were a small minority.[4] In November 1885, when pressing his remedial Irish plans on Salisbury, Churchill denounced 'those foul Ulster tories who have always been the ruin of our party'.[5] This was in the wake of the Maamtrasna debate, but it was not an uncommon reaction; Beach held similar views.[6] Yet at the same time the growing importance, as well as the potential usefulness, of Ulster unionism can never have been far from Churchill's mind, for all his dislike of the crudity and aggressiveness of its proponents at Westminster. And essentially his attitude towards this lobby moderated from the time of the Rosslea incident in late 1883, and was stiffened by Fitz-Gibbon's messages of increasingly embattled unionism in 1885-6. The course thus adopted was a departure from the 'catholic conservative' ideal which, given a calm social background of prosperity and a defused land problem, seemed once to have been capable of producing the kind of home rule which meant the opposite of

---

[1] See Savage, 'Origins of the Ulster Unionist party', and A. T. Q. Stewart, *The narrow ground: aspects of Ulster, 1609-1969* (London, 1977), pp 137-67. For southern nationalist reactions see, for instance, editorials in *Weekly Freeman*, 24 Jan. and 14 Feb. 1885.

[2] Northcote to Ashbourne, 5 Sept. 1883 (H.L.R.O., Ashbourne papers, B/71/26).

[3] See *Weekly Freeman*, 25 Oct. 1884, for their public speeches on Ulster and the franchise.

[4] See, for instance, 'Parliamentary correspondence' in *Weekly Freeman* throughout January 1886, and a widely quoted article by T. M. Healy in *Contemporary Review*, Nov. 1885, pp 723-31.

[5] Churchill to Salisbury, 16 Nov. 1885 (Salisbury MSS (Hatfield House), class E); Salisbury vaguely agreed, but kept clear (Salisbury to Churchill, 16 Nov. 1885; R.C.P., 1/ix/1066a).

[6] Beach to Churchill, 25 Sept. 1885 (Glos. R.O., D2455, PCC/20).

repeal: that chimera of—to take three oddly-assorted exponents—Gavan Duffy, Henry Bellingham, and J. E. Gorst.[1]

From 1884, though, Churchill was liable to use 'Parnellism', 'home rule' and 'repeal' interchangeably, despite the efforts of correspondents to point out semantic differences.[2] And the events of 1885–6 pushed him inexorably northwards. In early December 1885, an apprehensive Blunt noticed 'an odd mischievous look come over his face' at the mention of Ireland, and expected a change of direction.[3] In mid-December he warned Labouchere of his readiness in certain circumstances 'to agitate Ulster to resistance even beyond constitutional limits';[4] the election results and Gladstone's initiative supplied the necessary conditions. Labouchere at once passed the message on to Healy, as Churchill probably intended.[5]

In Dublin at Christmas, FitzGibbon and Holmes put Churchill in touch with Colonel Saunderson.[6] He then returned to London and contacted Lord George Hamilton, who enthusiastically assented to an Ulster venture.[7] Churchill followed this by carefully paying warm tributes to Saunderson in the house of commons, and urging

[1] Above, pp 254 and 264 n. 2. Such an idea had generally died out in Ireland by 1873 (see D. A. Thornley, 'The attitude of Irish conservatives to home rule from the disestablishment act to the national convention of 1873', *Bulletin of the Irish Committee of Historical Sciences*, no. 82 (Apr. 1958), and *Isaac Butt*, p. 55), but it had some enduring features.

[2] For a discussion of this point see C. Russell to Churchill, 14 Apr. 1889 (R.C.P., 1/xvii/3709).

[3] Blunt, *Land war in Ire.*, diary entry for 8 Dec. 1885, p. 6.

[4] See Churchill to Salisbury, 22 Dec. 1885 (W. S. Churchill, *Lord Randolph Churchill*, ii, 28–9; Labouchere told Winston Churchill that he had already been warned of such a plan by Lord Randolph; ibid.).

[5] Though the officially desired recipient was Herbert Gladstone (not his father). See Healy to Labouchere, 23 Dec. 1885 (Thorold, *Labouchere*, p. 258). Churchill and Healy had kept clear of each other since the end of the session (ibid., p. 285).

[6] Saunderson's biographer states that FitzGibbon effected the introduction (R. V. Lucas, *Colonel Saunderson, M.P.: a memoir* (London, 1908), p. 239); Holmes claimed in his unpublished memoir that he arranged the meeting (Cooke and Vincent, 'Ireland and party politics', pt I, p. 119).

[7] Hamilton to Churchill, 2 Jan. 1886 (R.C.P., 1/xi/1235).

Salisbury to sweeten the Ulster members in private meetings.[1] At the end of January the first press rumours of a Belfast visit appeared. Nationalist papers took an injured tone;[2] even tory ministers were rumoured to fear bloodshed.[3] Minds cannot have been set at rest by Churchill's first speech to his new constituents at Paddington, a week before he went to Ulster. This was a violent orange tirade, during which he unleashed a volley of backs-to-the-wall protestant clichés, to the surprise and delight of Ulster opinion, called up images of civil war, and repeatedly offered the assistance of English hearts and hands to their beleaguered coreligionists.[4] This speech (which referred to protestants rather than loyalists, and contained a direct attack on the catholic hierarchy) was far more extreme than anything he was to say in Belfast. There were at once some scandalised calls for his arrest;[5] more reasoned opinion saw it as evidence of the government's adoption of hard-line orthodoxy—the *Telegraph* describing it as 'restoring morality to politics'.[6] Churchill followed

---

[1] Churchill to Salisbury, 20 Jan. 1886 (ibid., 1/xi/1307b).

[2] 'If Lord Randolph Churchill goes to Belfast he will go on a mission of spite and vindictiveness', etc. etc.; *Weekly Examiner and Ulster Weekly News*, 6 Feb. and 20 Feb. 1886.

[3] Ibid.

[4] Only Gladstone's 'monstrous and unparalleled combination of verbosity and senility', Churchill remarked, could lead him to believe that protestants would obey the laws of a Dublin parliament 'of which Mr Parnell would be the chief speaker and Archbishop Walsh the chief priest'. They could not give their consent, which implied civil war. 'In a few days he was going to Belfast, upon the invitation of representatives there, to exchange ideas with the protestants of the north of Ireland on the present crisis, and he was sure that he might explain, not only that the meeting he was addressing sympathised, but that they would give their political assistance to the Irish loyalists [hear, hear] . . . Moreover he believed that there were hundreds and thousands of English hearts, and also hands, ready when the moment of trial came—when the protestants of Ireland were called upon, as they might be called upon, to give in a most practical and convincing form of demonstration a proof of their loyalty to the English throne—there would be hundreds of thousands of English hearts and hands beside and around and behind them [great cheering]' (Report in *Weekly Irish Times*, 20 Feb. 1886).

[5] From the *Pall Mall Gazette* and the *Freeman's Journal*; see report of newspaper reactions in *Belfast Newsletter*, 15 Feb. 1886.   [6] Ibid.

it up with a public letter of markedly diehard protestantism, denouncing Archbishop Walsh especially as a 'separatist';[1] he had learned that the bishops could no longer be used against home rule. The nationalist press, in tones of lugubrious disappointment, finally abandoned their hopes of Churchill; the editorial in the *Freeman* read like the most regretful of obituary notices.[2] Which, in a sense, it was.

But looked at from the north this new champion, despite his equivocal record, had been visible in the distance for some time. Ever since the Bradlaugh affair, he had been approached by belligerent anglican bishops with a view to becoming the spokesman of militant protestantism in parliament.[3] And after the Rosslea incident of October 1883, when Lord Rossmore had been expelled from the magistracy for endangering the peace during an orange-versus-nationalist demonstration,[4] Churchill took up the protestant martyr's case with ostentatious enthusiasm, sending a letter to Lord Arthur Hill in which he expressed violent approbation of Rossmore's action.[5] One reason for his speedy adoption of this cause may

---

[1] See Churchill to John O'Shea, 18 Feb. 1886 (R.C.P., 1/xii/1787). Bound in with his papers of this time are to be found copies of his father's diehard pronouncements after 1880 (ibid., 1/xi/1310).

[2] 'He had fought side by side with the Irish party through many a hard battle in the house of commons. His flippant jeer was almost as much dreaded by the dull orange wing as the sledgehammer blows of Healy, or the scathing eloquence of Sexton . . .' (*Weekly Freeman*, 20 Feb. 1886).

[3] And extricated himself by what Wolff described as 'a masterpiece of tact and statesmanship' (Wolff to Churchill, 30 Jan. 1884; R.C.P., 1/ii/288). See letters from Bishop of Sodor and Man, and Bishop of Liverpool, ibid., 1/ii/267–8, and Churchill to H. Spofforth, 27 Jan. 1884 (ibid., 1/ii/274).

[4] See J. Wallace Taylor, *The Rossmore incident* (Dublin, 1884), and D. W. M. Westenra, baron Rossmore, *Things I can tell* (London, 1912); also Cooke, 'A conservative party leader in Ulster', p. 83, n. 121.

[5] 'That dismissal, of which in my opinion Lord Rossmore may be proud, is but one of many proofs of the strong sympathy which has all along existed between her majesty's advisers and the Irish revolutionary party . . .' (Churchill to Hill, 17 Jan. 1884, R.C.P., 1/ii/259).

have been its popularity with tory democracy; among the letters of sympathy and support received by Rossmore there was a noticeably large proportion from conservative working-men's organisations,[1] and Churchill was at the time absorbed in his epic struggle for control of the national councils. He remained identified with the affair, speaking in Edinburgh about the union in uncharacteristically extreme terms soon afterwards;[2] the matter was raised in the house of lords by Churchill's friend and parliamentary ally, Lord Dunraven.[3] The Rosslea incident and its aftermath became a *cause célèbre*, monopolising the editorials in Irish papers for two months and raising at an early stage the issue of conservative support for Ulster unionism even in positions of doubtful constitutionalism. At one point Churchill engaged in a heated exchange with Parnell over it, daring him to put himself in the position of an Ulster orangeman and then be in favour of home rule (called, of course, 'repeal' by Churchill).[4]

None of this was necessarily incompatible with his dislike of 'foul Ulster tories', much less his initiative in catholic education. And he had contacts in Ulster which went back further than the hectic switches of 1885-6. Sir John Leslie, who had convened the Rosslea meeting, was connected to him by marriage; Leslie, heroically diehard, had proposed at Rosslea a resolution to exclude catholics from parliament.[5] His son, Lady Randolph's brother-in-law, was to accompany Churchill to Belfast in February 1886. Lord George Hamilton pressed his political friendship on Churchill after Rosslea, urging him to visit his father, the duke of Abercorn, at Baronscourt and view 'the northern farming class, who are the best conditioned

---

[1] Taylor, *Rossmore incident*, pp 62, 64, 79, 96, 98, 145, 146, 154.

[2] See above, p. 270.

[3] 18 Feb. 1884; *Hansard 3*, cclxxxiv, 1118-37.

[4] 8 Feb. 1884. This exchange, though reported at length in the *Weekly Irish Times*, 16 Feb. 1884, does not appear in *Hansard*.

[5] *Weekly Freeman*, 28 Nov. 1883. See also *Weekly Examiner and Ulster Weekly News*, 18 Jan. 1886, where he is taken to task for incitement. Also, for a notably anti-catholic speech delivered at Glaslough on 6 January 1886, see *Belfast Newsletter*, 6 Jan. 1886.

people in the United Kingdom'.[1] Churchill's reluctance to do so need not be taken as an aspersion on the northern farming class; he would also have had to meet Abercorn's daughter, the injured Lady Blandford, an innocent party in the scandal which had sent the Marlboroughs to Ireland nine eventful years before.

But the most recent of Churchill's Ulster contacts was the most important. This was the leader of the Ulster unionists in parliament, Colonel Saunderson (a glowing exception to the rule that anyone educated by the Jesuits at an early age is theirs for life).[2] An unlikely associate for Churchill, he mixed a taste for violent practical jokes with a matter-of-fact approach to revivalist religion, and was politically of an Adullamite liberal background. He only accepted orangeism in the 1880s, returning to politics by starring at a demonstration organised by William Johnston of Ballykilbeg in 1882. In 1884 he formally renounced the liberals, appearing with Plunket and Gibson at a Rotunda demonstration in Dublin. Besides emphasising the need for a rearmed orangeism, he was dedicated to 'giving it hot to Northcote',[3] which must have appealed to Churchill; he also seems to have been one of the M.P.s approached by Callan in his one-man campaign against Parnell in 1885.[4]

Churchill was impressed by Saunderson's public claims about exerting a balancing influence at Westminster in 1885. In the Christmas of that year, their meeting was arranged by the Howth circle of 'intelligent tories'.[5] According to Saunderson, Churchill said little, and Saunderson told him roundly that Ulster did not trust him.[6] In any case, Churchill must have been slightly nonplussed

[1] Hamilton to Churchill, 17 Sept. 1885 (R.C.P., 1/viii/1898). For Hamilton's association with Churchill, whom he did not personally like, see his *Parliamentary reminiscences and reflections*, i, 204, 279; ii, 20–21.

[2] As a child he had had a Jesuit tutor in the south of France (see Lucas, *Saunderson*).

[3] See a letter of 21 Feb. 1885, ibid., p. 80.

[4] See ibid., p. 91; Callan is not named, but the circumstantial evidence is overwhelming.

[5] See p. 272, n. 6, above.

[6] See R. R. James, *Lord Randolph Churchill*, p. 239.

by Saunderson, an uncompromising political innocent with something of the seventeenth century about him. For one thing, Saunderson all his life denounced the idea of an official catholic university as a trick of Satan; whereas Churchill would have scattered such foundations all over Ireland, including Armagh.[1] Their liaison was, however, made. Churchill returned to London and contacted Hamilton. He then started negotiations (along with Ashbourne) for Ulster unionist support at Westminster.[2] On 26 January 1886, Saunderson recorded, Churchill 'came to me and pledged himself at my disposal for a meeting in Ulster whenever I thought it necessary to hold one'.[3] 'It seems queer to me', he added, 'to become suddenly a political personage, hobnobbing with cabinet ministers. . . .'

The way was open to further contacts, like the celebrated William Johnston of Ballykilbeg.[4] As soon as Johnston heard of Churchill's projected visit, he determined to identify it with orangeism rather than simple unionism, and began a publicity campaign to this effect.[5] From the beginning of February until his speech on Churchill's platform in Belfast, it was obvious that he was trying to do what Northcote had so feared regarding himself in 1883: 'giving an orange character to the visit'.[6] Churchill's political friends in England reacted less energetically; Beach was surprised the visit was going ahead; he had thought of accompanying his colleague, but had decided activity in London would be more productive, and commiserated with Churchill on not being able to get out of it.[7]

[1] See p. 259, n. 5, above.

[2] See Lucas, *Saunderson*, pp 94, 96.

[3] Ibid., p. 96.

[4] On Johnston see Cooke, 'A conservative party leader in Ulster', p. 74, n. 63.

[5] See a letter from Johnston in *Belfast Newsletter*, 9 Feb. 1886; also comments in *Weekly Examiner and Ulster Weekly News*, 13 Feb. 1886.

[6] See Northcote's diary for 6 Oct. 1883; Cooke, 'A conservative party leader in Ulster', p. 79.

[7] Beach to Churchill, 12 Feb. 1886 (Glos. R.O., D2455 PCC/20; also R.C.P., 1/xii/1376).

Press leaks and the Paddington speech made Churchill's intention public. FitzGibbon wrote in excited approval.[1] The schedule for the visit took shape. At the principal meeting Churchill was to be proposed by Dr Kane—somewhat ironically, as Kane had once declared that if Churchill ever set foot in Ulster 'things would be made very hot for him',[2] and earlier still 'fear of Kane' had kept Churchill out of the province.[3] Lord Arthur Hill, Lord Deramore, Reverend Crawford and other stalwarts were also busily involved in preparations;[4] the strangeness of these bedfellows for Churchill did not go unremarked.

Churchill left London on 21 February with Lord Rossmore, W. E. McCartney, Robert O'Neill, Saunderson, and Jack Leslie.[5] He arrived the next morning to a muted welcome in Larne, suffering from his habitual seasickness. After lunch there, he made a brief speech and proceeded to Belfast via Carrickfergus on a special train. He arrived at the Northern Counties station in York Street to a tumultuous welcome. Addresses were presented, several harking back to the golden age of the Marlborough viceroyalty, a theme repeated by Churchill himself. Reporters noted his own gravity and thoughtfulness (or perhaps seasickness). He travelled to the Ulster Hall and received more addresses, those from orange lodges taking marked precedence; though some lodges had allegedly stayed away because of Churchill's suspected home-rule affiliations.[6] Despite the duke of Abercorn's habitual prominence at such gatherings, all the Hamiltons also stayed away; possibly for the same reason, or possibly out of solidarity with Lady Blandford. Churchill replied to

[1] FitzGibbon to Churchill, 14 Feb. 1886 (ibid., 1/xi/1380). The formal announcement was made on 13 February.

[2] Apropos of his action over the Irish franchise; see *Weekly Examiner and Ulster Weekly News*, 6 Feb. 1886.

[3] See above, p. 269.

[4] See details in *Weekly Irish Times*, 20 Feb. 1886.

[5] The details below come from contemporary newspapers, the fullest report being in the *Belfast Newsletter*, 23 Feb. 1886.

[6] *Weekly Freeman*, 27 Feb. 1886.

the addresses with a low-key speech, mostly about his Ulster ancestors.

That evening he returned to the Ulster Hall for the main meeting. At Larne he had told his audience that their privileges were worth fighting for, but that it might not come to that; here, however, he approached more nearly the appropriate tone, accusing Gladstone of an ambition to convert Trinity College into 'a Roman Catholic seminary' and calling up the horrors of 1641. Given his own record, there were in his strictures on the franchise and on Parnell's position many piquant self-contradictions.[1] On the religious issue, he adroitly presented an attack on the catholic church for encouraging sedition in the guise of an appeal to loyal catholics and a commiseration with their trials. Archbishop Walsh was—as had become usual for Churchill—singled out for special attack. And if the protestant faith was threatened they must remember 'No surrender' and give practical meaning to 'the forms and ceremonies of orangeism'. He instructed them to make their demonstrations orderly and, for the moment, to wait and prepare. The storm might blow over; but 'if my calculations should turn out to be wrong, then I am not of the opinion, and I have never been of the opinion, that this struggle is likely to remain within the lines of what we are accustomed to look upon as constitutional action'.[2] He rounded off with a reference to

---

[1] He emphasised, for instance, that Parnell's party never represented a majority of Irish opinion; but see L. J. Jennings, *The speeches of Lord Randolph Churchill* (London, 1889), ii, 44, for a speech at Hull on 31 Oct. 1881 ('There is only a very small section of the Irish people which does not gladly follow Mr Parnell') and also his speech about Irish education in the house of commons, 6 Aug. 1884, when he had remarked that 'the Irish gentlemen who sat behind him in that quarter of the house represented entirely and completely the feelings of the whole democratic and catholic population of the country' (*Weekly Freeman*, 9 Aug. 1884).

[2] An earlier passage ran: 'I will be no party to crippling the efforts of the cause which I am anxious to support, by any undue or hysterical indulgence of the sensibilities of timid or nervous persons. If we protestants, looking for all assistance, and trying in all good faith to broaden the labours of our action in this great national crisis, if we are disregarded or deserted by those whose assistance we have a right to claim, all I can say is that I as an Englishman,

the American civil war, and a promise of physical support from England in the dark hour.

One view of this speech is that he was attempting to defuse the situation and counsel calm;[1] if so, it only goes to show how little he understood Ulster. And exhortations to moderation in Churchill's speech seem more likely to have been directed towards preventing riots following the meeting. His fellow speakers followed the more belligerent emphasis, Saunderson promising another Boyne and adding a Nietzschean epigraph: 'my experience of the present age is this—that the age values one thing only, and that is force.' Johnston followed, and like Saunderson emphasised that Churchill's presence in Belfast represented a triumph for Ulster unionism, and orangeism in particular. As the guest of honour drove back to the house of his host, Sir Edward Harland, lord mayor of the city (and a friend of FitzGibbon), rioting broke out in the streets. Churchill stayed the night, lunched next day at the Ulster club, and left the province, never to return.

'Churchill's crusade' had a striking immediate effect. Salisbury swiftly congratulated him.[2] The nationalist press contrived to see it as a failure.[3] English conservative papers applauded it, though regretting the inevitably sectarian overtones.[4] From the other side, motions were drafted to accuse him of incitement to civil war; individual Irish nationalists were less upset (at least in private) than

having had the honour of filling a position which cannot be divested of much responsibility, I don't hesitate to confine my hopes of the salvation of the nation and security of the United Kingdom to the efforts of the protestants of Ireland, and essentially to the protestants of the great province of Ulster.'

[1] Cooke and Vincent, *Governing passion*, p. 377; for an analysis of the immediate political considerations governing his Belfast visit see ibid., pp 76–7.

[2] Salisbury to Churchill, 24 Feb. 1886 (R.C.P., 1/xii/1390a).

[3] The *Weekly Freeman* quoted Sydney Smith's description of Croker's attack on Macaulay: 'an attempt at murder ending in suicide' (27 Feb. 1886); the *Weekly Examiner and Ulster Weekly News* emphasised the absence of several prominent orangemen, describing Rossmore and Johnston as 'a shallow celebrity and a dismissed mackerel inspector' respectively (27 Feb. 1886).

[4] See quotations from the English press in *Belfast Newsletter*, 23 and 24 Feb. 1886; also *Weekly Irish Times*, 'Political gossip', 27 Feb. 1886.

disillusioned political innocents like Scawen Blunt.[1] Saunderson saw it all as 'a splendid success'; foreign arms firms began to send him catalogues for rifles.[2]

Immediate reasons of political advantage have been powerfully adduced as the only causes of Churchill's appearance in Belfast,[3] and whether it actually made a categoric difference to how affairs in Ulster immediately developed is highly doubtful.[4] But it can be seen as representing a long-term development in Churchill's career, as well as a process which has a wider importance in the sphere of Anglo-Irish relations. It is worth noting that after February 1886 his range of Irish contacts diminished; militant unionists and cranks predominate among his correspondents. At least one old acquaintance, however, had witnessed the Belfast epic, and applauded it. FitzGibbon's brother Henry, another Dublin tory, and professional man, had travelled to Belfast, drawn by solidarity with Ulster and 'I trust not a morbid desire to see and hear you as a public man.' From his hotel on Royal Avenue he watched Churchill's entry:

You can have no idea of the imposing sight it was . . . For a whole mile as far as the eye could reach there was a dense and orderly mass of respectable men marching after your carriage. I did not see a single drunken or disorderly person in the vast crowd. The contrast in this respect with the other demonstrations which it has been my misfortune to be a witness of was *most* striking. I congratulate you on your enterprise in coming here, and it cannot fail to open the eyes of the Saxon 'just a wee bit'.[5]

[1] William O'Brien recalls a cheery exchange with Churchill about the Belfast visit immediately after his return (*Evening memories*, p. 113); though elsewhere he subscribed to the orthodox horror at 'the orangemen, maddened by the guilty incitements of Churchill, drenching the streets of Belfast with blood' (ibid., p. 154). For Blunt's scandalised reaction see *Land war in Ire.*, pp 31–2.

[2] Lucas, *Saunderson*, pp 99, 101.

[3] Cooke and Vincent, *Governing passion*, pp 76–7.

[4] See Stewart, *The narrow ground*, p. 166, and Joseph Lee, *The modernisation of Irish society, 1848–1918* (Dublin, 1973), pp 132–3.

[5] Henry FitzGibbon to Churchill, 22 Feb. 1886 (R.C.P., 1/xii/1386). Gerald's youngest brother, he became President of the Royal College of Surgeons in Ireland and died in 1912.

Harland had got FitzGibbon into the Ulster Hall to hear Churchill's speech, 'which I would not have missed for anything; you have made a big score, and I hope you will accept my sincere congratulations as they are meant'.[1] Belfast had the blessing of the Howth symposium.

It is doubtful if Churchill saw the venture as presaging a departure any further into the orange spectrum. He detached himself from the Ulster unionists as swiftly as was decent, fulminating against their lack of parliamentary manners and vainly trying to keep Saunderson quiet. Statements like his admission a month after Belfast that he had 'for a considerable time hoped to be able to work in alliance with the Irish party' appalled Ulster.[2] But Saunderson implacably ignored his pleas for moderation, and Churchill's new allies continued to behave proprietorially towards him, asking for his support in local power struggles, and reiterating to him that they were unfairly vilified in the English press ('the tarring of the man Johnson at the Island has been tremendously exaggerated').[3] It was an alien subculture to Churchill, and he complained about its demands on him.[4] But his position was an awkward one; for instance, he had now to have police protection against catholic

[1] Ibid. At a later stage Gerald FitzGibbon believed that Churchill's disingenuous appeal to loyal catholics had had the effect of converting numbers of them to unionism (letter of 26 Sept. 1890, ibid., 1/xxvi/3640).

[2] See *Weekly Examiner and Ulster Weekly News*, 13 Mar. 1880.

[3] Saunderson to Churchill, 10 Aug. 1886 (R.C.P., 1/xiv/1653). Also see same to same, 23 June 1886 (ibid., 1/xiii/1549) for a commanding letter about electoral matters in Ulster; and Deramore to Churchill, 9 Aug. 1886 (ibid., 1/xiv/1648). Churchill's reactions were invariably evasive. He may have exerted some moderating influence; it is interesting to find Kane writing to him about conciliatory ideas on Irish policy to trump the home rulers (Kane to Churchill, n.d. but late 1886; ibid., 1/xiii/1571). But this was not typical. For Saunderson's reaction to Churchill's attempts to quieten him see Lucas, pp 112–13.

[4] See Churchill to Gibson, 30 Sept. 1886 (H.L.R.O., Ashbourne papers, B/32/4): 'Those Belfast beggars keep simmering, I wish they would settle down'; and Churchill to Morris, 6 Sept. 1886, complaining about the 'proceedings and manners of Ulster *soi-disant* tories' (Wynne, *An Irishman and his family*, p. 116).

fanatics,[1] and several conservative M.P.s upbraided him about identifying protestantism with loyalism.[2]

Some Ulster tories, of course, never trusted him—as Abercorn wrote triumphantly to Salisbury after Churchill's stunning resignation at Christmas 1886.[3] Out of office, he was a less and less likely champion for Ulster unionism.[4] In the wilderness he reverted to southern Irish initiatives (Beach had feared that he was after the chief secretaryship again in July 1886).[5] However, an orange aura remained, and made him less approachable; those trying to negotiate him into the liberal camp concentrated upon Ulster as a probable stumbling-block.[6] FitzGibbon still advised him as closely as ever; and on issues like land purchase and the *Times* commission, Churchill followed the FitzGibbon line exactly.[7] Educational intrigues had never ceased.[8] Even before his resignation, Salisbury had rejected

[1] See H. Matthews to Churchill, 25 Jan. 1887 (R.C.P., 1/xix/2365).

[2] See H. Farquharson to Churchill, 6 Mar. 1886 (ibid., 1/xii/413).

[3] Abercorn to Salisbury, 20 Dec. 1886, Salisbury MSS; for Saunderson's reaction see Saunderson to Churchill, 12 Jan. 1887 (R.C.P., 1/xix/2333).

[4] By 1893, ventures like that of February 1886 were cynically referred to in the Churchill family as 'Ulsterising'; see W. S. Churchill to Lady Randolph Churchill, 2 Apr. 1893, in R. S. Churchill, *Winston S. Churchill*, companion vol. I, pt 1, p. 372.

[5] See Cooke and Vincent, 'Ireland and party politics', pt II, p. 329. Holmes thought Beach went to Ireland to prevent 'an ideally bad appointment', that of Churchill. Churchill's conservative critics, however, believed that he dispatched Beach there in order to claim the leadership (see Lord George Hamilton, *Parliamentary reminiscences and reflections*, ii, 34). As chancellor, he continued to be preoccupied with Irish schemes—notably for railway nationalisation as well as for land purchase.

[6] See Labouchere to Churchill, 'Sunday' (early Jan. 1887) and 19 Jan. 1887 (R.C.P., 1/xviii/2289 and 1/xix/2394).

[8] From early 1886 FitzGibbon characteristically warned Churchill of the injustice of landlords getting out 'at the expense of the rest of us' (FitzGibbon to Churchill, 14 Feb. 1886; ibid., 1/xii/1380). For his line on the *Times* commission see same to same, 15 July 1888 (ibid., 1/xviii/3077). Morris was equally incensed by the illegality of the commission, FitzGibbon reported.

[7] In 1887 Churchill had hopes of bringing in an independent Irish education bill; FitzGibbon to Churchill, 3 Nov. 1887 (ibid., 1/xxi/2713), and much related correspondence.

an Irish local government plan backed by Churchill as 'too much like real home rule';[1] in 1889 Churchill recurred to such a scheme, collaborating with Carnarvon, FitzGibbon and Hartington.[2] By that year, Irish diehard opinion had begun once more to fear him as too progressive.[3]

But little ever happened—for reasons partly to do with Churchill's health, partly with Balfour's policy, partly with changes in Ireland itself. In 1890 Churchill drafted three long articles on Irish land purchase, denouncing the idea of bailing out landlords ('rent-chargers and encumbrancers') and advocating a scheme reliant upon wide measures of local government, Irish initiative being the only valid dynamic for legislation, and retreat from a policy that has been proved unwise being the only politic approach.[4] This could have stood as an epigraph for his own position *vis-à-vis* Irish affairs; but since February 1886 the verities had changed. The hardening of attitudes through the events of the eighties had caused even the heroically decisive FitzGibbon to have doubts. In February 1888 he watched from his drawing-room in Merrion Square as a Union of Hearts demonstration surged past en route from Ballsbridge to Rutland Square. Afterwards he wrote to Churchill:

The scene from our windows here was your Belfast entry by mud and rebellion out of torchlight, with T. D. Sullivan fresh from Tullamore jail as first gentleman, and Ripon K.G. and ex-governor-general of India and then Morley, freethinker from the privy council, both playing second. In ten minutes after the last band had played 'God Save Ireland' and the last star-spangled banner had gone by, my wife, daughters and I drove off to Dublin castle: never got there or back so quickly or so easily, and never saw there a

---

[1] See Salisbury to Churchill, 16 Sept. 1886 (ibid., 1/xv/1808).

[2] Hardinge, *Carnarvon*, iii, 246.

[3] R. Kelly to E. Wilmot, 18 Aug. 1889 (R.C.P., 1/xxiv/3247) and Fitz-Gibbon to Churchill, 10 Jan. 1892 (ibid., 1/xxvii/3793). Churchill's tory democrat supporters were equally worried, Louis Jennings frequently begging him to concentrate instead upon 'the decent English workman' (Jennings to Churchill, 24 Nov. 1889, ibid., 1/xiv/3733).

[4] Now in N.L.I., MS 2080; many similar ideas are to be found in Fitz-Gibbon's letters to Churchill throughout 1889.

larger or more 'brilliant' assembly. Which Rome is burning, and who is hero?[1]

This uncertainty prevailed; he could think of 'no new views on Ireland', being unsure about 'the reality of anything on either side'.[2] Like other intelligent unionists, he favoured moderate devolution by 1889; but, as he wrote to Churchill, what now loomed in the background was 'the impregnable Ulster unionist province'.

It cannot be made a subdivision of united Ireland, without depriving all the congenial inhabitants of the rest of the island of their only hope and support, and at the same time exposing the 'masses' living in Ulster to the most unbending and to them repugnant rule of the extreme Ulster party, and sacrificing all the 'loyalists' everywhere else. On the other hand it can't be kept as an England in Ireland without raising a frontier question of the most utterly insoluble character, and it can't be forced under the hateful yoke of home rule without destruction of its prosperity, if not without actual force.[3]

In 1886, FitzGibbon's emotional unionism had been amplified by his resentment at the terms of land purchase, and by what he saw as a general sell-out to the anti-English elements in the south at the expense of the Trinity-educated professional classes, traditionally faithful to the English connection.[4] He had introduced Churchill to Saunderson, encouraged his Belfast initiative, and backed him with all the accustomed weight of Howth toryism. By 1890 he had reverted to the idea of Churchill's completing the union by a positive, conciliatory Irish policy, probably in alliance with Rosebery: a notion shared by Churchill himself.[5] But the constructive unionist initiative was no longer sufficient answer; the spirit of the 1870s was

---

[1] FitzGibbon to Churchill, 3 Feb. 1888 (R.C.P., 1/xxii/2810).

[2] Same to same, 19 Feb. 1888 (ibid., 1/xxii/2823).

[3] Ibid.

[4] See his bitter complaints to Churchill about the arrogance of those who felt their time had come; FitzGibbon to Churchill, 14 Feb. 1886 (ibid., 1/xii/1380).

[5] See same to same, 9 July 1893 (ibid., 1/xxx/4272), and Churchill to Rosebery, 2 Sept. 1893 (ibid., 1/xxx/4375).

as dead as the seventh duke of Marlborough. And the kind of atavistic political emotions, and literal apprehensions of rhetoric, which Churchill played with in the north were essentially foreign to a flexible pragmatist like himself. Images of Faust as well as Pandora, over-simplifying though they are, remain inescapable.

The story of Churchill's orange card, seen in context, can be an enlightening one, both in terms of what was afterwards made of such a tactic, and how Churchill's behaviour was interpreted at the time. It is illustrative of Churchill's imaginative but imperfect apprehension of the Irish problem—made much of by contemporaries, but only recently reemphasised by historians. If he had nationalist contacts, they were not among those so assiduously maintained in Dublin; and wondering whether he was a covert home-ruler seems less relevant than considering the extent to which politicians used 'home rule' as it suited them, and what home rule actually meant, as opposed to what it stood for. Churchill may have been exceptional in his adaptability, and was capable of being exceptional in the specific nature of his policy statements. He was also exceptional in having a quasi-Irish background in the 1870s, and a permanent conditioning influence exerted upon him from Howth. How often, from education in 1877 to the *Times* commission in 1889 and land purchase in 1890, were Churchill's public ideas preceded by private advice from FitzGibbon; and Ulster came in between, at a juncture when the influence from Howth, the impressions left by his Irish stay, and the bewildering prism of high politics, combined to lead him out on to a political limb. Even without his self-destructive resignation, it is doubtful if he could ever have regained the creative initiative in Irish policy which—had he ever had his ambition of the chief secretaryship—he would once very likely have carried out.

Churchill had his own view of politics, not shared by everyone; Rosebery once wrote to him that he could not agree that the best ministry resembled 'a well-oiled weathercock'.[1] He also believed

---

[1] Rosebery to Churchill, 20 Jan. 1892 (ibid., 1/xxvii/3813).

in the dual nature of politics, public and private, his public reactions often being decided upon either flippantly or with a ruthless priority of manœuvre. In Belfast, however, he was nearly led into a Midlothian, conferring authority on an area of Irish policy which he probably never intended. Irish politics in many essentials operated outside the charmed circle of the English high political world— which can provide such a valuable, enlightening and entertaining reflection of how things were done at Westminster. Churchill failed to grasp this; and the educated Dublin tories from whom he took so much of his policy were also capable of misjudging reality in 1886. The result probably had a more decisive effect on Churchill's career than on the development of Irish history. But the interaction between the two remains an absorbing microcosm of the various shifts in balance, conflicts of interest, misapprehensions of intention and multiple varieties of insecurity which characterise Anglo-Irish politics in the 1880s.

The general election of 1892: the catholic clergy and the defeat of the Parnellites

C. J. WOODS

THE splitting, late in 1890, of the Irish nationalist party into Parnellites and anti-Parnellites as a result of the O'Shea divorce case in which Charles Stewart Parnell, the party's leader and co-respondent in the case, was effectively portrayed as an arch-deceiver, has been widely studied and needs no further exposition.[1] The purpose here is to consider the fate of the Parnellite faction at the subsequent general election in July 1892 and the role of the clergy of the Roman Catholic church in determining it.

When on 6 December 1890 Justin McCarthy formalised the split by withdrawing with 44 other dissidents from a meeting of Irish nationalist M.P.s in Committee-room Fifteen of the house of commons at Westminster, leaving Parnell, the chairman, with 27 loyal followers, 84 of Ireland's 102 seats were held by nationalists.[2] Parnell was to be able to count on 5 absentees, so that the Parnellite faction actually numbered 33 M.P.s (nearly 39 per cent of the nationalist body).[3] Between then and the general election in July 1892 the Parnellites suffered at by-elections a loss of two to the anti-Parnellites.[4] At the general election the Parnellites were reduced to

[1] The most syncretic study is F. S. L. Lyons's *The fall of Parnell, 1890–91* (London, 1960). There is new material in Dr Lyons's *Charles Stewart Parnell* (London, 1977), chs 15–17.

[2] Another Irish seat, vacant at that time, had been previously held by a nationalist. One English seat was held by an Irish nationalist. The complement of the Irish nationalist party was therefore 86.

[3] McCarthy and his 44 were to be joined by 7 absentees and by the successful candidate for the vacancy. These figures are worked out from information given in C. C. O'Brien, *Parnell and his party, 1880–90* (Oxford, 1964), p. 326.

[4] This figure is worked out from information given in B. M. Walker, *Parliamentary election results in Ireland, 1801–1922* (Dublin, 1978), p. 143. I am greatly indebted to this invaluable work for statistics on the 1892 election and to its author for his advice and encouragement.

a parliamentary membership of only 9 (or 11·3 per cent of the nationalist body).[1]

The debates of Committee-room Fifteen were carried from Westminster to every nationalist corner in Ireland; nationalist supporters divided for or against Parnell's continued leadership; the antipathy between the factions often turned into a bitterness which bred invective or even violence.[2] Parnell's death, on 6 October 1891 (three-and-a-half months after marrying Katharine O'Shea before a civil registrar), and the succession of John Redmond to the leadership of his faction, did not narrow but widened the split. The debate was in essence one which had been heard many times during the nineteenth century: would proponents of Irish autonomy better serve their cause by being independent of, or in alliance with, English politicians? Parnellites[3] argued that Gladstone and his liberals, having tried to remove Parnell from the nationalist leadership, could no longer be trustworthy allies; anti-Parnellites argued that unless Gladstone received the support of the nationalists he would not bring in an Irish home-rule bill when the liberals eventually as all expected, regained office. But there was more to the debate than the issue of parliamentary strategy. There was an issue which had never previously existed in the history of the movement for Irish autonomy: the moral fitness of the leader. Anti-Parnellites held that the moral turpitude of Parnell's relationship with Mrs Katharine O'Shea disqualified him from leadership. Some Parnellites may have been incredulous of the evidence heard

---

[1] The anti-Parnellites won 72 seats (including the English one); 19 of the remaining 23 Irish seats were won by unionists and 4 by liberal unionists (Walker, op. cit., pp 193–4).

[2] I have given greater treatment in my unpublished Ph.D. thesis, 'The catholic church and Irish politics, 1879–92' (University of Nottingham, 1968), ch. 6.

[3] I prefer the names 'Parnellites' and 'anti-Parnellites' as neutral. Parnellites called themselves 'nationalists' or 'independent nationalists' and were dubbed by their opponents 'factionists' or 'pledge-breakers'. Anti-Parnellites called themselves simply 'nationalists', and were dubbed by their opponents 'seceders' or 'whigs'.

in the divorce court; most considered the moral issue irrelevant. By the time of Parnell's death the moral issue had evolved into a religious issue: the authority of the catholic church.

The split was remarkable for the partisanship of the ecclesiastics of the catholic church; almost without exception they took the side of the anti-Parnellites. Though Parnell was nominally a protestant, his lieutenants were almost all practising catholics and his rank-and-file in Ireland were wholly so. Indeed the political party he led before the split was the edifice of what can be termed the 'catholic-consciousness movement': its power base was the catholic population; it represented the catholic interest; it had a formal relationship with the episcopal body and clergy of the catholic church. The faction Parnell led after the split was no less catholic in its power base or in the interest it represented, but it received only hostility from the bishops and priests of the church, whose authority it challenged and defied.

The seven parliamentary by-elections occurring in catholic areas of Ireland between the split in the nationalist party and the dissolution of parliament were indicators of the paucity of opinion in favour of the Parnellites and of the great political power wielded by the catholic priesthood among rural voters.[1] Four (Kilkenny North, Sligo North, Carlow, Cork city) were contested by the Parnellites and lost; two (Kilkenny North again, Wexford North) were not even contested; only one (Waterford city) was won.

Parliament was dissolved on 28 June 1892. The speaker's warrant for the issue of writs for elections to the new parliament reached the hanaper office in Dublin on the following day; these were issued and were forwarded immediately to the sheriffs of each county and parliamentary borough.[2] Nomination days varied from 2 to 12 July, and polling days from 6 to 19 July.[3] The electorate comprised all

[1] These elections are treated in Woods, op. cit., pp 377–84, 390–6; cf. Lyons, *Ir. parl. party*, pp 17–18, 26, 30–4; Lyons, *Fall of Parnell*, pp 159–77, 261–5, 276–8; Lyons, *C. S. Parnell*, pp 537–45, 581–4, 591–2.

[2] *Freeman's Journal* (hereafter *F.J.*), 30 June 1892, p. 5.

[3] Ibid., 1 July 1892, p. 4.

male heads of household, and also lodgers, but not sons or servants living in; it amounted in 1891 to little over half of all adult males or roughly one-sixth of the entire population.[1] Parnellites stood for 44 of the 103 seats; anti-Parnellites opposed them in every case and stood for 41 other seats besides; the remaining 18 seats (all but two were in Ulster) went uncontested by either nationalist faction. After a hard-fought campaign, which had begun even before the dissolution, the Parnellites were defeated in all but 9 constituencies, winning only 5 county seats (Clare East, Clare West, Dublin North, Galway North and Roscommon South) and 4 borough seats (Dublin College Green, Dublin Harbour, Dublin St Patrick's and Waterford). In the 43 constituencies where comparison is possible,[2] Parnellites and anti-Parnellites polled totals of approximately 70,000 and 100,000 respectively. Generally the Parnellites obtained a higher proportion of the nationalist vote in urban than in rural constituencies. There is ample evidence that in county constituencies they polled very much better in the towns than in the countryside. Ulster presented an exception: there the Parnellites polled universally badly.

What part did the catholic clergy take in electioneering on the anti-Parnellite side? Parish priests or their curates collected money locally for the national election fund and forwarded it to the trustees in Dublin, perhaps adding a donation from themselves. They comprised a significant proportion of the attendance at the county conventions held to adopt candidates; a leading M.P. always took the chair, but usually a priest would be the formal proposer of the agreed candidate and a locally-prominent layman would be the seconder.[3] In almost all those constituencies for which evidence has been found in the anti-Parnellite newspaper, the *Freeman's Journal*, priests signed the nomination papers submitted

[1] B. M. Walker, 'The Irish electorate, 1868–1915' in *I.H.S.*, xviii, no. 71 (Mar. 1973), pp 365–6, 392–9.

[2] One of the 43 (Cork city) had two seats.

[3] For numerous reports of remittances and conventions, see *F.J.*, June 1892, *passim*.

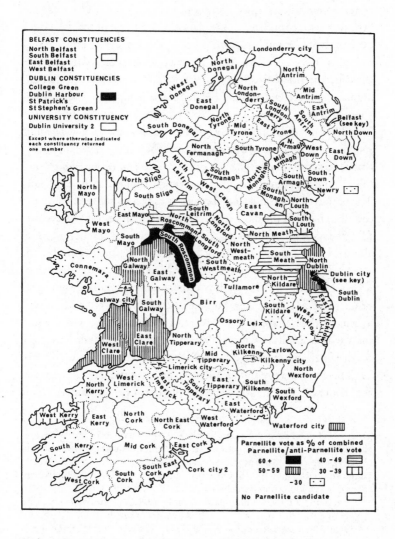

Irish parliamentary constituencies, 1892, showing the Parnellite vote as a
percentage of the combined Parnellite/anti-Parnellite vote

to returning officers, most commonly as proposers.[1] The evidence, however, is incomplete, as the papers were very probably lodged eventually in the public record office in Dublin and so must be presumed to have been lost in its destruction in 1922.[2] Another role filled by the priest was that of local aide to the candidate. For example, the Reverend Denis O'Hara, described as 'the veteran campaigner of Mayo', met two anti-Parnellite candidates for the county, John Dillon and Daniel Crilly, on their arrival by train at Manulla Junction on 30 June and accompanied them on their campaign.[3] Priests were also orators; hardly ever at a public meeting was one not to be found presiding, or at least speaking in support of the candidate. The preferred place and time for meetings was a spot adjacent to the catholic chapel at the close of a mass or other office. On the evening of Sunday 26 June immediately after devotions in the chapel at Cappamore, County Limerick, to give but one example, the Reverend John Shelley presided over 'a vast and orderly meeting' addressed by the anti-Parnellite candidate John Finucane; four other priests were in attendance.[4] Some priests electioneered inside as well as outside their chapels. The Reverend Patrick Skelly, while saying mass at Boardmills in County Meath on 10 July, provided a sample ballot paper and instructed his attentive congregation how to mark it.[5] There was a very similar incident on the same day elsewhere in the county.[6] Priests took every opportunity to canvass their

---

[1] Names of signatories on nomination papers for certain constituencies are given in *F.J.*: Dublin city, Dublin South, Kilkenny city, Cork city, Waterford city (5 July), Louth South, Limerick West, Westmeath North, Queen's County (Ossory), Roscommon South, Tipperary North (7 July), Meath North, Longford South, Sligo North, Queen's County (Leix) (8 July), Dublin North, Clare East (11 July), Longford North, Clare West (12 July).

[2] I am grateful to Miss Philomena Connolly, P.R.O.I., for confirming this.

[3] *F.J.*, 1 July 1892, p. 6.   [4] Ibid., 29 June 1892, p. 5.

[5] *South Meath election petition tried at Trim, November 1892: verbatim report reprinted from the 'Irish Daily Independent'* (Dublin, 1892) (hereafter *South Meath report*), p. 132.

[6] *North Meath election petition tried at Trim, December 1892: verbatim report reprinted from the 'Irish Daily Independent'* (Dublin, 1892) (hereafter *North Meath report*), p. 73.

parishioners for the anti-Parnellite side.[1] Clergy gave invaluable service on the day of the poll by getting voters to polling booths. In counties as far apart as Kerry, Westmeath and Mayo, priests headed or followed columns of electors marching from the countryside into the polling towns.[2] In the Louth North constituency there were only five polling stations: that at Dundalk served 3190 registered electors (out of a total of 5519), some of whom had to travel from as far away as Crossmaglen and Jonesborough on the Armagh border, which they did on cars apparently arranged by local clergy.[3] Supposedly the most important role assumed by priests on polling day was that of sub-agent or personating agent. Under the ballot act of 1872[4] a candidate could appoint agents, who had to make a statutory declaration of secrecy, to be present inside polling stations in order generally to guard against irregularities, the chief of which was by common consent personation. A catholic priest was ideally suited to this role, combining as he did familiarity with the local populace and immunity from intimidation. It is impossible to determine with exactitude how commonly priests were appointed as sub-agents or personating agents, for the official records were lost in the destruction of the public record office in 1922. In some cases information is forthcoming from newspapers: in Louth North it is known that priests were appointed to three of the five stations,[5] in Westmeath North to most stations,[6] in Kilkenny city to all six,[7] in Clare East to all twelve,[8] but in Cork city

[1] *The Times*, 4 July 1892, p. 7; *Irish Daily Independent* (hereafter *I.D.I.*), 12 July 1892, p. 6.

[2] *I.D.I.*, 11 July 1892, p. 6; 13 July, p. 6.

[3] More can be learnt from *F.J.* of Louth North than of most other constituencies, partly because the leading anti-Parnellite T. M. Healy was a candidate, partly because one voter from Tavanamore, near Crossmaglen, was attacked and killed on his way home (*F.J.*, 11, 14, 15, 19 July 1892). Healy's opponent, Philip Callan, was an independent nationalist with Parnellite support.

[4] 35 & 36 Vict., c. 33, pt III and 1st schedule.

[5] *F.J.*, 14 July 1892, p. 5.

[6] *I.D.I.*, 13 July 1892, p. 6.

[7] *I.D.I.*, 7 July 1892, p. 5; *F.J.*, 7 July 1892, p. 5.

[8] *I.D.I.*, 13 July 1892, p. 6.

to none.[1] Such a practice may have inhibited illiterate voters, obliged as they were to declare their choice orally and within the hearing of officials and agents. According to the Parnellite *Irish Daily Independent*, many illiterate voters in Waterford East (where they were 60 per cent of the total at some booths) wanted to whisper their choice to the presiding officer, and one altered his when made to declare it aloud.[2]

Only secular (i.e. parochial) clergy engaged actively in electioneering; no evidence has been found of regular clergy (i.e. ordained members of religious orders) doing so. Possibly regulars, based largely in towns, were less well placed than seculars to perform political functions, or perhaps spiritual, disciplinary or even social reasons existed for their aloofness.[3] Bishops were, with two or three notable exceptions, content to stay away from the hustings, though it is significant that their tolerance of the activities of their secular clergy was forthcoming. Any repetition of the episcopal body's forthright denunciation on 25 June 1891 of Parnellism for its 'hostility to ecclesiastical authority' would have been superfluous; the stance of the catholic church was well known. After a free fight in the town of Tuam (in the Galway North constituency) on 29 June, involving supporters of the Parnellite candidate Col. John Philip Nolan and of his anti-Parnellite opponent Dr Charles Tanner, and resulting in a certain Fr Heany having his teeth knocked out, the archbishop of Tuam, John McEvilly, went so far as to issue a pastoral denouncing what he called 'a most determined attempt to murder a clergyman'.[4] Individual bishops sent letters of support to local anti-Parnellite conventions.[5] Certain bishops signed nomina-

---

[1] *Cork Examiner*, 7 July 1892, p. 8.

[2] *I.D.I.*, 18 July 1892, p. 5.

[3] Cf. anon., 'Irish clericalism', in *The Times*, 29 June 1892, p. 15, 30 June, p. 7, 7 July, p. 8; there is a rejoinder from a Maynooth College priest in ibid., 5 July, p. 8.

[4] *I.D.I.*, 1 July 1892, p. 4; *F.J.*, 4 July 1892, p. 7.

[5] E.g. McEvilly of Tuam, MacCormack of Galway, Conway of Killala, Gillooly of Elphin (*F.J.*, 24 June 1892, pp 5–6, 28 June, pp 5–6).

tion papers: for example, the bishop of Ossory, Abraham Brown-rigg, who had become a staunch anti-Parnellite at the time of the Kilkenny North by-election in December 1890,[1] was the official proposer of Thomas Bartholomew Curran, candidate for Kilkenny city.[2] Some received anti-Parnellite candidates at their residences; for example, the bishop of Killala's residence at Ballina served as a refuge for Dillon and Crilly when they were attacked by hostile townsmen.[3] The priest who had recently been nominated coadjutor bishop of Killala, John Conmy, seems to have conducted Crilly all over the Mayo North constituency, and on the ugly occasion at Ballina referred to, as well as on a later occasion, received missiles in the face for his trouble.[4]

The most complete picture of electioneering by clerics, though not necessarily the most typical, is that of the two County Meath constituencies from which petitions were successfully lodged, under the corrupt and illegal practices prevention act of 1883,[5] by the defeated Parnellite candidates, James Joseph Dalton (South Meath) and Pierce Mahony (North Meath), for the unseating of the victorious anti-Parnellites, Patrick Fulham and Michael Davitt respectively, on the grounds of 'undue influence and intimidation ... by and through divers Roman Catholic clergymen'. This picture is to be viewed in the evidence given at the trials of the petitions at Trim: that for South Meath between 16 and 30 November 1892,[6] and that for North Meath between 15 and 23 December.[7]

The anti-Parnellite election effort apparently began in the bishop's house at Navan on 23 May when a dozen or so priests and Fulham (but not Davitt) met to make arrangements for the raising of a fund and the holding of a convention. The Reverend Peter Mc-Namee, parochial administrator of Navan, became treasurer jointly

[1] Lyons, C. S. Parnell, pp 543–5.
[2] F.J., 5 July 1892, p. 7. There were at least half a dozen other cases.
[3] The Times, 4 July 1892, p. 6.
[4] F.J., 5 July 1892, p. 6; 6 July, p. 5; 7 July, p. 5; 8 July, p. 6.
[5] 46 & 47 Vict., c. 51.
[6] South Meath report.   [7] North Meath report.

with a layman and levied the various parishes according to the 'national' (i.e. anti-Parnellite) support.[1] The Reverend Peter Kelly, parish priest of Slane, sent out a printed circular to every priest in the county requesting him 'to invite prominent nationalist laymen from the district' (presumably trusted anti-Parnellites) to a convention in the catholic seminary at Navan on 1 June for the purpose of adopting Fulham and Davitt as candidates.[2] Forty-eight priests and about twelve times as many laymen attended, and the recommended candidates, both of whom were in attendance, were duly adopted.[3] The evidence heard by the court at Trim does not make it clear whether the initiative for the nomination of Fulham and Davitt came from within the county or from without; it is likely that it came from McCarthy's parliamentary party or from his caucus, the Irish National Federation; the priests were probably content to support this initiative. What the evidence does make clear is that almost every single secular priest in the county—fifty or sixty in all (there were perhaps half a dozen exceptions)—exerted himself on behalf of the anti-Parnellites (as did some from across the county boundary), by private canvassing, by publicising forthcoming meetings, by public speaking, by acting as aide or host to the candidate, or by acting on polling day as personating agent or in some other capacity. At a public meeting at Drumconrath on 26 June, when Davitt took the opportunity to accuse his opponent, Mahony, of traducing 'the priests of Meath', over 25 clergymen were present; at Oldcastle three days later 30 were present; at Duleek on 3 July over 40 were present.[4] In many instances, of which much was made by counsel for the petitioners, priests spoke with strong disapproval of Parnellism from the very altars of their chapels.[5] Kelly had Davitt stay with him 'on and off' at the parochial house at Slane, which

---

[1] *North Meath report*, pp 133, 137–8.
[2] Ibid., p. 20.
[3] *South Meath report*, p. 10; *North Meath report*, p. 20.
[4] *North Meath report*, p. 15.
[5] *South Meath report*, pp 43, 91, 103, 132; *North Meath report*, pp 31, 34, 40, 47, 88.

Davitt gave on official documents as his address; the Reverend Joseph Flood, said to be of Inniskean, was also Davitt's host.[1] Every priest saying mass on 3 July read out the local bishop's pastoral letter on the elections, some of them giving supporting sermons. The Reverend Patrick Cantwell of Summerhill added: 'you cannot, after that, remain Parnellites and remain catholics.'[2] There is evidence that a few Meath priests, in the words of Davitt's counsel, T. M. Healy, 'were betrayed into some acts of violence'.[3] A Fr McDonnell of Kill allegedly advised anti-Parnellites going along to a meeting of their candidate at Longwood on 3 July to take sticks 'for their own defence', as he intended doing himself.[4] The Reverend Patrick Clarke struck and knocked down an elderly Parnellite named Owen Reilly outside the polling booth at Nobber; afterwards he was returned at Wilkinstown petty sessions for trial for assault.[5] A clerical colleague, Christopher Casey, struck and wounded a Parnellite, Patrick Byrne, with a blackthorn stick during a mêlée at Navan on polling day; he too was returned for trial.[6]

The bishop of Meath, Thomas Nulty, entered the fray on 29 June by issuing a pastoral letter to the clergy and laity of the diocese of Meath (which embraced the whole of the county of the same name, virtually of all of County Westmeath and parts of five other counties) denouncing Parnellism in the most frenzied terms. Ordered to be read out at all masses in catholic churches in the diocese on Sunday 3 July, it was published verbatim the day before in the *Drogheda Independent*, a newspaper which had a good circulation in County Meath and had Fulham among its directors.[7] The text, set solid in eight-point type, takes up six pages in the report of the trial

---

[1] Ibid., pp 21, 81, 168. The only priest named Flood in the Meath diocese was Joseph Flood, P.P. of Kingscourt, just inside County Cavan (*Irish Catholic Directory, 1892*, pp 123, 237, 264).

[2] *North Meath report*, p. 22.

[3] Ibid., p. 119.

[4] *South Meath report*, p. 96.

[5] *I.D.I.*, 2 Aug. 1892, p. 6; *North Meath report*, pp 52–6, 71–2, 104, 125–31.

[6] *I.D.I.*, 28 July 1892, p. 5; *North Meath report*, pp 86–7.

[7] *South Meath report*, p. 11; *North Meath report*, pp 75–6.

of Dalton's petition.[1] A few extracts will suffice to convey its import:

Parnellism, whose continued existence or practical extinction you will decide at these coming elections, is much more than a purely political question. Beyond all doubt it is an essentially and an intensely religious question as well, and one that will vitally influence your faith, your religious feelings, and the moral obligations and duties by which as Christians and catholics, you are conscientiously bound ... Parnellism strikes at the very root and saps the very foundations of catholic faith. All the successors of the apostles in this country—that is to say, the twenty-nine archbishops and bishops of Ireland—have solemnly warned and taught their respective flocks that Parnellism was unlawful and unholy, that it was in distinct, direct and essential antagonism with the principles of Christian morality and even dangerous to their faith as catholics, and consequently that they should shun and avoid it. They who refuse to accept that teaching or that principle on the unanimous authority of the whole Irish hierarchy deprive themselves of every rational ground or motive for believing in the truth of any of the other doctrines of their religion ... Parnellism, like paganism, impedes, obstructs and cripples the efficiency and blights the fruitfulness of the preaching of the gospel and of the diffusion of the divine knowledge without which our people cannot be saved ... The dying Parnellite himself will hardly dare to face the justice of his creator till he has been prepared and anointed by us for the last awful struggle ... I earnestly implore you, then, dearly beloved, to stamp out by your votes at the coming election this great moral, social and religious evil which has brought about so much disunion and bad blood amongst a hitherto united people ...

Despite his seventy-five years, Nulty preached against the Parnellites at both masses at Trim in the southern division of the county on 29 June, and again at Navan in the northern division on 3 July; he urged on the third occasion 'all the men of the county' (meaning anti-Parnellite males) to attend Davitt's public meeting on the following Sunday armed with 'heavy blackthorn sticks' for the purpose of repelling intruders.[2] It was Bishop Nulty who formally nominated Davitt, and on nomination day (7 July) he issued a public

---

[1] *South Meath report*, pp 11–16. It is also printed in *F.J.*, 4 July 1892, p. 7, and *I.D.I.*, 4 July 1892, p. 6.

[2] *South Meath report*, pp 111, 154, 157.

letter venting his displeasure with some local Parnellites who had awakened him the previous night by hurling abuse at his window.[1] As the bishop was inveighing against Parnellites in a sermon in his cathedral at Navan on 10 July, one of the congregation, James Lalor, the town clerk, caused a commotion by calling out 'You are a liar!'[2]

Polling day was 12 July in South Meath and 14 July in North Meath. In the South Meath constituency priests acting as personating agents were present inside nine of the ten polling stations (Athboy, Ballyvar, Clonard, Duleek, Dunboyne, Julianstown, Longwood, Summerhill and Trim); outside the tenth (Dunshaughlin) a priest watched and noted voters arriving.[3] In North Meath, priests were present inside seven polling stations (Drumconrath, Moynalty, Nobber, Oldcastle, Kells, Navan and Slane); outside the other two (Crossakiel and Wilkinstown) five or six priests watched.[4] Standing outside a polling station, with a register at hand (probably marked up from canvassing returns), was considered a means of maximising the vote for one's candidate; if the sentinel was a priest, the effect would be all the greater. It was however inside the stations, sitting near the presiding officer, that a priest could be of greatest use. While the purpose of the presence of agents was to prevent personation, a major effect was allegedly to inhibit the numerous illiterate voters, obliged as they were to declare their choice orally within the hearing of agents as well as of officials. Illiterates comprised 22·9 per cent of all voters in South Meath, and 23·7 per cent in North Meath.[5] At Slane polling station, according to a Parnellite personating agent, James O'Brien, two illiterate voters whispered 'Mahony' (the name of the Parnellite candidate) to the presiding

[1] *North Meath report*, pp 13–14.
[2] Ibid., pp 156–7.
[3] *South Meath report*, pp 10, 18–19, 43, 127–8.
[4] *North Meath report*, pp 13, 189.
[5] Calculated from figures given in *Return showing the number of persons who voted as illiterates at the general election of 1892 in the United Kingdom*, pp 9–12, H.C. 1893–4 (76), lxx, 713–16.

officer who then told them that they must speak out, within the hearing of all officials and agents present including the Reverend John Cassidy, curate of the parish and agent of the anti-Parnellite candidate; the two thereupon changed their minds and voted for Davitt, though Cassidy did not interfere with them.[1] It was at the same station that another illiterate, according to another Parnellite personating agent, 'walked in and threw himself on his knees before Father Cassidy and in a faltering voice . . . said "I will vote for Mr Davitt." He threw himself on his knees as if he was going to confession.'[2]

How typical was Meath? It will be evident that one of the considerations which made the Parnellites decide to challenge in the courts the returns of Fulham and Davitt was that Meath was an extreme case.[3] Certainly, the like of Nulty's pastoral was not heard elsewhere; the only other pastoral issued at this time with reference to the general election was that which Archbishop McEvilly ordered the priests of the archdiocese of Tuam to read out on 3 July, denouncing one local episode, not Parnellites in general. Certainly, the alacrity and zeal with which the priests of Meath rallied to the anti-Parnellite side could not have been surpassed elsewhere. Another consideration that may have influenced the bringing of the petitions was that the Parnellites' vote very nearly equalled that of the anti-Parnellites;[4] if it, therefore, could be shown that undue influence by the clergy had had even a marginal effect upon voters the inference would be that the Parnellites' defeat was due to the priests. Thus Meath was untypical; in most other constituencies, as will be seen, the imbalance in the vote was substantial.

A Parnellite priest was *rara avis*. In the first few months of

---

[1] *North Meath report*, pp 96, 111.

[2] *North Meath report*, p. 37. The curate's name is erroneously printed 'Kennedy'. O'Brien confirmed the story (ibid., pp 95–6), but Cassidy gave a quite different version (ibid., pp 121–2). Cf. *United Ireland*, 23 July 1892, p. 2, where the Parnellite version appears.

[3] See below, p. 307.

[4] Dalton obtained 2199 votes to Fulham's 2212, or 49·85 per cent of the total; Mahony obtained 2146 votes to Davitt's 2549, or 45·7 per cent of the total.

nationalist disunity a small but still significant minority of priests
was in evidence on the Parnellite side (much to the embarrassment
and alarm of their bishops), though 'in time they learned to keep
their views more to themselves.'[1] At the general election of July
1892 a mere three Parnellite priests showed themselves sufficiently
to come to the notice of the newspapers examined. One was the
Reverend Arthur Murphy, parish priest of Prior, County Kerry,
who was reported by an anti-Parnellite paper as being 'very energetic among his parishioners in support of . . . the Parnellite candidate for South Kerry'; after the 12 o'clock mass at Dungagon on
3 July Murphy addressed his congregation on the merits of Parnellism.[2] Another was Canon Dillon of the parish of Wicklow who,
according to a Parnellite source, 'never interfered with the opinions
of his flock', spent the week before the poll away from his parish,
and then returned to vote for the Parnellite candidate in the Wicklow East constituency, William Joseph Corbet.[3] One Meath priest,
Christopher Mullen, the parish priest of Moynalty, was said to be a
Parnellite, for which reason his parish was invaded by young priests
from County Cavan anxious to maintain the catholic church's
backing for the other side.[4] If Murphy, Dillon, Mullen and any
other sympathetic priests are discounted, the Parnellites had to do
without any clerical support whatever. No priest signed one of their
nomination papers, none chaired or addressed a meeting, none acted
as a Parnellite personating agent.

Let us now analyse further the results in the 43 constituencies
where there were Parnellite candidates. In the 11 such constituencies

---

[1] Emmet Larkin, 'Launching the counterattack: part II of the Roman
Catholic hierarchy and the destruction of Parnellism', in *Review of Politics*,
xxviii, no. 3 (July 1966), pp 361–5, 382; cf. Woods, op. cit., pp 380–81, 391–4,
424–5.

[2] *Cork Examiner*, 6 July 1892, p. 7.

[3] *I.D.I.*, 8 July 1892, p. 6.

[4] *United Ireland*, 23 July 1892, p. 2. Could Mullen have been 'A country
priest' who wrote to the editor of the Parnellite *Evening Herald* deploring the
activity of Bishop Nulty and his priests and referring knowingly to the
presence of Cavan priests in Moynalty (*I.D.I.*, 18 July 1892, p. 2)?

in Leinster, Munster and Connacht that can be classified as 'urban',[1] the Parnellites did very well, obtaining 30,500 votes against the anti-Parnellites' 22,956; in 7 of them their share of the combined Parnellite and anti-Parnellite vote (i.e. the nationalist or catholic vote) exceeded half; in only one of those remaining was their share below 40 per cent; and in the group as a whole it averaged 57·1 per cent. The results in the Dublin area are particularly striking: 19,874, or 70·4 per cent of the nationalist vote, went to the Parnellites and only 8365 to the anti-Parnellites (who failed to take a single seat). An examination of the geographical distribution of Parnellite sympathies within certain urban constituencies confirms the leanings of townsmen towards Parnellism and of countrymen to the contrary. According to an analysis in the *Freeman's Journal* of political opinion in the Limerick city constituency (which extended several miles into the surrounding countryside), there may have been majorities for the Parnellites in the Glentworth, Irishtown and Shannon wards, but in the rural parishes where 896 of the 5084 electors lived they had no support at all.[2] Similar situations existed in the Kilkenny city and Galway city constituencies.[3] Within the northern division of County Dublin, Parnellism was said to be much stronger in Kilmainham, which included industrial Inchicore, than in rural Tallaght or Naul.[4]

In the 28 'rural'[5] constituencies in Leinster, Munster and Connacht where the Parnellites fielded candidates they obtained 39,473 votes against the anti-Parnellites' 82,537; in only four did their share of the nationalist vote exceed half; in five it was between 40 and 50 per cent; in the group as a whole it was 32·4 per cent. The four rural

[1] I.e. the nine officially classified as 'borough constituencies' and the two County Dublin constituencies. The latter included such suburbs as Rathmines, Kingstown, Dalkey, Blackrock, Kilmainham, Drumcondra and Rathfarnham (*F.J.*, 7 July 1892, pp 5–6, 13 July, p. 5), and so can be regarded as substantially urban in character.

[2] *F.J.*, 29 June 1892, p. 5.

[3] *F.J.*, 7 July 1892, p. 5; *I.D.I.*, 22 July 1892, p. 2.

[4] *F.J.*, 16 July 1892, p. 6.

[5] i.e. those officially classified as 'county constituencies' except for the two County Dublin constituencies.

constituencies which returned Parnellite M.P.s (Clare West and East in Munster, Galway North and adjacent Roscommon South in Connacht) did so for no obvious reason. Generally it was in the urban centres that Parnellite support was evident. The *Freeman's Journal* reported that in Clare East the county town of Ennis 'turned the scale in the factionists' favour': of the 1500 or so townsmen who turned out to vote, 1300 voted for William Redmond the Parnellite nominee.[1] Redmond himself put the figure at 1200.[2] The *Irish Daily Independent* claimed that the towns of Athlone and Kilbeggan in the southern division of Westmeath were Parnellite by three to one.[3] Tralee, another county town, was stated to be a centre of Parnellism in Kerry West.[4] Matthias Bodkin, who succeeded in winning the Roscommon North seat for the anti-Parnellites by only 52 votes, later recalled that Boyle, Frenchpark and the other towns of the division had Parnellite majorities.[5] In Meath the county town of Navan was aggressively Parnellite: when Davitt was there for the anti-Parnellite convention he was faced with an effigy of himself dangling from a pole and was pelted with mud and stones.[6] However, in Wicklow East, while the county town of Wicklow was said to be 'solid' for the Parnellite faction, the fishing town of Arklow was said to be 'completely dominated by the curates', in consequence of which 600 of the 750 votes cast in the town went to the anti-Parnellite candidate, the other 150 to the unionist.[7]

---

[1] *F.J.*, 14 July 1892, p. 5.   [2] *I.D.I.*, 14 July 1892, p. 5.
[3] Ibid., 11 July 1892, p. 7.   [4] Ibid., p. 6.
[5] M. McD. Bodkin, *Recollections of an Irish judge: press, bar and parliament* (London, 1914), pp 180, 183. Bodkin was the only Irish nationalist politician to relate his personal experiences of the 1892 general election in his published memoirs (ibid., ch. 18). Bodkin also drew on his election experiences for material for chs 12 and 13 of his novel, *White magic* (London, 1897); in which, however, the scene is set in Ulster and (improbably) the townsmen are all orangemen, the countrymen all nationalists.
[6] *North Meath report*, pp 123, 133–4, 150–51, 160.
[7] *I.D.I.*, 8 July 1892, p. 6, 9 July, p. 2. Some evidence, partly from local newspapers, supports the view that the Parnellites did *not* generally fare better in the country towns than in the surrounding countryside (Joseph Lee, *The modernisation of Irish society, 1848–1918* (Dublin, 1973), pp 119–20).

In Ulster the Parnellites nominated candidates in only 4 of the 33 constituencies and collected a derisory total of 278 votes, compared with the anti-Parnellites' 12,200 in those 4 constituencies; their share of the nationalist vote ranged from 0·99 per cent in Down South to 5·6 per cent in the adjacent borough of Newry, averaging 2·2 per cent in the 4 constituencies. But the anti-Parnellites fielded candidates in only 12 other constituencies. Ulster politics clearly differed from politics elsewhere in Ireland.

Parnellites unhesitatingly put down their defeat to the activity of the catholic clergy, in particular to influence by them over timid or illiterate voters, as can be observed in their *Irish Daily Independent* for the days following the returns. After the declaration of the poll in Kilkenny city, the unsuccessful Parnellite candidate, John O'Connor, lamented 'that the voice of Kilkenny had been stifled by the priests and that Mr Curran [his anti-Parnellite opponent] would go to parliament to represent none but a few priests and 200 ignorant, timid and illiterate voters'.[1] A commentator in the *Independent*, writing on the Parnellite defeat in Mayo North, ascribed it to 'the poor illiterates who were driven to the booths like sheep to the slaughter', 1500 (out of 1797) plumping for Crilly, the priests' candidate.[2] The leader-writer in the Parnellite *United Ireland* of 16 July contended that the factors determining the Parnellite defeat were 'gross clerical intimidation, servile obedience to the priests on the part of the illiterate voters, clergymen canvassing in support of whiggery in their parishes or acting as personating agents in the polling booths'. A wag, bewailing the defeat in Tipperary South, by an unknown anti-Parnellite, of the Parnellite who had represented the constituency in the old parliament, expressed the opinion that 'were a broomstick nominated by the clergy it would sweep any division in Ireland'.[3] The ex-M.P. for Wicklow East, William Joseph Corbet, roundly blamed the priests of the division for his defeat, asserting that 'their influence over catholic voters has won at

---

[1] *F.J.*, 8 July 1892, p. 5.   [2] *I.D.I.*, 13 July 1892, p. 6.
[3] Ibid., 21 July 1892, p. 5.

the polls'.[1] The irascibly anti-Parnellite *Irish Catholic* also attached great importance to the influence of the clergy in bringing about the defeat of the Parnellites:

the alliance and unity of feeling between our priests and people . . . has been splendidly maintained. . . . Irish catholics have crushed by their own strength—a strength which has its origin in that union of the priests and people to which we have already referred—a revolt precisely similar in its nature, no matter what its outward signs or battle cries, to that with which religion and the church contend in France and Italy.[2]

John Redmond and his lieutenants contemplated lodging petitions against the return of the two anti-Parnellite candidates in Cork city, on the ground of intimidation by priests, in particular by the very popular Canon O'Mahony who had stated (amongst other things) that it would be 'a mortal sin of the deepest dye' to vote for Redmond's brother William or the other Parnellite candidate in the city;[3] but, for practical reasons and because of Bishop Nulty's pastoral, they decided to petition only against the return of Fulham and Davitt in County Meath, with results that have been seen.[4]

Was the defeat of the Parnellites due to the opposition of the catholic clergy? Whether the priests, by virtue of their position as spiritual and social leaders in their communities (combined with that of sponsors, publicists, organisers and general agents of the anti-Parnellite candidates), exerted an influence over catholic electors (particularly over timid or illiterate ones) sufficient to destroy the Parnellites' prospects of widespread success, is very doubtful. The possibility that any such influence was sufficient to take votes or even seats from within the Parnellites' grasp is, however, plausible and will be examined.

Clearly the Parnellites could not win very many seats in the new parliament, as they had nominated candidates for only 44, compared with the anti-Parnellites' 85. In large areas of Ireland, most notably in County Cork, the midlands and Ulster, there was scarcely

[1] Ibid., 23 July 1892, p. 5. [2] *Irish Catholic*, 16 July 1892, p. 4.
[3] *I.D.I.*, 26 July 1892, pp 5–6.
[4] Ibid., 23 July 1892, p. 2; 4 Aug., pp 4, 5; 5 Aug., p. 5.

a single candidate upholding what one Parnellite politician called 'the principles and policies of our lost leader'.[1] From the beginning of the election campaign the Parnellites appeared the weaker of the two nationalist factions.

1 *Parnellite vote in urban constituencies in Leinster, Munster and Connacht*

This and the following tables are compiled from figures given in B. M. Walker, *Parliamentary election results in Ireland, 1801–1922* (Dublin, 1978), pp 144–50, and *Return showing the number of persons who voted as illiterates at the general election of 1892 in the United Kingdom*, pp 9–12, H.C. 1893–4 (76), lxx, 713–16.

	Combined Parnellite and anti-Parnellite vote	Parnellite vote (total)	Parnellite vote (percentage)	Illiterate vote (percentage)
Dublin St Stephen's Green	3494	2878	82·4	1·3
Dublin St Patrick's	4804	3694	76·9	4·4
Dublin Harbour	5858	4482	76·5	2·2
Dublin College Green*	3684	2568	69·7	2·4
Dublin County South*	3713	2261	60·9	4·4
Dublin County North*	6687	3991	59·7	10·8
Waterford city	2969	1676	56·4	9·8
Galway	1237	593	47·9	20·7
Kilkenny city	1348	604	44·8	15·7
Limerick city	3368	1490	44·2	8·2
Cork city	16295	6263	38·4	13·1
Total	53,456	30,500	57·1	7·0

An asterisk indicates that there was also a unionist or liberal unionist candidate. In Dublin St Stephen's Green the liberal unionist (William Kenny, Q.C., a catholic) was elected, and in Dublin County South the unionist was elected. The illiterate vote is stated as a percentage of all votes cast.

[1] Ibid., 23 July 1892, p. 5.

2 *Parnellite vote in rural constituencies in Leinster, Munster and Connacht*

	Combined Parnellite and anti-Parnellite vote	Parnellite vote (total)	Parnellite vote (percentage)	Illiterate vote (percentage)
Roscommon South	6059	3815	63·0	24·6
Clare West	6749	3878	57·5	18·9
Galway North	3691	2040	55·3	46·9
Clare East	5962	3203	53·7	18·2
Meath South	4411	2199	49·9	22·9
Roscommon North	6450	3199	49·6	24·0
Meath North	4695	2146	45·7	23·7
Kildare North	3860	1707	44·2	22·3
Wicklow East★	2548	1115	43·8	17·3
Mayo North	3598	1397	38·8	48·9
Galway South	4034	1411	35·0	37·1
Kerry West★	3633	1143	31·5	31·0
Louth South	3577	1126	31·5	19·0
Westmeath South	3615	1080	29·9	22·9
				26·0
Waterford East	3605	1043	28·9	33·0
Limerick East	4077	1174	28·8	20·1
Kildare South	3617	975	27·0	20·6
Tipperary South	3344	773	23·1	19·4
Tipperary East	3889	891	22·9	20·5
Galway East	4356	974	22·4	35·3
Tipperary Mid	4171	887	21·3	19·6
Kerry North	3634	776	21·4	30·9
Galway (Connemara)	3235	598	18·5	56·1
Wicklow West★	3128	546	17·5	18·2
Limerick West	3773	516	13·7	23·5
Westmeath North	3257	379	11·6	22·5
Kerry South★	2321	225	9·7	35·5
Mayo East	2721	257	9·4	38·4
				27·3
Total	122,010	39,473	32·4	26·6

An asterisk indicates that there was also a unionist or liberal unionist candidate. The illiterate vote is stated as a percentage of all votes cast.

The effectiveness of clerical influence in the 43 constituencies where Parnellites were standing is not always exactly measurable. However, numerical testing is possible with the illiterate voters, as will now be shown. If the illiterate voters were in fact subject to extraordinary influence by the clergy, the Parnellites might have expected to obtain a larger share of the catholic vote in areas where the illiterates were fewer or where clerical activity was less, and vice versa. Now it is evident that the Parnellites did very well in and around Dublin, where illiterate voters were almost negligible and where priests were absent from the polling stations as well as from the hustings, and that they did fairly well in all other urban constituencies, in most (if not all) of which similar circumstances prevailed; whilst in rural constituencies, where the percentage of illiterate voters ranged from 17·3 to 56·1 and where the priests often, after playing a major role as publicists, manned the polling stations on polling day, the Parnellites' polls were, with a few exceptions, disappointing to themselves. But there is no direct correlation between the figures for the Parnellites' share of the combined Parnellite and anti-Parnellite vote and the figures for the illiterates' share

3 Parnellite vote in Ulster

	Combined Parnellite and anti-Parnellite vote	Parnellite vote (total)	Parnellite vote (percentage)	Illiterate vote (percentage)
Newry	961	54	5·6	17·9
Tyrone Mid	3790	123	3·2	22·9
Armagh South	3498	59	1·7	28·2
Down South	4249	42	0·99	20·6
Total	12,498	278	2·2	23·1

In every case there was also a unionist or liberal unionist; none was elected. The illiterate vote is given as a percentage of all votes cast.

of the total vote.[1] An examination of table 2, in which the 28 rural seats in Leinster, Munster and Connacht contested both by Parnellites and anti-Parnellites are listed in order of the Parnellites' share of the combined vote, will show that, while the Parnellite share is 40·4 per cent in the upper half and 20·4 per cent in the lower half, the illiterates' share of the total vote is virtually the same: 26·0 and 27·3 per cent respectively.[2] Individual cases also tell against the view that a causal relationship existed between illiteracy, clerical activity at the hustings and booths, and Parnellite defeat. In the Galway North constituency no less than 1758, or 46·9 per cent, of the 3746 voters, declared themselves illiterates (only two other constituencies had higher illiteracy rates); some voters there could neither read, write nor even speak English, and could only state in Irish that they wished to vote for 'the soggarth' (the priest); the priests, evidently intrepid campaigners on the anti-Parnellite side, seem to have acted as personating agents;[3] none the less, the Parnellite candidate triumphed. In the Clare East constituency, though there was a priest inside every single polling station, Parnellism was also victorious.

Whether the election effort of the clergy was effective, if not upon illiterate voters, then upon those who were timid, impressionable, deferential or merely apathetic, is impossible to determine by the same sort of numerical analysis. But again individual cases provide some evidence that the priests' effort was not effective. County Meath is one. The success of the petitions and the unseating of Fulham and Davitt, on grounds of intimidation by Bishop Nulty and his priests,[4] led to fresh elections in the county in February 1893.

[1] See tables 1 and 2. The figures are not strictly comparable; the total vote, of which the illiterates are given as a percentage, includes unionists or liberal unionists (in eight cases) and (apparently) spoilt ballots; but it is unlikely that this discrepancy is very significant. Ulster is ignored, as its political behaviour is exceptional and as the number of cases (four) is too small for generalisation.

[2] A rank correlation coefficient of +0·13 obtained from the figures in columns 4 and 5 seems to indicate only a very slight correlation between Parnellite and illiterate votes. There are too few constituencies in tables 1 and 3 for similar analyses to be meaningful.

[3] *I.D.I.*, 11 July 1892, p. 5; cf. above, p. 296.

[4] *Return . . . of the judgments delivered by the judges selected for the trial of election petitions*, pp 25–45, H.C. 1893–4 (25), lxx, 829–49.

This time the clergy were cautious: while priests canvassed for the anti-Parnellite candidates, chaired and addressed public meetings, and busied themselves inside as well as outside nearly all polling stations on polling day (17 February in Meath South, 21 in Meath North), they did not preach politics in their chapels and the bishop refrained from alluding to the election in his Lenten pastoral.[1] The result was that the Parnellite share of the vote was almost exactly the same: in Meath South, Dalton obtained 49·4 per cent (compared with 49·85 in July 1892); and in Meath North, Mahony obtained 47·4 per cent (compared with 45·7). It is significant that Patrick O'Brien, in a hard-hitting anti-clerical speech at Trim on 26 February, a few days after the declaration of the polls, did not accuse the clergy of undue influence but merely chided them with 'taking one side and promoting strife'.[2] Evidently the extraordinary activity of the clergy at the general election had made little or no difference to the result. This time, after again being narrowly defeated, Parnellites made no complaints about intimidation. Limerick city was another individual case in point. The Limerick city constituency was unique for the complete absence of priests from electioneering, owing to the hostility of the local bishop, Edward O'Dwyer, to the anti-Parnellite candidate, Francis O'Keeffe;[3] yet the Parnellites fared worse in Limerick than in any other urban constituency except Cork. Evidently electors, even urban electors, had reasons enough to vote anti-Parnellite without prompting from the clergy. One anti-Parnellite M.P., Alfred Webb, made the point that 'Limerick is proof positive against the general charge of clerical intimidation.'[4]

Had the clergy, then, no influence over the electors? It is evident that they were unable significantly to win over voters to their point of view during the election campaign or on the days of polling in

[1] *I.D.I.*, esp. 13 Feb. 1893, p. 5; 17 Feb., p. 5; 18 Feb., p. 6; 22 Feb., p. 5; *Drogheda Independent*, esp. 21, 28 Jan. 1893, 4, 11, 18 Feb., *passim*.

[2] *United Ireland*, 4 Mar. 1893, p. 3.

[3] *Cork Examiner*, 22 June 1892, pp 5, 8.

[4] Ibid., 20 July 1892, p. 6.

July 1892, but it is still arguable that they influenced the election result in the long run. Priests surely did play a part in the formation of public opinion. The formation of public opinion was very much determined in the first place by the general disposition of the public; it involved various interest or pressure groups besides the catholic clergy; and with regard to the split it had probably been completed long before July 1892. It is doubtful whether the state of public opinion was likely to be much altered by any amount of electioneering, by priests or any other group, during the few weeks up to polling.

Though this is not the place to deal generally with the formation of public opinion with regard to the split, the division of the nationalist vote in 1892 between Parnellites and anti-Parnellites can be shown to have owed something to the influence of the clergy on public opinion and so some attention is necessary. The variation in the Parnellite vote between town and country, and also between the three southern provinces and Ulster, can be interpreted as reflective of a variation in the influence of the clergy in the formation of public opinion. Indeed the very absence of Parnellite candidates in more than half of the rural constituencies in the southern provinces and in all but four of the Ulster constituencies can bear the same interpretation.

The clergy in the towns, especially Dublin, were but one of several competing influences and not necessarily a major one. Their powerful rivals were the catholic bourgeoisie: professional men and prosperous business men who, like the priests, had education, leisure and financial independence enabling them to engage in public affairs and to seek to form public opinion. This class was much more numerous, relative to the clergy, in urban areas than in rural. This thesis has been tested by an analysis of information on a sample of 12 (out of 39) administrative counties given in the 1891 census reports.[1]

---

[1] *Census Ire., 1891: part I . . . vol. i: province of Leinster*, H.C. 1890–91 [C. 6515], xcv; *part I . . . vol. ii: province of Munster*, H.C. 1892 [C. 6567], xci; *part I . . . vol. iii: province of Ulster*, H.C. 1892 [C. 6626], xcii; *part I . . . vol. iv: province of Connaught*, H.C. 1892 [C. 6685], xciii.

A breakdown of occupations according to type, sex and religion is given in table XIX in each county report. A breakdown of 'occupations of males . . . 20 years and upwards in the principal towns' is given in table XXI. Unfortunately, religion is not indicated in table XXI and so it has been necessary to make an estimate (on the basis of the figures for the county as a whole) of the numbers of catholics. Another shortcoming is that the census enumerators' selection of 'the principal towns' is generally unsatisfactory. For example, the 'principal towns' of County Roscommon are designated as Athlone (part), Ballinasloe (part), Boyle and Carrick-on-Shannon (part); the market towns of Castlerea, Frenchpark, Roscommon and Strokestown are ignored. The occupations I have selected as 'influential' because they require or confer education, leisure and independence are as follows: lawyers; doctors and dentists; editors, journalists and other writers; engineers and surveyors; architects, musicians, actors, photographers, sculptors and artists; merchants, brokers, factors, auctioneers, accountants, etc.; bankers and other dealers in money; dealers in insurance. Excluded are teachers who, as employees of the clergy who managed most catholic schools, may have lacked independence. Also excluded are students of all kinds. In County Roscommon as a whole it has been found that there were, among the catholic population aged twenty or over and male, 75 priests, 13 lawyers, 21 doctors or dentists, 9 editors, etc., 19 engineers or surveyors, 17 architects, etc., 30 merchants, etc., no dealers in money, and one dealer in insurance—75 priests to 110 laymen in influential occupations. In the specified urban areas there were 6 priests to an estimated 38 laymen in influential occupations, a ratio of 1:6·33; in the remainder of the county (which we may designate 'rural') there were 69 priests to an estimated 72 laymen, a ratio of 1:1·04. Thus, while in the urban areas of County Roscommon the laymen outnumbered the priests by 6 to 1, in the rural areas the numbers were almost evenly balanced. In all other counties sampled the same sort of difference has been found between town and countryside. In the urban areas of County Meath (viz. Kells and Navan) there were 7 priests to 33 laymen (1:4·71), and in the rural areas 70 priests to 66 laymen (1:0·94). In the city of Dublin (for which all figures are actual, not partly estimated) there were 191 priests to as many as 1337 laymen in influential occupations. We may reasonably speculate that the imbalance between urban and rural areas would have been seen to be much greater if all of the numerous small towns and some of the larger villages that were a feature of the Irish countryside had been designated as urban by the census enumerators. A digest of the figures for the 12 administrative counties is given in table 4.

4 *Catholic priests and catholic laymen in influential occupations in urban and rural areas in twelve administrative counties*

For sources and definition of terms, see above, pp 313–14.

		Catholic priests	Catholic laymen in influential occupations	Ratio
Armagh	urban[1]	20	52	1:2·6
	rural	44	25	1:0·6
	total	64	77	1:1·2
Cork	urban[2]	61	193	1:3·2
	rural	216	292	1:1·4
	total	277	485	1:1·8
Cork city		80	514	1:6·4
Donegal	urban[3]	7	19	1:2·7
	rural	94	127	1:1·4
	total	101	146	1:1·4
Down	urban[4]	25	71	1:2·8
	rural	65	76	1:1·2
	total	90	147	1:1·6

[1] Armagh, Bessbrook, Lurgan, Newry (part), Portadown.
[2] Bandon, Bantry, Clonakilty, Dunmanway, Fermoy, Kinsale, Macroom, Mallow, Midleton, Mitchelstown, Queenstown, Skibbereen, Youghal.
[3] Ballyshannon, Letterkenny.
[4] Banbridge, Bangor, Belfast (part), Comber, Downpatrick, Dromore, Holywood, Lisburn (part), Newry (part), Newtownards.

4 *Catholic priests and catholic laymen in influential occupations in urban and rural areas in twelve administrative counties* (contd.)

		Catholic priests	Catholic laymen in influential occupations	Ratio
Dublin	urban[5]	151	633	1:4·2
	rural	83	122	1:1·5
	total	234	755	1:3·2
Dublin city		191	1337	1:7·0
Galway	urban[6]	47	165	1:3·5
	rural	117	183	1:1·6
	total	164	349	1:2·1
Meath	urban[7]	7	33	1:4·7
	rural	70	66	1:0·9
	total	77	99	1:1·3
Roscommon	urban[8]	6	38	1:6·3
	rural	69	72	1:1·0
	total	75	110	1:1·5
Waterford	urban[9]	15	9	1:0·60
	rural	102	59	1:0·58
	total	117	68	1:1·7
Waterford city		29	93	1:3·2

[5] Clontarf, Drumcondra, New Kilmainham, Pembroke, Rathmines and Rathgar, Balbriggan, Blackrock, Bray (part), Dalkey, Killiney and Ballybrack, Kingstown.

[6] Ballinasloe (part), Galway, Loughrea, Tuam.

[7] Kells, Navan.

[8] Athlone (part), Ballinasloe (part), Boyle, Carrick-on-Shannon (part).

[9] Carrick-on-Suir (part), Clonmel (part), Dungarvan.

Another, less powerful but effective rival group in the metropolis, cities, market towns and larger villages was the catholic *petite bourgeoisie* and *artisanat*: clerks, publicans, shopkeepers, tradesmen and millworkers. It has been shown elsewhere that it was such as these, and not farmers or agricultural labourers, who became fenians in the 1860s, and that Dublin contained nearly three times as many fenians relative to the catholic population as any other county.[1] The

[1] R. V. Comerford, 'Irish nationalist politics, 1858–70' (Ph.D. thesis, University of Dublin, 1977), pp 197–207.

fenians, because of their design to overthrow the government by force of arms, were politically alienated from the clergy to a much greater degree than any other body of catholics. In the market towns, such as those in County Roscommon mentioned above, the same occupational group (including some fenians or ex-fenians) made in 1879 a vital contribution to the rise of the land league into which the clergy were drawn only as success showed.[1] Thus by 1890, when the split occurred, there existed in urban areas a class which by its nature must have been much more numerous than the clergy and whose politicisation owed very little to the clergy.

These groups had in the formation of public opinion various advantages over the clergy drawn from the very nature of urban life: they were able to make the workplace, fair, shop or public house a venue for political discussion; they controlled the daily and weekly press which townsmen, being highly literate and close to news-vendors, were more likely to read than countrymen; they were able to stage massive political demonstrations, of which the biggest in Dublin for many years was Parnell's funeral; they controlled the city corporations or town commissions which were major sources of patronage. Little wonder, therefore, that in the metropolis the catholic-consciousness movement had never been under clerical influence, but on the contrary had for long been dominated by the bourgeoisie.[2]

The clergy in the countryside had to themselves the place that elsewhere was shared with, or even wholly occupied by, the middle-class laity.[3] In rural Ireland there was practically no other leisured

[1] Sam Clark, 'The social composition of the Land League', in *I.H.S.*, xvii, no. 68 (Sept. 1971), pp 447–69, and 'The political mobilization of Irish farmers', in *Canadian Review of Sociology and Anthropology*, xii, no. 4 (Nov. 1975), pp 483–99.
[2] Cf. Jacqueline R. Hill, 'Nationalism and the catholic church in the 1840s: views of Dublin repealers', in *I.H.S.*, xix, no. 76 (Sept. 1975), pp 371–95. There is no reason to believe that the clergy gained influence in Dublin between the 1840s and the 1890s.
[3] Cf. Michael Davitt, 'The priest in politics', in *Nineteenth Century*, xxxiii, no. 191 (Jan. 1893), p. 151.

and independent class. Hardly any of the gentry were catholic and the few who were had become alienated from the catholic-consciousness movement by its support for the tenant-farmer class in the land war. The 'strong' farmers, who by definition possessed leisure and independence, were in many cases not catholic and as a class were not numerous, except in eastern counties like Kildare and Meath. The priest had the attention of the entire parish for an hour every Sunday; he controlled the parish school and could count on the loyalty of the schoolmaster; he usually presided over the local branch of the Irish National League or (after the split) the Irish National Federation, and as such was often involved on behalf of the very numerous tenant-farmer class in agrarian agitation, notably in the Plan of Campaign. His part in the formation of public opinion in his parish was therefore dominant. At the general election of 1892 counties like Cork, Limerick and Tipperary, where there had been much agrarian unrest in the late 1880s, 'were only saved . . . by the popularity of a few priests who had signalised themselves as leaders in the Plan of Campaign struggle', wrote William O'Brien, who was three times imprisoned for his own part in the agitation and who was himself, like most leading agitators, an anti-Parnellite parliamentary candidate.[1] In County Cork there were no Parnellite candidates whatever; in the counties of Limerick and Tipperary there were five, all of whom fared very badly. While it was always 'an axiom of Irish politics that clerical influence was much greater in rural areas',[2] the prominent part played by the clergy in the Plan of Campaign (fourteen were, like O'Brien, imprisoned for it[3]) seems to have given them an additional advantage in the formation of public opinion after the split.

Ulster, like rural parts of Leinster, Munster and Connacht, lacked a catholic middle class, though for quite different reasons. Throughout Ulster the professional men and prosperous businessmen were

---

[1] William O'Brien, *An olive branch in Ireland* (London, 1910), pp 23–4.

[2] J. H. Whyte, 'The influence of the catholic clergy on elections in nineteenth-century Ireland', in *E.H.R.*, lxxv, no. 295 (Apr. 1960), p. 251.

[3] Woods, op. cit., ch. 4.

by and large protestants, not catholics, and so, with rare exceptions, took no part in the catholic-consciousness movement. In the three Ulster counties sampled (Armagh, Donegal and Down) the ratios of catholic priests to catholic laymen in specified 'influential' occupations are lower than in 7 of the 9 other counties and cities sampled.[1] The clergy therefore played a greater role in the formation of opinion within the catholic community.[2] There was a non-clerical factor to boost anti-Parnellite strength. In much of Ulster the catholic population was small or even negligible, for which reason the power-base of the catholic-consciousness movement was thin. Elsewhere in Ulster, in counties such as Monaghan and Cavan, though the catholics made up the majority of the population, they felt less secure than their co-religionists further south, fearing as they did the still numerous protestants with their unionist or liberal unionist politics. In consequence greater solidarity existed among the catholics of Ulster. Therefore Irish nationalism in Ulster was anti-Parnellite, and almost universally so.

It is not argued that urban interests, rather than rural, were served by Parnellism or that professional and business men, clerks, shop-keepers and tradesmen were necessarily Parnellites. What is contended is that while in rural areas (where the group that had a quasi-monopoly of forming public opinion was duty bound to urge the anti-Parnellite case or to remain silent) the Parnellite case was not much heard, in urban areas those who influenced public opinion differed frankly, and the issues that divided the two sides were aired and contested freely, so that Parnellism obtained widespread acceptance. Ulster was peculiar in that catholics sank their differences and plumped for the anti-Parnellite faction from grave fear of the protestants with whom their differences were much more serious.

The catholic clergy contributed to the defeat of the Parnellites in 1892 not by hectic electioneering but by steady influence. There were very many catholics who voted against Parnellism without taking any advice from their priests.

[1] See table 4.
[2] Cf. Peter Gibbon, *The origins of Ulster unionism* (Manchester, 1975), p. 93.

The historical work of T. W. Moody

J. G. SIMMS

IRISH history has been revolutionised in the last generation. The origins of that revolution are to be found in the initiative and determination of two graduate students of the University of London, T. W. Moody and R. Dudley Edwards, one of them from Belfast and the other from Dublin. They were the founders and first editors of *Irish Historical Studies*, launched in March 1938 as the joint journal of two societies, the Ulster Society for Irish Historical Studies and the Irish Historical Society, which they had respectively founded in 1936. With the collaboration of a succession of coeditors T.W.M. has continued to edit the journal up to the completion of the eightieth number and twentieth volume in 1978. The journal has set the stamp of accuracy and objective scholarship on the whole range of Irish historical writing during the last forty years.

The new concept of Irish history was further advanced by a number of monographs, in a series edited throughout by T.W.M., with a succession of coeditors, under the general title 'Studies in Irish History'. The first volume was *Irish public opinion, 1750–1800*, by R. B. McDowell, published by Faber and Faber in 1944. Altogether seventeen volumes have been published, seven by Faber and Faber, and ten by Routledge and Kegan Paul, the most recent being *The Church of Ireland, 1869–1969* (1975), also by R. B. McDowell.

That such research and revision should be synthesised in a co-operative historical work, or works, was the theme of T.W.M.'s presidential address to the Irish Historical Society, delivered on 4 December 1962. His project was adopted and an organisation set up, under the auspices first of the Irish Committee of Historical

[321]

Sciences, and then of the Royal Irish Academy, with substantial help from the Irish government. The *New history of Ireland*, planned in nine volumes and edited by T.W.M. in collaboration with Professors F. X. Martin and F. J. Byrne, is being published by Oxford University Press. The first volume to appear, in 1976, was volume III, covering early modern Ireland from 1534 to 1691. Work is in active progress on further volumes, of which the next to appear will be volumes VIII and IX, comprising between them a chronology, succession lists, parliamentary sessions and elections, and a historical atlas. In addition a parallel series of ancillary volumes is in progress, the work of individual scholars, supplementing the *New history* in a number of special fields—bibliography, statistics, parliamentary history, medieval texts. The first of these, P. W. A. Asplin's bibliography, *Medieval Ireland, c. 1170–1495*, was published in 1971; three further volumes appeared in November 1978. All such ancillary volumes appear under the imprint of the Royal Irish Academy.

In the meanwhile a forerunner of the larger project appeared in 1967 as *The course of Irish history*, edited by T.W.M. and Professor Martin and published by the Mercier Press, Cork. It was based on twenty-one television programmes, each scripted by a specialist but aimed at a wide audience. The book has proved extremely popular and has already been reprinted many times.

The following list of T.W.M.'s publications has been divided into themes, many of which reflect his special interests, ranging over five centuries of Irish history. Within each category the listing is by date of publication. Reviews have not been included.

1 *General history of Ireland*

(Editor, with H. A. Cronne and D. B. Quinn) *Essays on British and Irish history in honour of James Eadie Todd.* Pp xvi, 336. London: Muller, 1949.
The Irish. In *Oxford junior encyclopaedia* (2nd edition, 1964), i.

(Editor, with F. X. Martin) *The course of Irish history.* Pp 404. Cork: Mercier Press; New York: Weybright and Talley, 1967. Second printing, with revisions, May 1967; the American edition is of the second printing.

Fenianism, home rule and the land war (1850–91). In *The course of Irish history* (see above), pp 275–93.

(Editor) *Historical Studies: papers read before the Irish Conference of Historians,* vi (Dublin, 2–5 June 1965). Pp viii, 182. London: Routledge and Kegan Paul, 1968.

(Editor, with F. X. Martin and F. J. Byrne) *A new history of Ireland.* Vol. iii: *Early modern Ireland, 1534–1691.* Pp lxiv, 736. Oxford: Clarendon Press, 1976.

Early modern Ireland. In *A new history of Ireland,* iii (see above), pp xxxix–lxiii.

(Editor, with F. X. Martin and F. J. Byrne) *A new history of Ireland.* Vols viii and ix: *A companion to Irish history,* parts I and II. Oxford University Press (in the press).

(With J. G. Simms and C. J. Woods) A chronology of Irish history, 1603–1976. In *A new history of Ireland,* viii (see above).

2 *Ulster history* (see also ¶ 10 below)

(Editor) The revised articles of the Ulster plantation, 1610. In *Bulletin of the Institute of Historical Research,* xii, no. 36 (Feb. 1935), pp 178–83.

The Londonderry plantation, with special reference to the resulting relations between the crown and the city of London, 1609–41. In *Bulletin of the Institute of Historical Research,* xiii, no. 39 (Feb. 1936), pp 168–72 (summary of Ph.D. thesis, University of London, 1934).

Redmond O'Hanlon (*c.* 1640–1681). In *Proceedings and Reports of the Belfast Natural History and Philosophical Society,* 2nd series, i, pt 1 (1937), pp 17–33.

The treatment of the native population under the scheme for the plantation in Ulster. In *I.H.S.,* i, no. 1 (Mar. 1938), pp 59–63 (Historical Revision II).

(Editor) Ulster plantation papers, 1608–13. In *Analecta Hibernica*, no. 8 (1938), pp 179–298.

(Editor) Schedules of the lands in Ulster allotted to the London livery companies, 1613. In *Analecta Hibernica*, no. 8 (1938), pp 299–311.

Sir Thomas Phillips of Limavady, servitor. In *I.H.S.*, i, no. 3 (Mar. 1939), pp 251–72.

The Londonderry plantation, 1609–41: the city of London and the plantation in Ulster. Pp. 487. Belfast: William Mullan and Son, 1939.

(Editor) The school-bills of Conn O'Neill at Eton, 1615–22. In *I.H.S.*, ii, no. 6 (Sept. 1940), pp 189–204 (Select Documents I).

(Editor, with J. C. Beckett) *Ulster since 1800: a political and economic survey*. Pp 133. London: B.B.C., 1954. Second printing, with corrections, 1957.

A general survey [of Ulster since 1800]. In *Ulster since 1800: a political and economic survey* (see above), pp 121–33.

(Editor, with J. C. Beckett) *Ulster since 1800, second series: a social survey*. Pp 240. London: B.B.C., 1957. Second printing, with corrections, 1958.

The social history of modern Ulster. In *Ulster since 1800: a social survey* (see above), pp 224–35.

(Editor, with J. G. Simms) *The bishopric of Derry and the Irish Society of London, 1602–1705*. Vol. i, 1602–70. Pp [vi], 430. Dublin: Stationery Office, for the Irish Manuscripts Commission, 1968. Vol. ii (1670–1705) to be published in 1978.

The Ulster question, 1603–1973. Pp x, 134. Dublin and Cork: Mercier Press, 1974.

3 *The Irish parliament*

The Irish parliament under Elizabeth and James I: a general survey. In *Proceedings of the Royal Irish Academy*, xlv, sect. C, no. 6 (1939), pp 41–81.

(With R. Dudley Edwards) The history of Poynings' Law: part I, 1494–1615. In *I.H.S.*, ii, no. 8 (Sept. 1941), pp 415–24 (Historical Revision IV).

4 *The United Irishmen and Theobald Wolfe Tone*

The political ideas of the United Irishmen. In *Ireland To-day*, iii, no. 1 (Jan. 1938), pp 15–25.

(Editor, with R. B. McDowell) The writings of Theobald Wolfe Tone. A comprehensive edition, from all the known sources, including many documents hitherto unprinted. Oxford University Press (forthcoming).

5 *Thomas Davis*

Thomas Davis, 1814–45. Pp 64. Dublin: Hodges, Figgis, 1945.

The Thomas Davis centenary lecture in Newry. In *An t-Iubhar*, 1946, pp 22–6.

Thomas Davis and the Irish nation. In *Hermathena*, ciii (1966), pp 5–31.

6 *The fenian movement*

(Editor) *The fenian movement*. Pp. 126. Cork: Mercier Press, 1968.

The fenian movement in Irish history. In *The fenian movement* (see above), pp 113–26.

(Editor, with Leon Ó Broin) The I.R.B. supreme council, 1868–78. In *I.H.S.*, xix, no. 75 (Mar. 1975), pp 286–332 (Select Documents).

7 *Michael Davitt*

Michael Davitt in penal servitude, 1870–1877. In *Studies*, xxx, no. 120 (Dec. 1941), pp 517–30; xxxi, no. 121 (Mar. 1942), pp 16–30.

Michael Davitt and the 'pen' letter. In *I.H.S.*, iv, no. 15 (Mar. 1945), pp 224–53.

Michael Davitt, 1846–1906: a survey and appreciation. In *Studies*, xxxv, no. 138 (June 1946), pp 199–208; no. 139 (Sept. 1946), pp 325–34; no. 140 (Dec. 1946), pp 433–8.

Michael Davitt and the British labour movement, 1882–1906. In *Transactions of the Royal Historical Society*, 5th series, iii (1953), pp 53–76.

Michael Davitt. In *Collier's encyclopaedia* (New York, 1961).

Michael Davitt. In J. W. Boyle (ed.), *Leaders and workers* (Cork: Mercier Press, [1965]), pp 47–55.

Introduction to Michael Davitt, *Leaves from a prison diary: or lectures to a 'solitary audience'* (2 vols, London, 1885; reprinted, Shannon: Irish University Press, 1972), pp vii–xiv.

Davitt and Irish revolution, 1846–82. Oxford University Press (forthcoming).

8 *Home rule and the land war*

The new departure in Irish politics, 1878–9. In *Essays on British and Irish history* (see above, p. 322), pp 303–33.

(Editor) Parnell and the Galway election of 1886. In *I.H.S.*, ix, no. 35 (Mar. 1955), pp 319–38 (Select Documents XV).

The Irish home-rule movement and the British liberal party. In *Topic* (Washington and Jefferson College, Pa), 13 (spring 1967), pp 44–59.

The Times versus Parnell and Co., 1887–90. In *Historical Studies*, vi (see above, p. 323), pp 147–82.

Anna Parnell and the land league. In *Hermathena*, cxvii (1974), pp 5–17.

(Editor, with Richard Hawkins) The Irish journal of Florence Arnold-Forster, 1880–82. Oxford University Press (forthcoming).

9 *The Irish in America*

The Ulster Scots in colonial and revolutionary America. In *Studies*, xxxiv, no. 133 (Mar. 1945), pp 85–94; no. 134 (June 1945), pp 211–21.

Irish and Scotch-Irish in eighteenth-century America. In *Studies*, xxxv, no. 137 (Mar. 1946), pp 85–94.

Irish-American nationalism. In *I.H.S.*, xv, no. 60 (Sept. 1967), pp 438–45.

10 *University education in Ireland*

Higher education. In *Ulster since 1800: a social survey* (see above, p. 324), pp 192–203.

The Irish university question of the nineteenth century. In *History*, xliii, no. 148 (1958), pp 90–109.

(With J. C. Beckett) *Queen's, Belfast, 1845–1949: the history of a university*. 2 vols: i, pp lxviii, 1–452; ii, pp xvi, 453–983. London: Faber and Faber, 1959.

(Part-author and joint editor)[1] *Commission on higher education 1960–67: I presentation and summary of report* (Pr 9326), pp iv, 119 (Mar. 1967); *II report*, vol. i (Pr 9389), pp xxvii, 1–492 (July 1967); vol. ii (Pr 9588), pp xxiv, 493–976 (Apr. 1968). Dublin: Stationery Office.

The university merger. In *Studies*, lvi, no. 222 (summer 1967), pp 172–8. (Contribution to a symposium on the proposed 'merger' of Trinity College and University College, Dublin.)

11 *Historiography*

Twenty years after. In *I.H.S.*, xi, no. 41 (Mar. 1958), pp 1–4. (Retrospect of the first twenty years of *I.H.S.*).

A new history of Ireland. In *I.H.S.*, xvi, no. 63 (Mar. 1969), pp 241–57.

(Editor) *Irish historiography, 1936–70*. Pp viii, 155. Dublin: Irish Committee of Historical Sciences, 1971.

Thirty-five years of Irish historiography. In *Irish historiography* (see above), pp 137–55.

A new history of Ireland. In *Ireland Today: Bulletin of the Department of Foreign Affairs*, no. 898 (15 Dec. 1976), pp 6–8.

The first forty years. In *I.H.S.*, xx, no. 80 (Sept. 1977), pp 377–83. (Editorial retrospect; cf. above, Twenty years after.)

Irish history and Irish mythology. In *Hermathena*, cxxiv (summer 1978), pp 7–23.

---

[1] As member of the commission and (with Cearbhall O Dálaigh and Eoin O'Malley) member of its drafting consultative committee.

12 *Bibliography*

The writings of Edmund Curtis. In *I.H.S.*, iii, no. 12 (Sept. 1943), pp 393–400.

Ireland. In W. H. Burston and C. W. Green (ed.), *Handbook for history teachers* (London: Methuen, 1962), pp 509–13; 2nd edition, rewritten and enlarged (London: Methuen, 1972), pp 838–44.

Rules for contributors to *Irish Historical Studies*, revised edition. In *I.H.S.*, supplement I (Jan. 1968), pp 71–124; 2nd revised edition (Dublin, 1975) reprinted from *I.H.S.*, xix, no. 76 (Sept. 1975), pp 467–79.

The fenian movement: a select bibliography. In *The fenian movement* (see above, p. 325).

A bibliography of modern history. Pp 47. Dublin: University Press, 1977.

13 *Other topics*

Edmund Curtis, 1881–1943. In *Hermathena*, lxiii (1944), pp 69–78.

Edmund Curtis. In *Dictionary of national biography, 1941–1950* (London: Oxford University Press, 1959), pp 193–4.

The Thomas Davis lectures. In *Radio Éirean handbook, 1955* (Dublin: Stationery Office), pp 53–6.

(Part-author)[1] *A view of Irish broadcasting.* Pp 32. [Dublin]: Radio Telefís Éireann, May 1971.

(Editor) An Irish countryman in the British navy, 1809–1815: the memoirs of Henry Walsh. In *Irish Sword*, iv, no. 16 (summer 1960), pp 149–56; no. 17 (winter 1960), pp 228–45; v, no. 18 (summer 1961), pp 41–55; no. 19 (winter 1961), pp 107–16; no. 20 (summer 1962), pp 146–54; no. 21 (winter 1962), pp 236–50.

(Editor) *Nationality and the pursuit of national independence.* Pp xvi, 178. Belfast: Appletree Press, 1978. Historical Studies xi.

Introduction to *Nationality and the pursuit of national independence* (see above), pp ix–xv.

---

[1] As member of R.T.E. authority and (with Dónall Ó Moráin and Michael O'Callaghan) of a drafting committee.

Index

Index

De Cobain, E. S. W., 91
Delany, Bp, of Cork, 240, 259
Denieffe, Joseph, 150, 153, 156
Denvir, John, 87, 100–2
Deramore, Lord, 278
Derrygonnelly, Co. Fermanagh, 230
De Valera, Eamon, 16, 20
Devoy, John, 85, 169; *Recollections of an Irish rebel*, 85–6
Dickson, Thomas, 91, 227–8, 231
Dillon, John, 97, 229, 260, 294, 297
Dillon, Myles, 13
Disraeli, Benjamin, 238, 243, 248
Doheny, Michael, 66, 152
Donegal, County, 319; distress in, 216; Dunfanaghy, police and soldiers at, 132–3; Leitrim estates in, 177–8; Murray Stewart estates in, 190, 193, 194–5
Douglas, Archie, 2
Down, County, 319; Hall estate in, 177; party processions in, 146
Down South, 306
Downpatrick, Co. Down, 231
Doyle, James, bp of Kildare and Leighlin, 73–4
Drennan, William, 69–70, 71, 74, 82, 107
Drogheda, 92; election (1868) and disturbances, 122–3, 129 133
Dromore, Co. Tyrone, 234
Drumconrath, Co. Meath, 298, 301
Dublin, city, corporation, 45–6; protestant working class in, 35–68 *passim*; Dublin Castle, 66, 76, 90, 117, 154, 238, 241, 248, 249, 264
Dublin College Green, 292
Dublin Harbour, 292
Dublin North, 292
Dublin Protestant Operative Association and Reformation Society, 36–7, 39, 41–2, 45–7, 50–52; response to repeal movement, 53–7; sense of Irishness, 57–9; attitude to Britain, 59–60, 60–64, 65–7
Dublin St Patrick's, 292
Dublin University, *see* Trinity College, Dublin
Dufferin, Lord, on Irish estates, 188
Duffy, Charles Gavan, 77, 80, 82, 272
Duignan, W. H., 262

Duleek, Co. Meath, 298
Dundalk, Co. Louth, 295
Dunfanaghy, Co. Donegal, 132–3
Dungannon, Co. Tyrone, 233
Dunraven, Lord, 275

Edgar, Dr John, 70, 72, 75, 92
Edwards, Robin Dudley, 4, 5, 6, 11
Elections, British army at, 119–25; general election (1892), 289–319 *passim*; polling procedure, 295; *see also* Illiterate voters
Emmet Monument Association, 150, 152
Enniscorthy, Co. Wexford, 105
Enniskillen, Co. Fermanagh, 229
Enniskillen, earl of, 216
Erne, earl of, estates, 177, 178, 180, 190, 208, 216, 217, 219, 221, 234
Errington mission, 256
Evictions, 174; British army and, 127, 128, 140–43; in Ulster, 201–2, 205, 208, 217, 222–4; used to discourage land league, 223–4
Ewart, William, 91

Father Mathew Total Abstinence Society, 109
Fenians, 83, 98, 125–6, 317; and drink question, 84–90; infiltration of British army, 117–18; and Anglo-French tension, 152–71; and prospects of European war, 169–70; *see also* Irish Republican Brotherhood
Fermanagh, County, 209, 212, 214, 216, 217; Archdale estate in, 177; distress in, 216; 'defence association' in, 232; Erne estate in, 177, 178, 190; land league in, 228, 229; orange order and tenant-right movement, 227
Fermanagh Impartial Reporter, 218
Findrum, Co. Tyrone, state of (1880), 215
FitzGibbon, Gerald, 241–2, 243, 247, 251, 252, 256, 257, 258–60, 263–4, 267, 268, 269–70, 271, 272, 278, 280, 284–5, 286
FitzGibbon, Henry, 281–2
Fitzpatrick, P. V., 78
Flood, Revd Joseph, 299
Flying columns, 126, 128
Forster, William Edward, 92, 247, 256
France, nationalist hopes of, 150–71

Index

Freeman's Journal, 241, 245, 249, 250, 257, 264–5, 274, 292, 304, 305
Fulham, Patrick, 297, 298, 299, 307, 311
Furlong, Nicholas, bp of Ferns, 103, 105

Gaelic Athletic Association, 111
Gaelic League, 101
Galway North, 296, 305, 311
Gibson, Edward, 241, 242, 243, 244, 252, 264, 265, 269, 270, 271, 276, 277
Gilbert and Sullivan, 238
Gladstone, Herbert, 260
Gladstone, William Ewart, 18, 29–30, 31, 124, 127, 244, 245, 256, 262, 272, 290
Glangevlin, 221, 231
Gorst, Sir John, 252, 253–4, 272
Gosford, Lord, estates of, 190, 223, 228, 231
Granard, Co. Longford, 125
Gray, Edmund Dwyer, 245–6, 248–9, 258
Gregg, Tresham Dames, 36–7, 39–41, 46–8, 48–50, 51–2, 54, 55, 56, 57, 58, 62–4, 65–6, 67
Gregory, W. H., 48, 51
Gregory, Sir William, 240, 248, 251
Griffith, Arthur, 111
Griffith's valuation, 218–20
Gwynn, R. M., 29

Hamilton, Lord Claud, 266
Hamilton, Lord George, 272, 275
Harland, Sir Edward, 280, 282
Harland and Wolff, 2
Hartington, marquis of, duel with Churchill, 261; 284; committee, on elections, 122, 124, 129
Haughton, James, 88
Hawarden kite, 264, 266
Hayden, Mary, 5
Healy, Fr, 244, 251, 252
Healy, Maurice, 94–5
Healy, T. M., 94, 255, 299
Henderson, W. D., 206
Henry, R. M., 4
Hibernian Temperance Society, 71, 72
Hill, Lord Arthur, 91, 274, 278
Hillery, Dr Patrick J., 25
Hobson, Bulmer, 112
Holmes, Hugh, 258, 266, 268, 272

Home Rule Confederation of Great Britain, 100
Howth, FitzGibbon circle at, 251–2, 260, 266, 276, 282, 286

Illiterate voters, 296, 301–2, 306, 307, 310–11
Inchiquin, earl of, estate, 177, 189, 190, 195; income from, 189–92
Indian mutiny, 118, 151, 152
Institute of Historical Research, 3, 4
Ireland, John, bp of St Paul, Minnesota, 102–4, 107
Irish Association for the Prevention of Intemperance, 94
Irish Broadcasting Authority, 20
Irish Broadcasting Council, 20
Irish Catholic, 307
Irish Committee of Historical Sciences, 5, 24
Irish Daily Independent, 305, 306
Irish Historical Society, 5
Irish Historical Studies, 5–7, 22
Irish Literary Society, 101
Irishman, 155, 156, 158, 167, 168
Irish Manuscripts Commission, 21
Irish National Federation, 298, 318
Irish National Land League, 126, 128, 202–3; spreads in mid-Ulster, 217, 221–4, 228; use of evictions against, 223–4; and tenant-right movement, 228; setback in Tyrone, 231–2; meetings, 228–31; dispersal of meetings, 144; orange counter-demonstrations, 228–9; fenians and, 317
Irish National League, 101, 128, 318; formation, 232, 233, meetings, 233–4; dispersal of meetings, 144; orange counter-demonstrations, 233–4
Irish parliamentary party, and drink question, 91–8, 109–10; and Lord Randolph Churchill, 255–8; split (1890), 109, 289–90
Irish People, 88–9
Irish Republican Brotherhood, 112, 149, 153, 168, 169, 170; *see also* Fenians
Irish Times, 245

James, Henry, 268
Jeune, Mrs, 255